WHAT IS AN *Aspen RoadMap?*

Aspen RoadMaps™ are comprehensive course outlines that lead you, step by step, through your law school courses—helping you prepare for class and study for exams. With a clean, modern design that is as easy to use as it is visually appealing, your RoadMap will guide you from the "big picture" to the details you need to know.

WHAT MAKES THE *ASPEN ROADMAP*™ FOR CRIMINAL LAW THE BEST?

The Aspen RoadMap™ for Criminal Law:

- Represents the newest, most up-to-date outline available.
- Is brought to you by the publishers of the successful *Examples and Explanations Series.*
- Is based upon the insights and teaching methods of Professor Laurie Levenson, one of America's best classroom teachers of Criminal Law.
- Illuminates areas of subtlety and ambiguity in criminal law.
- Offers the most complete set of study tools available to help you reinforce your learning and prepare for exams.
- Includes analyses that help you to apply and understand criminal law.

THE PRACTICAL COMPONENTS OF YOUR *ASPEN ROADMAP*™

- ***The Casebook Correlation Chart*** helps you match sections of your casebook to this *RoadMap*™.
- ***The RoadMap™ Capsule Summary*** provides a "big picture" view anytime you need it.
- ***Chapter Overviews***, each no more than two pages long, highlight key concepts.
- ***Minority Positions*** are clearly explained, and the effects of rival approaches are clarified.
- ***Hypotheticals*** are interwoven throughout to help further clarify important concepts.
- ***Examples***—complete with accompanying analyses—are included in each chapter to provide lively and memorable illustrations of key points.
- ***Chapter Review Questions***—complete with answers—reinforce your understanding.
- ***Exam Tips*** help you target what you really need to know in order to maximize your study time and do well on exams.
- ***Sample Exam Questions***, presented as short essays, are accompanied by model answers.

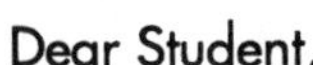 ASPEN LAW & BUSINESS Educational Division

Dear Student,

I'd like to take this opportunity to welcome you to the *Aspen RoadMap*™ for Criminal Law. I am Laurie Levenson, Associate Dean at Loyola Law School—where I have taught Criminal Law for more than eight years. Prior to joining the faculty at Loyola, I practiced criminal law as a prosecutor for almost a decade.

During my years in the classroom and in the many hours I've spent talking with students outside of class, I have come to learn when and why you, as a student, might occasionally have difficulty with this course. From what other students have told me, I have developed specific approaches and effective techniques that can help you navigate your way through potential problems.

Criminal Law is the study of how, why, and when society punishes people for conduct that violates society's standards of behavior. Like society, these laws evolve over time. In this way, the study of criminal law is an inquiry into our society and our time. Armed with your *RoadMap*™, you will be able to orient yourself in any criminal law casebook and gain the confidence you need to succeed in this course. But, more importantly, you will be better equipped to appreciate the intricate relationship between the law and the criminal justice system, and how they both reflect the values and conflicts of our time.

Your *RoadMap*™ introduces the basic terms for the different elements of crime. It shows you how those elements are interpreted and applied in specific crimes such as murder, conspiracy, theft, and rape. As you explore the finer points and subtleties of criminal law, (for example, theories of accomplice liability), your *RoadMap*™ will guide you with well-marked signposts every step of the way. Such signposts include plenty of examples, case discussions, summaries of the law, and exam tips.

Good luck, and please remember that this book is not intended to replace your casebook and assigned primary material, but rather to help you orient yourself in your reading, in the classroom, and at exam time. I think you're going to enjoy this journey into criminal law, and I'm pleased to be able to be a part of it.

Sincerely,

Laurie L. Levenson

Laurie L. Levenson
Associate Dean

P.S. I'd welcome your suggestions for making the *RoadMap*™ even more useful. Please write to me at Aspen Law & Business, Law School Division, One Liberty Square, 10th floor, Boston, MA 02109 or e-mail me at j.barmack@aspenpubl.com

Aspen Publishers, Inc. A **Wolters Kluwer** Company

1185 Avenue of the Americas, New York, NY 10036

Criminal Law

Laurie L. Levenson

Associate Dean
Loyola Law School

ASPEN LAW & BUSINESS
A Division of Aspen Publishers, Inc.

This publication is designed to provide accurate and authoritative information in regard to the subject matter covered. It is sold with the understanding that the publisher is not engaged in rendering legal, accounting, or other professional services. If legal advice or other professional assistance is required, the services of a competent professional person should be sought.

—From a *Declaration of Principles* jointly adopted by a Committee of the American Bar Association and a Committee of Publishers and Associations

Permissions
Aspen Law & Business
1185 Avenue of the Americas
New York, NY 10036

Third Printing

Printed in the United States of America
ISBN 1-56706-459-0

Library of Congress Cataloging-in-Publication Data

Levenson, Laurie L., 1956–
Criminal law / Laurie L. Levenson.
p. cm.
Includes index.
ISBN 1-56706-459-0 (pbk.)
1. Criminal law—United States. 2. Criminal procedure—United States.
3. Criminal justice, Administration of —United States.
I. Title.
KF9219.L388 1997
345.73—dc21 97-16998
CIP

Summary of Contents

CONTENTS

6 The Death Penalty 143

CONSPIRACY 243

13 THEFT OFFENSES AND OTHER CRIMES AGAINST PROPERTY 379

CASEBOOK CORRELATION

Aspen Roadmap	Kaplan, Weisberg & Binder **Criminal Law: Cases and Materials** 1996 (3d ed.)	Kadish & Schulhofer **Criminal Law and its Processes: Cases and Materials** 1995 (6th ed.)	Johnson **Criminal Law: Cases, Materials, and Text** 1990 (4th ed.)	Dressler **Cases and Materials on Criminal Law** 1994
1. THE STUDY OF CRIMINAL LAW				
A. Introduction				1-3
B. Development of the Criminal Law	10-16, 17-18			3-5
C. Classification of Offenses	207-210	237-244	208	
D. Overview of the Criminal Justice System	2-10, 20-27	1-59	483-505, 535-566	5-6, 8-15
E. Role of the Jury	936, 983	59-74	505-535	6-8, 15-20
F. Role of Counsel		74-96	472-483	798-800
2. JUSTIFICATION OF PUNISHMENT				
A. Types of Punishment	29-118	97-101		21-23
B. Purposes of Punishment	30-96	101-131		23-35
C. Case Studies	661-667	131-146	387	35-45
D. Sentencing	108-117	146-153	103-122	38-45
E. Proportionality	96-108	282-294		45-63
F. Criminalization and Decriminalization		153-169		
G. Legality	161-194	294-314	81-103	64-80
3. ELEMENTS OF A CRIME				
A. Introduction—"Elements" of a Crime	119-120			
B. Actus Reus—Culpable Conduct	121-161	171-203	49-61	81-102
C. Mens Rea—Culpable Mental States	195-199, 221-238	204-225	1-9, 61-75	103-128
D. Mistake of Fact	238-263	225-235	14-18	146-156
E. Strict Liability	199-221, 245-256, 263-264	235-257	28-49	128-146
F. Mistake of Law	263-302, 449-461	257-282	18-28, 75-80, 606	156-173
4. RAPE				
A. Introduction		315		
B. Types of Rape				
C. Perspectives on Rape		315-319		320-327
D. Elements of Rape	1099-1128	320-361		327-340, 357-364, 368-371
E. Rape Reform Legislation	1138-1153	361-369		346-357, 364-368
F. Problems of Proof	1128–1137	369-384		340-346, 371-387
G. Model Penal Code Approach	1110, 1113, 1131, 1136			383-384
H. Statutory Rape	139-147, 1153-1155	226-234		149-153

Aspen Roadmap	Kaplan, Weisberg & Binder **Criminal Law: Cases and Materials** 1996 (3d ed.)	Kadish & Schulhofer **Criminal Law and its Processes: Cases and Materials** 1995 (6th ed.)	Johnson **Criminal Law: Cases, Materials, and Text** 1990 (4th ed.)	Dressler **Cases and Materials on Criminal Law** 1994
5. HOMICIDE				
A. Introduction	383-384	385		194-197
B. Definition of Homicide	168-173	385-386	236-252	201-207
C. Levels of Homicide	385-398	386-394	162-169	197-201
D. Murder	399-416	394-405	159-160, 169-188, 255-261	207-216, 839-842
E. Manslaughter	416-461, 463-498	405-468	146-162, 188-199, 201-208	216-257
F. Felony-Murder Doctrine	498-542	468-476, 478-509	208-235, 261-263	257-285
G. Misdemeanor—Manslaughter Rule [Unlawful-Act Doctrine]	511-514	476-478	208	285-286
H. Homicide Review				
6. THE DEATH PENALTY				
A. Historical Development of Death Penalty in the United States	543-550		122-125	286-287
B. Policy Considerations	545-546	510-522		287-299
C. Administration of the Death Penalty	550-563	524-536	136-137	299-319
D. Constitutional Limitations on Imposition of the Death Penalty	543-550, 563-590	522-545	125-145	286-305
7. CAUSATION				
A. Introduction	317-320	547-548		174-176
B. Common Law Approach to Issues of Causation	320-336, 337-381	548-581	252-254, 263-271	174-193
C. Model Penal Code Approach	322-323, 336-337	588-589	271-272	190-191
8. ATTEMPT				
A. Introduction	781-783	581-582		
B. Historical Background	783-786	582		650-653
C. Policy Considerations		582-585		653-659
D. Elements of Attempt	786-810	585-599, 601-617	571-587	659-685, 701-704
E. Defenses to Attempt	810-815, 822-848	599-600, 623-640	567-571, 594-606	685-701
F. Solicitation	815-822	617-623	583-586, 587-589	705-714
9. ACCOMPLICE LIABILITY				
A. Introduction	849-851, 861-863	641-644	642-643	789-792
B. Requirements for Accomplice Liability	851-906	644-671	642-646, 650-657	792-827
C. Relationship Between the Liability of the Parties	906-917	671-683	633-642, 646-650	827-836
D. Abandonment/Withdrawal Defense	595-597	683		836-838
E. Exam Tips				

Aspen Roadmap	Kaplan, Weisberg & Binder **Criminal Law: Cases and Materials** 1996 (3d ed.)	Kadish & Schulhofer **Criminal Law and its Processes: Cases and Materials** 1995 (6th ed.)	Johnson **Criminal Law: Cases, Materials, and Text** 1990 (4th ed.)	Dressler **Cases and Materials on Criminal Law** 1994
10. CORPORATE LIABILITY				
A. Liability of the Corporate Entity	997-1018, 1021-1032	199-201, 683-705	199-201	863-876
B. Liability of Corporate Agents	1018-1020, 1031-1032	705-719		857-863
11. CONSPIRACY				
A. Introduction	919	643	587-589, 590-594	715-716
B. Consequences of a Conspiracy Charge	920-931, 937-939	720-733	622-627	716-724
C. Conspiracy as a Form of Accessorial Liability	951-961	734-743	633-642, 662-666	854-857
D. Elements of a Conspiracy	931-951	743-764	580-583, 607-614, 650-662	724-748
E. Scope of Agreement—Single or Multiple Conspiracies	968-975	764-774	627-632	749-761
F. Parties	961-967	774-780	614-622	761-770
G. Summary of Conspiracy Law				
H. Exam Tips				
I. Criminal Enterprises and RICO	975-995	781-799	666-685	770-778
12. DEFENSES				
Part I Justification Defenses				
A. Rationale Behind Justification Defenses	591-601	131-136, 860-880	373-375	388-405
B. Self-Defense	604-643	801-836, 837-846	388-434	405-452
C. Defense of Another	607-609	836-837	432-433	452-456
D. Defense of Property	655-661	846-852	434-446	456-463
E. Law Enforcement Defense	643-655	852-860	426-431	463-472
F. Necessity	661-693	860-880	375-388	472-493, 506-513
G. Euthanasia	367-372	201-203, 880-892		842-853
Part II Excuse Defenses				
A. Duress	693-712	896-913	363-373, 374	499-520
B. Intoxication	307-315, 762-765	913-929	9-14, 72-75, 328-339, 356-362	520-557
C. Insanity	713-762, 765-772, 774-777	929-999	273-328	557-632
D. Diminished Capacity	303-307, 772-774	999-1011	340-356	632-643
E. Infancy				643-649
F. Entrapment	894	617-621, 623-625, 649-650, 671-675, 1044-1046	449-471	822
G. Consent	253-255, 1033-1035	329, 333-355, 561-564, 880-892	446-449	
H. Developments in Excuse Defenses		1011-1037	328-339	

Aspen Roadmap	Kaplan, Weisberg & Binder **Criminal Law: Cases and Materials** 1996 (3d ed.)	Kadish & Schulhofer **Criminal Law and its Processes: Cases and Materials** 1995 (6th ed.)	Johnson **Criminal Law: Cases, Materials, and Text** 1990 (4th ed.)	Dressler **Cases and Materials on Criminal Law** 1994
13. THEFT OFFENSES AND OTHER CRIMES AGAINST PROPERTY				
A. Historical Development of Crimes Against Property	1039-1042, 1053-1057	1039-1041		877-878
B. Theft Crimes	1037-1039, 1048-1051, 1075-1095	1041-1064, 1079-1088, 1090-1094	686-690, 697-701, 717-737, 754-756	878-885, 886-902
C. Fraud Crimes	1042-1048	1064-1079	691-697, 701-709, 741-754	885-886, 902-905
D. Consolidated Theft and Fraud Crimes	1054	1088-1090		877
E. Expanding Concept of "Property"	1051-1053	1094-1102	709-717	
F. Mail and Wire Fraud	1057-1075	1102-1114	737-741, 754-756	
G. Defenses to Theft and Fraud Crimes		1114-1125		
H. Other Crimes Against Property	1095-1098	602-604		462-463
I. Summary of Theft Crimes				
J. Summary of Other Crimes Against Property				

CAPSULE SUMMARY

This Capsule Summary is intended for review at the end of the semester. Reading it is not a substitute for mastering the material in the main outline. To quickly find specific information in the main outline, use the Detailed Table of Contents or the Index.

THE STUDY OF CRIMINAL LAW

A. INTRODUCTION

1. **Nature of Criminal Law.** Criminal law is the study of offenses against society. Unlike tort law, crimes are offenses against the entire community, not just an individual victim.

2. **Approaching the Study of Criminal Law.** The study of criminal law breaks down into four basic components: 1. elements of crimes; 2. theories of accomplice liability; 3. preliminary offenses; and 4. elements of defenses.

B. DEVELOPMENT OF THE CRIMINAL LAW

1. **Common Law vs. Statutory Law.** American criminal law is derived from English common law. In general, the common law no longer governs in America. Now, criminal offenses are governed by statutory law that relies on common law definitions of key legal terms.

2. **Model Penal Code.** The Model Penal Code is a model statute drafted by the American Law Institute. It is not binding on legislatures, but has been influential.

C. CLASSIFICATION OF OFFENSES

1. **Types of Offenses.** Modernly, there are three different types of crimes:

   a. **Felonies.** Punishable by more than one year in jail.

   b. **Misdemeanors.** Punishable by less than one year in jail.

   c. **Violations.** Punishable by fine or less than six months in jail.

2. **Malum in se vs. Malum prohibitum.** At common law, crimes were also divided by their level of danger:

   a. **Malum in se.** Inherently immoral or dangerous.

   b. **Malum prohibitum.** Regulatory violations.

D. OVERVIEW OF THE CRIMINAL JUSTICE SYSTEM

1. **Proof beyond a Reasonable Doubt.** The key protection for defendants against improper conviction is the burden on the prosecution to prove guilt beyond a reasonable doubt. This standard of proof applies regardless of whether the criminal case is a felony, misdemeanor, or violation.

2. **Burden of Production.** The prosecution has the burden of presenting evidence to support its case against the defendant, once the government has proved affirmative defenses.

3. **Jury Trial.** The Sixth Amendment guarantees the right to a jury trial for all crimes carrying a term of more than six months imprisonment. There is no constitutional requirement of unanimity or a jury of 12 citizens.

4. **Role of Counsel.** All defendants are entitled to counsel in criminal cases.

JUSTIFICATION OF PUNISHMENT

A. PURPOSES OF PUNISHMENT

There are four purposes of punishment:

1. **Retribution.** Punishment because the defendant deserves to be punished.

2. **Deterrence.** Punishment for the utilitarian purpose of providing a disincentive for the defendant or others to commit future crimes.

3. **Rehabilitation.** Punishment to correct criminal behavior.

4. **Incapacitation.** Punishment to prevent defendant from causing future harm.

B. **SENTENCING** Punishment for crimes occurs at sentencing. Punishment must be proportional to the crime.

C. **LEGALITY** Not all bad acts are punishable as crimes. Under American law, a person may not be punished unless that person's conduct was defined as criminal before committed.

Elements of a Crime

A. **ELEMENTS OF CRIMES**

A.R. + M.R. + (Circum.) + (Result) = Crime

1. **Actus Reus.** Every crime has an actus reus, which is a voluntary physical act. An actus reus may be a positive act or an omission when there is a duty to act. An act must be voluntary to be an actus reus.

   a. **Voluntary acts.** Voluntariness is defined as any act that is the result of conscious and volitional movement. It includes everything that is not involuntary, as that term is narrowly defined. Under the Model Penal Code, involuntary acts include:

      i. reflex or convulsion;

      ii. bodily movement during unconsciousness or sleep;

      iii. hypnosis or under hypnotic suggestion (MPC);

      iv. bodily movement of the defendant by another.

   b. **Omissions.** Generally, there is no legal duty to help another facing harm. Therefore, failure to act only constitutes an actus reus when there is a duty to act. Duties to act may arise from:

      i. a statute;

ii. status relationship (e.g., parent-child);

iii. contractual relationship (e.g., babysitter);

iv. voluntarily assuming the care of another;

v. putting the victim in peril (may also be seen as positive act).

2. **Mens Rea — Culpable Mental States.** Acts alone do not constitute a criminal offense, even if they cause harm. Culpability is the extent to which a defendant's mental state shows the defendant deserves to be punished for his or her acts. The mens rea requirement focuses on levels of awareness and intentionality with which the defendant acted.

a. **Common law terminology.** A variety of words were used at common law to describe criminal intent. They include:

i. **Maliciously.** Acting in disregard to the risk to another;

ii. **Intentionally.** Acting with the purpose to cause a specific harmful result;

iii. **Negligently.** Acting without exercising the standard of care a reasonable person would exercise under the circumstances;

iv. **Specific intent.** Acting with the intent to commit a crime or an intent to cause a specific result;

v. **General intent.** Acting with the intent to commit the act.

b. **Model Penal Code terminology.** The Model Penal Code has been greatly influential in defining the mens rea requirements for crimes. The language of culpability used by the Model Penal Code includes:

i. **Purposely.** Defendant acts with the goal or aim to achieve a particular result;

ii. **Knowingly.** Defendant is virtually or practically certain that her conduct will lead to a particular result;

iii. **Recklessly.** Defendant consciously disregards a substantial and unjustifiable risk that her acts will harm another person;

iv. **Negligently.** Defendant is unaware and takes a risk that an ordinary person would not take.

c. **Motive vs. intent.** Motive is the underlying reason why the defendant engages in criminal behavior. Prosecutors need not prove motive. Intent is the defendant's mens rea for a crime and is an element of the offense.

d. **Minimal level of mens rea required for crimes.** For most crimes, defendant must act at least recklessly. The more serious the crime, the higher the required mens rea.

e. **Applying the mens rea requirement to material elements.** Material elements are those elements of a crime for which the defendant must have a mens rea. Although each circumstance defining a crime must exist for the defendant to be guilty, the defendant need not be aware of each circumstance's existence.

i. **Example.** It is a crime to assault a federal officer. Although the prosecution must prove defendant assaulted a federal officer, that circumstance is not material and the defendant is still guilty whether or not she realized the person she was attacking was a federal officer.

ii. **Jurisdictional elements.** If an element is not material, it may also be referred to as a "jurisdictional element."

B. MISTAKE OF FACT

1. **General Rule.** Ignorance or mistake of fact is a defense when it shows that the defendant did not have the mens rea for a material element of the crime. In other words, if the defendant does not know something she must know to be guilty of a crime, her ignorance or mistake is a defense.

a. **Determining material elements.** In order to decide whether a mistake is a defense, it is critical to know which elements of the crime the defendant must know. That determination can be made by the language of the statute, its legislative history, and an understanding of what elements of the crime defined the moral wrong being punished. Ordinarily, a defendant must know that aspect of her conduct that makes the conduct wrong.

b. **Honest mistake sufficient.** Generally, an honest mistake is sufficient to negate an element of a crime. However, in some jurisdictions, the defendant is required to have both an honest and reasonable mistake.

C. STRICT LIABILITY

1. **Definition.** Strict liability crimes are offenses with no mens rea requirement as to the key element of the offense that makes the defendant's behavior wrong. The defendant is guilty of a crime even if he honestly and reasonably believed his conduct was proper.

2. **Types of Strict Liability Crimes.** Strict liability is typically imposed for two types of crimes:

   a. **Public welfare offenses.** Regulatory offenses affecting health, safety, and welfare are often strict liability offenses. Indications that a crime is a strict liability offense include:

      i. highly regulated industry;

      ii. affecting public welfare;

      iii. no mens rea language in statute;

      iv. large number of prosecutions;

      v. relatively light penalties.

   b. **Morality offenses.** There are also a number of common law morality offenses that are treated as strict liability offenses:

      i. statutory rape;

      ii. bigamy;

      iii. adultery.

3. **Strict Liability Crimes Disfavored.** Generally, common law offenses are presumed not to be strict liability crimes even if the statute does not expressly mention a mens rea requirement. Morissette v. United States, 342 U.S. 246 (1952). A minimum level of recklessness is required for most common law crimes.

4. **Vicarious Liability.** Vicarious liability is a defendant's responsibility for the criminal acts of another without proof that the defendant had a culpable mens rea as to those acts.

5. **Defenses to Strict Liability Crimes.** A defendant charged with a strict liability crime cannot assert mistake or ignorance of fact. The defendant can, however, challenge whether there was a voluntary actus reus.

D. MISTAKE OF LAW

1. **General Rule.** Mistake or ignorance of the law is not a defense.

2. **Exceptions.** Mistake of law is a defense when:

   a. The defendant has been officially misled as to the law by:

      i. reliance on an invalid statute (misreading of a statute is insufficient);

      ii. reliance on a judicial decision;

      iii. reliance on an administrative order;

      iv. reliance on an official interpretation.

   b. Because of ignorance or mistake of the law, the defendant lacks the mens rea for the crime;

   c. Lack of reasonable notice of the law. See Lambert v. California, 353 U.S. 225 (1957).

RAPE

A. ELEMENTS OF RAPE

Rape is defined as "unlawful sexual intercourse with a woman without her consent by force, fear, or fraud." The elements of rape include:

1. **Sexual Intercourse.** The slightest penetration is sufficient for rape. There need not be a completed sexual act.

2. **Unlawful.** Traditionally, a husband cannot be guilty of raping his wife.

3. **Without Consent.** The crime of rape requires that the defendant be aware he is acting without the victim's consent. Lack of consent is a material element of the crime of rape.

   a. **Resistance.** Lack of consent is generally established through proof of resistance.

   b. **Victims incapable of providing consent.** In some situations, the law presumes that the victim is incapable of giving consent:

      i. statutory rape (sex with minor);

      ii. mentally incompetent victim;

      iii. unconscious victim;

      iv. deception by defendant.

4. **By Force, Fear, or Fraud.** Because of difficulties in ascertaining when a woman has consented to sex, the prosecution must also prove intercourse was accomplished by force, fear or fraud.

   a. **Force.** The requirement of force or threat of force has been traditionally interpreted very narrowly by the courts. It has not included intimidation and nonphysical threats. It has, however, included the threat of physical force.

   b. **Deception.** Traditionally, deception was insufficient for rape. Modern legislation now recognizes situations where deception is used to create a fear of unlawful physical injury.

B. **MISTAKE AS A DEFENSE** Traditionally, an honest mistake as to consent constitutes a defense to rape. Regina v. Morgan, [1976] A.C. 182. The modern view is that the defendant's mistake must be both honest and reasonable.

C. **PROBLEMS OF PROOF** Rape cases, especially acquaintance rape cases, are traditionally among the most difficult cases to prove. Procedural obstacles have included:

1. **Corroboration.** Traditional common law did not require corroboration of the rape victim's testimony, but some modern statutes do have that requirement for nonforcible rape cases.

2. **Special Jury Instructions.** Many jurisdictions admonish jurors to evaluate a rape victim's testimony with care.

3. **Attacks on Woman's Character.** Traditionally, a defendant would attack the victim's character during a rape case. To prevent such attacks, many jurisdictions have now adopted special procedural protections for rape victims.

   a. **Rape shield laws.** Rape shield laws limit the scope of cross-examination of a rape victim. Evidence of a victim's prior sexual history is inadmissible unless it involves prior consensual sexual intercourse with the defendant.

D. **STATUTORY RAPE** Sexual intercourse with a girl under a certain age, often 18 years old, is strictly prohibited by most jurisdictions. In these cases, the defendant's mistake of fact as to the victim's age is irrelevant.

Homicide

A. **DEFINITION OF HOMICIDE** Homicide is the unlawful killing of another human being. The elements of the crime are:

A.R.	—	An act that causes death ("killing")
M.R.	—	Depends on the grade of homicide
Cir.	—	Another human being
Result	—	Death

1. **Killing.** A killing occurs when the defendant ends a person's life. Many different methods of killing (e.g., shooting, stabbing, poisoning, etc.) satisfy the actus reus for homicide.

   a. **Death.** Each jurisdiction defines when life ends. Commonly, it is when the brain ceases to function or the moment the victim's heart stops.

   b. **Year-and-a-day rule.** Under common law, death must occur within a year and a day of the defendant's acts to constitute the killing.

2. **Mens Rea.** The level of mens rea defines the type of homicide committed. Murder requires "malice aforethought." The common law term for malice is "abandoned and malignant heart."

3. **Another Human Being.** Homicide requires the killing of another human being. Each jurisdiction may define what constitutes a human being.

   a. **Fetus.** A fetus is not considered a human being unless the laws of the jurisdiction expressly state otherwise. Keeler v. Superior Ct., 2 Cal. 3d 619 (1970).

   b. **Born alive rule.** Injuries inflicted upon a child while in the mother's womb may be the basis for a homicide charge if the child is then born alive but subsequently dies from in utero injuries.

   c. **Suicide.** Killing of one's self is suicide, not homicide. Helping another commit suicide may constitute homicide.

   d. **Infanticide.** Killing a young child is infanticide.

   e. **Patricide.** Killing one's parents is patricide.

B. **LEVELS OF HOMICIDE** Common law did not divide murder into degrees. The modern approach is to divide homicides into degrees. The two main categories of homicides are murder and manslaughter. In addition, there may be varying degrees of murder. Manslaughter is typically divided into voluntary and involuntary manslaughter.

1. **Murder.** Murder is the killing of another human being with malice.

   a. Malice has several meanings:

      i. intent to kill;

      ii. intent to cause serious bodily harm;

      iii. callous or extreme disregard for human life (gross recklessness);

      iv. killing during the commission of a felony.

CAPSULE SUMMARY

b. **Degrees of murder.** Each jurisdiction may decide whether and how to divide its murders by degrees. A standard approach is to view premeditated murders as the most serious types of killings.

i. **First-degree murder.** In many states, murder with premeditation constitutes first-degree murder. Thus, first-degree murder is malice plus premeditation.

(a) **Premeditation.** Premeditation requires cool, deliberate thought. Different approaches are used to judge whether there has been sufficient deliberate thought to constitute premeditation:

- **Carrol approach.** The broadest definition of premeditation only requires that the defendant acted deliberately or with purposeful conduct. No time is too short to form premeditation. Commonwealth v. Carrol, 412 Pa. 525 (1963).
- **Anderson approach.** In some jurisdictions, premeditation requires that the defendant act with a "preconceived design." People v. Anderson, 70 Cal. 2d 15 (1968).

(b) **Defenses to premeditation.** Diminished capacity and intoxication are defenses to premeditation.

ii. **Other degrees of murder.** All killings with malice constitute murder. Malice may include an intent to kill but it also may be mere gross recklessness. If a defendant consciously acts with an unusually high and unjustifiable risk of death, the defendant acts with malice.

2. **Manslaughter.** Manslaughter is the killing of another human being without malice.

a. **Voluntary manslaughter.** Killings made in the "sudden heat of passion" after provocation constitute voluntary manslaughter. Common law voluntary manslaughter requires:

i. **Actual heat of passion.** The defendant must be actually provoked. If the defendant is not enraged at the time of the intentional killing, she is acting with malice.

ii. **Legally adequate provocation.** There are several approaches used to determine what is legally adequate provocation.

(a) **Traditional common law used a categorical approach.** Only the following types of provocation satisfy:

- assault or battery on the defendant,
- mutual combat,
- defendant's illegal arrest,
- injury of a close relative,
- sudden discovery of spouse's adultery.

Words alone are insufficient provocation.

(b) **Modern objective standard.** The provocation must be of such a nature that it would inflame a reasonable person to kill. Courts vary in how objectively they view the reasonable person. Most courts will permit the jury to consider the defendant's and victim's physical characteristics in determining provocation.

(c) **Model Penal Code approach** The Model Penal Code does not require a specific act of provocation. A defendant who kills while in extreme emotional distress has not acted with malice.

iii. **Insufficient cooling time.** If too much time has elapsed between the act of provocation and defendant's response, the heat of passion doctrine will not apply. The length of time between the act of provocation and defendant's reaction is expanded in some jurisdictions by two doctrines:

(a) long-smoldering reaction;

(b) rekindling doctrine

b. **Model Penal Code manslaughter.** Under the Model Penal Code, a killing which would otherwise constitute murder is reduced to manslaughter if it is committed under the influence of extreme mental or emotional disturbance for which there is a reasonable explanation or excuse. MPC 210.3(1)(b). The Model Penal Code approach differs from the traditional law of voluntary manslaughter in the following ways:

- **i.** No specific act of provocation is required.
- **ii.** The Model Penal Code approach is more subjective.
- **iii.** There is no cooling time limitation.
- **iv.** Words alone may be sufficient.
- **v.** Diminished capacity may be considered.
- **vi.** The victim need not be the person who provoked the defendant.

c. Involuntary manslaughter. Unintentional homicides, if committed without due caution and circumspection, constitute involuntary manslaughter. The minimum level of culpability for involuntary manslaughter is gross negligence.

- **i. Distinguishing civil and criminal liability.** Ordinary negligence results only in civil liability. For a defendant to be guilty of involuntary manslaughter, the magnitude of risk created by defendant's behavior must substantially outweigh the social utility of the defendant's conduct. In other words, there must be "gross" negligence.
- **ii. Dangerous instrumentality doctrine.** If a defendant acts negligently with a dangerous instrumentality, such as a gun, knife, or car, the defendant's behavior may automatically constitute gross negligence and satisfy the requirements for involuntary manslaughter.
- **iii. Model Penal Code approach.** Under the Model Penal Code, homicide is manslaughter when it is committed recklessly, i.e., the defendant was conscious of the risk of death. A separate, lesser offense of "negligent homicide" applies if the defendant acts with a "failure to appreciate a risk of death of which the actor should be aware." MPC 2.02(2)(d).

d. Murder vs. manslaughter. The difference between murder and manslaughter is malice. Reckless conduct by a defendant may constitute murder or manslaughter depending on how extreme it is. If the defendant acts with wanton disregard or gross recklessness, the defendant has acted with malice. However, if the defendant has acted recklessly, but has an explanation as to why he risked danger to others, the conduct may only constitute involuntary manslaughter.

C. FELONY-MURDER DOCTRINE

1. **Basic Felony-Murder Doctrine.** If a defendant causes a death during the commission of a felony, the prosecution need not prove that the defendant acted with an intent to kill. Under the felony-murder doctrine, the defendant is guilty of "constructive murder" because the intent to commit the felony substitutes for the intent to kill or malice.

2. **Requirements to Prove Felony Murder.** To prove felony murder, the prosecution must prove: a. defendant committed a felony; b. during the course of the felony, the defendant or an accomplice caused a death.

3. **Limitations on the Felony-Murder Doctrine.** In an attempt to limit the impact of the felony-murder doctrine, modern courts have adopted limitations on its application. These include:

   a. **Inherently dangerous felony limitation.** Only an underlying felony that is "inherently dangerous to human life" will trigger the felony-murder doctrine. Most jurisdictions evaluate the felony in the abstract, not as actually committed in a particular case.

   b. **Independent felony limitation/merger doctrine.** If the underlying felony is an "integral part" of the homicide itself, the felony-murder doctrine is not applied. A felony must have an independent purpose other than killing or gravely harming the victim to qualify for the felony-murder doctrine.

   c. **During the course of the felony.** The felony-murder rule only applies to felonies that occur during the course of the felony.

      i. **Duration of felony.** Typically, a felony begins when defendants begin to prepare for their crime and does not end until the defendants are in custody or have reached a position of temporary safety.

C A P S U L E S U M M A R Y

ii. **In furtherance of felony.** Unanticipated actions by a co-felon not in furtherance of the common purpose of the felony may not be charged under the felony-murder doctrine.

iii. **Acts of co-felons.** Traditionally, only deaths at the hand of a co-felon qualified for prosecution under the felony-murder rule. This is referred to as the agency theory. Some jurisdictions hold a felon responsible for any death proximately resulting from the unlawful activity, even if caused by a third person. This is referred to as the proximate cause theory.

iv. **Death of co-felons.** Traditionally, a felon is not responsible for the death of a co-felon. Commonwealth v. Redline, 391 Pa. 486 (1958).

v. **Provocative act/Vicarious liability.** A doctrine related to the felony-murder doctrine is that of "vicarious liability." Under this doctrine, a co-felon's provocative acts create malice that make all the defendants responsible for murder.

D. MISDEMEANOR-MANSLAUGHTER RULE (UNLAWFUL-ACT DOCTRINE)

1. **Basic Doctrine.** A killing committed during an unlawful act, not amounting to a felony, constitutes involuntary manslaughter without a separate showing that the defendant acted without due caution or circumspection.

2. **Limitations on Unlawful-Act Doctrine.** Courts have reduced the harshest effects of the misdemeanor-manslaughter doctrine by adopting limitations on its application.

a. **Proximate cause limitation.** The misdemeanor-manslaughter doctrine only applies if there is a causal connection between the misdemeanor violation and the death that occurred.

b. **Malum in se vs. malum prohibitum.** In many jurisdictions, the violation must be malum in se ("wrong in itself") for the misdemeanor-manslaughter doctrine to apply. If the violation is only for regulatory purposes, the doctrine cannot be applied.

c. **Dangerous vs. nondangerous infractions.** In some jurisdictions, rather than distinguish between malum in se and malum prohibitum crimes, misdemeanor-manslaughter only applies to violations that are inherently dangerous.

DEATH PENALTY

A. ARGUMENTS IN FAVOR OF DEATH PENALTY The following policy arguments are raised by proponents of the death penalty:

1. **Sanctity of Human Life.** Retribution requires that a person who takes a life have her life taken to uphold the value of human life.

2. **Deterrence.** Although not proven, the death penalty may deter future murders.

3. **Incapacitation.** The death penalty is necessary to ensure that a person never kills again.

4. **Historical.** Historically, the death penalty has been recognized as an appropriate punishment for the most serious crimes.

B. ARGUMENTS AGAINST THE DEATH PENALTY The following policy arguments are raised by opponents of the death penalty:

1. **Sanctity of Human Life.** The State's taking of a human life cheapens the value of life.

2. **Deterrence.** The death penalty is not a proven deterrent. In fact, the notoriety accompanying capital punishment may encourage some people to murder.

3. **Incapacitation.** The death penalty is not needed to incapacitate dangerous criminals. Life imprisonment without parole is a suitable alternative.

4. **Expense.** With the current system of appeals, it is costlier to execute defendants than to incarcerate them for a life term.

5. **Error and Irrevocability.** Inevitable mistakes in the criminal justice system cannot be corrected when a defendant has been executed.

6. **Discriminatory Administration.** Sociological studies seem to demonstrate that racial and economic discrimination undermine attempts at fair administration of the death penalty.

C. ADMINISTRATION OF THE DEATH PENALTY

1. **Bifurcated Proceedings.** Capital trials involve two phases: 1. guilt phase to ascertain whether the defendant is guilty of the charged offense; 2. penalty phase to determine whether the defendant should receive the death penalty.

2. **Eligible Offenses.** The death penalty may only be imposed for intentional murders, although it may be applied in felony-murder cases as long as the defendant demonstrated "major participation in the felony committed, combined with reckless indifference to human life." Tison v. Arizona, 481 U.S. 137 (1987).

3. **Standards for Imposing Death Penalty.** Many jurisdictions ask the jury to balance the aggravating circumstances of the offense and the defendant's background against any mitigating circumstances.

4. **Death-Qualified Jurors.** In a death penalty case, the prosecutor may exclude for cause jurors whose views on the death penalty would substantially impair their performance as jurors. Wainwright v. Witt, 469 U.S. 412 (1985).

D. CONSTITUTIONAL LIMITATIONS ON THE DEATH PENALTY

1. **Due Process Challenges.** The death penalty does not violate procedural due process. McGautha v. California, 402 U.S. 183 (1971).

2. **Cruel & Unusual Punishment Challenges.** Capital punishment, if administered without any clear criteria for its imposition, may violate the Eighth Amendment prohibition of "cruel and unusual punishments." Furman v. Georgia, 408 U.S. 238 (1972).

   a. **Mandatory death penalty statutes.** A mandatory death sentence for any murder violates the Eighth Amendment. Woodson v. North Carolina, 428 U.S. 280 (1976).

   b. **Use of sentencing factors.** A set of standards to guide jurors in reaching their sentencing decision are sufficient to protect against unconstitutional arbitrariness. Gregg v. Georgia, 428 U.S. 153 (1976).

   c. **Victim impact evidence.** The Eighth Amendment does not bar the prosecution from presenting victim-impact evidence. Payne v. Tennessee, 501 U.S. 808 (1991).

3. **Other Eighth Amendment Limitations**

    a. **Age limits.** Execution of murderers under the age of 16 years at the time of the homicide violates the Eighth Amendment. Thompson v. Oklahoma, 487 U.S. 815 (1988) (plurality).

    b. **Mental retardation.** The Eighth Amendment does not bar execution of all persons with mental deficiencies. Penry v. Lynaugh, 492 U.S. 302 (1989).

    c. **Insane prisoner.** Execution of an insane prisoner is unconstitutional. Ford v. Wainwright, 477 U.S. 399 (1986).

4. **Equal Protection Limitations.** It is extremely difficult to prove an equal protection violation in the imposition of the death penalty. There must be clear evidence of purposeful discrimination. Statistical disparities in its imposition are insufficient to prove an equal protection violation. McClesky v. Kemp, 481 U.S. 279 (1987).

CAUSATION

A. **REQUIREMENT OF CAUSATION** Causation is only an issue for crimes that require a result. In such cases, the prosecution must prove that the defendant's acts led to the harmful result that forms the basis for the crime. Homicide is a crime for which causation must be proved.

1. **Actual Cause.** The prosecution must prove that defendant's acts formed a link in the chain of causation leading to the harmful result. This is commonly done by asking, "But for defendant's conduct, would the harmful result have occurred?" Actual cause is also called "legal cause" or "cause in fact." MPC §2.03(1)(a).

    a. **Accelerating the result.** A person who accelerates a result is considered an actual cause of the result.

    b. **Defendant's acts need not be sole factor leading to result.** The defendant's conduct need not be the sole cause of a result. It only needs to be a link in the chain of causation.

2. **Proximate Cause.** No specific formula exists to determine proximate cause. Probable cause is the determination that the defendant's conduct was

a sufficiently direct cause of the harmful result to warrant criminal punishment. Several factors are used to determine proximate cause:

a. **Foreseeability.** The most important factor in determining proximate cause is whether the resulting harm was foreseeable.

   i. **Harm must be foreseeable, but not the manner of the harm.** Ordinarily, defendants need not foresee the actual manner in which harm will occur, only the fact that such harm is likely to occur. However, when the defendant is engaged in otherwise socially useful conduct that leads to a harmful result, the court may require that the actual manner of the harm be foreseeable and preventable. People v. Warner-Lambert Co., 51 N.Y.2d 295 (1980).

   ii. **Vulnerability of the victim.** Generally, a defendant "takes his victim as he finds him." Thus, a defendant need not foresee a victim's peculiar frailties or vulnerabilities that may aggravate the harm.

      (a) **Victim refuses treatment.** If a victim refuses medical treatment, the defendant may still be responsible for the victim's harm.

   iii. **Transferred intent.** If the defendant intends to harm victim A but accidentally harms victim B, proximate cause exists. As long as the defendant intends to injure, the defendant need not foresee who the actual victim may be.

   iv. **Additional harm.** If the defendant intends to harm one victim but accidentally harms another more seriously, common law holds the defendant responsible for the more serious harm committed. Under the Model Penal Code, the trier of fact must determine whether the harm caused is too remote or accidental to have a just bearing on the defendant's liability. MPC §2.03(2)(b), (3)(b).

b. **Intervening acts.** The second part of the proximate cause analysis is to determine whether any intervening acts broke the chain of causation and thereby make it unjust to punish the defendant. If an intervening act breaks the chain of causation, it is referred to as a superseding or independent intervening act. If the act does not break the chain of causation, it is a dependent or concurrent intervening act.

i. **Foreseeability of intervening act.** If the intervening act is foreseeable, it is unlikely to be considered a superseding intervening act.

ii. **Type of intervening act.** Some acts are more likely to be viewed as breaking the chain of causation than others.

(a) **Acts of nature.** Ordinary acts of nature, such as inclement weather, do not generally break the chain of causation. However, unforeseeable freak acts of nature, like earthquakes, may be superseding acts.

(b) **Medical maltreatment.** Unless intentional or grossly incompetent, medical maltreatment does not break the chain of causation.

(c) **Intervening disease.** Diseases contracted by victims during medical treatment do not ordinarily break the chain of causation unless they are extremely rare.

(d) **Victim's acts.** Only voluntary acts by a victim can break the chain of causation. Because a victim's harmful acts ordinarily occur in response to the defendant's acts, they are not considered voluntary and do not break the chain of causation. This is particularly true of any injuries to the victim while trying to escape.

(e) **Additional perpetrators.** Courts have taken two approaches when there are multiple perpetrators.

- **Alternative #1.** If the defendant's act would have been sufficient to cause death, acts by another perpetrator will not break the chain of causation.
- **Alternative #2.** The first perpetrator is responsible for an attempt and the second perpetrator is responsible for the completed crime.

(f) **Failure to act.** Failure to help a person who has been put in danger by another, even if there is a legal duty to assist, does not ordinarily break the chain of causation.

(g) **Concurrent causes.** Courts differ over how to treat two individuals whose reckless conduct leads to a harmful result.

- **Alternative #1.** Only the defendant who most directly caused the result is responsible.
- **Alternative #2.** All defendants who jointly participate in the enterprise are responsible.

8 ATTEMPT

A. BACKGROUND Attempt is a separate crime that punishes a defendant for conduct before it causes a harmful result. The defendant is punished for trying to commit a crime. Attempt is an inchoate crime.

1. **Punishment.** In most jurisdictions, attempt carries a lesser punishment than the completed crime. However, some jurisdictions, including the Model Penal Code, punish attempt to the same extent as the completed crime. MPC §5.05(1).

2. **Policy Considerations.** Punishing attempts allows law enforcement to get involved before actual harm is caused. However, there should not be punishment until the evidence shows the defendant's clear purpose to cause a harmful result and her actions toward fulfilling that goal.

B. ELEMENTS OF ATTEMPT For a charge of attempt, the prosecution must prove:

1. **Mens Rea.** Defendant's purpose was to commit the completed offense. At common law, this was referred to as specific intent.

   a. **Knowledge is insufficient.** In most jurisdictions, knowledge of the likely consequences of one's acts is insufficient to prove attempt even if it would have been sufficient for the completed offense. People v. Kraft, 133 Ill. App. 3d 294 (1985).

   b. **Model Penal Code approach.** Under the Model Penal Code, the defendant's purpose or belief that she will cause a prohibited result satisfies the mens rea for attempt. MPC §5.01(1)(b).

   c. **Mens rea requirement for attendant circumstances.** In a majority of courts, the defendant need not act purposely as to circumstances that the defendant would not need to know to be guilty of the completed crime. MPC §5.01. A minority of jurisdictions require purposefulness as to all elements of the crime.

2. **Actus Reus.** There are several tests for determining whether a defendant's actions cross the line from mere preparation to criminal attempt.

   a. **Last step.** Under early common law, a defendant was not guilty unless she had done all she could to commit a crime and external forces prevented her from causing a harmful result.

   b. **Proximity approach.** Under the traditional proximity approach, the focus is on how much the defendant has physically done and how physically close the defendant has come to completing the crime.

   c. **Unequivocality test.** Under the unequivocality test, also called the Res Ipsa Loquitor Test, a defendant's acts were viewed in the abstract to determine whether they showed an unequivocal intent to commit a crime.

   d. **Model Penal Code approach.** A majority of courts now adopt the Model Penal Code's standard for attempt. The defendant must take a "substantial step strongly corroborative of the actor's criminal purpose." MPC §5.01(2).

C. DEFENSES TO ATTEMPT

1. **Abandonment.** Common law did not recognize abandonment as a defense to attempt. Once the defendant took enough steps to be guilty of attempt, there was no turning back.

2. **Model Penal Code renunciation.** Modern laws and the Model Penal Code recognize renunciation (i.e., abandonment) as a defense. If a defendant completely and voluntarily renunciates her criminal purpose, she is not guilty of attempt. MPC §5.01(4).

3. **Impossibility.** The defense of impossibility arises when a defendant has done everything possible to commit a crime, but unexpected factual or legal circumstances prevent the crime from occurring.

   a. **Factual impossibility.** If an unexpected factual circumstance, such as a gun being unloaded, prevents a crime from being completed, the defendant is still guilty of attempt. The court asks the question, "Had the circumstances been as defendant believed them to be, would there have been a crime?'' If the answer is yes, the defendant is still guilty of attempt and impossibility is not a defense.

b. **Legal impossibility.** Under common law, legal impossibility is a defense to attempt. True legal impossibility arises when the defendant consciously tries to violate the law but there is no law prohibiting defendant's behavior. For example, if the defendant performs an abortion believing it is unlawful, but, in fact, abortion is legal in that jurisdiction, the defendant is not guilty of attempt. The problem in applying this rule is that it is often difficult to distinguish legal impossibility from factual impossibility.

c. **Hybrid impossibility.** Some situations present a hybrid of factual and legal impossibility. In these cases, if the facts had been as the defendant believed them to be, the defendant would have been guilty of a crime. However, the ''fact'' is that the defendant was wrong about the legal status of some of the circumstances related to her conduct. For example, the defendant who receives property believing it to be stolen but, in fact, it is not stolen. Some courts view these cases as providing a legal impossibility defense; others consider them factual impossibility cases and do not provide a defense.

d. **Model Penal Code approach.** Instead of trying to distinguish between factual and legal impossibility, the Model Penal Code takes an alternative approach. MPC §5.01 does not recognize impossibility as a defense. However, under MPC §5.05, in situations where an attempt is so inherently unlikely to result or culminate in the commission of a crime that neither the conduct nor the actor presents a public danger, the court has the discretion to dismiss or mitigate the level of the offense.

4. **Merger.** If an attempt succeeds, the defendant is only guilty of the completed substantive crime. Attempt merges with the completed substantive offense.

D. RELATED CRIMES

1. **Stalking.** To allow for earlier intervention into potential criminal behavior, some legislatures have adopted stalking statutes. Typically, they prohibit a person from intentionally harassing another and placing that person in immediate and reasonable fear for her safety.

2. **Solicitation.** Solicitation is a separate crime from attempt. It consists of recruiting, encouraging, directing, counseling, or inducing another person

to commit a crime. No substantial step need be taken toward completion of the crime, but the defendant must have the purpose/specific intent to promote or facilitate completion of the crime.

9 ACCOMPLICE LIABILITY

A. THEORY OF LIABILITY

1. **Not a Separate Crime.** Accomplice liability is not a separate crime. Rather, it is a theory by which the defendant is guilty of a substantive offense.

2. **Eliminating Common Law Distinctions.** At common law, there were distinct categories and labels for participants in crimes. These included: principal in the first degree, principal in the second degree, accessory before the fact, and accessory after the fact. The modern approach eliminates these categories and, except for accessory after the fact, all persons who participate in a crime are considered accomplices or aiders and abettors.

3. **Using Another Person as an Instrument to Commit a Crime.** If a person unknowingly or unwittingly participates in a crime, that person is not an accomplice but is considered a mere instrument by which the actual perpetrator committed the offense.

B. REQUIREMENTS FOR ACCOMPLICE LIABILITY

1. **Mens Rea.** For accomplice liability, the defendant must help another in the commission of a crime with the purpose of having the crime succeed.

   a. **Mere presence.** Mere presence at the commission of a crime is insufficient to constitute aiding and abetting unless the defendant has agreed in advance to be present to provide moral support or assistance to the principal.

   b. **Knowledge insufficient.** To be guilty as an accomplice, a defendant must not only know that his acts may assist in the commission of a crime, but must also have the specific purpose of having the crime succeed. United States v. Peoni, 100 F.2d 401 (2d Cir. 1938).

   c. **Determining purpose.** The greater a defendant's stake in the venture, the more likely that the defendant is participating with the purpose of having the crime succeed.

d. **Model Penal Code approach.** The Model Penal Code also requires a purpose of promoting or facilitating the commission of a crime. MPC §2.06(3)(a).

2. **Actus Reus.** The slightest act of encouragement or assistance may suffice for accomplice liability.

a. **Mere presence.** Mere presence is sufficient if there is a prior understanding that the defendant's presence is offered as a form of encouragement.

b. **Help need not contribute to criminal result.** A person is guilty of aiding and abetting a crime even if the criminal result would have occurred without defendant's assistance.

c. **Principal need not be aware of accomplice's acts.** A person can aid and abet a crime even though the principal is unaware of the accomplice's help.

d. **Attempted complicity.** The common law did not recognize attempts to assist that could not actually provide assistance. By comparison, the Model Penal Code recognizes accomplice liability if a person attempts to aid another in the commission of a crime. MPC §2.06(3).

e. **Failure to protect a victim.** Accomplice liability may be based upon an omission when there was a legal duty for the defendant to intervene and the defendant purposely did not do so to allow the principal to inflict harm.

C. RELATIONSHIP BETWEEN THE LIABILITY OF THE PARTIES

1. Accomplice and Principal Liability Do Not Depend Upon Each Other

a. **Feigned accomplice.** A person who acts as an accomplice in an effort to apprehend the principal during the commission of a crime is not guilty of aiding and abetting the offense.

b. **Excused principal.** Accomplice liability does not depend on conviction of the principal for the underlying offense. Principals may be excused from crimes for many reasons, including immunity, specialized defenses, or the principal's cooperation with law enforcement. As long as a crime was committed, and the accomplice purposely assisted in its commission, the accomplice is guilty of the crime even if the principal is not convicted.

D. DEFENSES TO ACCOMPLICE LIABILITY

1. **Abandonment/Withdrawal.** At common law, abandonment was not a defense to accomplice liability. Some jurisdictions have added a statutory defense for defendants who voluntarily and completely renounce involvement in a crime and make substantial efforts to prevent it.

2. **Model Penal Code.** The Model Penal Code recognizes an abandonment defense if the defendant terminates her complicity prior to the commission of the offense, either: 1. depriving the plan of its effectiveness, or 2. providing sufficient warning to law enforcement to prevent commission of the crime.

10 CORPORATE LIABILITY

A. NATURE OF CORPORATE LIABILITY

At common law, corporations could not be guilty of crimes. Today, corporations can be guilty of crimes, including those that require purposeful conduct. Corporate criminal liability is constitutional. New York Central & Hudson River Railroad Co. v. United States, 212 U.S. 481 (1909).

B. REQUIREMENTS FOR CORPORATE LIABILITY

Corporate criminal liability is a form of vicarious liability.

1. **Respondeat Superior Approach.** The traditional approach used to determine corporate liability holds a corporation criminally liable if its agent:

   a. commits a crime;

   b. within the scope of her employment;

   c. with the intent to benefit the corporation.

2. **Model Penal Code Approach.** The Model Penal Code narrows the scope of corporate criminal liability. The respondeat superior approach only applies to minor infractions and nonpenal offenses. For serious crimes, there is only criminal liability if a high managerial agent or board of directors authorizes, commands, solicits, or recklessly tolerates the wrongdoing.

C. LIABILITY OF CORPORATE AGENTS

1. **Vicarious Liability.** An individual working in the corporate setting may have responsibility both for her own acts, as well as for those employees working under her supervision. This indirect liability is called "vicarious liability." Under both the Model Penal Code, MPC §2.07(6), and prevailing case law, a person operating in a corporate setting is responsible for:

    a. any crimes that person personally commits; and

    b. reckless failure to discharge a duty for which the corporate agent has primary responsibility.

2. **Responsible Relationship Doctrine.** For strict liability offenses, a supervisor is responsible for criminal violations by his or her subordinates if there is a "responsible relationship" between the defendant and the subordinate's acts or omissions.

3. **Impossibility Defense.** Even where courts recognize vicarious liability, they ordinarily allow a defense if the corporate agents show it was "objectively impossible" to avoid the harm.

Conspiracy

A. NATURE OF CONSPIRACY CRIME

1. **Definition.** A conspiracy is an agreement by two or more persons to commit a crime. It is an inchoate crime.

2. **Separate Crime.** Unlike accomplice liability, conspiracy is a separate crime. A defendant may be guilty of both conspiracy and the substantive crime that was the object of the conspiracy.

3. **Conspiracy Punishes Preparatory Conduct.** Conspiracy punishes the mere act of agreeing, even if there is no substantial step toward completing the crime.

4. **Procedural Consequences of Conspiracy Charge.** A conspiracy charge allows the joinder of multiple defendants for trial, the introduction of hearsay evidence, extension of the statute of limitations, and greater latitude in selecting venue for the trial.

5. **Duration of a Conspiracy.** A conspiracy remains in effect until it has been abandoned or its objectives have been achieved.

B. ELEMENTS OF CONSPIRACY

1. **Actus Reus.** The actus reus of a conspiracy is an agreement to commit a crime.

   a. **Nature of agreement.** An agreement to commit a crime may be expressed or implied. It may be proven by concerted action. Mere presence at a crime scene is ordinarily not enough to establish agreement.

   b. **Agreement with unknown parties.** A conspirator need not know or have contact with all other members of a conspiracy.

   c. **Joining ongoing conspiracy.** A person who joins an ongoing conspiracy is responsible for her co-conspirator's prior acts. They may be used as evidence against the defendant on the conspiracy charge, but, if they involved separate crimes, the defendant does not have co-conspirator liability for those offenses.

2. **Overt Act Requirement.** At common law, there was no requirement of an overt act to prove conspiracy. Merely agreeing to commit an illegal act was sufficient. Under modern statutes, an overt act is required for conspiracies involving less serious offenses.

   a. **Definition of overt act.** An overt act is any legal or illegal act done by any of the conspirators to set the conspiracy in motion.

      i. Only one conspirator needs to commit an overt act;

      ii. An overt act may be in itself an innocuous act.

3. **Mens Rea.** Conspiracy requires two mens rea: a. an intent to agree; b. a purpose to have the crime succeed.

   a. **Knowledge is insufficient.** Knowledge alone is insufficient to establish the mens rea for conspiracy, at least for conspiracies to commit serious crimes. Defendant must join the conspiracy with the purpose of having the crime succeed. People v. Lauria, 251 Cal. App. 471 (1967).

   b. **Inferring purpose.** Purpose may be inferred when:

      i. The defendant has a stake in the venture.

ii. The defendant's goods or services serve no legitimate use.

iii. The volume of business with the illegitimate enterprise is grossly disproportionate to that of legitimate businesses.

c. **Mens rea for attendant circumstances.** If knowledge as to attendant circumstances is not required for the substantive offense, then such knowledge is also not required for conspiracy to commit that offense. For example, a conspiracy to assault a federal officer does not require that the victims know that their intended targets are federal officers. United States v. Feola, 420 U.S. 672 (1975).

C. CONSPIRACY AS A FORM OF ACCOMPLICE LIABILITY

1. **Pinkerton Liability.** A conspirator is responsible for all acts of her co-conspirators during the course of and in furtherance of the conspiracy. Pinkerton v. United States, 328 U.S. 640 (1946).

a. **Proof of accomplice liability not required.** A co-conspirator is automatically responsible for criminal acts of co-conspirators in furtherance of the conspiracy regardless of whether she knew of or participated in those crimes.

b. **Co-conspirator liability is not retroactive.** A conspirator is not responsible for substantive offenses committed before she joined the conspiracy, but acts committed by the defendant's co-conspirators before she joined the conspiracy can be used as evidence for general conspiracy charges.

c. **Model Penal Code.** The Model Penal Code rejects *Pinkerton* liability. It requires proof of accomplice liability.

2. **Scope of the Agreement—Single vs. Multiple Conspiracies**

a. **Scope of conspiracy defines defendant's potential *Pinkerton* liability.** Because a defendant is responsible for the criminal acts of all co- conspirators, it is important to define the scope of a criminal agreement. There are two general configurations for conspiracies: wheel conspiracies and chain conspiracies. Some conspiracies are hybrids of these two types.

b. **Wheel conspiracy.** If conspirators are each working with the same middleman, the arrangement is called a wheel conspiracy. In order for a wheel conspiracy to be considered one conspiracy, the individuals working with the middleman must themselves be tied together by common interests in a single venture. If they are not, then there is not one conspiracy but multiple conspiracies with the same hub. If there is one conspiracy, each conspirator is responsible for the criminal acts of each person interacting with the common middleman. If there are multiple conspiracies, the person interacting with the middleman is only responsible for her and the middleman's criminal acts. Kotteakos v. United States, 328 U.S. 750 (1946).

c. **Chain conspiracy.** In a chain conspiracy, conspirators participate in a single conspiracy by performing different roles along a single distribution line. Each is responsible for the criminal violations of others on the distribution line. Blumenthal v. United States, 332 U.S. 539 (1947).

3. **One Conspiracy with Multiple Objectives.** A single conspiracy may have multiple objectives. If a conspiracy has as its goal to commit several crimes, it is still ordinarily viewed as one conspiracy. This is called the *Braverman* rule.

D. PARTIES

1. **Gebardi Rule.** A person that a particular law is intended to protect cannot be a party to a conspiracy to violate that law.

2. **Wharton Rule.** If it is impossible to commit the substantive offense that is the objective of the conspiracy without cooperative action, an agreement to commit that offense is not an indictable conspiracy, e.g., dueling, bigamy.

3. **Bilateral Rule.** At traditional common law, a conspiracy requires at least "two guilty minds." Thus, if one of two persons charged with a conspiracy cannot be prosecuted for the crime, there is no conspiracy. This rule applies only when there are two co-conspirators. The following situations raise concerns under the bilateral rule:

   a. **Feigned conspirator.** Conspiracy with police informant or undercover officer.

   b. **Acquittal of all co-conspirators.** The acquittal of all co-conspirators in the same trial triggers the bilateral rule.

   c. **Special defenses for one conspirator.** If a conspirator has a defense that does not address the existence of the conspiracy, it will likely not affect a conspiracy charge against the remaining co-conspirator. These defenses include: diplomatic immunity, insanity, spousal privilege.

d. **No requirement that all conspirators be tried.** The bilateral rule requires only that there be two or more defendants eligible for prosecution. It does not require that all defendants be tried.

4. **Unilateral Approach.** The Model Penal Code and many state jurisdictions have adopted the unilateral concept of conspiracy. Under this approach, as long as the defendant believes she is conspiring with another person to commit a crime, she is guilty of conspiracy regardless of whether the other person can be convicted. MPC §5.04(1)(b).

E. DEFENSES TO CONSPIRACY

1. **Abandonment.** If everyone in a conspiracy abandons the plans of the conspiracy, the defendant is only responsible for crimes that were committed when the conspiracy was still active.

2. **Withdrawal from Ongoing Conspiracy.** Under common law, if a defendant withdrew from an ongoing conspiracy, she was still responsible for the initial crime of conspiracy, but would no longer be responsible for ongoing crimes of the conspiracy. To withdraw, a conspirator must notify her co-conspirators of her withdrawal.

3. **Model Penal Code Approach.** The Model Penal Code allows for a defense to the underlying conspiracy charge, as well as to ongoing co-conspirator liability.

   a. **Withdrawal.** Under the Model Penal Code, if a person either informs her co-conspirators that she is withdrawing or notifies the authorities that she is terminating her association with the conspiracy, she is not responsible for ongoing acts of her co-conspirators. MPC §5.03(7)(c).

   b. **Renunciation.** Under the Model Penal Code, if the defendant successfully thwarts the success of a conspiracy, she may also escape liability for initially joining the conspiracy. MPC §5.03(6).

F. CRIMINAL ENTERPRISES AND RICO

1. **RICO.** The Racketeer Influenced and Corrupt Organizations Act (RICO) prohibits participation in an enterprise through a pattern of racketeering activity. 18 U.S.C. §§1961-1963. The RICO statute allows the prosecution to charge multifaceted, diversified conspiracies. It requires proof of the following elements:

a. **Enterprise.** An organization, legal or illegal, engaged in ongoing activities.

b. **Pattern.** A pattern exists of at least two related acts of racketeering activities. "Continuity plus relationship" is used to define when activities are related.

c. **Racketeering activity.** The prohibited acts of "racketeering activity" are defined by statute. They include a wide range of state and federal crimes.

d. **Conduct and participation.** To be guilty of RICO, an individual must be involved in either the operation or the management of the enterprise. Mere advisors, like accountants, are not covered by the statute as participants.

DEFENSES

A. JUSTIFICATION VS. EXCUSE DEFENSES Two different types of affirmative defenses are recognized by the criminal law: justifications and excuses.

1. **Justification Defense.** A justification defense recognizes that the defendant made the right decision given the circumstances. Justification defenses include:

   a. Self-defense

   b. Defense of others

   c. Defense of property

   d. Law enforcement

   e. Necessity (choice of evils)

2. **Excuse Defense.** The law recognizes a limited number of defenses where the defendant made the socially wrong choice by engaging in certain conduct, but was either not fully capable of controlling her behavior, or for other policy reasons, should be excused from criminal liability. Excuse defenses include:

a. Duress

b. Intoxication

c. Insanity

d. Diminished capacity

e. Infancy

f. Consent

g. Entrapment

B. **SELF-DEFENSE** Self-defense is a type of necessity defense. It allows the use of force when a defendant is facing the threat of force.

1. **Common Law Elements.** Self-defense has long been recognized as a defense under common law. It requires:

a. Defendant has an honest and reasonable fear of death or great bodily harm. People v. Goetz, 68 N.Y.2d 96 (1986).

i. **Reasonable person in defendant's situation.** The reasonableness standard for self-defense is not strictly objective. The jury may consider:

(a) The physical attributes of defendant and the assailant;

(b) Defendant's prior experiences;

(c) Physical movements and comments of the potential assailant.

ii. **Honest but unreasonable fear.** In some jurisdictions, if the defendant has an honest but unreasonable fear, the defendant's crime is mitigated to voluntary or involuntary manslaughter.

iii. **Impact of battered spouse syndrome on reasonableness requirement.** Recently, courts have been willing to accept evidence on battered spouse's syndrome so that the jury can decide whether a reasonable person in the battered spouse's situation would have believed she was in imminent danger of death or serious bodily injury.

b. The perceived threat to the defendant is unlawful and immediate.

   i. **Objective requirement.** Traditional common law uses an objective standard to determine whether the defendant faced the threat of imminent harm.

   ii. **No preemptive strikes.** Under the traditional approach, a defendant is not allowed to launch a preemptive strike if she fears danger in the future. Other lawful alternatives must be found.

c. Defendant reacts with a proportional response, not excessive force.

   i. **Deadly force.** As part of the proportionality requirement, deadly force may only be used when the defendant faces the threat of deadly force or serious bodily injury. In some jurisdictions, deadly force may also be used against the threat of certain serious felonies, including, for example, kidnapping, forcible rape, or robbery.

   ii. **Force may only be used against attacker.** Self-defense only authorizes the use of force against one's attacker; it is not a justification for using force against a third person.

d. Defendant was not the initial aggressor.

   i. **Initial aggressor.** An initial aggressor loses the right to use deadly force, but retains the right to use nondeadly force.

   ii. **Reclaiming right to use self-defense.** An initial aggressor may reclaim the right to use self-defense by communicating to his adversary his intent to withdraw and attempting to do so in good faith.

e. Defendant has a duty to retreat before using deadly force.

   i. **No duty to retreat at traditional common law.** At traditional common law, a person did not have a duty to retreat before resorting to deadly force. However, many jurisdictions have added this requirement.

   ii. **When duty arises.** The duty to retreat only arises if the defendant uses deadly force.

iii. **Ability to reach complete safety.** Even when there is a duty to retreat, the defendant only has a duty to do so when he knows he can reach complete safety by retreating.

iv. **Exception to retreat rule.** Under the "Castle Rule," a defendant does not have the duty to retreat when he is attacked in his own home.

2. **Model Penal Code.** The Model Penal Code takes a more flexible approach to self-defense. It allows for self-defense when the "actor believes that such force is immediately necessary for the purpose of protecting [the defendant] against the use of unlawful force. . . ." MPC §3.04.

a. **Honest belief by actor that force is immediately necessary.**

i. **Subjective standard.** Unlike the common law, the Model Penal Code uses a subjective standard for determining when the use of force is necessary.

- **Limitation.** If the defendant is reckless or negligent in his belief that self-defense is necessary, he is responsible for any crimes that only require recklessness or negligence, such as manslaughter or negligent homicide. MPC §3.09(2).

ii. **Flexible concept of immediacy.** The immediacy of the threat facing the actor is viewed from the actor's subjective standpoint.

b. **Use of deadly force.** Under the Model Penal Code, deadly force may only be used when the actor believes such force is necessary to protect himself against the following threats:

i. death;

ii. serious bodily injury;

iii. kidnapping;

iv. forcible sexual intercourse.

c. **Initial aggressor rule.** The Model Penal Code also recognizes the initial aggressor limitation on the use of self-defense.

d. **Duty to retreat.** There is a duty to retreat before using deadly force if the defendant knows he can do so with complete safety. Exceptions are made when defendant is in his dwelling, workplace, or is a public officer performing his duty. MPC §3.04(2)(b)(ii).

e. **Injury to third party.** A defendant can assert self-defense when he accidentally hits a bystander, unless he has acted recklessly or negligently with regard to the bystander's safety. MPC §3.09(3).

C. DEFENSE OF ANOTHER

1. **Majority Reasonableness Standard.** A defendant may use force to protect another person if the defendant reasonably believes the use of force is justified. MPC §§3.05, 3.09(2).

2. **Minority Alter Ego/Act At Peril Rule.** In some courts, the defendant "stands in the shoes" of the person being defended. Defense of another is authorized only if the person being defended had the right to use defensive force.

D. DEFENSE OF PROPERTY

1. **Common Law.** At early common law, deadly force was permissible to prevent any felony. However, today deadly force may *not* be used solely to defend property.

2. **Spring Guns.** Mechanical devices may not be used to defend property if they constitute the use of deadly force.

E. LAW ENFORCEMENT DEFENSE

1. **Force in Apprehending Misdemeanants.** Both common law and the Model Penal Code allow law enforcement to use only nondeadly force in apprehending a misdemeanant. Durham v. State, 199 Ind. 567 (1927); MPC §3.07.

2. **Force in Apprehending Felons.** In *Tennessee v. Garner*, the Supreme Court held that deadly force may not be used to prevent a felon's escape unless the officer reasonably believes the suspect poses a significant threat of death or serious physical injury.

F. NECESSITY (Choice of Lesser Evils)

1. **Common Law Elements**

a. **Defendant faces a choice of evils.**

i. Economic necessity alone will not justify commission of a criminal act.

b. **There are no apparent legal alternatives.**

i. Necessity is a defense of last resort. If there is a lawful alternative, the defendant must select it.

c. **There is an immediate threat.**

i. The threat of future harm does not warrant use of the necessity defense.

d. **Defendant chooses the lesser harm.**

i. **Objective standard.** The jury decides whether the defendant, from society's point of view, picked the lesser evil.

ii. **Greater vs. lesser evils.** In general, loss of life is a greater evil than loss of property. It is a more difficult question whether fewer lives may be sacrificed to save more. Most courts avoid this question by not allowing necessity in homicide cases.

2. **Limitations on Use of Necessity Defense**

a. **Not self-created**

i. **Limit on necessity defense.** A defendant cannot create a necessity and then use that necessity as an excuse to violate the law.

ii. **Compare Model Penal Code.** Under MPC §3.02, a defendant who creates her own necessity may still assert a necessity defense to intentional crimes. However, the defendant may be prosecuted for negligent offenses because she was negligent in creating the dangerous situation.

b. **No contrary legislative intent**

i. **General rule.** The necessity defense may not be used when the legislature has already decided that the defendant's alleged necessity does not outweigh society's support for a particular law.

ii. **Civil disobedience cases.** Necessity is often claimed but rarely succeeds in civil disobedience cases. Often, the harm faced is not imminent, defendants have other lawful alternatives to change the law, and the protester's arguments are contrary to legislative judgment on the issue.

c. **Economic necessity insufficient.** Economic necessity alone will not justify commission of a criminal act. The Model Penal Code does not have a specific restriction against economic necessity, although it is unlikely its harm would outweigh the harm of violating the law.

d. **Surrender requirement in prison escape cases.** Necessity is recognized as a defense to prison escape, but there is an additional requirement that the escapee surrender immediately upon reaching a place of safety. United States v. Bailey, 444 U.S. 394 (1980).

e. **Necessity in homicide cases.** The majority rule is that necessity is not a defense in intentional homicide cases. For a minority of jurisdictions, necessity is permitted if one sacrifices fewer lives to save more lives. The Model Penal Code does not prohibit the use of a necessity defense in homicide cases.

3. **Model Penal Code.** MPC §3.02 provides for a choice of evils defense. A defendant may engage in criminal conduct to avoid harm if:

   a. The harm avoided is greater than the harm done.

   b. There is no specific prohibition to the use of a choice of evils defense for this offense.

   c. There is no clear legislative purpose to exclude the choice of evils defense in defendant's situation.

G. EUTHANASIA

1. **Changing Law.** In most jurisdictions, euthanasia is still unlawful. However, the law regarding the "right to die" is in flux. If the courts recognize a right to die, then the defense of euthanasia may be used as a type of necessity—the harm in taking a terminally ill person's life was outweighed by the good of ending the patient's suffering.

H. DURESS

1. **Excuse Defense.** Duress is an excuse defense. Because a defendant is compelled by another person's use of force or threat of force to commit a crime, the defendant is excused from punishment for his otherwise unlawful conduct.

2. **Common Law Duress.** The requirements of common law duress are:

   a. threat of death or grievous bodily harm;

   b. imminently posed;

   c. against the defendant or a close friend or relative;

   d. creating such fear that an ordinary person would yield;

   e. defendant did not put himself in the situation;

   f. defendant did not kill another person.

3. **Model Penal Code Duress.** The requirements of duress under MPC §2.09 are:

   a. threat of unlawful force;

   b. against defendant or any person;

   c. the type of threat that would cause a person of "reasonable firmness" in defendant's situation to yield;

   d. defendant did not recklessly put himself in the situation;

   e. the defense is available for any crime, including homicide.

4. **Comparison of Common Law and Model Penal Code Duress**

   a. **Threat of death or grievous bodily harm.** Under common law, a defendant must face a threat of death or great bodily harm to have a duress defense.

      i. **Compare Model Penal Code.** The Model Penal Code only requires a threat of "unlawful force." The more serious the threat, the more serious a crime the defendant is allowed to commit. MPC §2.09.

      ii. **No economic duress or threat to reputation.** Neither the common law nor the Model Penal Code recognizes a duress defense when the threat is of economic harm or damage to the defendant's reputation.

b. **Imminently posed.** Under the common law, there is an objective requirement that the threatened harm be imminent.

i. **Compare Model Penal Code.** The Model Penal Code does not have a separate imminency requirement. However, the imminency of the threat may be a factor in deciding whether a reasonable person would have yielded to the threat.

c. **Against the defendant or a close friend or relative.** Under early common law, the defendant himself had to be threatened. Modern common law recognizes threats to close relatives of the defendant.

i. **Compare Model Penal Code.** Under the MPC, the threat may be to any person. MPC §2.09. However, the closer the relationship to the defendant, the more likely a trier of fact will find a reasonable person would have yielded to the threat.

d. **Creating such fear that an ordinary person would yield.** An objective standard is used under the common law to determine whether the defendant properly yielded to the threat against him.

i. **Compare Model Penal Code.** Under the MPC, the trier of fact must look at "a person of reasonable firmness in defendant's situation." This is a mixed objective and subjective standard which allows the jury to consider such subjective factors as the defendant's size, strength, age, and health.

e. **Defendant put himself in the situation.** The common law denies the duress defense to anyone who puts himself into a coercive situation.

i. **Compare Model Penal Code.** The Model Penal Code also denies a duress defense if the defendant puts himself into a coercive situation, but it is a bit more forgiving than the common law standard. It only applies the restriction to defendants who "recklessly" put themselves into the situation.

f. **Homicide cases.** The common law strictly precludes the use of a duress defense in murder cases.

i. **Compare Model Penal Code.** The Model Penal Code does not have a restriction on the use of a duress defense in homicide cases.

5. **Imperfect Duress.** In some jurisdictions, a faulty duress defense can be used to reduce a murder to manslaughter on the theory that a defendant who kills under duress is acting under extreme emotional distress.

6. **Duress vs. Necessity.** The threat of force by another person may raise either a duress or necessity defense. However, threatened harm by nature only raises a necessity defense.

I. INTOXICATION

1. **Involuntary Intoxication.** Involuntary intoxication can be a complete defense. It applies to intoxication by either alcohol or drugs.

   a. **Forms of involuntary intoxication.** Involuntary intoxication can take the following forms:

      i. **Unwitting intoxication.** Defendant is unaware that she has ingested drugs or alcohol.

      ii. **Coerced intoxication.** Defendant is forced to ingest drugs or alcohol.

      iii. **Pathological intoxication.** A medication or alcohol produces an unexpected grossly excessive effect.

2. **Voluntary intoxication.** In most jurisdictions, voluntary intoxication, if recognized as a defense, can only be used as a defense to specific intent crimes; i.e., crimes requiring proof of purposeful conduct. Intoxication is used to show that the defendant was unable to form the mens rea for the offense. The defendant is then ordinarily guilty of a general intent crime that does not require sober, sophisticated thinking.

   i. **Degree of intoxication.** Mere intake of alcohol or drugs is insufficient to demonstrate intoxication. There must be a "prostration of the defendant's faculties."

   ii. **No constitutional requirement for intoxication defense.** There is no constitutional requirement that an intoxication defense be afforded. Montana v. Egelhoff, 96 D.A.R. 6469 (1996).

   iii. **Prolonged intoxication leading to insanity.** Voluntary intoxication can lead to a complete defense if a defendant's prolonged use leads to a permanent mental disease or disorder.

J. INSANITY

1. **Competency vs. Insanity.** Competency examines the defendant's mental state at the time of trial. Insanity describes a defendant's mental state at the time of the crime. If a defendant is incompetent to stand trial, she is ordinarily committed until she is competent to stand trial or there are permanent civil commitment proceedings. A defendant who is adjudged insane is not guilty of a crime, but may later be subject to civil commitment.

   a. **Competency requirements.** A defendant must be competent to stand trial and, if applicable, be executed.

   b. **Competency to stand trial.** The test for mental competency to stand trial is whether the defendant has sufficient ability:

      i. to consult with her attorney,

      ii. to rationally understand the proceedings against her.

      Dusky v. United States, 362 U.S. 420 (1960).

2. **Requirements of Insanity Defense.** There are several tests used to determine whether a defendant is not guilty of a crime because of insanity. Common to all the tests is that requirement that the defendant be suffering from a mental disease or defect at the time of the crime.

   a. **Traditional M'Naghten test.** The traditional test for legal insanity requires proof that:

      i. at the time of the commission of the offense;

      ii. defendant was laboring under a defect or disease of the mind;

      iii. defendant did not know:

         (a) the nature and quality of his acts (defendant was operating in a hallucinogenic state); or

         (b) that his acts were wrong (morally or legally wrong).

   b. **Deific command exception.** Most jurisdictions, even those that follow the traditional M'Naghten test, also allow for an insanity defense when the defendant, due to a mental illness or disease, believes that God or a Supreme Being has ordered him to commit the crime.

c. **Irresistible impulse test.** Fewer jurisdictions recognize the irresistible impulse test. Under this test, an accused is legally insane if, due to a mental disease or defect, he would have been unable to stop himself even if a police officer had been at his elbow.

d. **Durham product rule.** In the past, a few jurisdictions have used a rule that simply asks whether the defendant's unlawful act was the product of mental disease or defect.

e. **Model Penal Code approach.** In a more flexible approach, the MPC holds that a person is not responsible for criminal conduct if due to a mental disease or defect:

i. he lacks substantial capacity

ii. to either:

(a) appreciate the criminality (wrongfulness) of his conduct; or

(b) conform his conduct to the requirements of the law.

3. **Disease or Mental Defect.** Mental disease is a legal, not medical, concept. Generally, it includes "any abnormal condition of the mind which substantially affects mental or emotional processes and substantially impairs behavior controls." McDonald v. United States, 312 F.2d 847, 850-851 (D.C. cir. 1962). A multitude of factors are used to determine when a mental condition is a disease or defect that can trigger an insanity defense.

K. DIMINISHED CAPACITY

1. **Nature of Defense.** Diminished capacity is a controversial defense abandoned by many jurisdictions. When applied, it is similar to voluntary intoxication — evidence of a defendant's mental condition is used to negate the prosecution's proof that the defendant formed the mens rea necessary for a specific intent (purposeful) crime. The diminished capacity defense is usually used when the defendant has a problem in prevailing on his insanity defense.

2. **Approaches to Defense.** Jurisdictions have taken three approaches to the diminished capacity defense:

a. **Reject defense.** The modern trend is to reject the diminished capacity defense. State v. Wilcox, 70 Ohio 182 (1982).

b. **Allow defense to mitigate specific intent crimes.** The majority of jurisdictions that allow the diminished capacity defense only allow it to reduce a specific intent crime to a general intent crime (e.g., first-degree murder to second-degree murder). United States v. Brawner, 471 F.2d 969 (D.C. Cir. 1972).

c. **Allow defense for any crime.** Under MPC §4.02(1), diminished capacity may be raised as a defense to any crime, even if it is a general intent crime and does not have a lesser included offense. Psychiatric evidence may be used to negate the mens rea for any crime.

L. INFANCY

1. **Common Law.** Children under age seven are conclusively incapable of forming mens rea for a crime. Children between ages 7-14 are presumed incapable of committing a crime. Youth over age 14 may be prosecuted for crimes.

2. **Statutory.** Each jurisdiction can set its own age limits for an infancy defense.

M. ENTRAPMENT

1. **Subjective Approach.** In federal court and many states, the test for whether a defendant was entrapped is the subjective "predisposition" test: Was the defendant predisposed to commit a crime? If the answer is "yes," defendant does not have an entrapment defense even if the government officers provide an opportunity for defendant to commit an offense.

2. **Objective Approach.** Alternatively, courts use an objective government misconduct test. The focus is on the government's behavior. The question asked is: Would the government's conduct have likely induced a law-abiding person to commit the crime? If the answer is "yes," defendant has an entrapment defense regardless of how predisposed she was to commit the crime.

3. **Model Penal Code Approach.** The Model Penal Code uses the objective approach but leaves the decision to the judge, not the jury. MPC §2.13.

N. CONSENT

1. **General Rule.** Consent is generally not a defense to a crime. It is only a defense if lack of consent is a material element of the crime, such as common law rape.

2. **Defective Consent.** Consent is ineffective under the following circumstances:

   a. victim legally incompetent to consent;

   b. victim incapacitated;

   c. forced consent.

13 THEFT OFFENSES AND OTHER CRIMES AGAINST PROPERTY

A. LARCENY

1. **Definition.** Larceny is the trespassory taking of the personal property of another with intent to permanently deprive that person of the property.

2. **Elements**

   a. **Trespassory taking and carrying away.** Defendant must take and carry away the property of another person.

      i. **Trespassory.** The taking must be without permission; i.e., trespassory.

      ii. **Asportation.** Slight movement of the property is sufficient.

   b. **Property.** Traditional theft laws cover only the taking of tangible personal property.

   c. **In possession of another.** The property must be taken from the lawful possession of another person, even if that person does not own the property. If a defendant is given temporary control over property, he can still be guilty of larceny if that control is deemed mere custody, not possession over the property.

   d. **With intent to permanently deprive.** The defendant must have the intent to deprive the victim permanently of the property at the time it is taken. If the defendant only intends to borrow the property, there is no larceny.

B. ROBBERY

1. **Definition.** Robbery is the taking of property from another person with force or intimidation.

2. **Elements**

   a. **Taking of property.** Like larceny, robbery is limited to the taking of personal property.

   b. **From victim's person or presence.** The property must be taken from the victim's person or the victim's presence.

   c. **By force or threat of force.** The defendant need not cause actual injury to the victim; slight force is sufficient. Threats of future force constitute extortion, not robbery.

C. EXTORTION

1. **Definition.** Extortion is the taking of property by threat of future violence. It sometimes goes by the name, "blackmail."

2. **Elements**

   a. taking of property

   b. from another

   c. by threat of future violence

D. MISAPPROPRIATION AND EMBEZZLEMENT

1. **Nature of Crime.** The courts and legislatures expanded theft crimes to include conversion of property that is already in the defendant's possession.

2. **Elements of Embezzlement**

   a. fraudulent

   b. conversion (misappropriation)

   c. of the property of another

   d. that the defendant already possesses.

E. FALSE PRETENSES

1. **Definition.** False pretenses is taking title of the property of another by false representations.

2. **Compare Larceny by Trick.** Larceny by trick is taking possession of the property of another by false representations.

3. **Elements of False Pretenses**

   a. taking title and possession of the property of another;

   b. by knowingly false representations;

   c. with regard to a material present or past fact;

   d. with intent to defraud.

F. LARCENY BY TRICK

1. **Definition.** Larceny by trick is taking possession of the property of another by false representations.

2. **Elements**

   a. taking possession of the property of another;

   b. by false representations or deceit;

   c. with intent to defraud.

G. DEFENSES TO THEFT AND FRAUD CRIMES

1. **Consent.** A taking must be against the owner's will or by fraud. If an owner knowingly consents to the permanent taking and there has been no fraud, then there is no theft crime.

2. **Claim of Right.** If a defendant is the true owner of goods or money, she may try to reclaim her right to it. Claim of right is not a defense to robbery or extortion, nor does it apply to larceny if the victim has lawful possession of the property when it is taken.

H. BURGLARY

1. **Definition.** Common law burglary is the breaking and entering of the dwelling house of another at nighttime with the intent to commit a felony inside.

2. **Elements**

   a. **Breaking.** Opening a door or window is breaking. Constructive breaking occurs when the defendant uses threats or misrepresentations to gain entry, or exceeds the scope of entry consented to by the victim.

   b. **Entering.** Partial entry is sufficient.

   c. **Dwelling house of another.** Common law burglary only covered residential buildings. Statutes have now expanded burglary to commercial buildings.

   d. **At nighttime.** At common law, illegal entry was burglary only if it happened at night.

   e. **Intent to commit felony inside.** Burglary is a specific intent crime because it requires that at the time of unlawful entry, defendant have the further intent to commit a felony inside the residence.

I. ARSON

1. **Definition.** The common law definition of arson is "the malicious burning of the dwelling house of another."

2. **Elements**

   a. **Burning.** Common law required actual charring of some part of the structure. Mere smoke damage or damage to the property inside the building is insufficient.

   b. **Dwelling House.** Common law only applied arson to the burning of residential buildings.

   c. **Of another.** The dwelling must be in the possession of another, even if the defendant is the owner of the building.

   d. **With malice.** A defendant must act with gross recklessness in burning the home.

The Study of Criminal Law

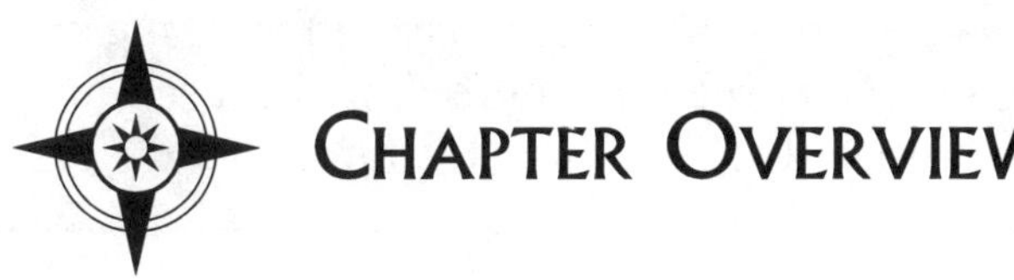

Chapter Overview

The criminal justice system is a complex combination of both substantive and procedural law. An initial study of criminal law focuses on the substantive principles defining crimes and defenses. It is helpful, however, to have an overview of how the criminal justice system operates, where laws originated from, and what procedural standards govern criminal cases. Therefore, Chapter 1 addresses:

- The Development of American Criminal Law
- Classification of Offenses
- An Overview of the Parties Involved in the Criminal Justice System
- An Overview of the Procedural Stages of a Criminal Case
- Concepts of Burden of Proof and Presumptions
- The Role of the Jury
- The Role of Counsel

A. INTRODUCTION

1. What Is Criminal Law?

Criminal law is the study of behavior punished by society. A course in criminal law will ordinarily include the study of: 1. theories of punishment; 2. legal definitions of crimes; 3. legal definitions of defenses; and 4. an overview of how cases are processed through the criminal justice system.

2. Criminal Law vs. Torts Law

Criminal law uses the power of the state to punish those who harm others or breach society's standards. A crime is an offense against the entire community, not just against the individual victim. While the same act may lead to both criminal and civil liability, civil liability is ordinarily limited to monetary penalties, whereas criminal convictions may lead to incarceration, capital punishment, and/or fines. There is often an additional societal stigma attached to conviction for a criminal offense.

STUDY TIP

While similar terms and concepts are used by both criminal law and torts, it is important not to confuse them. The same terms may have very different meanings in the study of each subject. For example, the term "proximate cause" has different connotations in criminal and tort law. See Chapter 7 infra.

3. Criminal Law vs. Criminal Procedure

Many first-year criminal courses focus on substantive criminal law issues, leaving criminal procedure to another course. Substantive criminal law involves the actual legal requirements of crimes and defenses. Criminal procedure addresses how a suspect is investigated, arrested, and processed through the criminal justice system.

4. Approaching the Study of Criminal Law

The study of criminal law breaks down into four basic components: 1. elements of crimes, 2. theories of accomplice culpability, 3. preliminary offenses, and 4. elements of defenses. The case study method is commonly used to learn these elements because it not only teaches the legal principles and rationales behind them but also gives examples of how those legal principles are applied.

STUDY TIP

Do not presume that every case in your casebook is included because it was correctly decided. Rather, it may be assigned to demonstrate a flaw in the court's reasoning or differing approaches to legal principles.

STUDY TIP

Often, the key information regarding a case is found in its footnotes or editor's notes. Because casebook authors typically edit cases, it is critical to read the footnotes that add perspective to the case.

5. Learning the Black Letter Law

Black Letter Law refers to the specific definitions of crimes and defenses and how the courts interpret those requirements. Each crime or defense is composed of "elements." An element is a requirement that must be proven in order for the crime or defense to be recognized.

STUDY TIP

When reviewing cases, it is important to focus on the court's instructions to the jury because that is where the court sums up the Black Letter legal requirements for the crime or defense.

B. DEVELOPMENT OF AMERICAN CRIMINAL LAW

1. English Criminal Law

American criminal law is derived from English common law. The common law was established through a series of case decisions creating principles of law. It is the development of legal principles through "case precedent."

2. Statutory vs. Common Law

Except in rare situations, the common law no longer governs in America. Both state and federal courts are governed by statutory law. However, the common law remains important because American statutes typically incorporate common law principles and terminology.

a. **Example.** Murder is statutorily defined as the "killing of another human being with malice." The definition of "malice" is found in the common law.

b. Exception. In People v. Kevorkian, 527 N.W.2d 714, 738 (Mich. 1994), the Michigan Supreme Court upheld the applicability of Michigan's savings clause statute prohibiting any acts that were offenses at common law. The court relied upon common law to determine Kevorkian's criminal liability for assisted suicide, but the common law was used in that case to limit, not expand, the scope of criminal liability.

3. The Model Penal Code

The Model Penal Code (MPC) is a model statute drafted by the American Law Institute. It is *not* binding on the legislatures or courts. Rather, it is a guide for drafting codes and has had a strong influence on states which have redrafted their codes since the MPC first was drafted in 1962.

STUDY TIP

The MPC provides a black letter statement of law that either reflects current law or may be used as a means to compare different approaches to criminal law issues.

C. CLASSIFICATION OF OFFENSES

1. Felonies, Misdemeanors, and Violations

At common law, crimes were divided into felonies and misdemeanors. However, as more regulatory crimes were enacted, the law created another category for the least serious offenses—criminal violations.

a. Felonies. Felonies are those offenses that carry a punishment of more than one year in jail. Felonies are more serious than misdemeanors.

b. Misdemeanors. Traditionally, misdemeanors are offenses subject to lesser punishment, ordinarily less than one year in jail.

c. Violations. Criminal violations are the least serious types of crimes and typically carry only a fine as punishment.

2. Malum in se vs. Malum prohibitum

At common law, crimes were also categorized by the level of danger a defendant's activities posed.

a. **Malum in se.** Crimes that are inherently immoral or dangerous are considered as malum in se, e.g., murder.

b. **Malum prohibitum.** Crimes where the defendant violated a regulation added to maintain the orderly functioning of society are considered malum prohibitum. Although there may be nothing immoral about the defendant's conduct, the defendant has violated a specific prohibition of the law, e.g., traffic violations.

D. AN OVERVIEW OF THE CRIMINAL JUSTICE SYSTEM

1. Overview of Participants

The key participant in the criminal justice system is the person being charged with the crime, the defendant. However, there are many other participants in the justice system. Each of these persons makes discretionary decisions that affect the outcome of the case.

Agency or Official	*Role*
Police	Apprehend suspects, investigate cases, and prevent crime
Prosecutors	Make filing decisions and prosecute cases
Magistrates	Provide initial review of charges against suspect
Judges	Supervise trials, sometimes determine guilt and impose sentence on guilty defendants
Probation Officers	Investigate case for sentencing and supervise defendants sentenced to probation
Parole Officers	Supervise defendants released from custody
Correctional Officers	Supervise defendants in custody

Note: Both the state and federal authorities have the power to enforce criminal laws. Cases that charge "United States vs." allege violations of federal law. Cases that charge "People/State/Commonwealth vs." allege violations of state law.

2. Overview of Procedures

The steps in a criminal case include:

Investigation	Law enforcement officers, often at the direction of prosecutors, interview witnesses, collect evidence, identify suspects.
Grand Jury	Body of citizens investigate and charge crimes.
Indictment	Grand jury files charges against the defendant.
Information/Complaint	Prosecuting agency files formal criminal charges.

Arraignment	Advisement of charges against the defendant and the defendant's constitutional rights
Bail	Release of defendant pending outcome of proceedings
Discovery	Exchange of information regarding a case
Preliminary Hearing	Hearing to determine whether there is probable cause to hold a defendant for trial
Plea Bargaining	Negotiations between prosecutor and defense counsel on outcome of case; used in 90% of cases
Diversion	Dismissal of case upon defendant's satisfactory completion of probation program
Guilty Plea	Defendant's admission of the guilt
Trial	Formal process to adjudicate guilt or innocence
Sentencing	Punishment for the offense. May take the form of incarceration, fines, restitution orders, and/or probation.

3. The Trial Process

The trial process is governed by rules of procedure and evidence. It includes:

Jury Selection	A jury is selected from a panel of potential jurors ("venire"). Jurors are questioned regarding their background and attitudes ("voir dire"). Jurors may be excused for bias ("for cause") or at the discretion of the litigants ("peremptory challenges").
Opening Statement	Each side has the opportunity to state to the jury what they expect the evidence to demonstrate.
Prosecution's case	Prosecution presents witnesses and evidence establishing defendant committed each element of the offense. "Direct examination" is questioning by the party calling the witness. "Cross-examination" is questioning by the opposing party. "Redirect examination" is follow-up questioning by the calling party.
Defense's case	Defense has the opportunity but no obligation to present evidence.
Rebuttal/Surrebuttal	Responsive evidence by each side
Closing Arguments	Each side argues why the evidence does or does not support the charges against defendant.
Jury Instructions	If there is a jury, the court instructs it on the law of the case.

Verdict	Decision by the jury
Sentencing	The court imposes its "judgment," which directs what type of punishment defendant will receive for the crime.

4. Presentation of Evidence

Not all evidence is admissible in a criminal case. Privileges and rules of evidence may preclude the introduction of evidence. For example, a defendant has a Fifth Amendment privilege not to testify. Likewise, the prosecution may not introduce prior criminal acts merely to show that the defendant has a propensity to commit crimes. Prior criminal acts are only admissible if they show motive, intent, modus operandi, identity, plan, preparation, or absence of accident or mistake.

5. Burdens of Proof

The burden of proof in a criminal case is proof beyond a reasonable doubt, In re Winship, 397 U.S. 358, 364 (1970).

a. **Beyond a reasonable doubt.** There is no set definition of "beyond a reasonable doubt." It is the highest standard of proof used under the law. It is designed to minimize the risk of convicting an innocent person. Jury instructions that refer to proof to "a moral certainty" are disfavored by the Supreme Court. Sandoval v. California, 511 U.S. 1, 114 S. Ct. 1239 (1994).

b. **Prosecution bears the burden of proof.** The burden is always on the prosecution to prove each element of a crime beyond a reasonable doubt. Patterson v. New York, 432 U.S. 197 (1977). However, the burden of proof to prove an affirmative defense may be placed on the defendant without violating due process. Leland v. Oregon, 343 U.S. 790 (1952).

c. **Burden of proof vs. burden of production.** Although the prosecution bears the ultimate burden of proof, the defense may face the "burden of production" to present evidence to raise a defense.

   i. **Example.** Defendant is charged with murder. The prosecution must prove that the defendant killed the victim with malice. If the defendant plans to argue that he acted in heat of passion or by self-defense, he must produce at least some evidence of those defenses.

   ii. **Affirmative defenses.** For some defenses, the defendant may have the burden of proving to the jury that the requirements of the defense have been met (e.g., insanity). However, the defendant will only bear this burden if the prosecution has already met its burden of proving beyond a reasonable doubt all the elements of the crime.

d. **Presumptions.** The court may instruct jurors regarding drawing inferences from the facts in a case. "Permissive presumptions" allow the jurors to decide whether to draw such an inference; "mandatory presumptions" require jurors to do so. Because presumptions ease the prosecution's burden, they can be unconstitutional.

Example. If the defendant is charged with "deliberate homicide" requiring an intent to kill, a jury instruction that the "law presumes that a person intends the ordinary consequences of his act" unconstitutionally relieves the prosecution of its duty to prove intent. Sandstrom v. Montana, 442 U.S. 510 (1979).

E. ROLE OF THE JURY

The constitutional right to a jury trial is a key component of the American criminal justice system. It protects individuals from arbitrary action by the government and ensures that criminal convictions and acquittals reflect the common sense judgment of representatives of the community.

1. Right to a Jury Trial

The Sixth Amendment guarantees the right to a jury trial for all serious crimes. Duncan v. Louisiana, 391 U.S. 145 (1968). There is no right to a jury trial for a petty offense carrying a maximum term of six months imprisonment. Baldwin v. New York, 399 U.S. 66 (1970). Recently the Supreme Court held that a defendant accused of such a petty offense has no right to a jury trial even when he is charged with multiple counts of the same offense and the aggregate maximum sentence is more than six months. Lewis v. United States, 116 S. Ct. 2163 (1996) (defendant was charged with multiple counts of obstructing the mail, each carrying a maximum sentence of six months).

2. Number of Jurors

Traditionally, juries have been composed of 12 citizens, but there is no constitutional right to a jury of 12. A six-member jury satisfies constitutional requirements. Williams v. Florida, 399 U.S. 78, 86 (1970).

3. Unanimous Verdict

Unanimity is not required in state criminal trials so long as a substantial majority of the jury supports the verdict. Apodaca v. Oregon, 406 U.S. 404 (1972).

4. Jury Nullification

Juries have the inherent power to disregard the law and render a verdict contrary to it. However, in most jurisdictions, the defendant does not have the right to a jury instruction advising jurors of their power to nullify. United States v. Dougherty, 473 F.2d 1113 (D.C. Cir. 1972).

5. General vs. Special Verdicts

In most cases, jurors issue "general verdicts" voting to acquit or convict the defendant. A "special verdict" requires the jury to answer specific questions regarding the case. "Special verdicts" are disfavored because they may direct the jury toward a particular verdict. United States v. Spock, 416 F.2d 165 (1st Cir. 1969).

6. Inconsistent Verdicts

Inconsistent verdicts occur when the defendant is charged with several interrelated offenses and the jury returns convictions and acquittals that are logically conflicting. In most jurisdictions, inconsistent verdicts are permitted for both jury and judge trials. United States v. Powell, 469 U.S. 57 (1984).

F. ROLE OF COUNSEL

In an adversarial system, defense counsel has the duty to zealously represent the client within the boundaries of the law.

1. Duty of Confidentiality

A primary duty of a lawyer is not to reveal confidential information. ABA Model Rule of Prof. Conduct 1.6. The duty of confidentiality is designed to encourage defendants to be candid with their counsel.

2. Duty of Candor Toward the Tribunal

Lawyers also have the duty not to knowingly make false statements of law or fact to a tribunal or fail to disclose material facts. ABA Model Rule of Prof. Conduct 3.3.

3. Duty When Client Wants to Present Perjured Testimony

A lawyer may not participate in the presentation of perjured testimony. ABA Model Rule of Prof. Conduct 3.3. However, jurisdictions split over the proper approach when such testimony is presented. In most jurisdictions, counsel may move to withdraw or have the defendant testify in narrative form and not use the perjured testimony in closing argument. In a minority of jurisdictions, a lawyer must reveal the fraud to the court.

a. **No constitutional right to present perjured testimony.** A defendant does not have the constitutional right to a lawyer who will assist him in presenting perjured testimony. Nix v. Whiteside, 475 U.S. 157 (1986) (counsel threatened to withdraw if defendant presented perjured testimony).

FIGURE 1-1

NATURE OF CRIMINAL LAW	
Criminal Law vs. Torts	Society is a victim of crimes. Individuals are victims of torts.
Common Law	Common law terms are now used to define statutory crimes.
Types of Crimes	Felonies (> 1 yr. jail) Misdemeanors (≤ 1 yr. jail) Malum in se (dangerous/immoral) Malum prohibitum (regulatory)
Burden of Proof	Beyond a reasonable doubt
Jury	Right for all serious crimes; No constitutional right to 12 jurors or unanimous jury.
Counsel	Right to counsel in all criminal cases.

REVIEW QUESTIONS AND ANSWERS

Questions: True or false?

1. Criminal law is the study of the legal requirements of crimes and defenses.
2. In order for a crime or defense to be recognized, at least one of the elements of the crime or defense must be proven.
3. The common law no longer governs in America but is still important for interpreting criminal laws in state and federal courts.
4. Since the emergence of the Model Penal Code, many jurisdictions have adopted the entire MPC as the governing code in their jurisdiction.
5. Criminal violations did not exist at common law.

6. If Joe were to be caught speeding at 80 m.p.h. in California, he would be committing a crime classified as malum prohibitum.

7. In the majority of all cases involving criminal conduct, an indictment is filed by law enforcement officers.

8. Upon a defendant's satisfactory completion of a probation program, he is placed on parole.

9. A defendant's decision not to present evidence in his favor entitles the prosecution to an automatic judgment.

10. A defendant was convicted of several burglaries. He used the same method of illegally entering each home—he cut a hole in the back door. Defendant served two years for his crimes. Six months after he was released, he was charged with the burglary of six more homes. In all six homes, there was a Christmas tree-shaped hole cut into the back door. Evidence of the defendant's prior criminal acts is admissible in the defendant's second burglary trial.

11. A burden of proof may be placed on the prosecution or the defense.

12. In order for a defendant's conviction to be constitutional, the verdict of the jury must be unanimous.

13. When Jim first consulted his lawyer Larry, he told him that he planned for several weeks to go to his girlfriend's house to kill her and her lover. After realizing this was not in his best interest, Jim tells Larry Lawyer that he wants to change his story and will now tell the jury that he shot his girlfriend and her lover when he caught them in bed together. As Jim's lawyer, he must zealously support Jim's testimony in court.

14. Jurors are required to draw specific inferences from the evidence presented in court.

15. The Sixth Amendment grants a defendant the right to a jury trial for all crimes.

Answers: 1. T; 2. F; 3. F; 4. F; 5. T; 6. T; 7. F; 8. F; 9. F; 10. T; 11. T; 12. F; 13. F; 14. T; 15. F

2 Justification of Punishment

Chapter Overview

Understanding the reasons society punishes criminals is critical to learning the principles of criminal law. Almost all discussion of criminal law issues leads back to the purposes of punishment. It is also essential to understand the limitations on the government's power to punish. Although criminal law is based upon society's mores, not all moral breaches are crimes. Chapter 2 addresses the following issues:

- Purposes of Punishment
  - Retribution
  - Deterrence
  - Rehabilitation/Reform
  - Incapacitation
- Approaches to Sentencing
  - Determinate vs. indeterminate
- Limitations on the Power to Punish
  - Proportionality
- Sources of Criminal Law
  - Criminalization and decriminalization
  - Legality

A. TYPES OF PUNISHMENT

Punishment may take many forms, including incarceration, fines, probation, and execution. In addition, the convicted defendant faces social stigmas. Incarceration is the most common form of punishment. It deprives a defendant of the privileges of the free community and may subject the inmate to harsher dangerous conditions in jail.

B. PURPOSES OF PUNISHMENT

There are at least four purposes for punishing a criminal defendant: retribution, deterrence (general and specific), rehabilitation (reform), and incapacitation. Not all of these purposes will be served in each case. In fact, these justifications often work at cross-purposes to one another. Underlying these purposes of punishment are two key philosophical theories of punishment: retributivism and utilitarianism. Criminal law often shows a tension and even a mixing of these conflicting theories of punishment.

1. Retribution

According to the retributivist theory, a defendant "deserves" to be punished because he or she has committed a crime. Immanuel Kant, Philosophy of Law. Retribution is a form of social revenge intended to repair the evil a defendant's crime has inflicted, reassert the values of society, and reestablish social order. Punishment constitutes the defendant's "just deserts" or "payback" for having committed the offense. Retribution is often associated with the ancient concept of *lex talionis* or "an eye for an eye."

a. **Deserved punishment.** Retributivists believe that criminals deserve punishment because they have exercised their free will to violate society's laws. Michael S. Moore, The Moral Worth of Retribution (1987). There are several theoretical bases for retribution:

i. **Punishment as revenge.** Punishment is justified because society, as well as the individual victim, has a right to seek revenge against the defendant. By avenging the crime, the victim is made whole and the need for private revenge is avoided. Additionally, some theorists believe it is morally right to hate criminals and therefore, punishment is justified. 2 James Fitzjames Stephens, A History of the Criminal Law of England 81-82 (1833 ed.).

ii. **Punishment as paying back a debt to society.** Punishment is justified because the defendant, by committing a crime, has taken something away from society and must repay a debt. Alternatively, retribution is seen as a way to maintain the social fabric. The defendant must repay a debt to society and thereby repair the tear in the social fabric. Emile Durkheim, The Division of Labor in Society 108-109 (Simpson transl. 1964).

iii. **Punishment as sending a message.** Punishment sends a message that society has certain moral norms that cannot be violated. Punishment reasserts society's standards for conduct.

b. Retribution looks backward. Retribution requires punishment of a defendant even if it will not deter future criminal conduct. Retribution looks backward at previous conduct to determine whether it deserves punishment irrespective of any future benefit to society.

c. Criticism of retributivism. Utilitarians criticize retributivism for:

- intentionally inflicting pain even when it cannot be shown that punishment will promote the greater good;
- legitimizing vengeance;
- relying on emotion, not reason, to determine the imposition of punishment;
- punishing those who are forced to commit crimes because they are subjected to unfair social conditions.

2. Deterrence

Under a utilitarian theory, punishment is used to deter the commission of future offenses. The premise of a deterrence theory is that defendants weigh the advantages and disadvantages of their acts before committing a crime. Punishment increases the costs of criminal behavior and thereby provides a disincentive to commit future crime. Jeremy Bentham, Principles of Penal Law. There are two types of deterrence: general and specific.

a. General vs. specific deterrence. There are two types of deterrence: general and specific.

i. General deterrence. Punishment of the individual defendant is used as an example to deter others from committing the same crime.

Example. Defendant is convicted of bank robbery. Because of defendant's old age and failing health, the judge knows there is little risk the defendant will ever rob again. The judge imposes a stiff sentence anyway to deter other potential criminals from robbing banks.

ii. Specific deterrence. Punishment may also be used to discourage the individual defendant from repeating criminal behavior.

Example. Defendant purposely fails to file her income tax returns. To insure that the defendant will not fail to file future returns, the court imposes a lengthy sentence and significant fine.

b. Criticisms of deterrence theory. The deterrence theory of punishment has been criticized for:

i. being ineffective in cases where the criminal is motivated to act by emotional concerns. Deterrence theory presumes the decision to commit a crime is a rational decision in which the defendant coolly weighs the benefits and costs of her actions. In reality many crimes are spontaneous or emotionally driven.

ii. improperly punishing one person solely to benefit another. Philosopher Immanuel Kant asserted that individuals should never be treated merely as a means to benefit the rest of society. In the worst case scenario under a deterrence theory of punishment, an innocent person who appears guilty may be punished in order to deter others and benefit society as a whole.

c. Retributivism vs. deterrence. There are two key differences between retributivism and deterrence.

i. Deterrence is a utilitarian concept that looks forward to determine whether punishment will discourage future wrongful conduct. Retributivism looks backward to determine whether punishment is justified.

ii. Deterrence is premised on a belief that humans will act in their own interest unless sufficient limits are imposed by the law. Retributivism is based upon a belief that humans possess free will to do what is right and therefore must be punished when they choose to violate society's norms.

3. Rehabilitation/Reform

Punishment may provide the defendant with opportunities to remedy personal deficiencies that led him or her to commit the crime. Reforming methods range from having the defendant recognize guilt and repent to providing vocational training and psychological treatment.

a. Criticisms of rehabilitation theory. Reform/rehabilitation theory is criticized for:

i. wrongly allocating precious societal resources to those who least deserve them;

ii. seeking to remake human beings with a belief that society knows what is "for their own good"; and

iii. assuming that all people who commit crimes are merely sick and can be reconditioned not to commit further crimes.

4. Incapacitation

Punishment, in the form of imprisonment or execution, renders the defendant unable to cause further harm to society.

a. **Criticisms of incapacitation theory.** Incapacitation theory is criticized for:

i. being far too costly;
ii. being ineffective in reducing recidivism;
iii. not preventing criminal activities which may continue while a criminal is in prison.

C. CASE STUDIES

1. Regina v. Dudley & Stephens, 14 Q.B.D. 273 (1884)

Two seamen (Dudley and Stephens) stood trial for the murder of a fellow lifeboat passenger (Parker) whom they killed and ate when it appeared they all would otherwise die before rescue. The issue for the court was whether to punish or excuse the defendants for the killing. Deterrence was not an important goal of punishment given the rarity of such circumstances and the likelihood that a defendant facing certain death would risk future conviction. Rehabilitation and incapacitation were likewise inapplicable because it was unlikely that the defendants would find themselves in the same circumstances again and they posed no danger outside of that setting. Ultimately, the court convicted the defendants under a retribution theory: It was necessary to send the message that the defendants' conduct was wrong. Commutation of the defendants' capital sentences to six months imprisonment later softened the impact of that message on the individual defendants.

2. United States v. Bergman, 416 F. Supp. 496 (S.D.N.Y. 1976)

A rabbi/philanthropist was convicted of Medicaid fraud. The trial court issued an opinion explaining its decision to impose imprisonment. The court recognized that prison would not serve as rehabilitation, especially for a defendant like Bergman. Likewise, the court found no need for specific deterrence or incapacitation because Bergman was not a dangerous man and had learned his lesson. Two grounds justified the sentence: general deterrence and retribution. White collar crimes are among the most deterrable offenses because offenders calculate the benefits and risks of their behavior before acting. Retribution was necessary to proclaim the court's judgment that the offenses were grave, not minor or purely technical.

3. **State v. Chaney, 477 P.2d 441 (1970)**

The appellate court reviewed the defendant's one-year sentence for rape and robbery and found it too lenient. The apologetic tone of the sentence would not convey to the defendant or to the community the proper condemnation of defendant's conduct, a key purpose of sentencing under a retribution theory of punishment.

Note. The *Chaney* case is unusual because it involved an appellate court increasing a sentence. In most jurisdictions, the appellate court only has authority to decrease a sentence.

4. **United States v. Jackson, 780 F. Supp. 1508 (N.D. Ill. 1991)**

A repeat offender received a life sentence under a career criminal statute. The case raises the issue of whether career offender statutes go too far in incarcerating defendants and how long a sentence is necessary to deter criminal conduct. Does it make sense to lock up people until they die or just until they are so old they are unlikely to commit crimes? Do extra-long sentences achieve more deterrence? "Three strikes" sentences raise the same issues.

EXAM TIP

When asked whether a sentence is proper, students should evaluate the sentence under all theories of punishment—retribution, deterrence, incapacitation, and rehabilitation.

D. SENTENCING

Indeterminate (discretionary) and determinate (guideline) sentencing provide two models for sentencing authority.

1. Indeterminate Sentencing

Traditionally, judges had broad discretion in imposing sentences. Under an indeterminate sentencing model, the judge may select a sentence from a wide range set forth in the statute. The parole authorities also had the discretion to determine when the defendant would be eligible for release on parole.

Criticism. Indeterminate sentences were viewed as creating unacceptable disparities in sentencing. Defendants who committed the same crime might get vastly different sentences depending on the leniency of the sentencing judge.

2. Determinate Sentencing

Recently, state and federal courts have moved to a guideline approach to sentencing, which greatly limits the trial judge's discretion. The court must select a sentence based upon the nature of the defendant's offense and criminal history. There is little discretion to tailor the sentence for the individual. Only under extraordinary circumstances may a court depart from the guidelines. See, e.g., United States v. Johnson, 964 F.2d 124 (2d Cir. 1992) (departure from guidelines permitted because of effect on defendant's family).

Criticism. Determinate sentencing has been criticized as being unduly harsh because it does not tailor sentencing to the particular facts of a case and background of the defendant. There is also growing evidence that determinate sentencing has not resulted in more consistency in sentencing because of the discretionary departures often authorized even in determinate sentencing schemes.

E. PROPORTIONALITY

An underlying principle of criminal law is that the punishment should be proportional to the seriousness of the crime. MPC §1.02. Too little punishment will not deter criminal behavior and allow a defendant to profit from the crime. Too much punishment creates sympathy for the defendant and disrespect for the law.

1. Constitutional Principles

In 1983, the Supreme Court held that the Eighth Amendment prohibition against "cruel and unusual" punishment requires that a sentence not be disproportionate to the crime. Solemn v. Helm, 463 U.S. 277 (1983) (life imprisonment without possibility of parole for repeated minor crimes unconstitutional). However, some members of the Court have recently stated that they would abandon the proportionality analysis and only use the Eighth Amendment to outlaw specific unacceptable modes of punishment. Harmelin v. Michigan, 501 U.S. 957 (1991) (mandatory term of life imprisonment without possibility of parole upheld) (Scalia, J.).

2. Test for Proportionality

Three factors are used to determine proportionality: 1. the inherent gravity of the offense, 2. the sentences imposed for similarly grave offenses in the same jurisdiction, and 3. sentences imposed for the same crime in other jurisdictions. The Eighth Amendment does not require strict proportionality between crime and sentence. It only forbids extreme sentences that are "grossly disproportionate." See *Harmelin v. Michigan* (Kennedy, J. concurrence).

3. Examples

Grossly disproportionate sentences include: a. 20 years imprisonment for slapping one's wife, Thomas v. State, 634 A.2d 1 (Md. 1993); and b. a mandatory 40-year imprisonment term for statutory rape. State v. Bartlett, 830 P.2d 823 (Ariz. 1992).

F. CRIMINALIZATION AND DECRIMINALIZATION: WHAT TO PUNISH?

Criminal laws are based upon societal values. They are society's effort to protect those values. However, not all immoral or improper behavior constitutes a crime. Restraints are put on the criminal justice system because of the dangers of overcriminalization.

1. Determining Society's Values

Moral values provide the basis for society's criminal laws. Patrick Devlin, The Enforcement of Morals. However, society's values may change faster than its laws. Thus, it can be difficult to ascertain whether a law expresses the current values of society or those of the past.

EXAMPLE AND ANALYSIS

In Bowers v. Hardwick, 478 U.S. 186 (1986), the Supreme Court reviewed the constitutionality of Georgia's statute criminalizing sodomy. It found the state's prohibition of homosexual practices "deeply rooted in this Nation's history and tradition." Thus, it held the statute did not violate the due process clause. Chief Justice Burger's concurrence underscored the Judeo-Christian moral and ethical foundation for the law. By contrast, the dissent argued that society's values have changed and there is a more compelling social value in protecting the right to privacy.

Note. *Bowers v. Hardwick* was decided by a 5-4 vote. Two years after the decision, Justice Powell stated that he had incorrectly voted with the Majority.

2. Victimless Crime

A fundamental principle of criminal law is that an offense is a crime against the community, not just the victim in the case. The common moral bonds of society therefore justify criminalizing what might otherwise be deemed "victimless crimes"; i.e., criminal acts to which the victim consents. These include euthanasia, suicide, dueling, abortion, and incest.

Corollary. Because all crimes are considered offenses against *society*, the victim's consent is *not* a defense to most crimes.

3. Dangers of Overcriminalizing

Not all moral wrongs are crimes. There are several reasons to limit the list of immoral acts that are subject to criminal punishment:

- lack of consensus about what conduct is immoral;
- lack of respect generated for law when laws no longer reflect a change in social morality and therefore are not enforced;
- dangers of discriminatory enforcement;
- diversion of limited investigative and prosecutorial resources;
- invasion of constitutional rights such as privacy or due process; and
- ineffectiveness of the law in deterring behavior.

G. LEGALITY

Under common law, the courts had residual power to determine when a violation of society's morals constituted a crime. Today, the legislature determines the legality of behavior.

1. Principle of Legality

In American criminal jurisprudence, a person may not be punished unless that person's conduct was defined as criminal before the defendant acted. This is the principle of "legality." In Latin it is stated, *nullum crimen sine lege, nulla poena sine lege* ("no crime without law, no punishment without law").

a. **Not all harmful or immoral acts are crimes.** Because of the principle of legality, not all harmful or immoral conduct constitutes a crime. Conduct must be specifically prohibited by law before it may be punished.

b. **Rationale for principle of legality.** The principle of legality serves:

- to provide notice as to what conduct is unlawful;
- to confine the discretion of the police in their enforcement of the laws;
- to prevent judges and juries from arbitrarily creating new crimes; and,
- to ensure that the criminal law only operates prospectively.

c. **Correlating constitutional principles.** The principle of legality is mandated by principles of American constitutional law:

i. **Prohibition against bills of attainder or ex post facto laws.** Art. I, Secs. 9 and 10 of the Constitution prohibit punishing a person for an offense that was not created until after the defendant's act.

ii. **Due process clause.** The basic principle of due process, as expressed in the 5th Amendment and 14th Amendment of the Constitution, requires notice before a person may be convicted of a crime, clarity as to the meaning of the law, and sufficient specificity to prevent arbitrary enforcement by law enforcement authorities.

2. Cases Addressing Legality

a. **Shaw v. Director of Public Prosecutions (1962), A.C. 220.** The defendant was convicted of several crimes associated with the publication of a directory of prostitutes. One offense charged was "conspiracy to corrupt public morals." The vague nature of the charge allowed the jury to decide on a case-by-case basis whether improper behavior should constitute a crime. In the United States such a law would have violated the principles of legality, but the conviction was upheld in the English court.

b. **Keeler v. Superior Court, 2 Cal. 3d 619 (1970).** The defendant was convicted of murder for killing the fetus inside his pregnant wife. By statute, murder was defined as the unlawful killing of a "human being." It was unclear, however, whether a "human being" included a fetus. The appellate court held that the common law definition of "human being" did not include a fetus. Thus, defendant's conduct, while "immoral" and "improper," did not constitute a crime. Due process and ex post facto principles prohibited retroactive application of the definition of "fetus." Under the principle of legality, new legal definitions may only be applied prospectively.

c. **Papachristou v. City of Jacksonville, 405 U.S. 156 (1972).** The defendants were convicted under a vague statute prohibiting loitering and vagrancy. The Court overturned the conviction because the vague statute allowed for arbitrary and discriminatory enforcement by the police.

3. Warning: Not All Imprecise Statutory Language Violates Principles of Legality

A statute may have imprecise language without violating principles of legality or constitutional norms. It is not uncommon for statutes to use common law terms, such as "negligently" or "cruel and inhumane treatment," without defining those terms. The fact that a statute requires a jury to exercise discretion in its assessment does not automatically make the statute invalid.

Example. In Nash v. United States, 229 U.S. 373 (1912), the trial court dismissed the indictment as too vague because it charged conspiracies "in restraint of trade" and "to monopolize trade." The Supreme Court held that the statutes did not violate due process even though they granted the jury broad discretion to determine what was reasonable conduct and what constituted criminal behavior.

FIGURE 2-1

Purposes of Punishment	
Retribution	"Deserves to be punished; "paying back" society; "sending a message"
Deterrence	Utilitarian: Costs of crime > benefits Prevent future crime
Rehabilitation	Correct criminal behavior
Incapacitation	Protect society from individual

Review Questions and Answers

THEORIES OF PUNISHMENT

Question: Which of the following theories of punishment has the court primarily relied on in each of the sentencing scenarios below?

a. Retribution

b. General Deterrence

c. Specific Deterrence

d. Rehabilitation

e. Incapacitation

1. James Chow, a 21 year-old college junior is arrested for driving under the influence on his way home from a weekend fraternity party. James pleads guilty to the offense, but the judge sentences him to the maximum six months in the county jail. At the sentencing hearing the judge addresses James regarding the sentence: "I'm doing this to teach you a lesson, so that for the rest of your life if you've been drinking, you will never go anywhere near the driver's seat of an automobile."

2. Same scenario as #1 but the judge tells James: "I'm not sure that you really deserve to go to jail for six months, but I don't really care. What I care most about is sending a message to you and all the other frat boys like you at all the universities in this state. Fun and parties are all well and good, but when people who have been drinking get behind the wheel, they become a menace to everyone on the road. Your case will show them that we do not tolerate drinking and driving in this jurisdiction."

3. Junior Blaine, a 56 year-old repeat sex offender, is convicted of kidnapping and rape. Upon sentencing Junior to the maximum 25 years in state prison, the judge says: "Mr. Blaine, I'm happy to be able to put you away until beyond your 80th birthday. You deserve this punishment, but most importantly, I will sleep well tonight knowing that you will be off the streets until you are too old and feeble to be a threat to anyone."

4. Tina Martino, a 16 year-old high school dropout is convicted on a first offense for burglarizing a neighborhood liquor store with an older friend who is a repeat felon. Tina claims she needed the money to help feed her brothers and sisters. Upon sentencing Tina to two years in the custody of the Youth Authorities, the judge tells Tina: "Ms. Martino, I know two years may seem like a long time, and your counsel has suggested that I give you probation or release you to the custody of your mother. But I'm sending you to the Youth Authorities because I think it will provide you with an opportunity to turn your life around, to make a fresh start. I suggest you take full advantage of this opportunity and finish your high school education.

5. David Stengle is convicted of murdering his wife after a domestic dispute. Mr. Stengle pleads to the judge that he is sorry for what he has done, and that he has already suffered terribly and considered suicide. Defense counsel further points out that there is no danger that Mr. Stengle will ever commit such a crime again. The judge, however, sentences the defendant to the maximum sentence stating: "Mr. Stengle, you are clearly sorry for what you have done, and society has little to fear from you in the future. But what you have done is wrong, very wrong, and to a certain degree can never be forgiven. This court and the rest of society must condemn what you have done in the strongest terms possible. We must give you the full punishment that your evil act deserves. Your victims and the People have come to this court for justice and they will get it."

Answers: 1. c; 2. b; 3. e; 4. d; 5. a

Elements of a Crime

Chapter Overview

Crimes are defined by their elements. The goal of the first-year law student is to learn the legal components of a crime and to be able to apply those legal standards to the facts of a particular case. This chapter reviews the basic legal requirements for crimes. In evaluating whether a crime has been committed, a student must look for these basic characteristics. In addition, the student must understand the consequences if one of the requirements is missing. Therefore, Chapter 3 discusses:

- Elements of a Crime
  - Actus reus (criminal conduct)
    - Positive acts and voluntariness requirement
    - Omissions and duty to act
  - Mens rea (culpable mental state)
    - Common law terms
    - Model Penal Code standards
    - Strict liability
  - Mistake of fact
    - Transferred intent
  - Mistake of law

A. INTRODUCTION—ELEMENTS OF CRIMES

All crimes are defined by elements. A defendant has engaged in criminal behavior only if each element of a crime was present. If the facts of a case do not satisfy each element, the defendant has not committed a crime.

The elements of a crime commonly include:

1. Actus Reus (physical act);
2. Mens Rea (culpable mental state);
3. Attendant Circumstances (e.g., status of victim);
4. Result (harm caused).

A.R. + M.R. + (Circum.) + (Result) = crime

Not every crime will require each of these elements. However, almost all crimes have an actus reus and mens rea requirement. Therefore, this chapter will discuss those two key elements, as well as how attendant circumstances operate to define a crime. Results and causation are discussed in Chapter 8.

Note. The Model Penal Code's definition of "elements" of a crime includes only "conduct, attendant circumstances, or results." MPC §1.13(9). Mens rea is treated as a standard of culpability applied to each of the elements.

FIGURE 3-1

ELEMENTS OF A CRIME	
Actus Reus	Physical act
Mens Rea	Mental state
Circumstance	Other requirements for criminal offenses, such as location of act or status of victim
Result	Harm caused

B. ACTUS REUS—CULPABLE CONDUCT

1. General Rule

All crimes require a defendant to commit a voluntary criminal act—an actus reus. The actus reus may be a positive act, such as hitting another, or an omission, which is a failure to act when there is a legal duty to do so.

2. Purpose of Actus Reus Requirement

The law does not punish people for bad thoughts alone. If it did, it would punish too many people. An actus reus requirement limits law enforcement by focusing its efforts on identifiable occurrences and separates those who seriously intend to commit harm from those with mere fantasies.

3. Identifying the Actus Reus

The definition of each crime will include an actus reus. There may be many different types of physical action that satisfy the actus reus of a crime.

Example. Homicide. Homicide is defined as the "unlawful killing of another human being." The act required is "killing," which may be accomplished in many different ways, including pulling the trigger of a gun or pouring poison in a drink. The victim's death is the result of the defendant's actions. However, only a defendant's physical acts leading to that result are considered the actus reus.

4. Words Alone

Verbal conduct may be sufficient to constitute the "actus reus" of a crime such as treason, sedition, solicitation, conspiracy, or aiding and abetting.

Example. An army officer tells the enemy the time and place of an attack. The words alone are sufficient actus reus for the crime of treason.

5. Positive Acts vs. Omissions

Both affirmative acts (positive acts) and failures to act when there is a duty to do so (omissions) may constitute the actus reus of a crime.

Examples. Shooting a gun or taking the property of another are positive acts. Failing to rescue one's drowning child is an omission.

6. Positive Acts

a. **Voluntariness requirement.** All physical acts must be voluntary to constitute an actus reus. A "voluntary" act is any act that is the result of conscious and volitional movement.

i. **Automaton.** If the defendant is acting as an automaton whose mind is not engaged at the time of the act, there is no valid actus reus.

Example. People v. Newton, 8 Cal. App. 3d 359 (1970). Defendant shot a police officer after being shot himself. He claimed he was unconscious at the time his hand, in a reflexive action, pulled the trigger. The court ruled defendant was entitled to argue to the jury that there was no voluntary actus reus.

ii. **Movement by another.** If defendant is physically moved by another, there is no actus reus.

Example. Martin v. State, 31 Ala. App. 334 (1944). Defendant was convicted of being drunk on a public highway after police had forcibly moved him from his house where he was intoxicated and placed him onto the highway. The court held that because defendant was not present on the highway due to his own volitional movement, he could not be punished.

iii. **Narrow concept of voluntariness.** As used in the actus reus context, "voluntariness" only refers to whether the defendant is conscious of an act and is capable of volitional movement. It does not address the issue of whether the defendant was free of coercion when engaging in those movements.

Example. Defendant is forced at gunpoint to rob a bank. Defendant's act is a voluntary actus reus because she was conscious of her actions and performed them herself. Even though defendant's acts may have been coerced, they are still considered "voluntary." The question of whether defendant has a legal defense of duress is a separate issue. See Chapter 12, infra.

iv. **Rationale for voluntariness requirement.** Punishment for an involuntary act does not satisfy two key purposes of punishment: deterrence and retribution. A person who is unaware that she is acting ordinarily cannot be deterred and the retributivist theory of punishment is based upon the assumption that the defendant freely chose to commit a crime.

b. **MPC involuntary acts.** MPC §2.01 defines a voluntary act as any act that is not involuntary. Involuntary acts include:

i. **Reflex or convulsion.** People v. Newton, 8 Cal. App. 3d (1970) (defendant claimed he shot police officer out of unconscious, reflexive action).

ii. **Bodily movement during unconsciousness or sleep.** *People v. Cogdon*, (defendant killed her daughter while sleepwalking).

iii. **Hypnosis or under hypnotic suggestion.** *Warning.* Most jurisdictions have *not* adopted "hypnosis" as a basis for "involuntary" act because hypnosis may simply make it easier for a defendant to commit an act she had already intended to commit.

iv. **Bodily movement not otherwise the product of the effort or determination of the actor, either conscious or habitual.** Martin v. State, 31 Ala. App. 334 (1944) (defendant was physically carried out of his home and charged with being intoxicated in a public place).

c. **Special applications of voluntary act rule**

i. **Habit.** Actions done by habit are still considered voluntary acts. While consciousness is a matter of degree, habitual acts are still considered voluntary. MPC §2.01(2)(d).

Example. Defendant routinely speeds down a particular street. One day, she hits someone because defendant is unaware she is speeding. Defendant is still responsible for speeding.

ii. **Possession.** Because a person may be in a conscious state but nonetheless unaware that he possesses an item, most jurisdictions hold that possession is not an act unless the possessor knew of his control of the item for a sufficient period to have been able to terminate his possession. MPC §2.01(4). This approach interjects into the actus reus element, an issue of the defendant's mental state.

Example. Defendant is stopped at the airport while carrying a suitcase. Unbeknownst to defendant, another person has slipped a narcotic into his suitcase. Defendant has not committed a voluntary act because he was unaware of his possession of the narcotic.

d. **Extending the period of the actus reus.** By extending the period of the actus reus, an act that might otherwise be viewed as involuntary is deemed a voluntary act. The Model Penal Code provides for such extension by focusing on whether the defendant's conduct includes a voluntary act or omission at some earlier point in time. MPC §2.01(1).

i. **Epileptic reflexes.** Ordinarily, reflex or seizure actions do not constitute a voluntary act. However, if a defendant is aware that she is susceptible to such problems, the court may stretch the period of the actus reus to include the time when the defendant knowingly took the risk of an attack. Analyzed in this way, the act is in fact voluntary.

Example. Defendant who knows he is subject to epileptic attacks decides to drive anyway. He has an attack while driving and kills another. Defendant has committed a voluntary act because his actus reus began when he decided to drive with his condition. People v. Decina, 2 N.Y. 2d 133 (1956).

ii. **Revisit Martin v. State.** In *Martin v. State*, supra, the issue was whether the defendant voluntarily "while intoxicated . . . appear[ed] in any public place . . . and manifest[ed] a drunken condition." It was crucial for the court to determine the exact actus reus of the crime. If the actus reus was getting intoxicated and appearing in public, then the actus reus could be extended to include defendant's voluntary act of getting drunk before being ejected onto the highway. The court, however, implicitly held that the statutory actus reus was "appearing" in a public place while intoxicated, and therefore, it was irrelevant that defendant had voluntarily become intoxicated in his home. By so ruling, the court declined to extend the period of the actus reus.

7. **Omissions**

a. **General Rule.** Generally, there is no legal duty to help another facing harm. Therefore, failure to act only constitutes an actus reus when there is some other specific duty to act. MPC §2.10(3).

EXAMPLES AND ANALYSIS

Pope v. State, 284 Md. 309 (1979). The defendant witnessed the beating of a child and failed to come to the child's aid. The defendant had no criminal liability because she had no specific duty to come to the child's aid.

Jones v. United States, 308 F.2d 307 (1962). A ten month-old baby, unrelated to defendant, died while living in defendant's house. The child died from abuse and mistreatment, even though the defendant had the means to provide food and necessities to the child. Defendant's conviction was overturned because the jury was never instructed that in order to find defendant guilty, it must first find he had a legal duty to help the child.

---

i. **Kitty Genovese case.** In 1964, a woman was stabbed to death while numerous witnesses watched and failed to help. It took twenty minutes for anyone to call the police. While morally troubling, the spectator's failure to assist was not criminal.

ii. **New Bedford rape case.** In 1983, a woman was gang-raped in a tavern in New Bedford, Massachusetts while patrons watched. The patrons were not guilty of any offense.

Note. Following the incident, the State passed a controversial statute making failure to report a crime to the police a misdemeanor.

b. **Rationale for general rule.** Although there may be a moral obligation to help others in need, there is no general responsibility under Anglo-American law. American law does not compel active benevolence among people. Rather, it only requires that one not cause others harm. Reasons for this laissez-faire approach include:

- the American tradition of individual freedom;
- the difficulty of knowing how much help one must provide others in life;
- the fear of diverting attention from the perpetrator of the crime to the bystander;
- the possibility that Good Samaritans may face undue risk of harm.

c. **Criticisms of general rule.** The general rule not requiring a duty to act is troubling. Objections to it include:

- There is no moral difference between failing to help when one can do so with no peril to oneself and actively causing the harm;
- The general rule ingrains a callousness and indifference into how members of society interact with each other.
- The general rule may embolden violators to commit more crimes because they know people are not required to assist the prospective victims.

d. **Duty to act.** Sometimes, through a relationship with the victim or a legal responsibility under a statute or contract, a person gives up a portion of her freedom and assumes the duty to help another. In such situations, if the person fails to act, the failure to help constitutes an "actus reus" by omission. The duty to act may arise from:

i. **A statute.** Either a criminal or civil statute may create a duty to act.

ii. **Status relationship.** Typically, parent-child, employer-employee, spouse-spouse, owner-customer. Informal relationships do not ordinarily trigger a duty of care. See People v. Beardsley, 150 Mich. 206, 113 N.W. 1128 (1907).

iii. **Contractual agreement. Example.** babysitters and caretakers.

iv. **Voluntarily assuming care of another**

(a) See Regina v. Stone & Dobinson, (1977) Q.B. 354, 357-378 (part-time care of co-occupant triggered duty of care).

(b) See People v. Oliver, 210 Cal. App. 3d 138, 258 Cal. Rptr. 138 (1989) (inviting intoxicated person into home triggered duty of care).

v. **Putting the victim in peril.** Once the defendant has put the victim in peril, a duty to help is triggered.

(a) **Example.** Jones v. State, 220 N.D. 384, 43 N.E. 1017 (1942) (defendant's rape of a 12 year-old girl triggered duty to save her when she jumped into a creek to kill herself).

(b) **Example.** Commonwealth v. Cali, 141 N.E. 510 (1923) (defendant accidentally started a fire and then decided not to put the fire out so that he could collect money from the insurance company).

(c) **Positive or negative act?** This category may also be viewed as an actus reus by "positive act" if one considers the actus reus to begin as soon as the defendant puts the victim in peril.

e. **Active vs. passive euthanasia.** A physician's discontinuance of medical care for a terminally ill patient is typically treated as a failure to provide help for someone in the physician's care. Absent a duty to continue care, the physician's act of omission is not considered culpable conduct. Barber v. Superior Court, 147 Cal. App. 3d 1006, (1983).

i. Medical ethics distinguishes between active and passive euthanasia. Active euthanasia, such as administrating a drug to a patient to hasten death, is ordinarily prohibited. By contrast, passive euthanasia is permitted even though it involves "pulling the plug" from life support systems causing death. The theoretical basis for this distinction is questionable.

ii. Active participation in assisting suicide may be prosecuted as a common-law felony. People v. Kevorkian, 527 N.W. 2d 714 (Mich. 1994).

f. **Ability to help and knowledge of duty.** In most jurisdictions, there is a duty to help only if the defendant can do so without risk of serious harm to himself and if the defendant knows of those facts that create the duty to act.

g. **Good Samaritan laws.** A few jurisdictions have adopted Good Samaritan laws that impose an obligation to rescue a person in emergency situations, e.g., Minnesota and Vermont. Others have enacted reporting laws. By contrast, most European countries enforce a general duty to help another in distress.

h. **Misprison of felony.** At common law, one who fails to report a crime could be charged with a separate crime of "misprison of felon." The common law offense of misprison of felony is no longer a crime in American jurisdictions. Today's misprison of felony statutes require active concealment of the felony; mere failure to report is not sufficient. United States v. Johnson, 546 F.2d 1225 (5th Cir. 1977). By contrast, misprison of felony is a common offense in European jurisdictions.

EXAM TIP

Students should begin their analysis of whether a crime exists by first evaluating whether there is a valid actus reus for the crime, either by a positive voluntary act or by omission when there was a duty to act.

8. Status Offenses

A defendant may not be convicted for merely having a status or condition. There must be a positive act or failure to act when there is a duty to do so. Thus, the Supreme Court has held that punishing a defendant simply for being a narcotics addict is unconstitutional. Robinson v. California, 370 U.S. 660 (1962). Similarly, a court has held that a state may not punish persons for the condition of being HIV-positive. Anderson v. Romero, 72 F.3d 518 (7th Cir. 1993). The Supreme Court has also implied that while a state may criminalize homosexual acts, it may not criminalize the mere status of being a homosexual. Bowers v. Hardwick, 478 U.S. 186 (1986).

a. **Powell v. Texas, 392 U.S. 514 (1968).** A plurality of the Court upheld a conviction of an alcoholic for being drunk in a public place. The Court held that the statute did not punish the defendant for the status of being an alcoholic, but for his conduct of getting drunk.

b. **Public policy considerations.** The courts are wary of extending the "status" exception because it limits society's ability to use its criminal laws to control ongoing social problems such as alcoholism and drug addiction.

FIGURE 3-2

ACTUS REUS	
General Rule	All acts must be voluntary.
Involuntary Acts	Automatism does not constitute a voluntary act. Involuntary acts include: 1. reflex or convulsion 2. unconscious or sleep movements 3. hypnosis (some jurisdiction) 4. bodily movement of defendant by another
Positive Act	Physical acts by the defendant; Must be voluntary
Omissions	Failure to help is not an act unless there is a legal duty to do so by: 1. statute 2. by status relationship 3. by contractual relationship; or 4. by voluntarily assuming the care of another

REVIEW QUESTIONS AND ANSWERS

ACTUS REUS

For each of the following hypotheticals determine whether the defendant has engaged in a voluntary act.

Question: Carmen regularly participates in class. On her second day, the professor asks a question Carmen has mastered. She quickly raises her hand to respond. In doing so, she slaps the head of the student beside her. If Carmen is charged with assault, is there an actus reus for the crime?

Answer: Yes. Carmen was conscious at the time she engaged in the *positive act* of raising her hand.

Question: Carmen falls asleep in her criminal law class. During her sleep, she fantasizes about impressing her fellow students and the professor by answering a tough question on the law. While having this dream, Carmen quickly raises her hand and slaps the head of the student beside her. If Carmen is charged with assault, is there an actus reus for the crime?

Answer: No. Carmen can claim somnambulism or unconsciousness.

Question: While Carmen is sitting in class, a cockroach bites her arm. She swings at the insect but hits her neighbor instead. If Carmen is charged with assault, is there an actus reus for the crime?

Answer: Yes. Carmen chose to *swing at* the insect. If her arm's reaction had just been a reflex, then there would be no actus reus.

Question: While Carmen is sitting in class, she accidentally hits her elbow against her desk. The spasm caused by the bump causes Carmen to hit her neighbor. If Carmen is charged with assault, is there an actus reus for the crime?

Answer: No. A reflex movement is considered automatism, not a voluntary act.

Question: Poor Carmen. After she finally settles into her criminal law class, a fight breaks out between the two students behind her. One of the students pushes Carmen into another classmate. If Carmen is charged with assault, is there an actus reus for the crime?

Answer: No. Carmen's bodily movement is *not* the product of her own conscious effort.

Question: Michael works as a doctor at a local prison. One of the inmates who was convicted of a particularly heinous crime comes to Michael with an infection. Michael fails to treat him and the inmate dies. If Michael is charged with homicide, is there an actus reus for the crime?

Answer: Yes. Michael had a contractual duty to provide care for the inmate. Failure to do so constituted an actus reus by omission.

Question: The legislature has recently passed a statute requiring motorists to stop and offer aid to any person with a disabled car on the highway. Michael is late to work one day, so he decides not to stop when he sees a stranded motorist. The motorist is later injured. If Michael is charged with the motorist's injury, is there an actus reus for the crime?

Answer: Yes. Michael had a statutory duty to offer assistance.

Question: Jerry Babushi comes to Susan's house for a party. Unbeknownst to Susan, Babushi is Susan's half brother. While he is there, Babushi suffers an epileptic fit while drinking the punch. As Susan stands by and watches, Babushi chokes to death. If Susan is charged with Babushi's death, is there an actus reus for the crime?

Answer: Yes. As the host of the party, Susan may have a duty to help. However, she does *not* have a duty because Babushi is her half brother. First, she does not know of the relationship. Second, the only relationships that traditionally trigger a duty to help are husband-wife and parent-child.

C. MENS REA—CULPABLE MENTAL STATES

Ordinarily, acts alone do not constitute a criminal offense, even if they cause harm. The classic maxim is *actus non facit reum, nisi mens sit rea.* There is no crime without a vicious will. A vicious will is the mental state required for the crime. Culpability is the extent to which a defendant's mental state shows the defendant deserves to be punished for his acts.

Different crimes require different mental states. However, not all possible mental states are relevant under the law. For example, it is irrelevant whether a defendant acts regretfully or arrogantly. The mens rea requirement focuses on levels of awareness and intentionality with which the defendant acted; e.g., Did the defendant purposely cause a harm or was the harm the result of defendant's carelessness?

1. **Rationale for Mens Rea Requirement**

   The purposes of punishment rely heavily on the premise that the more a defendant intends to commit a wrongful act, the more that person should be punished.

   a. **Retribution.** The person who intends to violate the law is ordinarily viewed to be more deserving of punishment than the person who accidentally commits the same act.

   b. **Deterrence.** The more a person considers the wrongfulness of her actions, the more the risk of punishment can serve to deter the defendant's acts.

   c. **Rehabilitation.** The more a person intends to violate the laws or cause harm, the more that person's attitudes need to be reformed.

   d. **Incapacitation.** The most dangerous persons in society are often those who have carefully thought over their evil deeds and nonetheless decide to commit them.

2. **Mens Rea Terminology**

   The common law developed a variety of terms to describe the mental state required for different types of crimes. These terms, however, were often confusing and not used consistently by the courts. As a result, the Model Penal Code developed a set of terms to more precisely define the culpability/mental state required for different types of crimes. While many laws still use the language of the common law, the Model Penal Code has assisted courts in defining and applying those common law terms.

   a. **Common law terminology.** At common law, courts have used a variety of terms to describe the mental state required for crimes:

      i. **Maliciously.** Older cases and statutes, especially in England, refer to a defendant acting "maliciously." Although the term seems to suggest that the defendant must act in a wicked manner or with ill will, that is not the legal definition of the term.

Rather, "maliciously" simply means that the defendant realizes the risks her conduct creates and engages in the conduct anyway. The Model Penal Code term for this level of intent is "recklessness."

(a) **Regina v. Cunningham, 2 Q.B. 396 (1957).** Defendant almost asphyxiated a woman when he tore a gas meter off a wall adjoining her building. Unbeknownst to defendant, gas seeped through the wall and almost asphyxiated the woman. Although the law required that the defendant act "maliciously," the court held that maliciousness does *not* mean with evil or wicked intent. Rather, it means only that the defendant foresaw that his acts might cause harm, but nevertheless engaged in them; i.e., defendant acted recklessly.

(b) **Regina v. Faulkner, 13 Cox. Crim. Cas. 550 (1887).** A sailor went into a ship's hold to steal some rum. While he was there, he lit a match, causing the rum and ship to catch fire. Defendant was convicted of "maliciously" setting fire to the ship. Although the sailor's actions were wrong, he could not be guilty of acting "maliciously" in setting the fire unless he considered the risk of causing a fire and disregarded it; i.e., unless the defendant acted recklessly.

ii. **Intentionally.** Another confusing common law term is "intentionally." In some situations it would mean that the defendant has the purpose to cause a specific harmful result. In other situations, the defendant need only be aware that his acts may cause a specific result.

Example. Defendant wants to destroy a set of plans his competitor is taking to a prospective client. Defendant therefore puts a bomb on the competitor's airplane. Defendant does not want to kill his competitor; he only wants to destroy the plans. But he realizes that the bomb is likely to kill. Defendant has still acted "intentionally" as to his competitor's death.

iii. **Negligently.** Even the term "negligently" can be confusing when used in the criminal context. Criminal negligence is different from civil negligence. When the moral condemnation and stigma of criminal law will apply, the courts require a higher showing of carelessness than in tort, although common law is vague as to exactly what degree of negligence is required. In general, it means not exercising the standard of care a reasonable person would under the circumstances. Santillanes v. New Mexico, 115 N.M. 215 (1993).

iv. **Willfully.** The word "willful" has many meanings under the common law. Sometimes, it means doing an act with the purpose of violating the law. However, it can also mean intentionally doing an act knowing its likely consequences. Finally, it can mean simply that the defendant intended his act and that act had harmful or illegal consequence.

v. **General intent vs. specific intent.** One of the most confusing areas of criminal law is the common law use of "general intent" and "specific intent" to describe the mens rea level for certain crimes. The following are simplified definitions for each.

(a) **General intent crimes.** Crimes that only require that the defendant intend to commit an act are referred to as "general intent" crimes. The defendant need not intend the consequences of his acts.

- **Example.** The defendant is charged with battery for hitting a victim. Battery is a general intent crime which means that the defendant need only realize that by engaging in the physical act, there is a substantial likelihood that he or she would harm another. The defendant need not intend to cause a specific harm.
- **Model Penal Code equivalent.** Recklessly.
- **Proving general intent.** General intent to commit an act ordinarily can be inferred from the defendant's actions. Ordinarily, it is the lowest level of mens rea for common law crimes.

(b) **Specific intent.** Certain crimes require a higher level of intent. At common law, they are referred to as "specific intent crimes." The defendant must act with either the intent to commit a crime or an intent to cause a specific result.

- **Example.** The defendant is charged with burglary which requires that the defendant enter a building with intent to commit a felony therein.
- **Model Penal Code equivalent.** Specific intent crimes correspond with the Model Penal Code stan-

dard of "purposely," and in some circumstances, "knowingly."

- **Common law language.** Statutes may use the word "intentionally" or "with intent to" to describe the mens rea requirement for a specific intent crime.

vi. **Unlawfully.** The term "unlawfully" does *not* refer to a mens rea standard, although it is often mentioned in the same phrase. It simply means that there is no legal excuse for the defendant's behavior.

b. **Model Penal Code approach (MPC §2.02).** Because of the difficulties in interpreting and applying common law mens rea terms, courts have been receptive to the mens rea/culpability terms of the Model Penal Code. The Model Penal Code recognizes four levels of mens rea:

i. **Purposely.** A person acts purposely if it is the defendant's goal or aim to engage in particular conduct or achieve certain results. MPC §2.02 (2)(a).

(a) **Example.** The defendant wants to kill his enemy so he aims at him and pulls the trigger. The defendant has acted "purposely."

(b) **Example.** Burglary is defined as entering a building with the intent to commit a crime therein. The phrase "intent to" requires that the defendant enter with a specific purpose in mind.

(c) **Common law terminology.** "Intent to," "with specific intent," or "intentionally."

(d) **Purposely is ordinarily not required.** For most crimes, the mens rea standard will not be set as high as purposely. The defendant's knowledge of the consequences of his acts will suffice. However, there are a few crimes where the prosecution must prove that the defendant had a specific purpose in mind and intended the harmful consequences of his acts. Ordinarily, these are the most serious offenses.

- **Example.** The crime of treason requires that the defendant have the purpose to help a foreign nation.

- **Example.** The crime of first-degree murder requires that the defendant have the purpose to kill.

ii. **Knowingly.** A person acts knowingly if she is virtually or practically certain that her conduct will lead to a particular result. MPC §2.02 (2)(b).

(a) **Example.** The defendant puts a bomb on a plane with the goal to destroy cargo aboard it, but is virtually certain the plane's passengers will be killed as well. With regard to the death of the passengers, the defendant has acted knowingly.

(b) **Willful ignorance/deliberate ignorance doctrine.** Under the "willful blindness" ("ostrich defense"/"deliberate ignorance") doctrine (MPC §2.02(7)), if a defendant strongly suspects the fact but consciously avoids learning the truth so he or she will not be certain, the courts will nonetheless find that the defendant acted "knowingly." The "willful blindness doctrine" essentially elevates reckless thought into knowledge.

Example. United States v. Jewell, 532 F.2d 697 (1976) (drug defendant did not look in secret compartment so he could claim that he did not know he was transporting marijuana; court found constructive knowledge based upon deliberate ignorance doctrine).

(c) **Common law terminology.** "Intentionally," "willfully," or sometimes, "specific intent."

iii. **Recklessly.** A person acts recklessly if he or she realizes there is a substantial and unjustifiable risk that his or her conduct will cause harm but consciously disregards that risk.

(a) **Example.** The defendant drives 60 mph past a school during school hours. Although the defendant does not intend to hit anyone, he realized the risk that he may do so and continues speeding anyway.

(b) **Subjective standard.** "Recklessly" is a subjective standard. It requires that the defendant personally realized the risk and disregarded it.

(c) **Nature of risk.** The Model Penal Code requires that the risk be of such a nature and degree that, even knowing the nature and purpose of the defendant's actions, his conduct still involves a gross deviation from the conduct of a law-abiding person in the same situation.

(d) **Minimum level for crimes.** For most crimes, the minimal level of mens rea required is "recklessly."

(e) **Recklessly vs. knowingly.** The difference between "knowingly" and "recklessly" is a matter of degree. If a defendant is so aware of a risk that he or she is virtually certain it will occur, then the defendant is acting knowingly. However, if the defendant is aware of a risk, but not as certain it will occur, the defendant may be acting recklessly.

(f) **Common law terminology.** "General intent," "maliciously."

iv. **Negligently.** A person acts negligently if he or she is unaware and takes a risk that an ordinary person would not take.

(a) **Example.** The defendant is unaware that his child is suffering from a life-threatening illness and fails to seek medical treatment. An ordinary person would have been aware of the risk, and sought the care. The defendant has acted negligently.

(b) **Objective standard.** Negligence is an objective standard. The focus is not on the defendant's state of mind, but what risks the defendant should have known he was taking. By acting negligently, the defendant is acting below the standard of care an ordinary person would have met.

(c) **Rarely used for criminal offenses.** The mental state for crimes is rarely set as low as negligence. When it is, it is usually because the result of the defendant's acts involve such grave consequences, such as negligent homicide, and the standard for negligence requires a "gross" deviation from the standards used by the ordinary person. Santillanes v. New Mexico, 115 N.M. 215, 849 P.2d 358 (1993).

(d) **Common law terminology.** "Without due care," "negligently."

c. **Common law vs. Model Penal Code mens rea standards.** For a summary of common law vs. Model Penal Code standards, see Figure 3-3.

FIGURE 3-3

Common Law	*Model Penal Code*
Maliciously	Recklessness
Specific Intent	Purpose
General Intent	Recklessness or Knowledge
Intentionally	Purpose or Knowledge
With intent to	Purpose
Willfully	Purpose or Knowledge

d. **Motive vs. Intent.** Intent (mens rea) is a requirement of a crime; motive is not. Motive is the underlying reason why the defendant engages in criminal behavior. Common motives include: jealously, greed, and hatred. Intent is the defendant's state of mind as to the consequences of his or her acts. A defendant may be guilty of a crime even with a good motive.

i. **Example.** The defendant's ailing wife begs him to kill her to end her misery. Even though the defendant may have a good motive, if he kills her, he has acted with criminal intent.

ii. **Using motive to prove intent.** Most often, motive is used to prove that the defendant acted with sufficient intent. The more the defendant has a motive to commit a crime, the more likely it is he or she intended to do so.

iii. **Motive used for sentencing.** Whereas motive may be irrelevant to criminal liability, it is often used by courts to determine an appropriate sentence for a crime.

3. **Minimal Level of Mens Rea Required for Criminal Offenses**

For most crimes, the minimal level of mens rea that must be proved is that the defendant acted recklessly. MPC §2.02(3).

a. **Rationale.** The purposes of punishment depend, in large part, on the defendant deciding to take the risk of causing harm or violating the law. Thus, unlike in tort law, the minimum level of mens rea required for most crimes is "recklessly."

4. Strict Liability

Some crimes have no mens rea requirement. MPC §2.05. If an offense does not require that the defendant subjectively realize the risk that he or she is taking, or even act negligently, it is a strict liability crime.

a. **Absolute liability.** Strict liability crimes are also referred to as absolute liability.

b. **Minor offenses.** The strict liability standard is usually reserved for minor, regulatory offenses carrying minimal punishments. See discussion infra.

Study Tip

Use these routinely studied cases to test yourself on the meaning of the mens rea standards:

Regina v. Cunningham (1957) 2 Q.B. 396. Defendant was charged with "unlawfully and maliciously" asphyxiating his future neighbor by stealing a gas meter from a wall and thereby allowing gas to seep into the victim's room. The defendant argued that he only intended to steal the meter, not harm the victim. Which mens rea standard is described in each of the following hypotheticals?

- Cunningham wanted Mrs. Wade to inhale the poison gas because he wanted her to suffer. (Purposely)
- Cunningham hoped by some miracle that Mrs. Ward would not inhale the poison gas, but he knew that it was virtually certain that she would do so. (Knowingly)
- Cunningham did not know for sure that Mrs. Ward would inhale the gas, but he considered the possibility that she might do so and decided to take the meter anyway. (Recklessly)
- Cunningham did not think of the possibility that Mrs. Ward might inhale the gas, but an ordinary person would have realized there was a significant risk. (Negligently)
- Cunningham did not realize that there was any risk of Mrs. Ward inhaling the gas, and even a reasonable person would have been unaware of the risk. (Strict liability)

- Defendant wanted to steal the meter to buy his future mother-in-law a gift. (Mens rea is unclear; these facts point to the defendant's motive.)

Regina v. Faulkner, 13 Cox. Crim. Cas. 550 (1877). Defendant set a ship on fire when he went down into its hold to steal some rum. He was charged with maliciously setting fire to a ship (arson). Assuming the following facts, which level of mens rea is described in each of the following hypotheticals?

- Faulkner's goal in lighting the match was to burn the ship. (Purposely)
- Faulkner's goal in lighting the match was to steal the rum, but he knew that it was virtually certain that the match would cause a dangerous fire. (Knowingly)
- Faulkner's goal in lighting the match was to steal the rum, but he realized there was a substantial possibility that the match would cause the ship to burn. (Recklessly)
- Faulkner did not realize there was any possibility that the match might ignite a fire, but any rational person would have realized that risk. (Negligently)
- Faulkner did not realize there was any possibility that the match might start a fire, and neither would any other reasonable person in his situation. (Strict liability)
- Faulkner lit the match because he hated the captain. (Defendant's motive may be evidence of purposefulness.)

5. Identifying Mens Rea Requirements for Crimes

Frequently, a statute will describe the mens rea level for a crime. However, it may use common law or Model Penal Code language. Because common law language may be confusing and inconsistent, it is helpful to try to determine the equivalent MPC culpability standard being described in the statute. Additionally, some crimes omit mens rea language altogether. In these situations, an understanding of the appropriate mens rea level must be determined from traditional rules of statutory construction.

a. **Example.** "A person is guilty of assault on an officer if he intentionally, knowingly, or recklessly causes bodily injury [to the officer]." (Me. Rev. Stat., §752-A). This statute sets forth the mens rea requirement in clear Model Penal Code terms.

b. **Example.** A person is guilty of destruction of property if he or she "maliciously" cuts down or destroys shrubs, trees, etc. Unless otherwise provided, the term "maliciously" means the defendant must act recklessly.

c. **No mens rea level mentioned in statute.** If the statute is silent as to the mens requirement, the general rule is that the minimum level of mens rea is applied, i.e., recklessness. MPC §2.02(3). The legislature must expressly indicate in the statute or its legislative history if it imposes strict liability.

d. **Minimum level stated.** The mens rea level for a crime is the minimum level of culpability the prosecution must prove. More will, of course, also satisfy. MPC §2.02(5).

6. Applying the Mens Rea Requirements to Material Elements

Crimes are composed of elements. If the element has a mens rea requirement assigned to it, it is a material element. MPC §1.13(10).

a. **Material element.** The term "material element" describes those elements that relate directly to the harm or evil sought to be prevented by the law. Non-material elements include elements relating exclusively to statute of limitations, jurisdiction, and venue. MPC §1.13(10). Ordinarily, mens rea is required for the material elements. MPC §2.02.

b. **Attendant circumstances.** A separate element of a crime may require proof that a certain circumstance existed at the time of defendant's acts. Without proof of that circumstance, defendant is not guilty of the crime.

i. **Example.** A statute provides: "It is an offense to rob a federally insured financial institution." Unless the victim bank is federally insured, defendant is not guilty of the crime.

ii. **Relationship to mens rea requirement and material elements.** Although each attendant circumstance must exist for the defendant to be guilty of the crime, the defendant need not necessarily be aware of its existence. For example, a defendant is guilty of robbing a federally insured bank, regardless of whether she knew the bank was federally insured. If the defendant must be aware of the circumstance to be guilty of the crime, the attendant circumstances is considered a material element. See Mistake of Fact discussion, infra.

c. **Mens rea level for a material element.** Unless the grammatical structure of the definition of the crime suggests otherwise, the same mens rea level applies to all material elements of that offense. However, there are occasions where a different mens rea level will apply to different material elements within the definition of a crime.

Example. Burglary is defined as "knowingly entering a building with intent to commit a crime." The material elements of burglary are:

Actus Reus	entering building ("knowingly")
Circumstance	to commit a crime ("purposely")

In analyzing whether a crime has been committed, one must determine the material elements of the crime and the level of mens rea to be proven as to each.

d. **Principles of statutory interpretation.** The Model Penal Code provides guidance for the difficult issues that arise in statutory interpretation.

i. **Level of mens rea is the same for all material elements of an offense unless otherwise stated.** Under the Model Penal Code, if a law prescribes the standard of culpability, that same standard is used for all material elements of the offense unless the legislative purpose is to the contrary.

EXAMPLE AND ANALYSIS

Defendant is charged with burglary, which is defined as "knowingly entering a building with the intent to commit a crime therein." The first mens rea standard, knowingly, describes the defendant's mens rea for the act of entering the house. "With intent to commit a crime" adds another mens rea requirement to the crime; i.e., entering with the purpose to commit a crime therein. MPC §2.02 (4).

ii. **Default level of mens rea is recklessness.** If a law does not set forth the level of culpability required, under the Model Penal Code, "purposely," "knowingly," or "recklessly" will suffice. MPC §2.02(3). Thus, the lowest level of mens rea required, if a statute does not provide otherwise, is "recklessness."

e. **Failure to prove mens rea.** If the prosecution cannot prove the defendant acted with the necessary mens rea for an offense, the defendant is not guilty of the crime.

i. **Lesser included offenses.** There are some crimes that have different levels of culpability. For those offenses, a defendant may be guilty of a lesser crime if the mens rea proven is less than that required for the more serious offense.

(a) **Example.** Defendant is charged with first-degree murder that requires purposeful conduct. If the defendant only acts recklessly, he or she may still be guilty of a lower level of homicide, such as murder or manslaughter. See Chapter 5 infra.

FIGURE 3-4

MENS REA — CULPABLE MENTAL STATES	
Common Law Terminology	
Maliciously	recklessly
Intentionally	with purpose or knowledge
Specific Intent	with purpose to violate law or cause harmful result
General Intent	intent to commit physical act
Model Penal Code Terminology	
Purposeful	goal or aim to achieve result
Knowingly	virtually or practically certain that conduct will lead to a particular result
Recklessly	conscious disregard of substantial and unjustifiable risk of harm
Negligently	unconscious disregard of substantial and unjustifiable risk an ordinary person would not have taken
Application of Mens Rea	
Material Elements	The mens rea typically applies to the material elements of a crime.
Jurisdictional Elements	Required circumstances of a crime that do not require a culpable mens rea by the defendant
Default Level of Mens Rea	"Recklessly" unless strict liability or negligence crime specifically defined

Review Questions and Answers

IDENTIFYING MENTAL STATES

Question: 18 U.S.C. §700 provides: "Whoever knowingly casts contempt upon any flag of the United States by publicly mutilating, defacing, defiling, burning, or trampling upon it shall be [guilty of an offense against the United States.]" What level of mens rea is required for a violation of the statute?

Answer: Knowingly.

If a defendant shreds a flag with the purpose of protesting the deployment of troops to Bosnia, has he or she violated this statute?

Answer: Yes. The defendant's "motive" may be to protest, but he or she has "knowingly" mutilated the flag.

Question: 18 U.S.C. §707 provides: "Whoever, with intent to defraud, wears, or displays the sign or emblem of the 4-H clubs [shall be guilty of an offense against the United States]."

What level of mens rea is required for a violation of the statute?

Answer: Purposely (Specific Intent).

If a defendant wears the green four-leaf clover sign of the 4-H club on St. Patrick's day to avoid being pinched, has he or she violated this statute?

Answer: No. In wearing the 4-H emblem, it was not the defendant's purpose to defraud.

Question: 8 U.S.C. §1082 provides: "Whoever transports, aids, harbors, or conceals an illegal alien [shall be guilty of an offense against the United States.]" What level of mens rea is required for a violation of the statute?

Answer: Recklessly. The absence of statutory language does *not* mean the statute is strict liability. Rather, it is assumed the minimal level of culpability, recklessness, applies.

If a defendant hires a domestic worker who speaks no English, has recently arrived in the United States, and refuses to discuss his or her background, has the defendant violated the statute?

Answer: Yes. Given the circumstances, if defendant realized there was a substantial risk that the worker was illegal and disregarded that risk, the defendant acted with recklessness.

APPLYING MENS REA STANDARDS

Question: Al and Bill are standing next to a swimming pool that is ten feet deep. Bill tells Al that he cannot swim, and that he completely panics when thrown into water. An argument ensues after which Al pushes Bill into the pool. Al does not want Bill to die and hopes that by some miracle Bill will be able to save himself. Al knows, however, that Bill is virtually certain to drown unless someone rescues him. Al ignores Bill's cries for help and Bill drowns.

What is Al's mental state with respect to the act of pushing Bill into the pool?

Answer: Purposely. It is Al's goal or purpose to push Bill into the pool.

What is Al's mental state with respect to Bill's death?

Answer: Knowingly. Al may not want Bill to drown but he is virtually certain he will.

Question: Larry and Nancy plan a surprise party for their friend, Maggie. Maggie tells Nancy that she has recently visited the doctor, who told her not to have any excitement because a sudden shock could cause her to have a heart attack. With all of the party preparations, Nancy does not tell Larry about this conversation. Larry and Nancy continue to plan the surprise party.

On the evening of the party, Larry, Nancy, and others jump out of their hiding places and surprise Maggie. Maggie suffers a heart attack and dies.

What is Nancy's mental state with respect to Maggie's death?

Answer: Recklessness. Even though Nancy did not intend to harm her friend, if she realized the risk of shocking Maggie, she has acted recklessly. If Nancy does not realize the risk, she has acted with negligence.

What is Larry's mental state with respect to Maggie's death?

Answer: None. Larry was not told of Maggie's condition and a reasonable person in his situation would not have realized the risk.

Question: Uncle Sam is planning a Fourth of July celebration for his neighborhood. He lives in a canyon, surrounded by wood-framed homes. To entertain his friends, Sam decides to buy some fireworks. Because he is afraid that the warnings on the box might indicate he should not use the fireworks in his area, Sam never reads the box warnings before using the fireworks. Sam uses the fireworks and sets a neighbor's house on fire.

If a statute prohibits "knowingly using fireworks in a dangerous manner," is Sam liable?

Answer: Yes, under the deliberate ignorance doctrine. Sam realizes there may be a risk posed by his behavior but intentionally avoids confirming his suspicion. Under the "deliberate ignorance" doctrine, Sam will be deemed to have acted knowingly.

ACTUS REUS AND MENS REA HYPOTHETICALS

Question: Leslie sees her enemy, Paul, standing in a pool of liquid that smells like gasoline. She lights up a cigarette and drops it into the pool. When Paul screams for help, she refuses to help, even though she is standing next to two pails of water. Assume the crime of arson is defined as: "Anyone who sets fire to another individual is guilty of arson." Does Leslie have any criminal liability?

Answer: Yes.
Actus reus? Leslie has engaged in two types of actus reus. First, she has voluntarily and positively acted to drop the match in the gasoline. Second, she has failed to help when she put Paul in peril, which is an omission.

Mens Rea? Because the statute does not set forth the level of mens rea, one should assume it is "recklessness." It appears from the facts that Leslie realized her acts might set Paul afire and she chose to disregard those risks. At minimum, she acted recklessly. Additionally, strong arguments exist that Leslie acted knowingly and purposely. The purposeful nature of her behavior can be inferred from: a. the deliberate and harmful nature of her acts; and b. her motive to retaliate against an "enemy."

Question: Doug, a bus driver for the local school district, suffered from fatigue and periodic blackouts for ten months. The blackouts all occurred while Doug was off-duty in his home. Doug planned to mention these incidents to his physician during his annual checkup on Wednesday. However, on Tuesday, Doug returned to work and passed out while driving the bus. The bus crashed into a house, killing several people inside. Doug was subsequently charged with recklessly causing another's death. Does Doug have criminal liability?

Answer: Yes.
Actus Reus? Although Doug may try to argue that the crash was caused by an "involuntary act," the court is likely to find that the defendant's actus reus began when he voluntarily took the risk of driving with his blackout condition.

Mens Rea? If Doug realized the risks associated with driving a school bus while suffering from blackouts, he acted recklessly. The fact that he planned to tell his doctor suggests he realized the risks. On the other hand, the blackouts always occurred at home and Doug may argue that he didn't believe there would be a risk at work.

D. MISTAKE OF FACT

On occasion, the evidence will show that the defendant did not form the mens rea necessary for the crime because he or she made a key mistake of fact. In such a situation, mistake of fact is a full defense because the defendant did not form the mens rea for the crime. MPC §2.04(1).

1. General Rule

Ignorance or mistake of fact precludes criminal liability if the mistake means the defendant lacks a mental state essential to the crime charged.

2. Model Penal Code §2.04(1)

"[I]gnorance or mistake is a defense when it negatives the existence of a state of mind that is essential to the commission of an offense. . . ."

3. Rationale

Although often referred to as a "defense," mistake or ignorance of fact is essentially a claim that the defendant did not have the mens rea for all of the material elements of the crime.

4. Application of Mistake of Fact Principles

In order to determine whether a mistake of fact defense applies, one must determine what facts the defendant needed to know to be guilty of the crime; i.e., the material elements of the offense. If the defendant is ignorant or mistaken as to a material element that does not require mens rea, then the defense will not apply.

a. **Example.** It is a crime to knowingly receive stolen goods. Defendant buys goods that are stolen, but he is unaware of it at the time. Defendant's mistake or ignorance of the facts precludes him from having the necessary mens rea for the crime.

b. **Example.** It is a crime to knowingly employ an illegal alien. Defendant knows his employee is illegally in the country, but he mistakenly believes the employee is from Russia, not Poland. Defendant's mistake is *not* a defense to the crime because it is not a requirement of the offense that the defendant know his employee's exact country of origin.

5. Determining Which Elements are Material

Because the mistake of fact defense depends on whether the defendant has made a mistake as to a material fact, it is crucial to determine what elements of a crime are material; i.e., what must the defendant know to be guilty of the crime?

a. **Statutory requirements.** The first place to look to determine what elements are material is the language of the statute. If a statute affixes a mens rea requirement to a particular fact, then the defendant must meet that mens rea requirement to be guilty of the crime. In other words, if a defendant needs to know something to be guilty of a crime, but he does not know it, he is not guilty.

Example. The law prohibits "knowingly using the credit card of another." Defendant uses a credit card without noticing that his name is not on it; a store teller has accidentally switched the defendant's card with that of another patron. Defendant is not guilty of knowingly using the credit card of another because he did not have the necessary mens rea for the offense.

b. **Common law offenses.** Many offenses, especially those at common law, did not use specific mens rea language that made clear what elements of the crime were material. Some crimes contained elements that the defendant did not need to know because defendant's conduct was still considered morally wrong regardless of his mistake as to one element of the crime. These additional elements were present to limit the number of moral wrongs the criminal courts would address.

Example and Analysis

In Regina v. Prince, L.R. 2 Cr. Cas. Res. 154 (1875), defendant was convicted of taking an unmarried girl under 16 years of age out of the possession and against the will of her father. Defendant claimed that he mistakenly believed that the girl was 18, when she was, in fact, only 14 years old. The court held that the defendant had no mistake defense because a violation of the law did not depend on whether the defendant knew the girl's age. The court found the material elements of the crime to be: 1. taking a girl (actus reus); 2. without her father's permission.

In the time and culture in which this case occurred, the morally wrong behavior in which the defendant engaged was taking a girl without her father's permission, because daughters were considered their fathers' possessions. Thus, the age of the girl was not a material element. It was jurisdictional because it served only to limit the number of such cases that the court would handle. The dissent [Brett, J.] argued that the true moral harm was taking an underaged girl from her father and that the defendant should, therefore, have a defense if he were mistaken as to that fact.

---

i. **Example.** White v. Case, 44 Ohio App. 331, 185 N.E. 64 (1993). The defendant was convicted of abandoning his pregnant wife. The defendant claimed that he was not guilty because he did not know his wife was pregnant. The court found that the morally wrong act was the defendant abandoning his wife and, therefore, it was irrelevant that he did not know she was pregnant.

ii. **Example.** United States v. Collado-Gomez, 834 F.2d 280 (2d Cir. 1987). Defendant was convicted of possessing crack cocaine for which he faced penalty enhancements because the cocaine was crack. Defendant claimed that he did not know the cocaine was of the crack variety. The court held there was no mistake defense because the defendant could not show that he was engaged in an activity that would have been innocent absent knowledge that the cocaine was crack.

iii. **Criticisms of morally wrong approach.** The moral-wrong approach to determine which elements are material is controversial, because it assumes that everyone in today's society has the same understanding as to what acts are morally wrong.

iv. **General intent v. specific intent crimes.** In trying to simplify which crimes allow a mistake of fact defense and which do not, some courts state that a mistake or ignorance of fact defense is only allowed for "specific intent" crimes. However, this rule is not very helpful because it is often difficult to distinguish between specific and general intent crimes.

v. **Model Penal Code approach.** The Model Penal Code acknowledges the moral-wrong approach by including a provision that holds that ignorance or mistake is not a defense when a defendant would be guilty of another offense had the situation been as he supposed. However, ignorance or mistake of fact can reduce the grade of the offense. MPC §2.04(2).

c. **Legislative intent.** Another way of determining which elements are material and whether a mistake of fact defense should be allowed is to examine the legislative history and purpose of a statute. If the purpose of a statute would be frustrated by allowing the defense, courts will find the contested element not to be material.

i. **Example.** In People v. Olsen, 36 Cal. 3d 638, 685 P.2d 52 (1984), the court held that a reasonable mistake as to the victim's age was not a defense to a charge of lewd or lascivious conduct with a child under the age of 14 years because the public policy of the statutes was to protect children as much as possible and, therefore, not allow a defense of mistake of fact, even if it is reasonable.

(a) **Mistake of age is generally not a defense.** Most jurisdictions do not allow a mistake of age defense to statutory rape, even if the defendant's mistake is reasonable. The Model Penal Code follows this approach for sex with a child under the age of ten. MPC §213.6(1). However, a substantial minority of states will allow a "reasonable" mistake of fact defense.

d. **Jurisdictional elements.** If an element of a crime is provided only to set limits on the jurisdiction of the court, the element is not material and a defendant's mistake regarding it is not a defense. This approach is used for federal crimes because federal courts have limited jurisdiction.

Example and Analysis

In United States v. Feola, 420 U.S. 672 (1975), the defendants attempted to rob men who turned out, unbeknownst to them, to be undercover FBI agents, and were charged with assaulting a federal officer. Defendants' claim that they did not know their victims were federal officers failed, because it would have been wrong to assault anyone and the statutory requirement that federal officers be the victims was only designed to establish the jurisdiction of the federal courts over such offenses. The

Court rejected defendants' claim that the "federal officer" requirement was more than jurisdictional because it exposed the defendants to increased punishment in federal court.

STUDY TIP

"Jurisdictional" elements are the same as "nonmaterial" elements.

e. **Summary.** Mistake or ignorance of the facts can seem confusing until one realizes that the only issue that must be resolved is what are the material elements of the crime; i.e., what facts does the defendant need to know to be guilty of the crime? If the defendant needs to know something and he does not, he has not met the mens rea requirements of the crime. On the other hand, if the defendant is ignorant or mistaken as to a fact, and knowledge of that fact is not a requirement of the crime, mistake of fact is not a defense. All of the above approaches (statutory interpretation, moral-wrong, legislative intent, and jurisdictional facts) can be used to designate which facts a defendant must know.

6. Reasonableness Requirement

Logically, if mistake of fact is a defense, an honest mistake by the defense should satisfy and the defendant's mistake need not be reasonable. Either the defendant has the mens rea for the crime or a mistake has negated his mens rea. MPC §2.04(1)(a) (an honest mistake is sufficient if it negatives the state of mind required for the crime). However, reaction to cases where an honest but arguably reasonable mistake was permitted led to a requirement in some jurisdictions that the defendant's mistake be reasonable.

EXAMPLE AND ANALYSIS

In Regina v. Morgan, (1976) A.C. 182, defendants were charged with forcible rape for having intercourse with a woman who struggled during the sex. Because defendants had been told by the woman's husband that she liked "kinky" sex and struggling was a way she got excited, defendants argued that they honestly, albeit mistakenly, believed she had consented. The court held that an unreasonable mistake of fact was still a defense, because an element of the crime was whether the defendants knew the woman was not consenting. Following *Morgan*, new statutes were adopted to require that the defendant make both an honest and reasonable mistake.

---

a. **Effect of reasonable mistake requirement.** By requiring that a mistake be reasonable, the court essentially makes negligent commission of an act sufficient for criminal liability because the standard is no longer what the defendant actually knew, but what a reasonable person would have known in his situation.

7. Transferred Intent

As long as the defendant has the requisite intent to commit a crime, it ordinarily does not matter if the defendant injures someone other than the intended victim. MPC §2.03(2)(a). See discussion of transferred intent in Chapter 7.

Example. Defendant tries to shoot victim A, but strikes victim B. Defendant's intent to harm victim A applies to the attack on victim B.

REVIEW QUESTIONS AND ANSWERS

MATERIAL ELEMENTS AND MISTAKE OF FACT

Question: A statute prohibits ''knowingly taking the property of another.'' (i.e., ''stealing'')
What level of mens rea is required for the crime?

Answer: Knowingly.
What are the material elements for the crime?

Answer: Taking (actus reus) and property of another (attendant circumstance). *Explanation*: There is nothing morally wrong with taking one's own property. Thus, the attendant circumstance that it be the ''property of another'' is material, not just jurisdictional.
What if the defendant honestly believes he is taking his own notebook?

Answer: The defendant has a mistake of fact defense because he has not formed the mens rea for a material element of the crime, i.e. the defendant does not know she is taking the property of another.
Question: A statute prohibits ''knowingly importing a controlled substance.''

What is the level of mens rea required for the crime?

Answer: Knowingly.
What are the material elements?

Answer: Importing (actus reus) and "a controlled substance" (attendant circumstance). *Explanation*: The language of the statute suggests that a material element of the crime is knowing that one is importing a controlled substance. There is nothing morally wrong with importing goods. Importing is only considered wrong when the goods are forbidden or if they are controlled substances.
What if the defendant believes he is importing cocaine, but it turns out to be heroin?

Answer: No mistake of fact defense because the statute only requires that the defendant know the substance is a controlled one, not that he know which controlled substance.
What if the defendant believes he is importing baby powder?

Answer: The defendant has a mistake of fact defense because he does not have the mens rea for a material element of the crime; i.e. he does not know the item is a controlled substance.
Question: A statute prohibits "knowingly receiving stolen property." Shelly is arrested when the police find a stolen bracelet in her home. In her defense, Shelly argues that she knew her boyfriend had stolen some goods, but she had no idea he was storing them in her home.
What is the level of mens rea required for the crime?

Answer: Knowingly.
What are the material elements for the crime?

Answer: Receiving (actus reus) and stolen property (attendant circumstance).
Does Shelly have a mistake of fact defense?

Answer: Yes. Although she knows that her boyfriend has stolen goods, she does not know that she has received any of them. The actus reus is a material element of the crime.
Question: It is a crime to "knowingly submit false statements to a federal agency." United States v. Yermian, 468 U.S. 63 (1984).
What is the level of mens rea required for the crime?

Answer: Knowingly.
What are the material elements?

Answer: Submitting statements (actus reus) and "false statements" (attendant circumstances). *Explanation*: The requirement that the false statements be submitted to a *federal* agency is only a jurisdictional element to ensure the crime can be prosecuted in federal court.

What if the defendant realizes he is submitting false statements but believes he is submitting them to a private contractor, not a federal agency?

Answer: No mistake of fact defense. Submission to a "federal agency" is a *jurisdictional* fact only. It is wrong to submit false statements to anyone. Thus, if the defendant makes a mistake as to whom he is submitting the false statements to, he has still satisfied all of the material elements of the crime.

Question: By statute, "anyone who intentionally accesses a federal interest computer, and . . . alters, damages, or destroys information . . . and thereby causes loss . . . aggregating $1,000 or more" is guilty of a federal offense. United States v. Morris, 928 F.2d 504 (1991).

What is the level of mens rea needed for the crime?

Answer: Intentionally (Knowingly or Purposely).

What are the material elements?

Answer: Accessing computer (actus reus). On the face of the statute it is unclear whether the defendant must intend to cause damage or loss. In reviewing the legislative history, the court found that it did not.

If the defendant intends to access the federal computer but believes he will cause no harm, does he have a mistake of fact defense if his access causes a virus to damage the computers?

Answer: No mistake of fact defense. It is sufficient that the defendant knew he was gaining unauthorized access to the computer.

E. STRICT LIABILITY (ABSOLUTE LIABILITY)

Strict liability crimes are offenses with no mens rea requirement as to the key element of the offense that makes the defendant's behavior wrong. Defendant is guilty of a crime, even if he honestly and *reasonably* believed his conduct was proper. The prosecution has no responsibility of proving a culpable mens rea. Strict liability is typically imposed for two types of crimes: public welfare offenses and common law morality crimes.

1. Public Welfare Offenses

In response to the Industrial Revolution, legislatures enacted statutes to deal with the new, highly regulated industries. As a regulatory device, strict liability crimes are used to address activities that can harm the public health, safety, and welfare.

a. **Examples.** Public welfare offenses include:

- illegal sales of liquor

- sales of impure or adulterated foods or drugs
- sales of misbranded articles
- criminal nuisances
- violations of traffic regulations
- violations of nuclear industry regulations

See Sayre, Public Welfare Offenses, 33 Col. L. Rev. 55, 73, 84 (1993).

b. **Example.** In United States v. Dotterweich, 320 U.S. 277 (1943), defendant, the president of a pharmaceutical company, was convicted of shipping misbranded and adulterated products. Although there was no evidence defendant knew, or should have known, that the products had been misbranded, he was held criminally responsible because the crime did not require a mens rea.

c. **Example.** Defendant drives in excess of the speed limit. He is guilty of speeding once he exceeds the speed limit. It is irrelevant whether he knew he was speeding or even if a reasonable person would have made the same mistake.

STUDY TIP

When strict liability crimes were first recognized, the sale of illegal narcotics, such as opium, was held to be a strict liability offense. For example, in United States v. Balint, 258 U.S. 250 (1922), the Supreme Court held that the Narcotic Act of 1914 did not require the prosecution to prove that the defendant knew he was selling a prohibited drug. Today, such statutes typically require a culpable mens rea.

2. Common Law Morality Offenses

There are also a number of nonpublic welfare offenses that impose criminal liability regardless of whether the defendant acted with a culpable mens rea.

a. **Examples.** Morality offenses imposing strict liability include:

- **Statutory Rape.** Defendant is guilty regardless of whether he honestly and reasonably believed the female was old enough to consent to sexual intercourse.

- **Bigamy.** Defendant is guilty even if the defendant has an honest and reasonable belief that she is no longer married to her prior spouse.
- **Adultery.** Defendant is guilty even if the defendant has an honest and reasonable belief that she is no longer married to her spouse.

STUDY TIP

The rationale for these common law strict liability crimes is slightly different than that for strict liability regulatory crimes. The above common law offenses are strict liability offenses in order to:

- deter immoral conduct as much as possible;
- protect certain classes of victims;
- avoid the difficulty of proving intent in cases involving intimate relations where witnesses will be limited.

3. Rationale for Strict Liability Doctrine

Various arguments are used to justify the use of strict liability for public welfare offenses. These include:

a. **Deterring risky behavior.** Because of the threat of prosecution, those engaging in high-risk activities will do so more carefully.

b. **Recognizing public's welfare is paramount.** Because the penalties for public welfare offenses are typically minor, the public's interest in safety outweighs the individual defendant's interest in being judged by his moral culpability.

c. **Easing prosecution's burden.** The strict liability doctrine allows prosecutors and courts to process a high volume of regulatory offenses that would otherwise be too time-consuming; e.g., traffic offenses.

4. Criticisms

Scholars generally disfavor strict liability crimes because the purposes of punishment are based upon showing that the defendant acted with culpable intent. Strict liability does not even require showing that the defendant acted negligently. Thus, a defendant may have taken all sensible precautions and will still be liable for a crime. The defendant's only option then is not to engage in the regulated activity at all, an option that may work to society's detriment.

5. Constitutionality

Strict liability crimes have been upheld as constitutional and not violative of due process as long as the penalty imposed is relatively light. United States v. Balint, 258 U.S. 250 (1922). The Supreme Court has never ruled on whether serious punishment for strict liability crimes would be cruel and unusual punishment.

6. Model Penal Code

Generally, the Model Penal Code rejects the concept of strict liability crimes and requires some form of culpability for each material element of an offense. MPC §2.02(1). However, the MPC recognizes strict liability (which it refers to as "absolute liability") for violations that cannot result in imprisonment or probation but may result in fines. MPC §2.05.

7. Identifying Strict Liability Crimes

a. **General rule.** Common law offenses are presumed *not* to be strict liability crimes even if the statute does not expressly mention a mens rea requirement.

   i. **Morissette v. United States, 342 U.S. 246 (1952).** In *Morissette*, defendant was charged with stealing spent bomb casings that were government property. Defendant claimed he did not know the property still belonged to the government. He thought they had been abandoned. The government claimed that because the statute did not state that the defendant must "know" he is taking the property of another, defendant's mistake should be irrelevant and the crime interpreted as a strict liability offense. After reviewing the history of strict liability/public welfare offenses, the Court held that the mere omission from a statute of any mention of intent does not make that crime a strict liability offense. For common law offenses, the presumption is against strict liability.

> **STUDY TIP**
>
> If a crime is not a strict liability offense, but no specific level of mens rea is required by the statute, the default level of culpability is recklessness.

b. **Legislative intent.** Because of the onerous effects of imposing strict liability, the legislature must expressly intend to eliminate a mens rea requirement for the crime. Legislative intent may be determined by the legislative history and purpose of the offense.

c. **Severity of penalties.** The strict liability doctrine is generally reserved for those crimes that carry relatively light punishment. The more severe the punishment, the less likely the crime is a strict liability offense.

d. **Number of possible offenses.** Strict liability is frequently used for those offenses that present a high volume of cases to the court, like traffic offenses.

e. **Evaluating a statute to determine strict liability.** In determining whether a statute imposes strict liability, one should examine:

- the language of the statute; (Warning: absence of mens rea language does not mean that a crime is strict liability);
- the legislative history;
- public policy factors:
  - Does it involve a highly regulated industry or a traditional common law offense?
  - Are the penalties relatively light?
  - Would proving mens rea put an undue burden on prosecution authorities?

8. Strict Liability Crimes Disfavored

Courts continue to disfavor strict liability crimes.

EXAMPLE AND ANALYSIS

In United States v. Staples, 114 S. Ct. 1793 (1994), the defendant was charged with possessing an unregistered firearm. On its face, the statute did not contain a mens rea requirement. Accordingly, the trial court refused to instruct the jury that the prosecution had to prove that the defendant knew his gun had characteristics that made it subject to registration requirements. The Supreme Court reversed. Even though the handling of firearms might initially appear to be a public welfare offense, the Court held that strict liability could not be imposed because violation of the statute subjected the defendant to a harsh penalty (ten years imprisonment) and there was no clear expression of legislative intent to treat the offense as a strict liability crime.

---

9. Other Strict Liability Concepts at Common Law

Even before the regulatory era, the courts recognized some strict liability crimes. They included statutory rape, adultery and bigamy. Strict liability principles also applied in felony-murder and misdemeanor-manslaughter cases. See Ch. 5 infra.

10. No Mistake or Ignorance of Fact Defense

Because there is no mens rea requirement, "mistake of fact" is not a defense to a strict liability crime, no matter how reasonable the mistake.

a. **Example.** Defendant is charged with having sex with an underage girl. Defendant claims that the girl lied to him as to her age, showed him a false birth certificate, had her parents lie to him as to her age, and looked and acted much older than she was. Defendant's mistake of age is still not a defense to a statutory rape charge.

b. **Example.** Defendant is charged with selling adulterated foods. Defendant claims that he tested the foods before selling them and took every precaution against adulteration. Nonetheless, the food became tainted during the delivery process. Defendant's ignorance of the tainting is not a defense to the strict liability crime.

11. Vicarious Liability

The principles of strict liability may also be imposed to find a supervisor responsible for the unlawful acts of a subordinate even though the supervisor did not know or have reason to know the subordinate was violating the law. "Vicarious liability" is the responsibility for the criminal acts of another without a showing that the defendant has a culpable mens rea.

State v. Guminga, 395 N.W.2d 344 (1986). Defendant owned a restaurant where a waitress was caught serving alcohol to an underage customer. The state statute imposed liability on the owner even though he was not directly involved in the offense and there was no proof that he knew of the practices. On review, the Minnesota Supreme Court reversed the conviction because it carried too heavy of a criminal penalty for a strict liability offense.

12. Defenses to Strict Liability Crimes

Even though there is no mens rea defense to a strict liability crime, a defendant may still challenge the actus reus component of the crime. Specifically, a defendant may claim that he or she did not engage in a voluntary act.

a. **State v. Baker, 571 P.2d 65 (1977).** Defendant was convicted of speeding. He claimed that his accelerator stuck while he was using the cruise control. The court held that speeding in that case was an "absolute liability" offense but left open the possibility that a defendant could claim, in the right circumstance, an "involuntary act" defense. Defendant in this case was not entitled to the defense because he voluntarily chose to use the cruise control.

b. **Hill v. Baxter, (1958) 1 Q.B. 277.** Defendant drove through a traffic light. He claimed that the violation occurred because he suffered a blackout. The court held that in theory "automatism" is a defense to a strict liability crime but found the evidence lacking in this case.

13. Alternative Approaches to Strict Liability Crimes

American law generally offers only two approaches: a. prosecution must prove mens rea; or b. mens rea is irrelevant. Some courts, however, are entertaining an alternative. The third approach would relieve the prosecution of the burden of proving the mens rea, but allow the defendant to prove he or she was not negligent.

a. **Canadian law.** In Regina v. City of Sault Ste. Marie, 85 D.L.R. 161 (1978), the court acknowledged three categories of offenses in Canada:

- offenses for which mens rea must be proved;
- offenses for which the prosecution need not prove mens rea, but the defendant can show he took all reasonable care to avoid harm;
- offenses for which the defendant's mens rea and exercise of reasonable care are irrelevant. (absolute liability).
  - In Reference Re Section 94(2) of the Motor Vehicle Act, 23 C.C.C.3d 289 (1985), the Canadian Supreme Court held absolute liability (corresponding to American strict liability) unconstitutional.

b. **American law.** Generally, American courts take an all-or-nothing approach. Either the prosecution must prove intent or intent is irrelevant. However, at least one court has recently adopted a version of the Canadian alternative to ameliorate the impact of strict liability laws.

i. **United States v. United States District Court (Kantor), 858 F.2d 534 (9th Cir. 1988).** The Ninth Circuit engrafted a "good faith defense" onto the federal child pornography statute in order to avoid finding it unconstitutional because of its impact on First Amendment rights and its severe penalties. The court held that though the statute did not require prosecutors to prove the defendant knew he was using an underage girl, the defense could present a defense of good faith belief or reasonable mistake as to the victim's age.

c. **Lady Wooton's proposal.** British criminologist Lady Barbara Wooton has proposed that the mens rea requirement be eliminated for all crimes and only be a consideration for sentencing. The problems with this proposal are: 1. mens rea lies at the heart of the American system of criminal justice; and 2. many more people might be prosecuted even though ultimately they may never be punished. Often the social stigma of a criminal conviction is as bad as the sentence itself.

FIGURE 3-5

STRICT LIABILITY	
Definition	No mens rea requirement for key elements
Types of Crimes	Public welfare and morality offenses
Characteristics of Statutory Strict Liability Crimes	1. Highly regulated industry 2. Affecting public welfare 3. No mens rea language in statute 4. High volume of prosecutions 5. Relatively light penalties

REVIEW QUESTION AND ANSWER

STRICT LIABILITY

Question: In an effort to protect the environment, Congress has passed a new statute making it a violation, punishable by 30 days in jail and a $10,000 fine, to discard used motor oil, except at specific recycling centers. During the Congressional debates on the statute, the author of the bill expressly states that there are thousands of people improperly discarding their motor oil everyday and that "even if the average citizen doesn't know it is wrong, it still is." The law that passes states: "It is violation of law to discard used motor oil except in designated recycling centers."

Ben is charged with violating the statute when he changes his oil in his front yard and pours the oil down the storm gutter. Ben claims that he had no idea that the oil needed to be recycled. Is he criminally liable?

Answer: Ben is most likely criminally liable because the statute appears to set forth a strict liability offense. Laws which involve minor regulatory offenses with minimal punishments are generally classified as strict liability crimes. A violation of a law classified as a strict liability offense triggers liability regardless of the person's mens rea.

In this case, there are a number of factors which indicate that this is a strict liability crime. First, the language of the statute in this case does not indicate a mens rea requirement. The legislative history of the bill also expressly states that the thousands of people improperly discarding their oil are still committing an act that is wrong, regardless of their knowledge. Also, the policy behind the statute fulfills an important goal—providing for the maximum protection of the environment. Further, the statute is a regulatory offense with a maximum penalty. Lastly, as with traffic cases, the number of cases this law will produce would place an undue burden on a prosecutor to prove the mens rea in each of these crimes. Therefore, Ben is liable regardless of his knowledge, because the law he violated is a strict liability offense.

F. MISTAKE OF LAW

1. General Rule

Mistake or ignorance of the law is generally *not* a defense. The law presumes that everyone knows its requirements because the laws themselves are based upon the community's standards for moral conduct.

2. Rationale

Laws are based upon society's common consensus as to what is proper behavior. Thus, simply by living in society, a person has notice of what conduct is expected of him or her. To allow a defendant to claim a mistake of law defense would put a premium on ignorance of the law.

3. Exceptions

There are three categories of exceptions where mistake of law is a defense:

- The defendant has been officially misled as to the law.
- The defendant does not have the necessary mens rea for the crime because of her ignorance or mistake as to legal requirements.
- The defendant has not received requisite knowledge of the law.

a. **Exception #1: Defendant misled by official authority. [MPC §2.04(3)(b)].** Because it is desirable to have people rely on official statements of the law, if a defendant does so and that statement later turns out to be incorrect, the defendant may assert a mistake of law defense.

i. **Reliance on invalid statute.** If the defendant relies on a statute that the courts later strike down, mistake of law is a defense. MPC §2.04(3)(b)(i).

(a) **Misreading of law insufficient.** A mistake of law defense cannot be claimed simply because the defendant misread the law. If that were the standard, every defendant would claim to have misinterpreted the law. People v. Marrero, 69 N.Y.2d 382, 507 N.E.2d 1068 (1987).

ii. **Reliance on judicial decision.** If the state's highest court had interpreted the law as permitting defendant's conduct, the defendant may rely upon that decision even if that court, or the Supreme Court, later changes its interpretation. MPC §2.04(3)(b)(ii).

(a) **United States v. Albertini, 830 F.2d 985 (9th Cir. 1987).** Defendant relied on a Court of Appeals ruling that the Supreme Court later overturned. Under such circumstances, defendant could claim mistake of law.

iii. **Reliance on administrative order.** If the defendant acts in accordance with an order of a controlling administrative agency, there is no criminal liability even if that order later turns out to be incorrect under the law. MPC §2.04(b)(3)(iii).

(a) **Cox v. Louisiana, 379 U.S. 559 (1965).** Defendant relied upon permission of the police and city officials to conduct a demonstration. Later prosecution was barred as a violation of due process.

iv. **Reliance on official interpretation.** If a controlling authority issues an interpretation of the law permitting the defendant's conduct, mistake of law may be a defense, (e.g., Attorney General's Opinions). MPC §2.04(3)(b)(iv).

(a) **Note.** Not all jurisdictions accept this exception. For example, in Hopkins v. State, 193 Md. 489, 69 A.2d 456 (1940), the court refused to overturn a conviction simply because the State's Attorney had advised the defendant his conduct would not be illegal.

(b) **Reliance on advice of counsel.** Relying on the mistaken advice of one's lawyer is ordinarily not sufficient to raise a mistake of law defense unless the lawyer's advice negates the defendant's mens rea for the crime. (See Exception #2 below.)

b. **Exception #2: Because of ignorance or mistake of the law, defendant lacks the mens rea for crime.** Some crimes require that a defendant know that his or her actions are in violation of the law or are "without authority of law." If a defendant does not know that he is acting without such authority because he has made a mistake of law, then the mens rea requirement of the crime has not been satisfied and mistake or ignorance of the law is a defense. In such situations, mistake of law operates in a manner identical to mistake of fact. The defendant does not have the mens rea required for the offense.

i. **MPC §2.04(1).** "Ignorance or mistake as to a matter of fact or law is a defense if: a. the ignorance or mistake negatives the purpose, knowledge, belief, recklessness, or negligence required to establish a material element of the offense. . . ."

EXAMPLES AND ANALYSIS

People v. Weiss, 276 N.Y. 384, 12 N.E.2d 514 (1938). Defendants are charged with kidnapping because they seize a person they believe to be a wanted murderer. The definition of "kidnapping" in that jurisdiction requires that the defendant act with the intent to confine the victim "without authority of law." Because the defendants mistakenly believed they had the "authority of law" to seize the murder suspect, they lacked the necessary mens rea for kidnapping.

Regina v. Smith (David) [1974] 2 Q.B. 354. Defendant is charged with "damaging any property belonging to another." He claims that he mistakenly believed that under the law the property he destroyed belonged to him. Because defendant must know that the property belongs to another, his mistake as to the legal status of the property was a mistake.

Liparota v. United States, 471 U.S. 419 (1985). Defendant is charged with the "unauthorized" use or acquisition of food stamps. He contends that he did not know that he was acquiring food stamps in a manner unauthorized by law. Because the statute requires that the defendant "know" that his acquisition is contrary to law, a mistake of law negates the necessary mens rea and is a full defense.

Cheek v. United States, 498 U.S. 192 (1991). Defendant is convicted of "willfully" failing to file a federal tax return. For purposes of this statute, "willfully" means defendant intentionally violated a known legal duty. Because defendant claimed he honestly, albeit unreasonably, believed that he was not required to pay taxes, defendant's good faith belief undermined the prosecution's claim that defendant acted "willfully."

---

ii. **Mere disagreement with law insufficient.** If a defendant knows what the law requires but simply disagrees with that law, there is no mistake of law defense.

(a) **Example.** Defendant is a tax protester who opposes income tax laws. He knows that income tax laws have been upheld by the courts, but his personal view is that they should be held unconstitutional. Defendant's opposition to the law is insufficient to negate his mens rea for the crime. He knows what his legal obligations are, he just chooses not to fulfill them. Cheek v. United States, 498 U.S. 192 (1991).

Study Tip

The Court's decision in Cheek v. United States, 498 U.S. 192 (1991) can be somewhat confusing. While the Court allowed the defendant a claim of mistake of law, it also stated that mere disagreement with the law or belief that the tax laws are unconstitutional would be insufficient for a mistake of law defense. If the defendant knows he is subject to the tax laws, but believes those laws are invalid, he should challenge those laws in the Tax Court, not fail to comply with the law. If, however, the defendant honestly believes the tax laws do not apply to him, he can claim a mistake of law defense. Thus, the Court seeks to draw a fine line between those who do not know their legal duty and those who know their duty but disagree with the law.

(b) **Proving disagreement with the law.** To prove that a defendant knew a law, but willfully failed to comply with it because he disagreed with it, the prosecution may rely upon the defendant's prior compliance with the law. *Cheek*, supra.

iii. **Mistake need not be reasonable.** An honest, good-faith mistake of law is sufficient to negate a defendant's mens rea, just as it is in mistake of fact situations. Of course, the more unreasonable a defendant's mistake, the less likely that the jury will believe that it was sincerely made.

Example. Defendant has protested the tax laws for years and, after previously filing tax returns, refuses to do so. Defendant's actions tended to show that he had a strong disagreement with the law, not a lack of understanding as to its requirements. However, it was up to the jury to determine whether the defendant had a good-faith misunderstanding of the law. Cheek v. United States, 498 U.S. 192 (1991).

iv. **Mistaken belief that violates a different law.** If a defendant believes that he is violating one law, and it turns out he is violating another, he is still guilty unless the offense with which he is charged requires that he "knowingly" act in violation of that law.

Example and Analysis

In Regina v. Taaffe [1983] 2 All E.R. 625 (Ct. App.), the defendant believed he was illegally transporting currency when, in fact, he was carrying narcotics. While defendant's actions may have been immoral, he did not violate the law because the specific statute with which he was charged required that the defendant "knowingly" import the drug. Transporting currency was not illegal. However, if transporting currency had also been illegal, defendant would be guilty even though he made a mistake as to which law he had violated.

(a) **Model Penal Code approach.** MPC §2.04(2) provides that an ignorance or mistake of law defense is not available if the defendant would be guilty of another offense had the situation been as the defendant supposed. In such cases, however, defendant's crime is reduced to the degree of the offense he thought he had committed.

v. **Interpreting statutes to determine whether defendant need know the requirements of the law.** As with mistake of fact, the most difficult step in deciding whether mistake of law is a defense is in interpreting the statute to determine whether the defendant need know its legal requirements. The same three steps apply:

- Read the language of the statute.
- Evaluate its legislative history.
- Determine whether public policy requires that the defendant know he is engaging in illegal conduct.

(a) **Ratzlaf v. United States, 114 S. Ct. 665 (1994).** Defendant was charged with illegally structuring cash transactions to avoid government reporting requirements. The language of the statute was ambiguous as to whether the defendant need only know she was structuring transactions or whether she also needed to know that the structuring would be an attempt to evade reporting requirements. The Court found the latter because currency structuring by itself is not so inherently evil as to provide the defendant notice that it would be contrary to law. There can be innocent reasons why transactions are structured such as avoiding audit or preventing others from knowing of one's wealth.

c. **Exception #3: lack of reasonable notice of the law.** In 1957, the Supreme Court carved out another narrow category of exceptions to the general rule that mistake of law is not a defense. The premise of this third exception is that due process requires that the defendant have sufficient notice as to what acts constitute a violation of the law. See also MPC §2.04(3)(a). The courts have interpreted this exception as narrowly as possible.

i. **Lambert v. California, 353 U.S. 225 (1957).** Defendant was charged with failing to register as a convicted person upon her arrival in Los Angeles. She had no notice of the reporting requirement and claimed ignorance of the law. The Court held that in the narrow circumstances of that case, Due Process required that defendant be afforded a defense. However, the *Lambert* exception has been limited to situations where:

- defendant's conduct is wholly passive;
- there was no actual notice of the law; and
- the violation involves a regulatory offense.

ii. **Model Penal Code, §2.04(3)(a).** The Model Penal Code would expand the *Lambert* exception to any case where a law-abiding and prudent person would not have learned of the law's existence.

4. Alternative Approaches to Mistake of Law

Some jurisdictions include more lenient standards for the mistake of law defense.

a. **Diligent pursuit provisions.** In New Jersey, the defendant may claim mistake of law if she "diligently pursues all means to ascertain the meaning and application" of the laws. N.J. Stat. Ann. tit. 2C, §2-4(c)(3) [based upon California Proposed Revision (1968)]. Thus, if a defendant seeks advice, including in part from private counsel, she may be excused if she later engages in unlawful conduct. Because this approach is subject to abuse; i.e., using lawyers to help fabricate a defense, most jurisdictions reject this approach.

b. **German approach.** In other countries, defendants are afforded a broad mistake of law defense. For example, in Germany, the only issue is whether the defendant was not aware that his conduct was unlawful and if proper application of his moral sensitivities would have led him to such awareness. If the defendant is unaware that he is violating the law, regardless of the source of his confusion, he is not culpable for the crime.

5. Cultural Defenses

Defendants are expected to live according to the standards of the community in which they live. Accordingly, cultural defenses are rarely allowed, although they may mitigate a defendant's punishment.

Example. A defendant who recently arrived from a foreign country beats his wife because she has committed adultery. Although such a practice may be accepted in his native culture, it is still a violation of American law.

FIGURE 3-6

Summary of Mistake of Law	
Gen. Rule:	Mistake or ignorance of the law is no defense.
Exceptions:	1. Defendant is officially misled as to the law. • Mere misreading of the statute is insufficient. 2. Mistake negates mens rea for the crime. 3. Lack of reasonable notice of the law.

Review Questions and Answers

Question: In 1992, a state statute prohibiting the sale of cigarettes was held unconstitutional by the State Supreme Court on the ground that it violated the interstate commerce clause of the Federal Constitution. Defendant, relying upon that decision, sold cigarettes in that state until 1995. In 1995, the United States Supreme Court ruled in another case that states may prohibit the sale of cigarettes. If defendant is charged with the unlawful sale of cigarettes from 1992 to 1995, does he have a mistake of law defense?
Answer: Yes. Defendant relied upon the State Supreme Court's ruling that his conduct was lawful.
Question: Defendant wanted to erect some advertisement signs in his city. Accordingly, he checked with his local police officer who said that he thought it would be permissible. As it turned out, state law prohibited the display. Would mistake of law be a defense?

Answer: No. A local police officer is not the type of official whose opinion can be relied upon in determining the law.

Question: Defendant was convicted of reckless driving. He decides to move to Alaska. Unbeknownst to him, Alaska has a law requiring all reckless drivers to register at City Hall within three days of arriving in the state. Failure to do so is a felony. Would mistake of law be a defense?

Answer: Yes, if defendant did not have actual notice of the registration requirement. The *Lambert* exception applies because the crime involves: 1. a regulatory offense; 2. passive crime; 3. no notice to the defendant.

Question: Defendant is charged with "knowingly selling unauthorized technology to a foreign nation." Defendant sold computers to another country but claimed that he did not realize that the computer was on a list of technology unauthorized for sale. Would mistake of law be a defense?

Answer: Yes. Because the statute requires that the defendant know what type of technology is unauthorized in order to be guilty of the crime. *Weiss/Liparota* exception.

Question: Defendant decides to open a child-care center. She reviews the laws in her jurisdiction and hires her staff. The laws provide: "No person who has been convicted of a crime may work in a child-care center." Defendant hires a defendant who she knew had a juvenile conviction for joyriding that was expunged. When charged with violating the statute, defendant claimed she had read the statute as covering only permanent, adult convictions. Would mistake of law be a defense?

Answer: No. Misreading a statute is not a defense. *Marrerro.*

Question: Defendant school teacher recently moved to the United States from Thailand. In Thailand, it is proper to cane students who misbehave in school. When defendant uses corporal punishment on a child in her class, she is charged with battery. Does she have an ignorance of the law defense?

Answer: No. There is no generally recognized "cultural defense" to crimes. Defendant must conform to the standards of the society in which she lives.

Question: Defendant Broderidge is the leader of a protest group opposing the fiscal policies of the United States government. Broderidge honestly believes that she is entitled to issue her own checks on the U.S. Treasury because the current government is illegally conducting its affairs. Broderidge is charged with unlawful counterfeiting of U.S. Treasury checks. Does Broderidge have a mistake of law defense?

Answer: Perhaps. If the counterfeiting laws require that Broderidge "knowingly" use a government check in a manner unauthorized by the law, Broderidge can claim she honestly believed that she was entitled under the law to use her own Treasury checks. However, if prosecutors can prove that Broderidge knew she was acting contrary to the law, but simply did so out of disagreement with it, she would *not* have a mistake of law defense. Additionally, her claim that she honestly believed in the legality of her checks would probably have little credibility with the jury.

RAPE

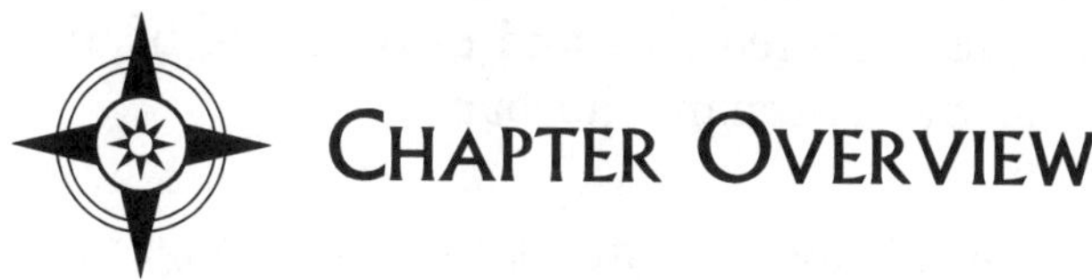

CHAPTER OVERVIEW

Rape is a specific crime against an individual. Many policy issues are raised by the changing definitions of the crime. Chapter 4 will review the common law and statutory definitions of rape, as well as the policy arguments underlying those definitions. The issues included for discussion are:

- Types of Rapes
- Perspectives on Rape
- Elements of Rape
  - Sexual intercourse
  - With a woman
  - Without her consent
  - By force, fear, or fraud
- Defenses to Rape
  - Honest belief of consent
  - Reasonable and honest belief of consent
- Rape Reform Legislation
- The Marital Exemption
- Problems of Proof
- Model Penal Code Approach
- Statutory Rape

A. INTRODUCTION

Rape is an example of a crime against a person, as are assault, battery, and homicide. However, because of public attitudes regarding the relationships between men and women, rape raises unique issues. Many of the principles of rape law are influenced by concerns about unfounded rape accusations and the need to have crimes proved beyond a reasonable doubt.

B. TYPES OF RAPE

1. Traditional Categories of Rape

Traditionally, the law has recognized two types of rape:

a. **Forcible rape.** At common law, the crime of rape was defined as a man's forcible intercourse with a woman who is not his wife. Intercourse required a man's penetration of a woman's vulva by his penis; it does not require sexual emission. Modern statutes have modified this definition to include same-sex forcible rapes, other types of sexual penetrations, sexual intercourse procured by fraud or drugging of the victim, and forced intercourse by a woman's husband.

i. **Acquaintance rape.** Rape may be committed by a stranger or an acquaintance. Nonstranger rape is estimated to be the most frequent type of rape. Acquaintance rape, also referred to as "date rape," typically involves a different type of force than that used in stranger rape. The woman may feel compelled to submit because of the man's position of authority or his continued aggression and pressure.

ii. **Gender-specific.** Traditionally, rape statutes have been gender-specific, limiting the crime to a man's nonconsensual sex with women. Under these statutes, only females can be victims of rape. Today, some jurisdictions recognize forcible sex with any person, including a person of the same sex, as rape or sexual assault, e.g., Cal. Pen. Code, §261.

b. **Statutory rape.** An ancient English felony statute also prohibited sexual intercourse by a male with a "woman child" under the age of ten years with or without her consent. This offense became a common law crime in the United States and is still prohibited in various forms by state statutes. The age of the victim who is legally incapable of giving consent varies according to the statute.

C. PERSPECTIVES ON RAPE

Frequently, men and women view the crime of rape differently. Most men will agree that forcible intercourse by a stranger constitutes rape. There is much less agreement, however, about when aggressive sexual conduct by an acquaintance ("date rape") constitutes a criminal offense. The broader questions raised by rape are:

- Do men and women have different perspectives on male sexual aggression and, if so, why?
- What constitutes harmful, illegal sexual aggression?
- What is the nature of the harm in rape? Is it a crime of violence or a crime of sexual intrusion?
- Has the law of rape kept up with changing sexual mores of society?

1. Statistics Regarding Rape

Rape is estimated to be one of the most underreported crimes in the United States. Although statistics vary, one government survey estimated that only 53 percent of all attempted or completed rapes are reported to the police. National Crime Survey, 1991. One recent study estimated that 27 percent of college women had been victims of at least one rape. Koss Study, Consulting & Clinical Psychol. 162 (1987).

2. Reasons for Underreporting

Rape is often not reported because of:

- the stigma attached to the victim of the crime;
- the difficulties rape victims have in being believed;
- law enforcement's unwillingness to take seriously and assist rape victims.

3. Social Stigma of Rape

Historically, both men and women have tended to blame the rape victim for her plight. Female behavior, whether it be dress, mannerism, or other conduct, has been blamed for bringing on the attack.

4. Victim's Relationship to Rapist

One key factor affecting attitudes toward rape has been the victim's relationship to the rapist. Stranger rape has traditionally been treated more seriously than rapes where the defendant is acquainted with the victim.

5. Historical Roots of Crime

To a large extent, the law of rape is influenced by its historical roots. The law of rape is rooted in ancient male concepts of property. A woman was viewed as the chattel of her husband or father. Rape was a property offense involving an unlawful taking. Modern law understands rape to be a crime of violence against the individual, not just a sexual taking.

D. ELEMENTS OF RAPE

1. Common Law

Rape is defined as "unlawful sexual intercourse with a woman without her consent by force, fear, or fraud." Regina v. Morgan [1976] A.C. 182. Thus, the elements of the crime of rape included:

a. **Sexual intercourse.** The actus reus for the crime of rape is "sexual intercourse" or "carnal knowledge." The slightest penetration is sufficient. There need not be completion of the sexual act.

b. **Unlawful.** At common law and under the Model Penal Code (MPC §213.1), a husband cannot be guilty of raping his wife. Women were considered the property of men and marriage constituted *per se* consent to intercourse. However, a defendant could be guilty of the rape of his wife if he aided and abetted another in having sexual intercourse with her against her will. *Regina v. Morgan* [1976] A.C. 182.

c. **Without consent.** The mens rea requirement for rape traditionally mandates that the defendant be aware he is acting without the victim's consent. Lack of consent is a material element of the crime of rape.

d. **By force, fear, or fraud.** Because of society's difficulties in ascertaining when a woman has or has not consented, common law also included a requirement that the prosecution prove intercourse was accomplished by force, fear, or fraud.

STUDY TIP

Rape =	A.R. (Penetration by force, fear, or fraud)	+	M.R. (Aware no consent)	+	Circ. (Unlawful)

2. Evaluating the Elements of Rape

Like other crimes, rape requires an actus reus, mens rea, and circumstances. However, the exact meaning of these requirements remains controversial.

a. **Mens rea.** The mens rea for rape is not clearly defined. Traditionally, the defendant must not only be aware he is having intercourse but also be aware that the victim does not consent. Some jurisdictions have now adopted a negligence standard which holds the defendant liable if a reasonable person would have known the woman was not consenting.

i. **Mistake as a defense.** Traditionally, an honest mistake as to consent constituted a defense to rape because it demonstrated the defendant did not have the necessary mens rea for the crime. In *Regina v. Morgan*, [1976] A.C. 182, Morgan and his three friends were charged with raping Morgan's wife. While they were out drinking, Morgan suggested to his codefendants that they should go to his home and have sexual intercourse with his wife. He described her as "kinky" and preferring to struggle during sex. When defendants were charged with rape, they claimed an honest belief that the victim had consented. The trial court rejected the defense because the belief was not reasonable. The appellate court held that an honest belief in consent, even if not reasonable, is a defense to rape because it negates defendant's mens rea for the crime.

- **Note.** Even though the appellate court held that the trial court had erred, it refused to reverse the defendants' convictions because no jury could have found that the defendants' had made a sincere, honest mistake of fact.
- **Response to Morgan.** In response to the *Morgan* decision, the British Parliament enacted a statute that made reckless disregard of whether there was consent a sufficient mens rea for rape. Sexual Offenses (Amendment) Act (1976), §1(1).

(a) **Modern view: reasonable mistake required.** Most American courts require that a defendant show he had both an honest and reasonable belief that the victim had consented. In other words, these courts have adopted a "negligence" standard that allows a mistake of fact defense only if a reasonable person in defendant's situation would also have believed the victim had consented. Commonwealth v. Sherry, 386 Mass. 682, 437 Mass. 682, 437 N.E.2d 224 (1942)(reasonable mistake of fact required for defense to rape).

(b) **Strict liability.** A small minority of jurisdictions provide no mistake of fact defense to rape even if the defendant honestly and reasonably believed the victim had consented. Rather, the defendant is strictly liable once a jury finds that the victim had not, in fact, consented. Commonwealth v. Ascolillo, 405 Mass. 456, 541 N.E.2d 570 (1989).

ii. **Practical effect of reasonableness standard.** Using an objective reasonable belief consent standard will only make a difference in rape prosecutions if society, in general, recognizes that when a woman says "no," she means "no." If the general public has misconceptions as to when women consent, then requiring that the defendant's mistake be reasonable will not alter the outcome of controversial rape cases.

iii. **Reasonable mistake defense not available in swearing contest between defendant and victim.** Some jurisdictions will not allow the "reasonable mistake" defense to be used when the victim unequivocally claims she resisted and the defendant claims she consented. The jury must instead choose between the credibility of the two parties rather than ascertain what a reasonable person would have believed under the circumstances. People v. Tyson, 619 N.E.2d 276 (Ind. App. 1993).

b. **Actus reus.** In addition to the requirement that the defendant have sexual intercourse with the victim, common law also required that defendant use force or fraud in obtaining nonconsensual sex.

i. **Force, threat of force, and resistance**. Traditionally, in order to demonstrate the victim did not consent, the prosecution must prove that defendant used force or threat of force. A victim's resistance is evidence that force was used. On occasion, intimidation may satisfy the force requirement.

(a) **Rationale.** Traditionally, courts have been concerned about the possibility that a victim's conduct could be misinterpreted as consent. In order to establish that the defendant acted without consent, the law would require that the defendant act with force or threat of force, which could be proven by evidence that the victim resisted the unlawful intercourse.

(b) **Criticism.** What constitutes "force or threat of force" depends on one's perspective. A woman may perceive a threat of force even when the defendant does not actually use physical violence, while a defendant may view aggressive male sexual behavior as normal. The force requirement makes it more difficult for prosecutors to charge rape. It may also place women at a greater risk of being seriously injured because they must show there is some kind of serious force they tried to resist.

EXAMPLE AND ANALYSIS

State v. Alston, 310 N.C. 399, 312 S.E.2d 470 (1984). In *Alston*, the court refused to find a "forcible" rape because the woman, who had been abused by the defendant on many previous occasions, submitted to his demand for sex. The court took a narrow view of force, limiting it to the defendant's actions immediately preceding intercourse. The woman's silence was interpreted as consent. The fact that the woman may have complied because of a long pattern of abuse and perceived lack of power was considered insufficient.

STUDY TIP

The issue of how much force is required for rape and whether women should not be expected to fight back raises the policy questions of whether it is patronizing to treat women as not having the power to resist sexual advances or whether there is an increased danger to women who choose to resist.

(c) **State v. Rusk, 289 Md. 230, 424 A.2d 720 (1981).** In the typical acquaintance rape situation, the defendant may argue that the victim consented because she did not resist defendant's advances, nor did he use any physical violence or express threat of harm. Although "lack of consent is generally established through proof of resistance," the jury is free to find that the victim reasonably feared the defendant even when there is no resistance.

(d) **Situations where proof of force not required.** In some situations, the law presumes the victim is incapable of providing consent and therefore does not require that there be proof of force, threat of force or resistance. These situations include:

- statutory rape (sex with minor)
- mentally incompetent victim
- unconscious victim
- deception by defendant (e.g., impersonation of husband)

(e) **Model Penal Code approach: defining rape offense by degree of force used, MPC §213.1.** The Model Penal Code shifts the focus of a rape case from how much resistance the victim offered to how much force the defendant used. The degree of force determines the degree of rape for which the defendant is culpable.

(f) **Resistance.** At common law, to ensure that the defendant acted with force, the courts would also require a showing of resistance by the victim. Resistance needed to be physical, not just verbal, often putting the victim at greater danger of serious physical injury. Accordingly, many modern jurisdictions have abandoned the resistance requirement and allow other evidence of the use of force or threat of force to suffice.

- **Note.** The "resistance" requirement places the focus of the case on the actions of the victim, not the defendant. Thus, the woman often feels as if she is the one on trial.
- **Reasonable resistance.** When resistance is a requirement, it is not at all clear how much resistance is considered "reasonable" under what circumstances. For example, when the defendant has a gun pointed at the victim's head, no resistance may be the appropriate response. Force should not be limited to situations where the defendant overpowers the victim. See Susan Estrich, Real Rape, 60-65, 69 (1978).

(g) **Alternative offenses approach.** Rather than eliminate the force requirement from the definition of rape, some jurisdictions offer the jury the option to convict on other offenses that do not have such a requirement. Unauthorized sexual intrusions are viewed as inherently coercive.

Examples and Analysis

In State in the Interest of M.T.S., 129 N.J. 422, 609 A.2d 1266 (1992), the court held that "sexual assault" is "any act of sexual penetration engaged in by the defendant without the affirmative and freely given permission of the victim . . . ." Force and violence are only factors that the fact-finder may consider in determining whether the victim freely gave affirmative permission for the sexual act.

In Commonwealth v. Berkowitz, 641 A.2d 1161 (Pa. 1994), the defendant was not guilty of rape because there was no showing of force, but the defendant was guilty of "indecent assault," a lesser included offense.

(h) **Nonphysical threats.** The terms "force" and "threat of force" have been traditionally interpreted very narrowly by the courts. Courts are reluctant to interpret "threat of force" to include nonphysical threats and intimidation. For example, a girl who submitted to sex because her principal threatened to prevent her from graduating did not act under "threat of force." State v. Thompson, 792 P.2d 1103 (Mont. 1990). Likewise, "force" did not include the threat to return the victim to a detention home unless she submitted to sexual advances. Commonwealth v. Milarich, 498 A.2d 395 (Pa. Super. 1985).

ii. **Deception.** In addition to force or threat of force, some jurisdictions now recognize that a defendant may also rape by deception. Traditionally, the use of deception was insufficient for rape because it did not constitute "force." However, recent statutes recognize that the use of deception precludes the victim from giving valid consent.

(a) **Traditional approach.** In those jurisdictions that limit rape to sexual intercourse by "force," deception was found insufficient to constitute rape.

Examples and Analysis

Boro v. Superior Court, 163 Cal. App. 3d 1224, 210 Cal. Rptr. 122 (1985). Defendant doctor deceived victim into believing that she must have intercourse with an "anonymous donor" in order to cure her alleged infectious disease. The court held that while the defendant's actions were reprehensible, they did not constitute rape.

People v. Evans, 85 Misc. 2d 1088, 379 N.Y.S.2d 912 (1975). The victim, a young college co-ed, had been tricked into allowing intercourse by a defendant who professed that he was just performing a psychological experiment on her. The court held that under New York state law, sexual intercourse by deception or intimidation did not constitute rape because it did not involve force or threat of force.

Rationale for Traditional Approach. Legislatures and courts were reluctant to expand rape to include intercourse by deception because there are situations, such as when the defendant promises travel, fame, or fortune, and later reneges on those promises, that the victim might claim rape.

(b) **Modern legislation on deception.** Rape procured by "false or fraudulent representation or pretense" has now been added to some state statutes, but it is generally still limited to situations where deception is used to create a fear of unlawful physical injury; e.g., Cal. Pen. Code, §266c).

c. **Circumstance—Marital rape exemption.** Under the common law and Model Penal Code, §213.1, a defendant cannot be convicted of raping his wife. Marriage constitutes a general waiver of the woman's right to say "no." Most states still retain some form of the marital exemption, either by making marital rape a lesser crime or by requiring aggravated force for proof of marital rape.

E. RAPE REFORM LEGISLATION

Although courts continue to make efforts to treat victims better, reform legislation has had little effect on rape victims' reporting behavior. The prevailing view continues to be that rape law is based upon male perspectives and stereotypes of male-female behavior, and that the real changes that need to be made are related to society's attitudes, not just the legal standards for rape.

Nonetheless, some reforms are being made in rape law:

- Elimination of the resistance requirement;
- Elimination or relaxation of the force requirement; (see State in the Interest of M.T.S., 129 N.J. 422, 609 A.2d 1266 (1992);
- Elimination of the marital exemption; (People v. Liberta, 64 N.Y.2d 152, 474 N.E.2d 567 (1984);
- The addition of a reasonableness requirement for a claim that the defendant mistakenly believed the victim consented; Commonwealth v. Sherry, 386 Mass. 682, 437 N.E.2d 224 (1982);
- Admission of expert testimony on rape trauma syndrome to explain the victim's reaction to the sexual assault.

F. PROBLEMS OF PROOF

The same concerns that have influenced the substantive law of rape—namely, concerns about unfounded accusations of rape—have influenced the procedural rules for the prosecution of rape cases.

1. Corroboration

Traditional common law did not require corroboration of a rape crime victim's testimony. However, some jurisdictions have imposed such a requirement to protect against false charges of rape. See United States v. Wiley, 492 F.2d 547 (1974). In these jurisdictions there must be independent corroborative evidence to conclude the victim's account is not a fabrication.

a. **Criticism.** The criminal justice system seems overly concerned with the risk of false reports of rape. Generally, victims of rape are reluctant to report the crime because of the stigma of society and the skepticism of juries. The need for a corroboration rule has also decreased as more women serve on juries and juries become more integrated.

b. **Modern approach.** Even though some jurisdictions require corroboration in some rape cases, no American state now requires corroboration in forcible rape cases.

2. Special Jury Instructions

Many jurisdictions still require that jurors be instructed that a rape complainant's testimony be evaluated with care. The Model Penal Code also requires such an instruction. MPC §214.6.

3. Cross-Examination and Shield Laws

Rape shield laws limit the scope of cross-examination of a rape victim to prevent the woman and her past from being put on trial, instead of the defendant. Typically, rape shield laws will prohibit the admissibility of evidence of the victim's prior sexual history. However, even rape shield laws allow evidence of prior consensual sexual intercourse with the defendant or testimony which directly refutes the rape claim. See State ex re. Pope v. Superior Court, 113 Ariz. 22, 545 P.2d 946 (1976).

a. **Defendant's right to a fair trial.** Courts are reluctant to enforce rape shield laws because they may impinge on the defendant's right to cross-examine and right to a fair trial. See State v. DeLawder, 28 Md. App. 212, 344 A.2d 446 (1975).

b. **Balancing probative value vs. prejudicial effect.** In deciding to what extent to admit evidence of a victim's sexual activities, courts generally balance the probative value of the evidence against its embarrassing effects on the victim and its likelihood of confusing and misleading the jury. Compare State v. Colbath, 130 N.H. 316, 540 A.2d 1212 (1988) (balance in favor of admitting evidence of victim's public displays of sexual conduct) with Wood v. Alaska, 957 F.2d 1544 (9th Cir. 1992) (court refused to admit pictures of victim posing for sexually explicit magazines and films).

c. **Probing victim's psychological condition.** Courts also have the discretion to order a psychiatric examination of the rape victim. Most courts will only do so if there is little or no corroboration to support the rape charge and clear evidence that the victim has a mental or emotional condition that may affect her credibility. Government of the Virgin Islands v. Scuito, 623 F.2d 869 (3d Cir. 1980).

4. Prior Behavior of Defendant

The trial court has the discretion to admit or preclude acts of prior sexual misconduct of the defendant.

G. MODEL PENAL CODE APPROACH

Like many states, the Model Penal Code sets forth many different types of sexual acts that may constitute criminal offenses. They range from indecent exposure to sexual assault to rape. MPC Art. 213: Sexual Offenses.

1. Rape

Under the Model Penal Code, rape is a felony. A defendant commits rape by purposely, knowingly, or recklessly having sexual intercourse with a female under any of the following circumstances if: 1. the female is less than ten years old; 2. the female is unconscious; 3. the female is compelled by force or threat of death, grievous bodily harm, extreme pain or kidnapping; or 4. defendant intoxicates his victim. MPC §213.1(1).

a. **Marital exception.** The Model Penal Code recognizes a partial marital exemption. If a man and woman live together as "man and wife," the man may not be charged with rape, although he may be guilty of gross sexual imposition. MPC §213.1(2) (a).

b. **Focus on defendant, not victim.** The Model Penal Code Approach, which defines the severity of sexual crime by the amount of force threatened or used by the defendant, tends to keep the focus of a rape case on the defendant, not the victim.

H. STATUTORY RAPE

By statute, jurisdictions prohibit sexual intercourse with a girl under a certain age, often 18 years old. The law conclusively presumes that a woman under that age is incapable of consent. No showing of force, fraud, or intimidation is required.

1. Mistake of Age

In most jurisdictions, the defendant's mistake of fact as to his victim's age is irrelevant. If the defendant has sex with a girl under the age of legal consent, defendant is guilty of statutory rape. Some jurisdictions, however, allow the defendant to use a reasonable mistake defense, which allows a mistake defense if a reasonable person would also have believed the victim was of lawful age to consent.

FIGURE 4-1

ELEMENTS OF RAPE	
Sexual intercourse with a woman	Any act of penetration
Unlawful	Husband cannot rape wife
Without Consent	Defendant must be aware victim is not consenting • C/L: Honest mistake is a defense. • Modern: Honest and reasonable mistake required for defense. Resistance is evidence of lack of consent.
By force, fear, or fraud	Threat or use of physical force required

Review Question and Answer

Question: James and Sheri met each other at a concert. After the concert, James asked Sheri for a ride home. Sheri did not know James, but had learned during the concert that they had several friends in common. Sheri agreed to give James a ride because she thought it might be fun to get to know him better.

On the ride home, Sheri and James discussed their personal lives. Sheri told James she had just broken up with her boyfriend and was looking for more excitement in her life. James told Sheri that he was "always available for fun," but wasn't ready for any commitments.

As they were driving, James gave Sheri directions to his house. He decided to take a route that led them past a beautiful view of the city. When they got to the viewpoint, James asked Sheri if they could stop for a moment. Sheri nervously agreed.

After staring out the window for a minute, James started to kiss Sheri. Sheri laughed and told James that he was "a fast worker" but she needed to get home. James said, "I'll make it quick." He then grabbed Sheri and started to remove her clothes. Sheri was too shocked and scared to move. She tried to turn on the ignition, but she couldn't reach it under the weight of James' body. By the time she could react, James had already penetrated her. Sheri reported the assault as soon as she got home.

Has James committed rape?

Answer: There is no clear answer as to whether James would be convicted of rape. The elements of rape are: 1. sexual intercourse, 2. with a woman, 3. without her consent, 4. by force, fear, or fraud.

Although there is no question that James had sexual intercourse with Sheri, the other issues are more difficult. First, although Sheri did not expressly consent, James is likely to argue that he reasonably believed she consented. Under common law, an honest belief was sufficient. Sheri discussed her personal life, voluntarily drove to an isolated spot, laughed when James kissed her and did not resist when he started to remove her clothes. On the other hand, she did try to get away by reaching for the ignition, she tried to stop the initial contact by telling James she needed to get home, and she immediately reported the contact as rape.

Second, the evidence is ambiguous as to whether James used force, fear or fraud. Although Sheri was shocked and scared, James made no express threats and did not use any physical violence, other than his body weight during intercourse. The question would be whether a reasonable woman would have been in fear.

Homicide

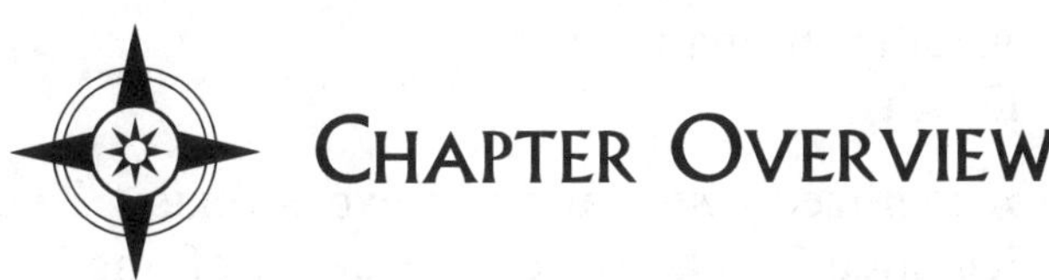

Chapter Overview

The specific crime most often studied in first year criminal law courses is homicide. The reasons for studying homicide are: 1. the law of homicide provides an excellent opportunity to study the impact of the common law on modern criminal offenses; 2. homicide cases raise the issue of the grading of offenses, i.e., distinguishing different levels of culpability for the same criminal act; and 3. homicide continues to be a frequent and serious occurrence in America.

Each jurisdiction sets forth its own definition of homicide. In some states, such as New York, the Model Penal Code has had a significant impact on the definition of homicidal crimes. In other states, the impact has been more limited, affecting primarily standards for voluntary manslaughter. Most state statutes still rely heavily on common-law principles of homicide, both in legislative drafting and statutory interpretation. Accordingly, Chapter 5 reviews:

- Legislative Grading of Homicide Crimes
- Definitions of Common Law Principles, including:
  - Premeditation
  - Provocation
  - Malice
  - Criminal negligence
  - Manslaughter
- Model Penal Code Homicide Provisions, including "Extreme Emotional Distress"
- Felony-Murder Principles, including Vicarious Liability
- Misdemeanor-Manslaughter

A. INTRODUCTION

Modern statutes and the common law do not treat all criminal killings alike. The punishment and name assigned to an unlawful killing depend on the level of mens rea the defendant possessed at the time of the act and the reason for the killing. A homicide vocabulary derived from common law must be mastered to understand the law of homicide.

B. DEFINITION OF "HOMICIDE"

Homicide is the unlawful killing of another human being. The elements of homicide are:

Actus Reus	Killing
Mens Rea	Depends on the grade of homicide
Circumstances	Another human being
Result	Death

A killing is unlawful if no legally recognized justification or excuse exists. The prosecution must prove that the defendant's acts caused the death of another human being. See Chapter 7 for *Causation* discussion.

1. Actus Reus: Killing

A killing occurs when the defendant ends a person's life. Many different methods of killing (e.g., shooting, stabbing, poison, physical blows, etc.) satisfy the actus reus requirement for homicide.

a. **Definition of "death."** Each jurisdiction defines when life ends. In most jurisdictions, death occurs when the brain ceases to function. Barber v. Superior Court, 147 Ca. App. 3d 1006 (1983); People v. Eulo, 63 N.Y.2d 341 (1984). However, an indefinite vegetative state does not constitute brain death even if the victim no longer has any higher cognitive brain functions. But see People v. Bonilla, 95 A.D.2d 396 (1983) (if enough brain death has occurred to warrant an organ transplant legal "death" has occurred even if the victim could have survived in a vegetative state). A minority of jurisdictions define death as the moment the victim's heart stops.

b. **Year-and-a-day rule.** Under common law, death must occur within a year and a day of the defendant's acts to constitute a "killing." Today, most jurisdictions have abandoned this requirement. However, it remains in force in federal courts.

2. Mens Rea

The level of mens rea defines the type of homicide committed. A homicide committed with malice aforethought is murder. On the other hand, a killing resulting from gross negligence only constitutes manslaughter. The common-law labels given to different mental states often have a variety of definitions. This chapter describes each mental state in detail. The most common terms include:

a. **Malice aforethought.** Killings committed with malice aforethought are considered murder. The term "aforethought" is superfluous. Malice refers to killings committed with callous disregard of human life. Malice may be proven by direct or circumstantial evidence.

i. **Malice.** Malice encompasses a variety of definitions and may include one or more of the following states of mind:

- an intention to cause death or great bodily harm;
- knowledge that death or great bodily harm almost certainly will occur;
- gross indifference to the risk of death or great bodily harm;
- an intent to commit a felony that results in a death (see felony murder discussion infra).

ii. **Abandoned and malignant heart.** At common law, other terms were also used to describe heinous and callous killings. Thus, a synonym for malice was a killing committed with an "abandoned and malignant heart." Some statutes still retain this language.

3. Circumstance — Another Human Being

Homicide requires the killing of a human being by a human being. Each jurisdiction may define what constitutes a human being.

a. **Fetus.** A fetus is *not* considered a human being unless the laws of the jurisdiction expressly state otherwise. Keeler v. Superior Court, 2 Cal. 3d 619, 470 P.2d 617 (1970). Viability, the point at which the fetus can survive independent of the mother, may or may not be an element of the offense of fetal murder. See People v. Davis, 872 P.2d 591 (Cal. 1994) (viability *not* element of California fetal murder; fetus only need be beyond eight weeks of embryonic stage).

b. **Born alive rule.** Injuries inflicted upon a child while in the mother's womb may be the basis for a homicide charge if the child is then born alive but subsequently dies as a result of the in utero injuries. Williams v. State, 316 Md. 677 (1989).

c. **Suicide.** If a person kills himself or herself, the homicide is suicide. Suicide is still a crime in a majority of jurisdictions; causing or assisting another to commit suicide may constitute homicide. People v. Kevorkian, 205 Mich. App. 180 (1994); Stephenson v. State, 205 Ind. 141 (1932).

i. **Assisted-suicide laws as unconstitutional.** Recently, the courts have struck down laws prohibiting physician-assisted suicide as unconstitutional violations of the right to privacy, See Compassion in Dying v. Washington, 85 F.3d 1440 (9th Cir. en banc), cert. granted, Washington v. Glucksberg, 117 S. Ct. 37 (1996) and of the Equal Protection Clause, Quill v. Vacco, 80 F.3d 716 (2d Cir.), cert. granted, 117 S. Ct. 36 (1996).

d. **Infanticide.** Killing a young child is infanticide. It may be included in the general prohibitions against homicide or it might constitute a separate offense.

e. **Patricide.** Killing one's parents is patricide. Ordinarily, it is considered simply another form of homicide.

C. LEVELS OF HOMICIDE

Jurisdictions now divide homicide into different levels or grades. The punishment for the offense depends on its grade. Initially, grading homicides served to confine the death penalty to the most heinous killings. Now, the grading of homicides distinguishes among defendants and the punishments they should receive. There are a variety of approaches to grading homicides. Some of these include:

1. Common Law

The common law in England did not divide murder into degrees. All murders were capital offenses. The common law eventually recognized the difference between murder and manslaughter.

2. General Modern Approach

Each state may adopt its own approach to grading degrees of homicide. In 1794, Pennsylvania was the first state to depart from the traditional approach of treating all murders the same. Rather, to confine the impact of the death penalty, degrees of murder were created. Today, many states have multiple degrees of murder and manslaughter. The approach in Figure 5-1 is common.

3. California Penal Code

California statutes divide homicide into the following categories and degrees, as shown in Figure 5-2.

4. Pennsylvania Penal Code

Pennsylvania divides homicide into the following levels, as shown in Figure 5-3.

5. New York Penal Code

New York divides homicide into different classes of felonies, as shown in Figure 5-4.

6. Model Penal Code

The Model Penal Code also divides homicide into levels, although its approach differs from common law jurisdictions in several ways. First, it does not recognize fetuses as human beings, whereas some common law jurisdictions do recognize the killing of a fetus as homicide. MPC 210.0(1). Second, it treats the felony murder doctrine as creating a presumption of gross recklessness and as a factor to be considered for sentencing. MPC 210.2(1)(b), 210.6(3) Third, it treats negligent homicide not as a form of involuntary manslaughter, as under common law, but as a separate lesser type of offense. Those offenses that constitute homicide are treated as different degrees of felonies depending on the defendant's mens rea. The levels of homicide under the Model Penal Code are as shown in Figure 5-5.

7. Foreign Approaches

Other countries have adopted a different approach to analyzing homicides, creating broad categories of offenses which presume killings are murders unless an overall view of the circumstances leads the court to impose a lesser punishment.

Example. In Sweden, anyone who takes another person's life is guilty of murder. However, mitigating circumstances may result in a determination of manslaughter or careless killing which are punished accordingly.

STUDY TIP

In analyzing a fact scenario to determine which, if any, offense has been committed, always start with the highest level of homicide and determine whether its mens rea requirement has been satisfied. Then systematically work down through the other levels of homicide.

FIGURE 5-1

Level of Homicide	*Mens Rea Requirement*
First-Degree Murder	premeditated killing or specific types of intentional killings or certain types of felony murder
Second-Degree Murder	malice or certain types of felony murder
Voluntary Manslaughter	provocation (no malice) or extreme emotional disturbance
Involuntary Manslaughter	gross negligence or misdemeanor-manslaughter

FIGURE 5-2

Level of Homicide	*Mens Rea Requirement*
First-Degree Murder* (Sec. 189) * Note: Only first-degree murders qualify for the death penalty, which may be imposed if there are "special circumstances." (See Chapter 6 infra.)	By specific means of killing listed in statute, with premeditation or during the commission of certain types of felonies
Second-Degree Murder	All other killings with malice

FIGURE 5-2 (*continued*)

Level of Homicide	*Mens Rea Requirement*
Manslaughter (Sec. 192)	Unlawful killings without malice
Three types:	
• Voluntary manslaughter	Heat of passion
• Involuntary manslaughter	During an unlawful act not constituting a felony (misdemeanor-manslaughter doctrine) or during a lawful act performed with gross negligence
• Vehicular manslaughter	Different punishments depending on whether committed with gross negligence and/or during unlawful act

FIGURE 5-3

Level of Homicide	*Mens Rea Requirement*
First-Degree Murder [sec. 2502(a)]	Intentional
Second-Degree Murder [sec. 2502(b)]	Felony murder
Third-Degree Murder [sec. 2502(c)]	All other killings with malice
Voluntary Manslaughter (sec. 2503)	Provocation or imperfect self-defense
Involuntary Manslaughter (sec. 2504)	Reckless, grossly negligent, or during a misdemeanor
Causing suicide (sec. 2505(a))	Intentionally with duress or deception (felony)
Aiding suicide (sec. 2505(b))	Intentionally (misdemeanor)

FIGURE 5-4

Level of Homicide	*Mens Rea Requirement*
First-Degree Murder (sec. 125.27)	Intentionally committed against certain types of victims or while defendant is in custody or during escape
Second-Degree Murder (sec. 125.25)	Intent to kill or felony murder
First-Degree Manslaughter	Intent to cause serious bodily injury or intent to kill because of extreme emotional disturbance
Second-Degree Manslaughter	Recklessness or intentionally aiding suicide
Negligent Homicide	Criminal negligence

FIGURE 5-5

Level of Homicide	*Mens Rea Requirement*
Murder	Purposely, knowingly, or acting with grossly reckless regard for human life
Manslaughter	Recklessly or under extreme emotional duress
Negligent Homicide	Negligently
Causing or Aiding Suicide	Purposely with force, duress, or deception

D. MURDER

Murder is the unlawful killing of another human being with malice aforethought.

1. Malice Defined

Intent to kill or cause serious bodily harm or acting with gross recklessness constitute malice or malice aforethought. All murders require proof of malice. However, as the most serious level of murder, first-degree murder also often requires premeditation.

a. **Types of malice.** As discussed in detail under second-degree murder infra, malice had several meanings:

- intent to kill;
- intent to cause serious bodily harm;
- callous disregard for human life; i.e., gross recklessness;
- killing during the commission of a felony.

2. First-Degree vs. Second-Degree Murder

Ordinarily, first-degree murder requires premeditation in addition to malice. The only exception is when first-degree murder is based upon felony murder. All other killings with malice constitute second-degree murder. See discussion infra §4. The distinction between first-degree and second-degree-murder is important because first-degree murder usually carries a more serious punishment and only first-degree murder makes a defendant eligible for the death penalty.

a. **Note.** Some jurisdictions do not distinguish between first- and second-degree murder. At common law, there were no such distinctions. The Model Penal Code also does not have different degrees of murder. MPC 210.2. However, many jurisdictions have divided murder into degrees. Most typically, first-degree murder is a killing with premeditation. Alternative approaches include classifying as first-degree murder:

- all intentional killings (Pa.);
- intentional killings of certain types of victims or while the defendant is in custody (N.Y.);
- killings that occur during certain types of felonies (Cal., N.Y.).

3. First-Degree Murder

The most serious type of homicide is first-degree murder. In most states, the mens rea required for first-degree murder is malice plus premeditation.

a. **Premeditation.** First-degree murder requires proof of mens rea beyond that of malice. The mens rea required for first-degree murder is "willful, deliberate, and premeditated" conduct. The terms "willful and deliberate" mean that the defendant intended to kill. The key requirement for first-degree murder is "premeditation."

i. **Cool, deliberate thought.** Premeditation requires that a defendant kill with "cool, deliberate thought."

(a) **Example.** The defendant decides to kill a business competitor. After purchasing a gun, the defendant waits until the victim is alone and then shoots him.

(b) **Rationale for premeditation standard.** The premeditation standard is based upon the belief that defendants who act "cold-bloodedly" are more dangerous, more deserving of punishment, and more easily deterred because they considered their acts and the consequences of them before killing.

(c) **Criticism of premeditation standard.** Empirically, it may not be true that one who kills after careful reflection is more dangerous than the killer who kills on impulse. For example, which defendant is more dangerous and deserving of punishment: A, who kills his parent after evaluating the senior's prolonged suffering, or B, who pushes a pedestrian into traffic on the spur of the moment?

ii. **No time too short.** In many jurisdictions, premeditation requires no specific amount of time. Premeditation can be formed in a matter of seconds.

Example. A defendant pulls a gun and shoots the victim three times. Premeditation may be formed as the killer is pressing the trigger. See Young v. State, 428 So. 155, 158 (Ala. Crim. App. 1982) or in the brief moments between deadly blows. See People v. Perez, 2 Cal. 4th 1117, 831 P.2d 1159 (1992); State v. Ollens, 107 Wash. 848, 733 P.2d 984 (1987).

Study Tip

Because premeditation requires a higher level of mens rea than malice, a defendant who is proven to have acted with premeditation will also have necessarily acted with malice.

b. **Differing approaches to premeditation.** Jurisdictions agree that first-degree murder requires proof of "premeditation"; however, they differ in their interpretations of what that term requires. In some courts, premeditation merely means acting with the purpose to kill. In others, premeditation requires purposeful conduct and a preconceived design.

i. **Carrol approach (purposeful).** The broadest definition of premeditation appears in Commonwealth v. Carrol, 412 Pa. 525, 194 A.2d 911 (1963). Under the *Carrol* standard, "premeditation" only requires that the defendant acted deliberately or with purposeful conduct.

(a) **Facts.** In *Carrol*, the defendant killed his wife, who had been abusing their children and was upset that the defendant would be leaving the home because of work. After a protracted argument, the couple went to bed. After thinking for five minutes about what his wife had done to their children, defendant reached for a gun that his wife had previously put at the head of their bed. He shot his wife twice in the back of her head. He then wrapped up her body in a sheet and dumped it in a desolate place.

(b) **Holding.** Any cool, deliberate thought, even if formed in a matter of seconds, is sufficient to demonstrate premeditation.

(c) **Implications of Carrol approach.** The *Carrol* approach makes it easier for the prosecution to prove premeditation. As long as the prosecution proves that the defendant acted with the conscious purpose to kill the victim, the jury can find premeditation. See Commonwealth v. O'Searo, 466 Pa. 224, 352 A.2d 30 (1976) (conscious purpose inferred from use of a deadly weapon).

ii. **Anderson approach (purposeful plus preconceived design).** Other jurisdictions require a higher standard of proof for premeditation. In People v. Anderson, 70 Cal. 2d 15, 447 P.2d 942 (1968), the court set forth evidentiary requirements to demonstrate that the defendant acted not only with deliberate thought, but also with "a preconceived design."

(a) **Facts.** In *Anderson*, the defendant stabbed a ten-year-old girl to death. The victim, found hidden in her home, was nude and had over 60 wounds. The defendant lived in the home as a boarder. On the day of the killing, he had been drinking and lied to family members as they tried to learn the whereabouts of the missing victim.

(b) **Holding.** The court reversed defendant's first-degree murder conviction. It found insufficient evidence of "premeditation,'' as that court interpreted the term. Premeditation requires preexisting reflection as demonstrated by two of the following three types of evidence: 1. planning activity, 2. motive, and 3. manner of killing. Because the killing seemed so out of control, there was no clear evidence of sexual abuse, and defendant made only limited efforts to conceal his crime, the court found there was insufficient evidence of premeditation. See also State v. Bingham, 105 Wash. 2d 820 (1986).

(c) **Reaction to Anderson.** Most courts have not adopted the strict *Anderson* approach because it narrowly constrains the prosecution's ability to prove premeditation. People v. Perez, 2 Cal. 4th 1117, 831 P.2d 1159 (1992). Although the courts will look at the defendant's manner, motive, and planning, these factors are not considered mandatory or exclusive.

c. **Summary of first-degree murder.** First-degree murder, other than by the felony-murder doctrine, requires that the defendant act with premeditation. Some courts equate ''premeditation'' with ''purposeful'' conduct. Other courts, however, impose a more restrictive approach and require proof of purposeful deadly conduct with a preconceived design. To determine whether there was a preconceived design, the court will look at the defendant's motive, manner, and planning activity.

STUDY TIP

Even though proof of manner, motive, and planning is *required* only under the *Anderson* approach, it is also helpful to examine these factors when analyzing purposeful conduct under the *Carrol* approach. *Anderson* and *Carrol* represent the ends of a continuum describing how much deliberation a defendant must engage in to be guilty of premeditated murder.

EXAMPLE AND ANALYSIS

In United States v. Watson, 501 A.2d 791 (1985), defendant shot and killed a police officer who was trying to arrest him. Defendant claimed that he panicked but the prosecution argued that premeditation was demonstrated by:

Motive:	Defendant was trying to escape from the officer.
Manner:	Defendant shot the officer directly in the chest.
Planning:	After an initial struggle with the officer, defendant chose not to escape but to stay and kill the officer who was pleading for his life.

d. **Alternative approaches to first-degree murder.** Some states have rejected premeditation and deliberation as the basis for identifying murders deserving the greatest punishment. Rather than the degree of preparation, the focus is on the aggravated nature of the killing. MPC §210.7. See, e.g., N.Y.P.C. §125.27.

i. **Example.** In New York, the intentional killing of a police officer is considered an aggravated killing that warrants a conviction for first degree murder. N.Y.P.C. §125.27.

ii. **Example.** Under the traditional approach, a mercy killing constitutes first-degree murder because the defendant typically acts with premeditation. A son who shoots his terminally ill father has acted with premeditation and is as guilty of first-degree murder as someone who shoots an enemy. State v. Forrest, 321 N.C. 186 (1987). However, in other jurisdictions, defendant's killing, while intentional, would not be aggravated level and would not constitute first-degree murder.

iii. **Model Penal Code approach.** Under the Model Penal Code, all intentional killings are murder. MPC §210.2. The facts underlying the killing are used as aggravating and mitigating circumstances for sentencing. MPC §210.6.

e. **Defenses to premeditation.** Because premeditation requires the highest level of intent, defendants may contest their ability to form cool, reflective thoughts.

i. **Diminished capacity.** In many jurisdictions, a defendant may argue incapacity to premeditate because of a psychological disorder. See, e.g., People v. Wolff, 394 P.2d 959 (Cal. 1964) (premeditation requires that defendant "maturely and meaningfully reflect on the gravity of the crime"); State v. Brooks, 97 Wash. 2d 873 (1982). However, the recent legislative trend has been to limit the impact of this defense by precluding expert testimony on diminished capacity. See, e.g., Cal. Pen. Code, §189 (enacted to overrule People v. Wolff).

ii. **Intoxication.** Intoxication is generally not a defense to murder. A defendant may form the intent to kill even when intoxicated. However, if a defendant is so intoxicated that he or she cannot form the cool, deliberate thoughts required for premeditation, intoxication may preclude a finding of the mens rea required for first-degree murder. State v. Brooks, 97 Wash. 2d 873 (1982).

4. Second-Degree Murder

All killings committed with malice and without premeditation constitute "murder." Depending on the jurisdiction, killings with malice may be classified as second-degree or third-degree murder. "Malice" is the standard that separates murder from manslaughter.

a. **Malice.** Malice is the intent to kill, cause great bodily harm, or act with gross recklessness toward human life.

i. **Intent to kill.** An intent to kill may be inferred from defendant's actions or statements, as well as from all other circumstances of the case.

(a) **Example.** Shooting a gun directly at a person or stabbing a person in a vital organ demonstrates intent to kill.

(b) **Deadly weapon presumption.** Use of a deadly weapon may create a presumption that defendant intended to kill. While most states will instruct jurors that they may make such an inference, it is not a mandatory presumption.

ii. **Intent to cause serious bodily harm.** An intent to cause great bodily harm also demonstrates malice. The intended injury must be serious, not trivial, although it need not pose an immediate threat of death. Serious bodily harm includes: loss of consciousness, bone fracture, disfigurement, or a wound requiring extensive suturing or other medical treatment.

(a) **Rationale.** Willingness to seriously injure another reflects a callous disregard for human life and creates a high and unacceptable risk of a resulting death.

(b) **Example.** Defendant swings with a baseball bat, intending to hit the victim in the chest. Instead, the bat hits the victim's head and the victim dies.

iii. **Gross/extreme recklessness (depraved heart) murder.** Common law also defined "malice" as "wanton indifference," "depraved mind," or "abandoned and malignant heart." A modern understanding of those terms is that the defendant acted with gross recklessness. A defendant who creates an unusually high and unjustifiable risk of death has acted with malice. Classic examples include: 1. shooting a firearm into a crowded room; 2. playing Russian roulette, and 3. driving in an extremely dangerous manner.

EXAMPLE AND ANALYSIS

Defendant shoots and kills the victim during a game of Russian Poker (loading a revolver with one bullet, spinning the chamber, and pulling the trigger). Defendant is guilty of murder, even if he never intended to kill or seriously injure the victim. It is sufficient if the defendant knows his conduct involved an unacceptably high risk of death. Commonwealth v. Malone, 354 Pa. 180, 47 A.2d 445 (1946).

(a) **Gross recklessness vs. recklessness.** One of the most difficult issues in analyzing homicide cases is determining whether the defendant acted with a gross disregard for human life, which would result in a second-degree murder conviction; or simply knew of the risk to human life, which may only lead to a manslaughter conviction. This issue is discussed in detail infra after an explanation of manslaughter. See Ch. 3 (C)(e)(3).

STUDY TIP

In many ways, second-degree murder may be considered the "catchall category" for intentional killings that have insufficient evidence of premeditation to be considered first-degree murder and insufficient evidence of provocation to be excused as voluntary manslaughter. If the jury finds that the defendant knowingly killed another, by default the defendant will be guilty of second-degree murder.

REVIEW QUESTION AND ANSWER

MURDER

Question: Punchy, a prison inmate, was charged with killing a prison orderly. The crime occurred in August while Punchy was in his cell. Punchy called for the orderly, a known prison informant, to bring him hot water for shaving. When the guard unlocked the door so that the orderly could deliver the water, Punchy threw the scalding water in the guard's face and lunged for the orderly. Punchy pulled a prison-made knife from the deep pocket of the heavy jacket he was wearing and with one stab to the heart, killed the orderly. Is Punchy guilty of murder and, if so, what degree?

Answer: First-degree murder in may jurisdictions requires premeditation. The "cool deliberate thought" required for premeditation may be formed in a matter of seconds. Under the *Carrol* approach, it is sufficient if the defendant acted with the intent to kill. Under the more stringent *Anderson* approach, the prosecution must show Punchy acted with a preconceived design to kill, as demonstrated by prior planning, motive, and a purposeful manner of killing.

Under the *Carrol* approach, Punchy clearly acted with premeditation. There was sufficient time for him to decide to kill his victim as the orderly walked to Punchy's cell. Throwing hot water on the guard would allow him access to his victim. Punchy had a weapon and was ready to use it to kill.

Even under the *Anderson* approach, there is a strong argument that Punchy acted with premeditation. Punchy's preconceived design to kill is demonstrated by:

1. *Planning Activity.* Punchy had made a prison knife. He had the opportunity to hide it under the jacket he chose to wear during the summer month of August. By asking for and throwing hot water on the guard, Punchy could gain access to his victim. All of this evidence shows planning.
2. *Motive.* Animosity toward an informant could be Punchy's motive.
3. *Manner of Killing.* Unlike in a frenzied, spontaneous killing where dozens of wild blows are landed, Punchy was determined enough in his efforts to kill his victim with one stab to the heart.

If the evidence is insufficient to prove premeditation, Punchy is still guilty of murder because he acted with malice. He had the intent either to kill or cause serious bodily harm by using a knife against another.

FIGURE 5-6

General Principles	
Definition	Killing with malice
Malice	1. Intent to kill or 2. Intent to cause GBH or 3. Gross recklessness or 4. Felony-murder

FIGURE 5-6 (*continued*)

Degree of Murder	
First Degree	Premeditation vs. preconceived [purposeful design] or Specific types of intentional killings or Certain types of felony-murder
Second Degree	Malice or Remaining types of felony-murder

E. MANSLAUGHTER

Manslaughter is the killing of another human being without malice. Traditionally, there are two types of manslaughter: voluntary and involuntary. By statute, some jurisdictions have added other categories, such as vehicular manslaughter.

1. Voluntary Manslaughter

A killing that may otherwise be considered murder because the defendant acted with the intent to kill may constitute only voluntary manslaughter if the defendant killed in a "sudden heat of passion" in response to legally adequate provocation. Traditionally, voluntary manslaughter applied only when a defendant was provoked. However, today jurisdictions apply it when there is: 1. provocation, 2. extreme emotional distress, or 3. imperfect self-defense.

Example. In State v. Thornton, 730 S.W.2d 309 (1987), the defendant shot a man he found in bed with his estranged wife. The court reversed the defendant's conviction for first-degree murder, finding the case a classic situation of voluntary manslaughter. The court found that as a matter of law "any reasonable person would have been inflamed and intensely aroused by this sort of discovery" and held that the defendant acted in the heat of passion, and not with malice.

a. **Rationale.** The concept of "malice" presumes a depraved and wanton heart; i.e., a person who has no concern for human life and kills for that reason. A defendant who is provoked or acts under extreme distress, has his reason obscured. Instead, he acts out of pure passion. Even if the law does not completely excuse the defendant's conduct, it is willing to mitigate culpability because society recognizes the "frailty of human nature." Glanville Williams, Provocation and the Reasonable Man (1954). Provocation is therefore considered a partial defense.

b. **Criticism.** Some commentators disagree with the underlying rationale for the provocation defense. In their view, reasonable people do not kill regardless of the provocation. The provocation defense injects a theory of comparative moral wrongdoing into the law. Moreover, it diminishes the value of the victim's life even though the victim did not pose a deadly threat to the defendant.

c. **Traditional voluntary manslaughter provocation.** Under common law, provocation reduces murder to manslaughter. Legal provocation requires proof of the following three elements: 1. actual heat of passion, 2. legally adequate provocation, and 3. absence of cooling time.

i. **Actual heat of passion.** The defendant must be actually provoked; i.e., in the actual heat of passion at the time of the killing. If the defendant is not enraged at that point, even though someone else in the same situation might have been, the partial defense of provocation does not apply.

Example. Defendant returns home to find his wife in bed with another man. He laughs at his discovery and then decides to shoot them both dead. The defendant has not acted in the actual heat of passion.

ii. **Legally adequate provocation.** Not all acts trigger the provocation defense. Because the doctrine is designed to provide leniency to individuals who act as another might in the same situation, it is limited to those situations in which a reasonable person might have been similarly provoked.

(a) **Traditional common law.** Traditional common law took a categorical approach to provocation. A defendant could claim provocation only under certain circumstances:

- extreme assault or battery upon the defendant
- mutual combat
- defendant's illegal arrest

- injury or serious abuse of a close relative
- the sudden discovery of a spouse's adultery

Girouard v. State, 321 Md. 532, 583 A.2d 718 (1991). Only if one of these circumstances were present, would the judge allow the jury to consider provocation.

- **Words alone insufficient.** Under common law and in a majority of jurisdictions today, words alone, no matter how insulting or inciteful, are insufficient provocation. *Girouard*, supra (wife's disparaging remarks regarding defendant's sexual ability legally insufficient provocation to justify stabbing); State v. Shane, 63 Ohio St. 3d 630, 590 N.E.2d 272 (1992) (merely informing husband of wife's adultery insufficient provocation).
- **Criticisms of traditional approach.** Critics have attacked the traditional approach as embracing too limited a view of what constitutes legal provocation and for institutionalizing a male-centered perspective which condones killing as an understandable reaction to adultery and sexual provocation. Compare Holmes v. Director of Public Prosecutions (1946) A.C. 588 (1946) (Sudden confession of adultery does not constitute provocation); with People v. Berry, 18 Cal. 3d 509 (1976) (sexual taunting sufficient provocation for manslaughter).

(b) Modern objective standard. Since the 1860s, there has been a trend away from specific categories of legally recognized provocation. Instead, the jury can determine whether the provocation might inflame a reasonable person. Maher v. People, 10 Mich. 212, 81 Am. Dec. 781 (1862). A general objective standard measures the defendant by societal norms but does not limit the defense to rigid, predetermined categories.

- **Characteristics of the reasonable person.** Courts differ over which of the defendant's characteristics they will allow jurors to consider in applying the reasonable person standard.
- **Purely objective standard.** The strictest approach instructs jurors to look at the reasonable person in the abstract and not to consider any of the charac-

FIGURE 5-7

PROVOCATION STANDARDS		
Objective	*Semiobjective*	*More Subjective*
Reasonable person with no particularized characteristics. (*Beddars*)	Reasonable person with defendant's physical characteristics, e.g. gender, age. (*Camplin*)	Provocation viewed from perspective of reasonable person in defendant's situation as he believes it to be. (MPC)

teristics peculiar to the defendant. Bedder v. Director of Public Prosecutions, (1954) 2 All E.R. 801 (jury not allowed to consider defendant's sexual impotency in determining adequacy of provocation).

- **Semiobjective standard.** Many courts adopt a position permitting the jury to consider at least some of the defendant's physical characteristics. Director of Public Prosecutions v. Camplin (1978) 2 All E.R. 168 (defendant's sex and age may be considered).
- **Model Penal Code more subjective standard.** The Model Penal Code provides the most subjective test for provocation. The jury must judge the reasonableness of the defendant's reaction from the viewpoint of a person under the circumstances as the defendant believes them to be. MPC 210.3(1)(b); People v. Casassa, 49 N.Y. 2d 668, 404 N.E.2d 1310 (1980). See also discussion of MPC "extreme emotional distress" doctrine infra. While not completely subjective, the Model Penal Code is the most subjective of the standards. See Figure 5-7 for a summary of the provocation standards.

(c) **Purpose of objective standard.** Most courts favor an objective or semiobjective standard for provocation. Without the requirement that the defendant's reaction be reasonable to a third person, an individual's idiosyncrasies of temper or mentality would justify the use of force.

(d) **Provocation by someone other than victim.** Most courts recognize provocation only when the defendant kills the person who provoked him or her. See Thibodeaux v. State, 733 S.W.2d 668 (1987) (no provocation defense when defendant killed two-month old baby after being provoked by the child's mother).

Exception. If the defendant intends to kill the provoking party, but accidentally kills another, the court may still allow the provocation defense. State v. Griego, 294 P.2d 282 (N.M. 1986).

(e) **Mistake concerning provocation.** A defendant may be entitled to the provocation defense even if he or she is mistaken as to the provocation if a reasonable person in defendant's situation would have believed adequate provocation existed.

iii. **Insufficient cooling time.** Too much time cannot have elapsed between the time of provocation and the act of killing. If it has, the defendant is not entitled to a provocation mitigation.

(a) **Traditional approach.** Historically, judges could decide not to give a provocation instruction if the time between the provocation and the killing were so long that the defendant was not likely to be in the heat of passion.

Examples and Analysis

A defendant learned that the victim had raped defendant's mother 20 years earlier. Many hours after the defendant learned this information, he attacked and killed the victim. The court properly refused to give a voluntary manslaughter instruction. United States v. Bordeaux, 980 F.2d 534 (8th Cir. 1992).

Defendant walked away after the first act of provocation but then later returned and shot the victim. The court found adequate cooling time as a matter of law. Stahl v. State, 712 S.W.2d 783 (Tex. App. 1986).

Defendant was sodomized and then taunted about it for two weeks. When defendant finally retaliated, the court found that as a matter of law there was sufficient cooling time and defendant did not have the right to argue provocation. State v. Gounagias, 88 Wash. 304, 153 P. 9 (1915).

(b) **Modern approach.** The prevailing view today is that the jury must determine whether sufficient cooling time has elapsed, making the defendant's reaction not an immediate response to the provocation. In making this determination, jurors may consider:

- **Long-smoldering reaction.** Even if considerable time has elapsed since the provoking act, the defendant may still be entitled to a manslaughter instruction if the heat of passion has been building up since the provocation. People v. Berry, 18 Cal. 3d 509, 556 P.2d 777 (1976) (repeated taunting by victim held to constitute "long course of provocating conduct").
- **Rekindling doctrine.** Reminders of the provocation may rekindle the defendant's passion, thereby justifying a reaction even after substantial time has passed.

Exam Tip

If a defendant takes too much time to respond to an act of provocation, the prosecution may argue that passions have cooled and defendant's reaction was "premeditated" revenge constituting first-degree murder.

Example and Analysis

In People v. Ellie Nesler, S056082, 109 D.J. 227 (Nov. 21, 1996), defendant shot and killed her son's molester three years after his alleged acts of molestation. Nesler claimed her passion was long-smoldering, but the prosecution claimed she was making good on a promise of vengeance. The jury agreed with Nesler and found voluntary manslaughter.

Note. This case shows how juries may at times improperly use provocation to mitigate a killing that they feel is in some way justified.

d. **Model Penal Code approach — extreme emotional disturbance doctrine.** In addition to providing a more subjective standard for evaluating the legal adequacy of provocation, the Model Penal Code also differs from the traditional provocation doctrine in other ways.

i. **Basic rule.** Under the Model Penal Code, a killing which would otherwise constitute murder is reduced to manslaughter if it is committed under the influence of extreme mental or emotional disturbance for which there is a reasonable explanation or excuse. MPC §210.3(1)(b).

ii. **Differences between traditional provocation doctrine and Model Penal Code approach.** There are five key differences between the traditional provocation defense and the Model Penal Code approach:

(a) **No specific act of provocation required.** The MPC does not require a specific act of provocation. It is sufficient if the defendant was acting under extreme emotional or mental distress. The MPC covers more than just the emotion of rage. Other emotional distresses may also apply.

(b) **More subjective viewpoint.** According to the MPC, an act of provocation is analyzed from the point of view of a reasonable person in defendant's situation. State v. Elliott, 177 Conn. 1 (1979). It is therefore a combination of subjective and objective elements, but allowing much more consideration of the defendant's viewpoint than traditional common law provocation.

(c) **No cooling time limitation.** The cooling time doctrine does not technically apply under the Model Penal Code because the focus is not on the defendant's reaction to a specific provocation, but on whether the defendant was under the influence of an extreme emotional or mental disturbance at the time of the killing. However, because the MPC requires the defendant to be acting under extreme emotional distress at the time of the killing, the prosecution may argue that the distress had abated making mitigation unavailable.

(d) **Words alone may be sufficient.** The Model Penal Code approach appears to allow words alone, under certain circumstances, to form the basis for legal provocation. MPC §210.3. But see People v. Walker, 473 N.Y.S.2d 460 (1984).

(e) **Diminished capacity may be considered.** Although diminished capacity is not a separate defense under the MPC, it can provide the basis for "extreme emotional disturbance."

(f) **Mistaken victim.** The MPC provides a defense when the defendant acted under an extreme emotional disturbance regardless of the source of the disturbance or the intended victim. MPC §210.3(1)(b).

Example and Analysis

In People v. Casassa, 49 N.Y.2d 668, 404 N.E.2d 1310 (1980), the defendant was devastated because the victim rejected his romantic advances. Defendant reacted in bizarre ways. He broke into her apartment, eavesdropped on her, and even disrobed and lay for a time in her bed. On his final visit, defendant reacted to the victim's rejection by stabbing and drowning the victim. Defendant claimed that he acted under extreme emotional distress.

Ruling: The traditional heat of passion doctrine would not have allowed the provocation defense because there was no act of provocation. However, under the MPC, the judge, acting as the trier of fact, considered the extreme emotional disturbance defense but rejected it because no reasonable basis existed even in defendant's emotional makeup for his reaction. Thus, while the *Casassa* court discussed the subjective nature of the MPC test, it ultimately held that the test is not purely subjective.

---

iii. **Limitations on Model Penal Code approach.** Even though the MPC views provocation very subjectively, it does not allow all responses by defendants. There must be something in the defendant's mental or emotional makeup to explain the reaction. A "reasonable explanation" must exist for the defendant's reaction. Mere personality disorders—hatred, anger, or extreme reaction to embarrassment—are not sufficient. *Casassa*, supra.

e. **Summary of voluntary manslaughter.** Voluntary manslaughter is an intentional killing without malice. Under common law, provocation, also known as the heat of passion, negated malice. Under the Model Penal Code, extreme emotional disturbance reduces a killing from murder to manslaughter. The common law requirements for a provocation defense are: 1. actual heat of passion, 2. legally adequate provocation, and 3. inadequate cooling time. The key issue in most cases is which, if any, of the defendant's characteristics may be considered in determining whether a reasonable person would have been provoked. Under the Model Penal Code, no specific act of provocation is necessary and the reasonableness of the defendant's response must be determined from the perspective of a person in the defendant's situation under the circumstances as defendant believes them to be.

FIGURE 5-8

VOLUNTARY MANSLAUGHTER	
Common Law	
Heat of Passion	1. Actual heat of passion 2. Legally adequate provocation • Categorical approach — battery — adultery • Reasonable person standard — Who is reasona ble person? 3. Inadequate cooling time • Long-smoldering • Rekindling
Model Penal Code (Manslaughter)	
Extreme Emotional Distress Differences from Common Law	Extreme mental or emotional disturbance 1. No specific act of provocation 2. More subjective 3. No cooling time limitation 4. Words alone sufficient 5. Acknowledges diminished capacity 6. Mistaken victim

REVIEW QUESTIONS AND ANSWERS

VOLUNTARY MANSLAUGHTER

Question: In Lopez v. State, 716 S.W.2D 127 (Tex. Crim. App. 1986) defendant Lopez goes to a party that he knows will be attended by people antagonistic to him. Defendant is very apprehensive about encountering these individuals because he has heard rumors that this rival family shot his mother and killed his brother during the preceding year. Accordingly, defendant brings a loaded gun with him to the party. Defendant draws the weapon when he sees the person he thinks was responsible for his mother's injury backing up his car in the general direction of the defendant. Fearing he would be run down and thinking about his mother's injury, defendant gets mad and cries. He then closes his eyes and shoots and kills the victim. Is the defendant guilty of manslaughter or murder?

Answer: Murder may be mitigated to manslaughter when the defendant demonstrates he was provoked to kill. Under the common law approach, defendant must show: 1. he was actually in the heat of passion; 2. there was legally adequate provocation; and 3. there was inadequate cooling time. In the instant case, defendant was actually in the heat of passion. He was mad and crying at the time he shot the victim. There is a question, however, as to whether there was legally adequate provocation. Traditionally, words alone provide insufficient provocation. In the instant case, there were not even words the night of the killing. Instead, there was only eye contact between the defendant and the victim and the victim backing up his vehicle. It is highly questionable whether a reasonable person in the defendant's situation would be provoked. Finally, defendant's provocation defense may fail because the most serious provocation, the victim's alleged assaults on the defendant's mother and brother, occurred at least one year prior to the killing. The killing might be seen as an act of revenge for his mother's death which is not allowed under the law. On the other hand, defendant may claim that he was long-smoldering in his rage, which was rekindled when he saw the victim move his car.

Defendant has a better chance for manslaughter under the Model Penal Code standard. He can claim that he was suffering from an extreme emotional disturbance at the time of the killing and that the victim's prior assaults on his family members provided a rational reason for his emotional state. Under the Model Penal Code, defendant need not show a specific act of provocation at the time of the killing and the jury can consider the long history of animosity between the defendant and the victim's family. Provocation must be analyzed from the defendant's viewpoint.

Question: Tommy Student had survived a semester of criminal law with Professor Flevinson. On the day of his final exam, he arrived exhausted from spending the previous three nights studying for her bone-cruncher test. Upon reading the final exam, Tommy became furious. His professor had humiliated him again in one of the exam's hypotheticals. Other students began to snicker during the exam. Unable to focus, Tommy stormed out of the room and headed for the professor's office. He was sure that his professor was out to destroy him. When Tommy arrived at his professor's office, Flevinson was laughing and gesturing wildly with a pencil. Tommy pulled out a small gun and shot and killed the professor. What crime, if any, has Tommy committed? If your analysis varies according to the Model Penal Code or Common law, apply each approach.

Answer: Tommy may be charged with criminal homicide. Homicide is the unlawful killing of another human being. Tommy killed Flevinson. They key issue is what level or grade of homicide applies in this case.

1. *First-Degree Murder.* The prosecution will likely argue that Tommy acted with the necessary mens rea for first-degree murder. The mens rea required for first degree murder is "premeditation." Premeditation may be shown by Tommy's motive to kill his professor (she had humiliated him repeatedly), his plan to kill his professor (he carried a gun to school), and his manner of killing her (a direct shot with the gun).

2. *Second-Degree Murder.* Alternatively, the prosecution will argue that even if Tommy did not plan the killing, he acted with "malice" and therefore is guilty of at least second-degree murder. Malice may be shown by Tommy's intent to kill (aiming the gun at his professor), intent to cause grave bodily harm (once again, using the gun), or gross disregard for human life.

3. *Voluntary Manslaughter.* In response, the defense is likely to argue that Tommy acted "in the heat of passion" after being provoked by his professor and is therefore only guilty of voluntary manslaughter. Provocation is a partial defense that mitigates the level of homicide. Under the common law, it requires that at the time of the killing: a. defendant was actually in the heat of passion, b. defendant was provoked by legally adequate provocation, and, c. there was insufficient cooling time between the provocation and defendant's response.

In this case, the professor's continued humiliating actions provoked defendant to act. Although he appeared actually in the heat of passion (he stormed out of the room), and his passions had not cooled, words alone and laughing are not legally adequate provocation. Provocation is that type of action by the victim that would cause the reasonable person in the defendant''s situation to lose control and act out of passion not reason. Even a victim gesturing with a pencil would not lead most reasonable persons to lose control. Accordingly, it is unlikely that under the common law provocation defendant's case would qualify as voluntary manslaughter.

Tommy may be more successful with a manslaughter argument under the Model Penal Code. The Model Penal Code treats as manslaughter a homicide which would otherwise be murder if it is committed under the influence of extreme mental or emotional disturbance for which there is reasonable explanation or excuse. The reasonableness of such an explanation or excuse shall be determined from the viewpoint of the person in the actor's situation under the circumstances as he believes them to be. The facts state that Tommy was in a state of exhaustion. He had been repeatedly humiliated and felt continuingly paranoid about his professor. He believed "she was out to get him." Using these facts, Tommy will argue that he killed under the influence of an extreme emotional disturbance and is therefore only guilty of manslaughter.

2. Involuntary Manslaughter

Unintentional homicides, if committed without due caution and circumspection, constitute involuntary manslaughter. Courts have used many terms to describe the standard for involuntary manslaughter, including: "gross negligence," "criminal negligence," and even "recklessness." All of these terms are used to describe situations in which a defendant acts in gross deviation from the standard of care that a reasonable person would exercise in the same situation. Most often involuntary manslaughter involves a defendant acting with gross negligence, i.e., defendant is not aware of the risk his conduct poses, but a reasonable person would have been.

EXAMPLE AND ANALYSIS

In an effort to show off his athletic ability, defendant rides his jet ski through the shallow swim area of the beach. Before he can swerve, a swimmer surfaces and is hit and killed by defendant. Even if defendant did not intend to kill a swimmer and may not have seen the swimmer, defendant may be guilty of involuntary manslaughter.

Although criminal liability ordinarily requires a conscious disregard of a risk of harm ("recklessness"), because the consequences of killing another person are so grave, gross negligence suffices for involuntary manslaughter. However, "gross negligence," because it leads to criminal punishment, reflects a standard higher than that required for civil negligence liability.

---

a. **Distinguishing civil and criminal liability.** To be criminally liable for a death, a defendant must act with gross negligence.

i. **Definition of gross negligence.** If a reasonable person would not pose the same risk to human life, the defendant has acted negligently. Negligence rises to the level of gross negligence when there is either a high likelihood of harm or risk of severe harm, or little or no social utility to the defendant's risky actions.

(a) **Descriptions of gross negligence.** Courts have found it difficult to define how much negligence criminal liability requires. It is more than that required for civil liability, but the question is how much more? To describe the extra carelessness required, courts use terms like "gross," "culpable," or even "reckless." State v. Barnett, 218 S.C. 415, 63 S.E.2d 57, 58-59 (1951). Ultimately, the jury must be convinced that the defendant exceeded conduct calling for mere compensation of the victim, and therefore deserves punishment by the state. Andrews v. Director of Public Prosecutions,

FIGURE 5-9

FACTORS FOR GROSS NEGLIGENCE	
Magnitude of Risk	*Social Utility of Conduct*
• Foreseeability of harm to victim • Seriousness of harm	• Cost of avoidance • Conduct's benefit to society
Remember: The degree of negligence required for criminal liability must ordinarily be greater than that needed for tort liability.	

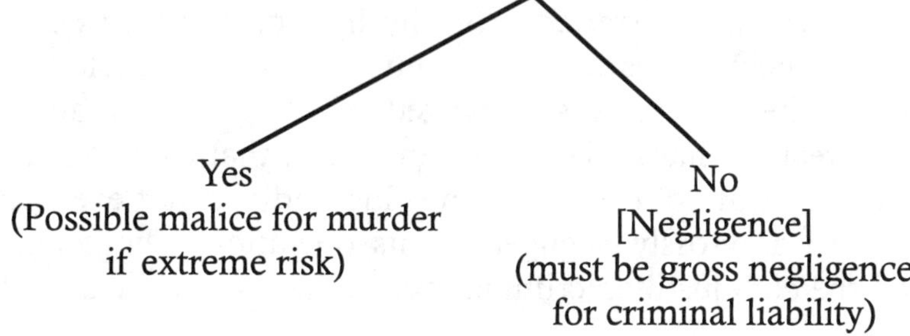
• Was the defendant aware of the risk taken?
Yes
(Possible malice for murder if extreme risk)
No
[Negligence]
(must be gross negligence for criminal liability)

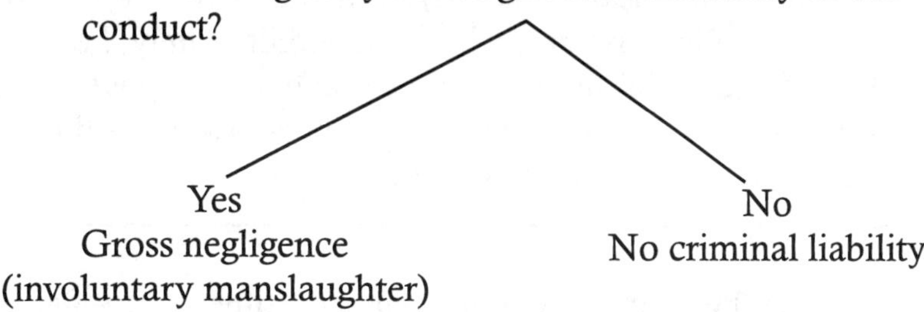
• Did the risk greatly outweigh the social utility of the conduct?
Yes
Gross negligence
(involuntary manslaughter)
No
No criminal liability

(1937) A.C. 576, 581-583. The Model Penal Code comments state the principle directly: Gross negligence "is more than the negligence required to impose tort liability." MPC §2.02, comment. Criminal negligence involves a gross deviation from the standard of care a reasonable person would observe in defendant's situation. MPC §2.02(2)(d).

(b) Distinguish ordinary negligence. Ordinary negligence is usually insufficient for criminal homicide. Either there must be a subjective awareness of the risk of death ("recklessness") or defendant's negligence must rise to the level of gross negligence.

ii. Determining gross negligence. The trier of fact will use many factors to determine whether a defendant acted with that type of negligence that should be criminally punished. Typically, these factors include: 1. How serious was the risk defendant's conduct posed? 2. What was the foreseeability of harm? 3. Why was the defendant involved in the high-risk activity? 4. Are there other reasons defendant's negligent conduct should not be punished such as the possible social utility of his conduct?

EXAMPLE AND ANALYSIS

In Commonwealth v. Welansky, 316 Mass. 383, 55 N.E.2d 902 (1944), the defendant owned a nightclub, the *New Coconut Grove*. The nightclub had inadequate emergency exits and was generally crowded and unsafe. One night, when the owner was in the hospital, a bar boy accidentally started a fire by lighting a match near some table decorations. The fire quickly spread, killing many patrons and employees trapped in the club. Defendant, the owner, was convicted of involuntary manslaughter and sentenced to fifteen years of hard labor. The court held that even though the defendant was apparently unaware of the risk at the club and was not even present when the fire occurred, he was grossly negligent in its operation. The conditions under which he operated the club justified criminal punishment once the accidental killing occurred.

Note. The court's opinion in *Welansky* is very confusing because the court uses the terms "recklessly" and "negligently" interchangeably. Ultimately, however, the court held that even if the defendant did not realize the grave danger posed by his conduct, he is responsible if an ordinary person would have been aware of the grave danger. The court's statement reflects a "gross negligence" standard.

---

b. **Dangerous instrumentality doctrine.** Some courts find that the use of a dangerous instrument automatically elevates behavior from mere negligence to criminally culpable negligence. Under this approach, a motor vehicle is considered a "dangerous instrumentality" and vehicular homicide is treated as involuntary manslaughter. State v. Barnett, 218 S.C. 415, 63 S.E.2d 57 (1951). Alternatively, vehicular homicides may be treated as a separate type of manslaughter not requiring gross negligence. See, e.g., Cal. Penal Code §192(c).

c. **Model Penal Code approach.** Under the Model Penal Code, homicide is manslaughter when it is committed recklessly, i.e., the defendant was conscious of the risk of death. A separate, lesser offense of "negligent homicide" is defined as a failure to appreciate a risk of death of which the actor should be aware." MPC §2.02(2)(d), 210.4.

   Example. Unaware of the risk their conduct poses, a group of fraternity students decide to drop large appliances out of a fourth story window as a prank. One of the appliances hits and kills a passerby. Under the MPC, defendants are guilty of negligent homicide because they should have been aware of the unjustifiable risk their conduct posed.

d. **Contributory negligence is NOT a defense.** Unlike in civil cases, in criminal law the contributory negligence of the deceased is not a defense.

Example. In Dickerson v. State, 441 So. 2d 536 (Miss. 1983), the defendant was speeding in his car when he smashed into the victim's car, killing him. Even though the victim had been negligent as to where he parked his car, the defendant was guilty of manslaughter.

e. **Objective vs. subjective standard.** At common law, a defendant need not be aware of the risk of death to be guilty of involuntary manslaughter. If an ordinary person in the same situation would have realized the high and unjustifiable risk of death, the defendant is grossly negligent. This objective standard raises questions about whether it is fair and proper to criminally punish defendants who are unaware of the risks they create.

   i. **Criticism of objective standard.** The negligence standard punishes people who have not considered the risk of harm. Mere ignorance may make the defendant culpable. Moreover, a defendant who is incapable of meeting the objective standard of care may be punished. Not only does punishment appear unjust, but it is also unclear how punishment can deter an inadvertent actor.

EXAMPLES AND ANALYSIS

Christian Scientist Cases. Some religions, such as the Church of Christ Scientist, teach that prayer rather than medicine should be used to cure illness. By applying the objective gross negligence standard, defendants who follow their faith may be convicted of involuntary manslaughter. Walker v. Superior Court, 47 Cal. 3d 112, 763 P.2d 852 (1988). The objective standard focuses on what the "reasonable person in the defendant's situation would do," "but the defendant's situation does not generally include one's religion."

In a similar case, in State v. Williams, 4 Wash. App. 908, 484 P.2d 1167 (1971), defendants were convicted of manslaughter for the death of their 17-month child. The defendants failed to seek medical attention for their child who had a serious tooth infection because they didn't realize how ill the child was and were afraid that authorities might try to take the child from them. When the child died, defendants were charged with manslaughter. The court upheld the conviction because it found that a reasonable person in the defendant's situation would have taken the child to the doctor. Even though the defendants loved their child and did not knowingly risk his life, they still acted negligently and were therefore guilty of manslaughter. This case highlights the problems in trying to identify who is the "reasonable person" and punishing under an objective standard.

---

ii. **Avoiding liability for involuntary manslaughter.** Because of the harsh consequences of applying the objective standard of care, sometimes courts avoid imposing liability on the defendant by holding that the defendant did not cause the death. See discussion of causation, infra.

FIGURE 5-10

INVOLUNTARY MANSLAUGHTER	
Basic Rule	Unintentional homicides committed without due caution and circumspection • Gross negligence • Criminal negligence/Mere recklessness
Gross Negligence	Unreasonable risk to human life • Magnitude of risk vs. social utility of conduct

REVIEW QUESTION AND ANSWER

INVOLUNTARY MANSLAUGHTER

Question: Jane, a bus driver for the Saybrook Unified School District, had been reprimanded twice for arriving late to work and warned that she would be fired if it happened again. Jane desperately wanted to keep her job because she loved driving the children. Nonetheless, on Monday morning Jane got another late start. When she began her route she had only half the time she needed to complete her course. As she approached one of her stops, Jane took a quick look at her watch. Just at that moment, a child stepped in front of the bus and was hit. Tragically, the child died from his injuries. What, if any, crime has Jane committed?

Answer: Nothing in the facts suggests Jane had an intent to kill or cause grave bodily harm. In fact, Jane liked the children. The facts also do not suggest that Jane *consciously* disregarded the risk to human life when she briefly glanced at her watch. Thus, it would be difficult to argue that she acted with the gross recklessness required to show malice for second-degree murder.

The most likely charge Jane would face is involuntary manslaughter. The prosecution would argue that by looking at her watch while she drove a bus and approached a bus stop, Jane took a risk to human life that an ordinary person would not take. Accordingly, Jane acted with negligence. The prosecution would argue that Jane's negligence was "gross negligence" because: 1. She was operating a deadly instrument (namely, the bus), and/or because 2. She took an unjustifiable risk by taking her eyes off the road because the social utility of her conduct, i.e., trying to save her job, did not outweigh the high possibility that she would seriously hurt or kill a child. Although Jane may believe that the social utility of trying to keep on schedule justified looking at her watch, a jury may find that rushing to keep her schedule did not justify the risks she took. Juries have broad discretion in evaluating the social utility of a defendant's conduct.

3. Second-Degree Murder vs. Involuntary Manslaughter

Gross recklessness constitutes murder; ordinary recklessness is only involuntary manslaughter. As with the issue of "gross negligence" versus "ordinary negligence," the dividing line between gross recklessness and mere recklessness is vague, and is ultimately a jury question. If the defendant consciously takes a risk that demonstrates a wanton disregard for human life, then "gross recklessness" or malice exists and the defendant is guilty of second-degree murder. If the defendant does not realize the risk or does not appreciate its seriousness, or shows there was some social utility in taking it, then the defendant is only guilty of involuntary manslaughter.

Second-Degree Murder	**Involuntary Manslaughter**
• Malice/Wanton Disregard	• No Malice
• Gross Recklessness	• Gross Negligence
	or
	• Mere Recklessness

a. **Gross recklessness.** In determining whether a defendant's conduct was sufficiently egregious to qualify as gross recklessness, courts will often consider the magnitude of the risk defendant took, as well as whether there was any social utility to the defendant's conduct. See discussion of gross negligence supra.

Examples and Analysis

In Commonwealth v. Malone, 354 Pa. 180, 47 A.2d 445 (1946), the defendant killed a fellow youth during a game of Russian Poker. Even though the defendant did not intend to kill the victim, by the nature of the game he knew there was a substantial and unjustifiable risk of death. It was considered a gross and unjustified risk because of the high risk of death or serious harm the negligible social utility inherent in the conduct. Accordingly, the court found defendant acted with "malice."

In People v. Berry, 208 Cal. App. 3d 783 (1989), defendant was charged with second-degree murder when his pit bull dog mauled a child who had wandered into the dog's area. The court found defendant had implied malice because he was actually aware of the dog's potential danger to human beings. The dog had been bred and trained to kill, and there was open access to the dog's area. Defendant consciously took a substantial and unjustifiable risk by owning such a dangerous dog to human life and was therefore guilty of murder.

In Commonwealth v. Feinberg, 253 A.2d 636 (Pa. 1969), defendant sold Sterno heating cans, knowing that local skid-row residents would consume them for their alcohol content. The cans were not designed for human consumption and resulted in the death of thirty-one persons. Because defendant knew that some of his customers were buying the Sterno for drinking purposes and was aware of its danger, he was guilty of second-degree murder.

---

b. **Model Penal Code approach.** The Model Penal Code also requires "extreme indifference to the value of human life" for murder. MPC §210.2(1)(b).

c. **Synonymous phrases.** Many different terms and phrases describe the level of intent required for second-degree murder. They are synonymous: malice, extreme indifference to human life, reckless and wanton disregard, gross deviation from the standard of conduct, depraved indifference, and a depraved and malignant heart.

d. **Omissions.** A defendant with a duty of care may engage in grossly reckless, malicious behavior by failing to provide the care necessary under the circumstances. See People v. Burden, 72 Cal. App. 3d 603, 616 (Dist. App. 1977) (gross neglect of a child constitutes murder if the parent is aware the child is starving).

e. **Gross recklessness vs. gross negligence.** The difference between second degree murder and involuntary manslaughter ordinarily depends on whether the defendant was consciously aware of the serious and unwarranted risk to human life.

   i. **Drunk driving cases.** Defendants accused of drunk driving often argue they should be convicted of only involuntary manslaughter, not second-degree murder, because they were too intoxicated to realize the risk they posed to human life. However, courts usually reject that argument, noting defendants are conscious of the risks when they decide to drink and drive, United States v. Fleming, 739 F.2d 945 (4th Cir. 1984), or "must have known" the risks because of the extremely careless manner in which they drove. People v. Watson, 30 Cal. 3d 290, 637 P.2d 279 (1981).

(a) **Vehicular murder.** To avoid the fiction of asserting that the defendant must have had actual awareness of the risk of fatal harm at the time of the accident, some jurisdictions have simply enacted a separate offense known as "vehicular murder." However, this approach raises the question of whether inadvertent killing should be punished as harshly as other murders. Compare Simmons v. State, 215 S.E.2d 883 (S.C. 1975) (life sentence for reckless driving upheld), with Pears v. State, 672 P.2d 903 (Alaska App. 1983) (20-year sentence held excessive).

(b) **Model Penal Code approach.** The MPC answers the question of whether a death caused by drunk driving should constitute murder or manslaughter. Although murder under the Model Penal Code ordinarily requires a conscious disregard of the risks involved, MPC §210.2(1)(b), an exception is made when a defendant is unaware of a risk because of self-induced intoxication. MPC §2.08(2). Accordingly, courts that apply the Model Penal Code generally treat vehicular homicide as murder. See State v. Dufield, 549 A.2d 1205 (N.H. 1988) (Souter, J.); People v. Register, 60 N.Y.2d 270, 457 N.E.2d 704 (1983).

FIGURE 5-11

SECOND-DEGREE MURDER VS. INVOLUNTARY MANSLAUGHTER

Second-Degree Murder	*Involuntary Manslaughter*
Malice	No Malice
Gross Recklessness	Mere recklessness or Gross negligence

Review Question and Answer

SECOND-DEGREE MURDER VS. INVOLUNTARY MANSLAUGHTER

Question: Johnny Racer's passion is skiing. He gets an enormous thrill from racing down the slopes of his local ski resort. Although he has been warned many times that he could knock over a less skilled skier, Johnny has confidence in his skiing ability. One day, as Johnny is barreling down the mountain, a novice skier unexpectedly darts out in front of him. Johnny tries to stop but is unable to do so in time and impales the skier with his pole. The novice skier dies. Is Johnny guilty of homicide?

Answer: Johnny did not premeditate the killing (first-degree murder) nor act in the heat of passion (voluntary manslaughter). Thus, the most severe charge the prosecution could seek is second-degree murder. Second-degree murder requires "malice" which can be shown by a callous disregard for human life, also known as "gross recklessness." In order to demonstrate recklessness, the prosecution must show that Johnny consciously disregarded the risk his skiing posed to human life. The prosecution would argue that Johnny received several warnings that he could hurt another skier but disregarded them. Accordingly, Johnny's skiing was grossly reckless.

By contrast, Johnny would argue that at the time he hit the novice skier, Johnny was not aware of the risk his actions posed because there was no warning that the skier would dart out in front of him. If Johnny were unaware of the risk, then his actions are at most grossly negligent which only constitutes involuntary manslaughter.

F. FELONY-MURDER DOCTRINE

The common law felony-murder rule gives prosecutors an alternative approach, a shortcut, to prove murder. Under the felony-murder rule, prosecutors need not show the defendant acted with the mens rea required for murder; i.e., intent to kill or cause grievous bodily harm, as long as they prove that the defendant caused the death during the commission of and in furtherance of a felony.

The felony-murder rule is controversial because it punishes a defendant for murder even though the death may have been accidental. Many courts disfavor the rule. To limit its impact, specific conditions often are required for its application. The felony must be inherently dangerous and independent from the killing, and the death must occur in furtherance and during the course of the felony.

Drafters of the Model Penal Code proposed eliminating the felony murder rule. Instead, the MPC creates a rebuttable presumption that a defendant has acted with the recklessness necessary for murder if the death occurs while the actor is engaged or is an accomplice in the commission of certain felonies, including robbery, rape, arson, burglary, kidnapping or felonious escape. MPC §210.2(1)(b).

The misdemeanor-manslaughter doctrine, unlawful-act doctrine, is a comparable rule that applies to killings arising out of the commission of an unlawful act that is not a felony. Such a killing constitutes involuntary manslaughter, without proof of the mens rea normally required for involuntary manslaughter; i.e., gross negligence. The Model Penal Code rejects the unlawful-act doctrine.

1. The Basic Felony-Murder Doctrine

If a defendant causes a death during the commission of a felony, the prosecution need not prove that the defendant acted with an intent to kill. Under the felony-murder doctrine, the defendant is guilty of "constructive murder" because the intent to commit the felony substitutes for the intent to kill or cause grievous bodily harm. Traditionally, the felony-murder doctrine is not limited to foreseeable deaths. A felon is strictly liable for all killings committed personally or by an accomplice in the course of the felony. But see §F(8)(C)(3) infra.

a. **Example.** In People v. Stamp, 2 Cal. App. 3d 203, 82 Cal. Rptr. 598 (1979), the defendant robbed a victim at gunpoint. The victim was forced to lie on the floor during the robbery. Shortly after the defendant fled, the victim died of a heart attack. Even though there was no evidence that the defendant intended to cause the victim's death, the defendant was still responsible for murder under the felony-murder doctrine.

b. **Nontraditional felony-murder doctrine.** In some jurisdictions, such as Michigan, the felony-murder doctrine is not used as a substitute to prove mens rea. Rather, it is solely a grading device; if the killing occurs during a specified felony and the prosecutor proves mens rea for murder, then the degree is automatically first degree. Most commonly, however, the discussion of felony-murder refers to the traditional doctrine that substitutes proof that the death occurred during the commission of a felony for proof of an intent to kill.

2. Rationale for Felony-Murder Rule

The rationales for the felony-murder rule include: a. deterring felons from killing, even accidentally, during their crimes (deterrence); b. vindicating society's loss when a felony results in death (retribution); and c. easing the prosecutional burden in cases where the defendant may have killed intentionally but claims the deaths were accidental (incapacitation).

3. Criticisms of Felony-Murder Rule

Many modern commentators reject the felony-murder rule, arguing that: a. a person cannot, by definition, be deterred from committing an accidental act; b. a harsher punishment levied against a defendant who accidentally causes a death is capricious and an unfair imposition of increased liability on the unlucky felon; c. the felony-murder rule does not reflect the defendant's actual culpability since the defendant had no intent to cause the death; and d. prosecutors do not need assistance in homicide prosecutions, especially since statistical evidence shows that homicides occur in felonies at a much lower rate than expected and, when a death occurs, there is usually evidence of the defendant's reckless intent.

4. History of Felony-Murder Doctrine

The felony-murder doctrine is a holdover from a time when all felonies were punishable by death. It made very little difference whether the defendant was convicted of a felony or a murder committed during that felony. A defendant involved in a felonious act, like shooting another person's deer, bore responsibility for any resulting harmful consequences. For a history of the felony-murder doctrine, see People v. Aaron, 409 Mich. 672 (1980).

EXAMPLE AND ANALYSIS

Regina v. Serne, 16 Cox. Crim. Cas. 311 (1887). Many criminal law books introduce the felony-murder doctrine with this case. In *Serne*, the defendant was charged with the murder of his son. The evidence suggested that the defendant set fire to his home in order to collect the insurance on his property and on the life of his imbecile son. The court instructed the jury that the defendant was guilty of murder if he acted with either knowledge that his actions would kill a person (malice) or an intent to commit a felony (felony-murder). Nonetheless, the jury returned a not-guilty verdict after the trial judge expressed his doubts about the scope of the felony-murder doctrine.

5. Modern Felony-Murder Law

English courts created the felony-murder rule but abolished it in 1957. Likewise, Canada has outlawed felony murder as impermissibly convicting a defendant in the absence of mens rea. By contrast, a majority of American court jurisdictions still recognize the felony-murder doctrine, although they have taken a variety of steps to limit its impact.

6. Model Penal Code Approach

The MPC rejects the traditional felony-murder rule. However, it creates a rebuttable presumption of extreme indifference to human life when a death occurs during a felony. MPC §1.12(5).

7. Prosecutors' Preference for Felony-Murder Doctrine

Prosecutors prefer using the felony-murder doctrine because it relieves the prosecutor from proving the most difficult element of homicide; i.e., defendant's mental state at the time of the killing. It also allows the court to impose liability on felons for the acts of their cofelons.

8. Requirements to Prove Felony Murder

To prove felony murder, the prosecution must prove:

- Defendant committed a felony.
- During the course of the felony, the defendant or an accomplice caused a death.

a. **Felony requirement.** In some states, the type of felony during which the death occurs may determine whether the felony-murder rule applies. Also, some states divide felony murder into degrees depending on the nature of the underlying felony.

i. **Example.** Commonly, serious crimes such as arson, rape, robbery, and burglary would trigger first-degree felony murder. All other felonies might trigger second-degree felony murder.

ii. **Example.** In Michigan, the prosecution must prove mens rea for any murder. If the murder occurs during a felony, it is elevated to first-degree murder.

b. **Causation.** The prosecution need not establish an intent to kill but it must still prove the defendant or accomplice "caused" the death. Traditionally, courts have interpreted causation for felony murder expansively. The defendant "takes his victim as he finds him" and is responsible for unforeseeable deaths, such as the victim's heart attack during a felony. See *Stamp*, supra.

9. Modern Limitations on the Felony-Murder Doctrine

Increasingly uncomfortable with the felony-murder doctrine, modern courts have adopted a number of limitations to its application. These limitations include:

- inherently dangerous felony limitation;
- independent felony limitation;
- limitation to killings "in furtherance" of the felony.

a. **Inherently dangerous felony limitation.** Only an underlying felony that is "inherently dangerous to human life" will trigger the felony-murder doctrine. Application of this doctrine ensures that courts will only find malice in cases in which the defendant has already caused a substantial risk to human life in the underlying felony.

i. **Example.** In People v. Phillips, 64 Cal. 2d 574, 414 P.2d 353 (1966), the defendant, a chiropractor, faced murder charges after he defrauded a child's parents into paying him for her treatment instead of opting for potentially life-saving surgery. One of the theories available to the jury was felony murder. The appellate court reversed defendant's conviction for second-degree murder because the underlying felony, grand theft, is not inherently dangerous to human life.

ii. **Determining whether a felony is inherently dangerous.** To determine whether a felony is inherently dangerous, courts either: a. analyze the felony in the abstract; or b. examine the facts of the case to ascertain how the felony was actually committed.

(a) **Dangerous in the abstract.** Most courts will analyze the felony in the abstract. A felony that can frequently be committed without creating a risk to human life is not "inherently dangerous." For this type of felony, the felony-murder doctrine is unavailable. Instead, the prosecution must prove the usual elements of homicide—actus reus and mens rea.

EXAMPLES AND ANALYSIS

In People v. Satchell, 6 Cal. 3d 28, 489 P.2d 1361 (1972), the court held that the felony of being an ex-felon in possession of a weapon is not inherently dangerous because a felon can possess a weapon without posing a danger to human life.

In People v. Henderson, 19 Cal. 3d 86, 560 P.2d 1180 (1977), the court held that the felony of "false imprisonment . . . effected by violence, menace, fraud, or deceit" did not trigger the felony-murder doctrine. The definition of the crime stipulates alternative ways to commit the crime which do not involve force or violence.

STUDY TIP

If a felony is not evaluated in the abstract, but according to the results in each case where prosecutors are seeking to use the felony-murder doctrine, then every such felony will be considered dangerous because a death occurred; e.g., *Phillips*, supra (death occurred when chiropractor failed to provide correct treatment).

(b) **Dangerous as committed.** A few courts will examine the circumstances in which a felony was committed to determine whether it was "inherently dangerous." This approach is more likely to find felonies to be inherently dangerous given the fact that there was a death in the case.

EXAMPLES AND ANALYSIS

In State v. Goodseal, 220 Kan. 487, 553 P.2d 279 (1977), a court found a felon's possession of a firearm inherently dangerous because it was used in a dangerous manner in that case.

Note. In People v. Patterson, 49 Cal. 3d 615, 778 P.2d 549 (1989), the appellate court did not consider other nondangerous crimes that were prohibited by the statute. Rather, the court focused only on the part of the statute under which the defendant was charged—the illegal distribution of cocaine, and held it to be an "inherently dangerous felony." This approach to analyzing a statute is more likely to find a felony inherently dangerous.

---

b. **Independent felony limitation (merger doctrine).** Just as the inherently dangerous limitation precludes the *least* serious types of felonies from eligibility for the felony-murder doctrine, the independent felony limitation blocks some of the *most* serious felonies from application of the doctrine. Under the independent felony limitation, if the underlying felony is an "integral part" of the homicide itself, the felony-murder doctrine is not applied. If the underlying felony is merely a step toward causing death, it merges with the resulting homicide. To use the felony-murder doctrine, there must be a separate purpose for punishing the underlying felony.

i. **Rationale for independent felony limitation.** This limitation serves many purposes:

- Prevents collapsing all homicide grades into felony murder. Without the independent felony limitation, any manslaughter would automatically become murder because a death occurred during the commission of a felony, namely the crime of manslaughter.
- Prevents confusing the jury with regard to the issue of intent. If the prosecution must prove intent to assault or kill for the underlying felony, felony murder would relieve the burden of proving malice for the murder.

- Prevents using the felony-murder doctrine where it can provide no independent deterrence. If one of the rationales for the felony-murder doctrine is that it may deter wrongdoers from committing felonies in a dangerous manner, the felony triggering the rule must be one the defendant can choose to perform violently or nonviolently (e.g., robbery v. theft).

Examples and Analysis

In People v. Smith, 35 Cal. 3d 798, 678 P.2d 886 (1984), the defendant was charged with felony-murder based on the underlying felony of child abuse. The court held that the felony-murder doctrine did not apply because the underlying felony required that the jury determine whether the defendant acted "under circumstances or conditions likely to produce great bodily harm or death." (fn. 4). Because proof of a deadly assault was required for the underlying felony, there was no independent felony to trigger the felony-murder doctrine.

In People v. Ireland, 70 Cal. 2d 522 (1969), the defendant faced felony-murder charges for drawing a gun and killing his wife. The underlying felony was assault with a deadly weapon. Because assaulting the victim with a deadly weapon was integral to proving the murder, it could not be used as an independent felony to charge felony murder. Absent this requirement, any felonious assault would automatically become murder if a death resulted.

A defendant is charged with manslaughter. The prosecution tries to elevate the charge to murder by claiming that the underlying felony is manslaughter and a death occurred during the commission of the felony. Obviously, the felony-murder doctrine cannot artificially elevate the manslaughter charge to murder.

---

ii. **Determining when a felony is independent.** To qualify for the felony-murder doctrine, a felony must include a purpose independent of killing or causing grave bodily harm to the victim. If it does not, it is an "integral part of" or "included in fact" in the homicide and the felony-murder rule does not apply.

(a) **Determining independent purpose of felony.** If the aim of a felony is other than killing or gravely harming the victim, it is an independent felony and qualifies for the felony-murder doctrine.

- **Examples.** In most jurisdictions, the felonies of robbery, burglary, kidnapping, rape, arson, and lewd conduct with a minor qualify as "independent" felonies.

- **Child abuse.** Courts have taken contradictory positions on whether child abuse qualifies as an "independent" felony. If the abuse includes an intent to kill or cause grave bodily harm, it likely will not qualify. Ironically, however, if the abuse is less than life-threatening, it may qualify because it is not part of an intentional attempt to fatally injure the child. See People v. Jackson, 218 Cal. Rptr. 637 (Cal. App. 1985). Moreover, some courts find child abuse by neglect qualifies as an "independent" felony, People v. Shockley, but single assaults do not. State v. Brown, 236 Kan. 800, 696 P.2d 954 (1985).
- **Burglary with intent to assault.** In California, burglaries based on an unlawful entry "with intent to assault" do *not* qualify for the felony-murder doctrine, because the intent to kill or injure is a requirement of the underlying felony. However, other jurisdictions, such as New York, allow any kind of burglary to qualify for felony murder.
- **Note.** The inconsistency in application of the "merger" doctrine reflects courts' differing levels of discomfort with the felony-murder rule.

(b) **Effect of independent felony limitation and inherently dangerous felony limitation.** Requiring the felony to be inherently dangerous yet separate from the act of killing excludes from the felony-murder doctrine deaths that occur during the least and most dangerous felonies.

Least Dangerous Felonies	____________ (F-M applies)	Most Dangerous Felonies
• Ineligible for F-M because of "inherently dangerous felony" limitation		• Ineligible for F-M because of "independent felony"

c. **Killings during the course of the felony.** Alternatively, courts can also limit the scope of the felony-murder doctrine by limiting which killings precipitated by the felon qualify for application of the rule. Accordingly, some courts determine application of the doctrine by considering:

- Who did the killing?
- Who was killed?
- When did it occur?
- Did it further the felony?

i. Who did the killing?

(a) Agency theory. Traditionally, only deaths directly caused by the defendant or a cofelon qualified for prosecution under the felony-murder rule. The majority of courts still follow this "agency" theory.

Example. In State v. Canola, 73 N.J. 206, 374 A.2d 20 (1977), the defendant faced felony-murder charges for the death of his cofelon, fatally shot by a jewelry store owner trying to resist their robbery. Applying the "agency" theory, the court held that the defendant was *not* guilty because the death did not occur by his hand or that of one of his agents (i.e., co-felons). Rather, the death was the result of an act by the victim.

(b) Proximate cause theory. Some courts are willing to apply the felony-murder doctrine to deaths beyond those directly caused by a cofelon. According to the "proximate cause" theory, the felon may be responsible for any death proximately resulting from the unlawful activity.

Examples and Analysis

Police officers responding to a crime scene accidentally kill another police officer while trying to apprehend the felons. Under the proximate cause theory, the felony-murder doctrine applies because the death "proximately resulted" from the unlawful activity. Commonwealth v. Almeida, 362 Pa. 596, 68 A.2d 595 (1949).

In "shield cases" the proximate cause theory has also been applied. In shield cases defendants use an innocent victim as a shield during a felony and law officers accidentally kill the shield. Taylor v. State, 55 S.W. 961 (Tex. Cr. App. 1900); Keaton v. State, 57 S.W. 1125 (Tex. Cr. App. 1900). They are guilty of felony murder.

ii. Who was killed?

(a) Exception for cofelons. In most jurisdictions, even those adopting the proximate cause theory of felony murder, a felon is not responsible for the death of a cofelon. Commonwealth v. Redline, 391 Pa. 486, 137 A.2d 472 (1958).

- **Rationale.** Felons are not responsible for the death of a cofelon because: a. the killing is viewed as justifiable, b. cofelons' lives are valued less than those of innocent victims, c. the death of a cofelon would not seem to be "in furtherance" of the felony, and d. felons "assume the risk" of dying when they participate in the felony.

- **Example.** Two felons decide to rob a bank. The police respond and shoot one of the felons. The cofelon is not liable under the felony-murder doctrine for his partner's death.

iii. When did the killing occur?

(a) During the course of the felony. In order for the felony-murder doctrine to apply, the death must occur "during the course" of the felony. Thus, if the felony has been completed and the cofelons are in custody, any subsequent death would not be covered by the felony-murder doctrine. However, killings that take place during a cofelon's attempted escape are considered "during the course of" the felony.

(b) Duration of the felony. Courts differ as to when the felony begins and ends depending on their view of the felony-murder doctrine. Typically, however, the felony commences when the defendants begin preparations for the crime and does not end until the defendants are in custody or have reached a position of "temporary safety." People v. Lopez, 16 Cal. App. 3d 184 (1981); People v. Gladman, 41 N.Y.2d 124 (1976).

iv. Did it further the felony?

(a) Separate criminal acts. Unanticipated actions by a cofelon not in furtherance of the common purpose of the felony may not be charged under the felony-murder doctrine.

- **Example.** Felons decide to rob a bank. While inside the bank, one of the felons decides to rape one of the customers and then kills her. The other felons would not be responsible or charged with the cofelon's unanticipated actions.

- **Note.** No firm rule governs when a cofelon's actions are "in furtherance of the felony." The issue is left to the jury. Juries use this requirement as a safety valve to acquit cofelons of murder if one felon's actions are so unpredictable and outside the common purpose of the felony that the cofelons should not be held responsible. See, e.g., United States v. Heinlein, 490 F.2d 725 (D.C. Cir. 1973) (cofelon stabbed rape victim when she slapped him; other rapists not held responsible for murder).

10. Vicarious Liability and Provocative Act Doctrine

To expand liability in felony-murder jurisdictions that have adopted the traditional "agency" approach, some courts have created the new doctrine of vicarious liability. Under vicarious liability, a felon bears responsibility for any killing attributable to the intentional acts of his or her associates committed with conscious disregard for life and likely to result in death, whether or not the cofelon directly caused the death. A cofelon's provocative acts create malice that make all the defendants responsible for murder.

a. **Applying vicarious liability doctrine.** Vicarious liability requires the prosecution to prove that the felons' acts created an atmosphere that would provoke life-threatening violence. All of the defendants would then bear responsibility for any killings resulting from this implied malice. The classic example is a cofelon starting a gun battle.

Example and Analysis

In Taylor v. Superior Court, 3 Cal. 3d 578, 477 P.2d 131 (1970), the defendant acted as the getaway driver in a robbery. While he waited in the car, his cofelons tried to rob a liquor store. After the defendants brandished their guns and repeatedly threatened the victim-owners, the victim-owners shot and killed one of the robbers. The defendant was charged with his cofelon's murder. Because the jurisdiction had adopted the agency theory of felony murder and someone other than one of the felons killed the cofelon, the court had to devise another theory to create liability. Notwithstanding contrary precedent case law (see People v. Washington, 62 Cal. 2d 777), the court held the defendant responsible because his codefendant's provocative conduct, as shown by "aggressive actions," caused the death.

---

i. **Provocative conduct/aggressive action.** There is no clear standard as to what constitutes "provocative acts" triggering vicarious liability. In *Taylor* the court held that repeated threats of "execution," together with the felon's nervous apprehension were sufficient to show a gross disregard for human life. However, in *Washington*, the court held that merely pointing a weapon during a felony did not constitute an act of implied malice.

"Aggressive Action" = Malice
("Provocative Conduct")

> ## STUDY TIP
>
> By adopting the provocative act doctrine as a form of vicarious liability, the *Taylor* court applied a type of proximate cause theory in a jurisdiction that generally follows the agency theory approach.

b. **Exception: Recklessness of the person killed.** Courts have limited the vicarious liability theory by holding it does *not* apply when the felon engaging in the malicious conduct dies as a result of those actions. Courts treat these situations as suicides, not homicides. See People v. Antick, 15 Cal. 79, 539 P.2d 43 (1975).

11. Summary of Felony Murder and Vicarious Liability

An alternative approach for prosecuting murder cases is to charge defendants under a felony-murder or vicarious liability theory. Under felony murder, the prosecution need not prove that the defendant intended to cause the victim's death. Malice will be presumed from the defendant's participation in the felony. Vicarious liability treats a defendant's aggravating actions during a felony as creating "an atmosphere of malice" supporting a charge of murder. Prosecutors may charge a murder case using either the traditional approach of proving intent or a felony-murder/vicarious liability approach, or both. A defendant may be convicted under multiple theories for murder but may only face punishment once for any given murder.

FIGURE 5-12

FELONY-MURDER DOCTRINE	
Basic Rule	Death during felony substitutes for proof of malice.
Limitations	1. Inherently dangerous felony 2. Independent felony 3. In furtherance of felony • Duration of felony • Acts outside scope • Death of cofelon
Vicarious Liability	Provocative acts of one felon create malice for cofelons.

EXAM TIP

If the factual scenario of an exam contains both a felony and a death, students should discuss homicide under both the traditional mens rea analysis and the felony-murder analysis.

REVIEW QUESTION AND ANSWER

FELONY MURDER

Question: James Keating owned a lakefront country home where he liked to vacation. His nearest neighbor was a safe distance away. As he sat before a roaring fire in his fireplace, Keating came upon an idea to remedy his recent financial reverses. He decided to burn down the old vacation home to collect the insurance

proceeds. Keating packed his belongings, removed the screen from the fireplace and drove off in his car. As the sparks began to ignite his house, a neighbor who had unexpectedly driven over to see how Keating was doing saw the sparks and dashed into the burning house to help extinguish the flames. Unfortunately, she tripped over a chair, struck her head and was knocked unconscious. Keating's neighbor died in the flames. Is Keating guilty of the murder of his neighbor?
Answer: Under a traditional mens rea analysis, it would be difficult to convict Keating of murder. He did not intend to kill or harm anyone, and he did not believe his actions posed a risk to any person because his house was located in a remote spot near the lake.

It would be much easier to convict Keating for murder under a felony-murder/ implied malice theory. Under the law of felony murder, if the neighbor's death occurred during Keating's commission of a felony, he is guilty of murder whether or not he acted with malice.

The prosecution's success in applying the felony-murder doctrine will depend on what underlying felony it uses for the charge because the prosecution must show: a. the felony is "inherently dangerous," b. the underlying felony does not merge into the homicide, and c. the death occurred "in furtherance of the felony."

a. *Insurance Fraud Felony Murder.* If the prosecution charges felony murder using insurance fraud as the underlying felony, it may run into problems because insurance fraud is not an "inherently dangerous" felony. If viewed in the abstract, there are many ways to commit insurance fraud that do not involve a risk to human life. Accordingly, felony murder would fail if the prosecution uses insurance fraud as the underlying felony. However, insurance fraud, as it was committed in this particular case, was very dangerous to anyone who might pass by and in fact caused the neighbor's death.

b. *Arson Felony Murder.* Arson has been traditionally recognized as a felony satisfying the limitations of the felony-murder doctrine. Arson is inherently dangerous, and it does not merge with the homicide because it has a purpose other than killing another human being. Finally, although Keating had left the scene, the death occurred while the arson continued and was not at the hands of another. Accordingly, it is viewed as occurring during the commission of and in furtherance of the felony.

G. MISDEMEANOR-MANSLAUGHTER RULE (UNLAWFUL-ACT DOCTRINE)

Just as the felony-murder rule substitutes for proving intent in a murder case, the misdemeanor-manslaughter rule may be used as a substitute for proving the necessary mens rea for an involuntary manslaughter charge.

1. The Basic Doctrine

Unintentional killings committed during an unlawful act, not amounting to a felony, constitute manslaughter. The commission of the unlawful act demonstrates that the defendant acted without due caution or circumspection.

Example. Defendant was charged with misdemeanor-manslaughter when his two Rottweiler dogs killed a passing jogger. Defendant violated a "safety" ordinance requiring that the dogs be restrained at all times. The safety ordinance satisfied the requirements of the misdemeanor-manslaughter doctrine because the ordinance was enacted to protect the health and safety of community members. State v. Powell 426 S.E.2d 91 (N.C. App. 1993).

2. Rationale

Misdemeanor laws usually prescribe the level of care a person must meet in order to avoid acting negligently. Thus, a violation of a misdemeanor law resulting in death shows, in a general way, that the defendant acted with at least gross negligence.

3. Criticisms of Unlawful-Act Doctrine

Like the felony-murder rule, the unlawful-act doctrine dispenses with proof of culpability and imposes liability for a serious crime, involuntary manslaughter, without reference to the actor's actual state of mind in relation to the death caused by the defendant's behavior.

4. Limitations on Unlawful-Act Doctrine

Courts have reduced the harshest effects of the misdemeanor-manslaughter doctrine by adopting limitations to its application.

a. **Proximate cause limitation.** The misdemeanor-manslaughter doctrine only applies if there is a causal connection between the misdemeanor violation and the death that occurred.

EXAMPLES AND ANALYSIS

Defendant was in an accident with a careless driver. The other driver died. Defendant was charged with misdemeanor manslaughter because he was driving with an expired driver's license. The court refused to apply the misdemeanor-manslaughter doctrine because defendant's violation did not lead directly to the death of the careless driver. Commonwealth v. Williams, 133 Pa. Super. 104, 1 A.2d 812 (1938).

Defendant stole $110 from a church collection plate and took off in his car when he was pursued by several congregants. One of these congregants had a heart attack during the chase, lost control of his vehicle and died. Defendant was charged with manslaughter on the theory that the victim's death was caused by defendant's petty theft. The court dismissed the indictment because the petty theft did not encompass the kind of direct, foreseeable risk of physical harm that should trigger the misdemeanor-manslaughter doctrine. Todd v. State, 594 So. 2d 802 (1992).

---

b. **Limiting types of misdemeanor offenses.** To restrict application of the unlawful act doctrine, courts will often limit it to those types of violations most likely to cause physical harm.

i. **Malum in se vs. malum prohibitum.** In many jurisdictions, a violation must be malum in se ("wrong in itself") for the misdemeanor-manslaughter doctrine to apply. If the violation only has a regulatory purpose and is not designed to protect the safety of others, it is often called "malum prohibitum" and cannot trigger the misdemeanor-manslaughter rule.

Example. Defendant was charged with misdemeanor-manslaughter when his two Rottweiler dogs killed a passing jogger. Defendant violated a "safety" ordinance requiring that the dogs be restrained at all times. The safety ordinance satisfied the requirements of the misdemeanor-manslaughter doctrine. State v. Powell, 426 S.E.2d 91 (N.C. App. 1993).

ii. **Dangerous vs. nondangerous infractions.** In some jurisdictions, rather than distinguish between malum in se and malum prohibitum crimes, misdemeanor-manslaughter only applies to violations that are inherently dangerous.

Review Question and Answer

MISDEMEANOR-MANSLAUGHTER

Question: Kara Godbout loves to race her jeep through the desert. She has been doing so for many years. Recently, state officials have passed a law that states:

"It is a violation of the law to drive an off-road vehicle in the desert without a permit. Violation of this law is punishable by six months in jail." Kara fails to obtain a permit but continues to race her jeep through the desert. As she drives over a sand dune, she accidentally plows into a hiker and kills him. Is Kara criminally liable for the death of the hiker?

Answer: There are two theories under which the government may prosecute Kara for involuntary manslaughter. First, the prosecution could argue that Kara should have known that there would be a hiker in the desert who she might strike and that it was grossly negligent for her to drive her jeep. Of course, this allegation may be difficult for the prosecution to prove if others regularly ride through the desert, and there was no indication that there might be hikers in the area.

Alternatively, the prosecution could use the misdemeanor-manslaughter (unlawful-act) doctrine to prosecute Kara. If Kara's violation of the permit law was the proximate cause of the hiker's death, Kara is automatically guilty of involuntary manslaughter even if the prosecution cannot prove she was acting grossly negligently. In order to determine whether the violation is the proximate cause of the death—i.e., is it the type of unlawful act triggering the misdemeanor-manslaughter doctrine, one must have some idea as to why the permit law was passed. If the law passed for environmental concerns—to limit the number of vehicles in the desert—then it is not malum in se and would not be the proximate cause of the death. If, however, the law was passed because the legislature recognized the danger off-road vehicles posed to hikers, then the violation is malum in se and would trigger the misdemeanor-manslaughter doctrine. Under that doctrine, defendant would be guilty of involuntary manslaughter.

FIGURE 5-13

MISDEMEANOR-MANSLAUGHTER RULE (UNLAWFUL-ACT DOCTRINE)	
Basic Rule	Unintentional killings committed during an unlawful act, not amounting to a felony, constitute involuntary manslaughter.
Limitations	Proximate cause limitation or Malum in se vs. malum prohibitum or Dangerous vs. nondangerous misdemeanors

H. HOMICIDE REVIEW

There are two approaches to prove a homicide. First, the prosecution can, after proving the actus reus and causation, establish intent by applying the standards for each level of homicide. Second, the prosecution can prove murder by using principles of felony murder or vicarious liability and prove involuntary manslaughter by using the unlawful-act/misdemeanor-manslaughter doctrine. Students should consider both approaches in addressing factual situations.

FIGURE 5-14

HOMICIDE REVIEW	
Murder 1	Premeditation (Fed./Calif. Approach) • Purposeful or Preconceived design standard? *Felony Murder involving burglary, arson, rape, kidnapping, robbery, mayhem.* or Killings involving particular victims (e.g., police officers) (NY approach)
Other Murders	Malice • Intent to kill or • Intent to cause GBH or • Gross recklessness or • *All other felony murders*
Voluntary Manslaughter	Provocation/Extreme Emotional Distress • Heat of passion or • Extreme emotional distress or • Imperfect self-defense (See §12B(2)(b) infra)
Involuntary Manslaughter	No malice • Gross negligence or • Mere recklessness or • *Misdemeanor-manslaughter/Unlawful-Act Doctrine*

THE DEATH PENALTY

CHAPTER OVERVIEW

The death penalty is the punishment reserved for the most serious criminal offenses. Capital punishment remains controversial and is not used in all jurisdictions. Presently, federal law and the laws of 36 states authorize the death penalty. Both its justification and its administration raise many important issues that are discussed in Chapter 6. This chapter's discussion of the death penalty includes:

- The History of the Death Penalty in the United States
- Policy Arguments for and against the Death Penalty
- Rules for Administration of the Death Penalty
- Constitutional Limitations on the Death Penalty's Application

A. HISTORICAL DEVELOPMENT OF DEATH PENALTY IN THE UNITED STATES

Capital punishment has existed in the United States since this country was founded. The Constitution refers to capital crimes. Const., Amend. V. Each state developed its own laws proscribing how and when the death penalty should be imposed. Additionally, early federal laws authorized the death penalty.

In 1972, opponents of the death penalty asked the Supreme Court to declare capital punishment unconstitutional. Furman v. Georgia, 408 U.S. 238 (1972). Instead of abolishing the death penalty altogether, the Court held that its imposition without clear criteria and fair procedures violates the "Cruel and Unusual Punishment" prohibition of the Eighth Amendment to the Constitution. As a result of the ruling in *Furman*, many state and federal death penalty laws were held unconstitutional. In response to *Furman* and its progeny, the death penalty provisions of state and federal laws were revised. Now, a series of decisions, discussed infra, governs the proper administration of the death penalty.

B. POLICY CONSIDERATIONS

Traditional sentencing principles apply to a discussion of capital punishment but take on greater importance because of the irrevocable nature of the penalty.

1. Purposes of Punishment and the Death Penalty

a. **Retribution.** Authorities are divided on whether retribution justifies the imposition of the capital punishment. Proponents of capital punishment argue that a person who takes a life deserves to have his life taken and the death penalty is necessary to uphold the sanctity of human life. Abolitionists argue that the death penalty cheapens life and should be rejected.

i. **Religious beliefs.** Religious faiths differ in approach to capital punishment. However, the death penalty has historically been part of several major religious traditions including Greco-Roman, Judaic, Islamic, and Christian.

b. **Deterrence.** Authorities are divided on whether the death penalty serves as a deterrent. Isaac Ehrlich's 1975 study concluded that it does. See Ehrlich, The Deterrent Effect of Capital Punishment: A Question of Life and Death, 65 Am. Econ. Rev. 397 (1975). Prior studies, however, had reflected similar homicide rates regardless of the death penalty. Sellin, The Death Penalty (1959). Other experts have also contested Ehrlich's conclusions and asserted that the death penalty deters criminal behavior no more effectively than life imprisonment does. The notoriety accompanying a capital trial may actually encourage some defendants to murder. In some circumstances, the death penalty is promoted as the only possible deterrent. Execution may be the only way to discourage a defendant serving a life sentence from future murder while incarcerated.

c. **Incapacitation.** The death penalty serves as the ultimate form of incapacitation. A person who is executed cannot commit further crimes. Opponents of capital punishment argue that a defendant may also be incapacitated by a sentence of life imprisonment without parole. This argument assumes, however, that a prisoner cannot take any more lives while in custody.

d. **Rehabilitation.** When the death penalty is used, rehabilitation, other than in the spiritual sense, is abandoned.

2. Other Policy Considerations

a. **Error and irrevocability.** A major concern in imposing the death penalty is that there is no margin for error. The execution of an innocent person is an error that cannot be corrected. An estimated 23 innocent people have been wrongfully executed in America in this century. Bedau & Radelet, Miscarriages of Justice in Potentially Capital Cases, 40 Stan. L. Rev. 21 (1987). Nonetheless, some commentators believe that even the certainty of error does not justify abolishing the death penalty because certain crimes deserve that punishment and its imposition achieves more justice. Ernest Van Den Haag, Punishing Criminals (1975).

b. **Discriminatory administration.** Abolitionists also complain that the amount of discretion held by prosecutors, judges, jurors, and governors has led to hopelessly discriminatory administration of capital punishment. Difficulties with eliminating arbitrariness and racial discrimination in the administration of the death penalty led Justice Blackmun to proclaim that he would "no longer . . . tinker with the machinery of death" because, in his view, "no combination of procedural rules or substantive regulations ever can save the death penalty from its inherent constitutional deficiencies." Callins v. Collins, 114 S. Ct. 1127 (1994) (Blackmun, J. dissenting).

STUDY TIP

A complete discussion of capital punishment requires consideration of the traditional purposes of punishment (retribution, deterrence, and incapacitation), as well as moral and legal issues unique to this punishment. These issues include the effect of an erroneous decision to impose death, the morality of state-authorized killing, and the difficulties of imposing the death penalty in a fair and nondiscriminatory manner.

C. ADMINISTRATION OF THE DEATH PENALTY

Capital trials typically are "bifurcated proceedings" involving two phases: 1. the guilt phase; and 2. the penalty phase. In the "guilt phase," the trier of fact determines whether the defendant is guilty of the most serious type of murder. Many states codify "special circumstances" that make a murder serious enough to qualify for the death penalty. Special circumstances may include multiple murders, murder of a law enforcement officer, murder for profit, murder of a witness, murder by an explosive device, murder by torture, or murder during the commission of a particular type of felony. Following the defendant's conviction in the guilt phase and a finding of "special circumstances," a "penalty phase" decides whether or not to administer the death penalty.

1. Eligible Offenses

Generally, the death penalty may be imposed only for intentional murders. In Coker v. Georgia, 433 U.S. 584 (1977), the Supreme Court held that the death penalty is excessive punishment for rape.

a. **Felony murder.** The Supreme Court has allowed application of the death penalty in felony-murder cases where the defendant neither committed the killing nor actually intended to kill, as long as the defendant demonstrated "major participation in the felony committed, combined with reckless indifference to human life." Tison v. Arizona, 481 U.S. 137 (1987).

b. **Open questions.** The Supreme Court has not yet considered whether capital punishment may constitutionally be imposed for crimes such as espionage or aircraft hijacking if no death occurs. While historically crimes like treason have been punished by the death penalty, new laws enacted since the Supreme Court set forth standards for imposition of the death penalty, remain untested. See 18 U.S.C. 3591 et. seq.

2. Standards for Imposing Death Penalty

To avoid constitutional challenges to the death penalty, [see discussion in Ch. 6 (C)], state and federal authorities have adopted various criteria for its imposition. In most jurisdictions, the jury must balance the aggravating circumstances of the offense and the defendant's background against any mitigating circumstances. Only if the jury finds that the statutory aggravating circumstances outweigh the mitigating circumstances may it recommend death.

a. **Aggravating circumstances.** Jurisdictions may adopt their own list of aggravating circumstances. This list provides a guide to judges and juries in applying the death penalty in that jurisdiction. Gregg v. Georgia, 428 U.S. 153 (1976). Common factors include:

- the circumstances of the crime, including:
  - the number of victims
  - the method of death

   - other felonies committed at the time of the killing
   - the reason for the murder; e.g., Was it a murder for hire?
- the identity of the victim (e.g., police officer);
- the defendant's prior criminal conduct;
- the defendant's age at the time of the crime;
- the defendant's level of participation;
- the probability that the defendant will continue to commit criminal acts of violence and pose a threat to society.

b. **Mitigating circumstances.** Generally, jurors may consider any aspects of the defendant's character or the crime in determining whether to impose the death penalty. This list cannot be closed by statute or the judge. Mitigating factors may include:

- defendant's lack of prior criminal conduct;
- defendant's age at the time of the crime;
- whether the victim had induced or facilitated the offense;
- whether defendant committed the offense as a result of provocation or coercion;
- whether defendant's psychosis or mental deficiency caused the offense;
- whether the defendant played a minor role in the offense;
- the defendant's good behavior while awaiting trial.

c. **Factors that may be either aggravating or mitigating circumstances.** Recently, the Supreme Court held that a state law requiring the sentencer to consider the defendant's age at the time of the crime was not unconstitutionally vague. The defendant had challenged the California statute because it did not state whether age should be an aggravating or mitigating factor in the sentencer's determination. The Supreme Court held that there is nothing wrong with a factor potentially being both mitigating and aggravating. Both the defense and the prosecution may present arguments regarding the significance of age in a particular case, leaving the judge or jury to decide whether age mitigates or aggravates the offense. Tuilaepa v. California, 114 S. Ct. 2630 (1994).

3. Model Penal Code Approach

The Model Penal Code does not take a position on whether the death penalty should be authorized for murder, as reflected by the brackets around MPC §210.6. Instead, the MPC provision outlines how those jurisdictions that have adopted the death penalty should impose it. See MPC §210.6. The MPC approach requires a bifurcated proceeding. First, a court or jury determines the defendant's guilt. The court then weighs the enumerated aggravating factors supporting the death penalty against any mitigating circumstance sufficiently substantial to call for leniency.

4. Selecting a Death Penalty Jury

Special rules apply in the selection of a jury for a death penalty case.

a. **Death-qualified jurors.** Jury selection in a death penalty case differs from the process used in noncapital prosecutions. In a death penalty case, the prosecutor may exclude for cause jurors whose views on the death penalty would substantially impair their performance as jurors. Wainwright v. Witt, 469 U.S. 412 (1985). Accordingly, only those who would be willing under proper circumstances to impose the death penalty are qualified for a death penalty jury.

b. **Practical impact of death-qualified juries.** It is widely believed that the death-qualified juries, because their members are willing to impose the death penalty, are also more likely to favor the police and prosecution in the guilt phase of the trial.

D. CONSTITUTIONAL LIMITATIONS ON IMPOSITION OF THE DEATH PENALTY

Until the 1950s, death penalty opponents fought to abolish it through legislative reforms. When that approach proved unsuccessful, opponents attempted to challenge the death penalty on constitutional grounds. To date, the Supreme Court has refused to abolish capital punishment. It has, however, upheld limited constitutional challenges to the scope of the death penalty. The constitutional challenges that may be made to the death penalty include:

- Due Process Challenges
- Cruel and Unusual Punishment Challenges
- Equal Protection Challenges

1. Due Process Challenges

In McGautha v. California, 402 U.S. 183 (1971), the Supreme Court held that the death penalty does not violate procedural due process, even when the jury has unlimited decision-making discretion. However, as discussed infra, unlimited discretion may violate the Eighth Amendment prohibition of "cruel and unusual punishments."

2. Cruel and Unusual Punishment Challenges

In 1972, the Supreme Court held in Furman v. Georgia, 408 U.S. 238 (1972), that capital punishment, as then administered without any clear criteria for its imposition, violated the Eighth Amendment prohibition of "cruel and unusual punishments." However, the Court did not hold the death penalty per se unconstitutional. The Court also did not clarify what administrative systems would satisfy constitutional concerns. In particular, it did not rule on whether states should adopt mandatory death penalty statutes or sentencing guidelines to avoid arbitrary punishments.

a. **Mandatory death penalty statutes.** Some states responded to *Furman* by enacting mandatory death penalty statutes. Those statutes quickly came under challenge and the Court struck them down.

   i. In Woodson v. North Carolina, 428 U.S. 280 (1976), the Supreme Court held that a mandatory death sentence for any first degree murder violates the Eighth Amendment. Writing for three justices, Justice Stewart rejected the mandatory sentence approach, citing three rationales: 1. a mandatory death penalty is inconsistent with contemporary standards of decency; 2. mandatory sentences fail to provide the jury with sufficient guidance; and 3. individual dignity requires a particularized consideration of the relevant aspects of the crime and defendant's character and record. A majority of justices left open the question of the constitutionality of all mandatory death penalty statutes.

   ii. In Sumner v. Shuman, 483 U.S. 66 (1987), the Court struck down mandatory death sentences for prisoners who kill while serving life sentences without possibility of parole. The Court stressed that the Eighth Amendment requires consideration of the character, record, and circumstances of the particular defendant and offense.

b. **Guided discretion standards.** To avoid arbitrariness challenges to death penalty statutes, many states adopted a sentencing guidelines approach, which prescribed the factors for jurors to consider in deciding whether to impose the death penalty. The challenge was then and remains today to delineate these factors narrowly enough to avoid arbitrary and capricious sentencing but broadly enough to allow for individualized consideration of the defendant's background and crime. The Court heard constitutional challenges to the guidelines approach to death penalty sentencing as states began to draft laws in an effort to satisfy the Court's holding in *Furman*.

   i. **Use of sentencing factors.** In Gregg v. Georgia, 428 U.S. 153 (1976), the Supreme Court held that the death penalty is not a per se violation of the Eighth and Fourteenth Amendments. Noting that the constitutional framers accepted capital punishment and that a majority of states enacted it again in the wake of *Furman*, the Court determined that it continues to serve two important social purposes: retribution and deterrence. The Court also decided that the death penalty is not disproportionate punishment for murder. It held that states could constitutionally use a set of standards to guide jurors in reaching their sentencing decisions and that such standards are sufficient to protect against unconstitutional arbitrariness.

ii. Requirements for sentencing factors. In Walton v. Arizona, 497 U.S. 639 (1990), and Lewis v. Jeffers, 497 U.S. 764 (1990), the Supreme Court held that, to satisfy the Eighth and Fourteenth Amendments, a capital sentencing scheme must "suitably direct and limit" the sentencer's discretion "so as to minimize the risk of wholly arbitrary and capricious action." The state must "channel the sentencer's discretion by clear and objective standards that provide specific and detailed guidance, and that make rationally reviewable the process for imposing a sentence of death." Even so, states are afforded broad leeway in what factors may be used to guide the jurors' discretion.

(a) Broad leeway is allowed in defining aggravating and mitigating factors. In Arave v. Creech, 507 U.S. 463, 113 S. Ct. 1534,123 L. Educ. 2d 188 (1993), the Court held that a state could use as an aggravating circumstance the fact that the defendant acted with "utter disregard for human life." This circumstance was not considered unconstitutionally vague because a judge applied it by using existing case law that further defined the phrase as requiring a finding that defendant was a "cold-blooded, pitiless slayer."

(b) Victim impact evidence. The Eighth Amendment does not bar the prosecution from presenting evidence from the victim's family regarding the impact of the murder. Although such evidence is naturally emotional, it is not inconsistent with deliberative process in death penalty cases. Payne v. Tennessee, 501 U.S. 808, 111 S. Ct. 2597, 115 L. Educ. 2d 720 (1991).

(c) Mitigating factors should not be limited. In Lockett v. Ohio, 438 U.S. 586 (1978), the Court struck down a sentencing scheme that mandated a death sentence when the range of mitigating circumstances was too limited. Although the Court was widely split in its reasoning, four justices found that "the sentencer, in all but the rarest kind of capital case, [must] not be precluded from considering as a *mitigating factor*, any aspect of a defendant's character or record and any of the circumstances of the offense . . . ." Id. at 604. Accordingly, the Court has struck down sentencing approaches which proscribed consideration of:

- **Defendant's personal background and emotional circumstances**. Eddings v. Oklahoma, 455 U.S. 104 (1982).
- **Defendant's good behavior in jail while awaiting trial**. Skipper v. South Carolina, 476 U.S. 1 (1986).
- **Defendant's mental retardation and age**. Penry v. Lynaugh, 492 U.S. 302 (1989). However, a state may limit to what extent the jury may consider a defendant's age and mental condition. Graham v. Collins, 113 S. Ct. 892 (1993) (defendant's condition could only be considered in determining whether defendant posed a "continuing threat").

c. **Limited-discretionary standards.** Some states have adopted an approach that requires jurors to impose the death penalty under specific circumstances. In deciding the constitutionality of these standards, courts consider whether the statutes allow the sentencing authority sufficient discretion to consider individual mitigating factors, thereby avoiding arbitrary administration of the death penalty. In general, the Supreme Court has approved of this approach. Jurek v. Texas, 428 U.S. 262 (1972).

Example and Analysis

The Supreme Court upheld a Pennsylvania statute requiring a death sentence if the sentencing jury finds at least one of a list of "aggravating circumstances" and no mitigating circumstances. The jury must also impose the death penalty if the aggravating circumstance "outweighs" any mitigating factors. The Court held that such a scheme does not violate the Eighth Amendment because the statute does not mandate an automatic death sentence and allows the jury to consider any mitigating circumstances offered by the defendant. Blystone v. Pennsylvania, 494 U.S. 299 (1990).

d. **Other Eighth Amendment limitations.** In addition to requiring standards for application of the death penalty, the Eighth Amendment may place limits on whether particular defendants may be executed.

i. **Age limits.** Execution of murderers who were under the age of 16 years at the time of the homicide has been found unconstitutional as contrary to Eighth Amendment's "evolving standards of decency." Thompson v. Oklahoma, 487 U.S. 815 (1988) (plurality opinion). However, the execution of a 16 year-old or 17 year-old does not constitute cruel and unusual punishment per se. Stanford v. Kentucky, 492 U.S. 361 (1989).

ii. **Mental retardation.** The Eighth Amendment does not bar the execution of all persons with mental deficiencies. See Penry v. Lynaugh, 492 U.S. 302 (1989).

iii. **Insanity.** The execution of a murderer who has lost his sanity while on death row is unconstitutional. Ford v. Wainwright, 477 U.S. 399 (1986).

(a) **Forced use of antipyschopathic drugs.** Some states have attempted to force medication on death row inmates in order to render them sane for execution. The United States Supreme Court has not addressed this issue directly, but has held that a mentally ill inmate may be forcibly treated with antipsychopathic drugs when "the inmate is dangerous to himself or others and the treatment is in the inmate's medical interest." Riggins v. Nevada, 504 U.S. 127, 112 S. Ct. 1810, 1815 (1992). State courts have interpreted this holding to mean that drugs may not be administered solely to make the defendant sane for execution because such treatment is not in the defendant's "medical interest." State v. Perry, 610 So. 2d 746 (La. 1992).

3. Equal Protection Limitations

It has been extremely difficult to eliminate arbitrariness and racial discrimination from the administration of the death penalty. Even so, a majority of the Court has rejected attempts to prove that capital punishment violates the Equal Protection Clause of the 14th Amendment.

a. **Racial discrimination.** In McClesky v. Kemp, 481 U.S. 279 (1987), the Supreme Court confronted complex statistical evidence showing racially discriminatory administration of the death penalty. The Baldus study demonstrated that black defendants who kill white victims are much more likely to receive the death penalty than whites who kill blacks. The Court held that an equal protection challenge to the death penalty required clear evidence of purposeful discrimination and rejected this study as merely proof of discriminatory impact.

b. **Gender discrimination.** The Court has not yet considered equal protection attacks on the death penalty based on gender discrimination. Women are underrepresented on death row. Additionally, defendants who kill women are much less likely to receive the death penalty than defendants who kill men.

FIGURE 6-1

DEATH PENALTY	
Arguments in Favor vs. Arguments Against the Death Penalty	
1. Sanctity of human life; Appropriate retribution 2. Deterrence 3. Incapacitation 4. Historical use	1. Sanctity of human life 2. No proven deterrence 3. Alternative methods for incapacitation 4. Expense 5. Error and Irrevocability 6. Discriminatory Administration
Administration of the Death Penalty	
1. Bifurcated proceeding	Guilt phase vs. penalty phase
2. Eligible offenses	Intentional murders or certain felony murders or treason
Constitutional Limitations	
1. Procedural Due Process	No per se violation
2. Cruel & Unusual Punishment	Mandatory or arbitrary death sentences
3. Limitations	Under age 16 yrs. No limitation because of mental retardation No execution of insane
4. Equal Protection	Requires proof of purposeful discrimination

Review Questions and Answers

DEATH PENALTY

Questions: True or false?

1. The death penalty is a proven deterrent.
2. Arbitrary standards for imposing the death penalty violate a defendant's 14th Amendment right to due process.
3. Death penalty cases are handled in bifurcated proceedings.
4. In *McClesky v. Kemp*, the Supreme Court opened the door for more challenges to the death penalty based upon equal protection violations.
5. Evidence of mental retardation and age must be allowed as mitigating circumstances in death penalty cases.
6. Good behavior in jail is not a legitimate factor to be considered in death penalty sentencing.
7. Capital punishment constitutes cruel and unusual punishment if imposed in an arbitrary manner.
8. The death penalty is not allowed in felony-murder cases.

Answers: 1. F; 2. T; 3. T; 4. F; 5. T; 6. F; 7. T; 8. F

Question: Defendant Enrique Muñoz, age 18, is charged with killing his mother and father with a shotgun. At trial, the prosecution proved that Muñoz shot his parents at close range while they were sitting on the family couch filling out his college applications and eating ice cream. When his mother tried to crawl away, he went out to his car, reloaded, and shot her again. Defendant had purchased the gun with a false driver's license and enlisted friends to serve as his alibi. Muñoz stood to inherit at least $2 million from his parents. After the guilt phase of the trial, the jury returned a verdict of first-degree murder. It further found that Muñoz was eligible for the death penalty because he had engaged in multiple murders and had acted with a profit motive.

At the penalty phase of trial, the defense called an expert witness who testified that Muñoz had been psychologically abused by his parents. The expert witness also suggested that the defendant may be mildly retarded. Muñoz himself claimed that he was sexually abused but offered no physical evidence to support this allegation. In rebuttal, the prosecution called family members who testified that Muñoz was never abused and that the family wanted Muñoz to be executed for what he had done. The defense called other family members who testified that they wanted Muñoz's life spared. They acknowledged that the crime was particularly heinous, but they pointed out that Muñoz had never been in trouble before and the family could not bear another loss.

Assuming the jurisdiction permits imposition of the death penalty, would it be appropriate in Muñoz's case? Is there anything about the defendant's background that prevents the imposition of the death penalty?

Answer:

1. *Appropriateness of Death Penalty.* In most jurisdictions, there are a series of mitigating and aggravating factors that the jury must consider that guides its discretion in penalty. In this case, the prosecution will argue that the defendant's crime is aggravated by its particularly brutal nature, the fact that the defendant would be willing to commit such a crime at such a young age, the defendant's sole responsibility for the killing, and the enormous pain the crime has inflicted on the victim's family.

In response, the defense will argue that the defendant has no prior criminal record, was provoked by his parents to commit the crime, acted out of an emotional deficiency, poses no danger to society if he spends his life in jail, and committed this crime because of his youth and lack of maturity.

Ultimately, the jury must balance these factors to determine whether the aggravating factors outweigh the mitigating factors justifying the most extreme of sanctions—the death penalty.

2. *Limitations on Imposition.* There are two factors about the defendant which may affect the imposition of the death penalty. The first is the possibility that the defendant may be mildly retarded. However, this will probably not prevent capital punishment because the Eighth Amendment does not necessarily bar the execution of persons with mental deficiencies. The second factor is the defendant's age. The defendant's youth may prevent the use of the death penalty. The execution of murderers under the age of 16 at the time of the homicide has been found unconstitutional due to the Eighth Amendment's "evolving standards of decency." In order to decide if the defendant's age will prevent the imposition of the death penalty, more evidence is needed to determine if the defendant was under the age of 16 at the time of the murders.

CAUSATION

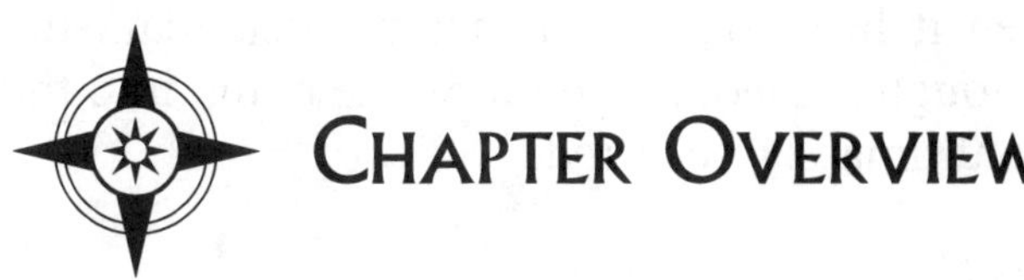

CHAPTER OVERVIEW

If a crime requires that a defendant's conduct lead to a particular result, issues of causation may arise. For example, homicide requires that the defendant's acts result in the death of the victim. An intended death that occurs in an unintended way or an unintended death resulting from the defendant's action raises causation issues.

There is no precise test to determine causation. The issue is presented to the jury for its general consideration. Nonetheless, common law has developed some standards for determining causation which also appear in the Model Penal Code.

Chapter 7 addresses the following causation issues:

- But-for *or* Actual Cause
- Proximate Cause
  - Foreseeability
  - Intervening acts
  - Subsequent acts
- Transferred Intent

A. INTRODUCTION

Causation issues arise only in the context of those crimes requiring a specific result. The most important of these crimes is homicide. When a court decides that a defendant has caused an unlawful result, the law holds that the defendant should be punished for his or her acts. However, if the result that occurs is too attenuated or distant from defendant's acts, the law will not punish the defendant. Public policy principles play a key role in any discussion of causation.

1. Examples

a. Defendant places poison by his sick wife's bedside, intending that she drink it. During the night she dies of a heart attack without having consumed the drink. Although the defendant's act could have led to his wife's death, the actual result was not directly related to defendant's act and the law would not punish him for the death.

b. Defendant throws a live hand grenade into a room. Before the bomb can explode, a person in the room tosses it outside. The bomb falls into the crowded street, exploding and killing several persons. If the court finds causation, then it has determined that the defendant deserves punishment even though someone else threw the bomb into the location where the deaths ultimately occurred.

2. Comparison with Tort Law

Issues of causation are relatively rare in criminal law. Most crimes do *not* require a harmful result. Causation issues are much more prevalent in tort cases. Although tort law uses a similar vocabulary for causation, the same rules may not apply because of the differing consequences of civil and criminal liability.

3. Lack of Statutory Standards

Most state codes have no explicit rules for determining causation. The courts generally resolve causation on the basis of evolving common law principles.

4. Model Penal Code

The Model Penal Code addresses causation in Sec. 2.03. Approximately 12 states have adopted the Model Penal Code approach, discussed infra.

5. Omissions as Legal Causes

Both affirmative acts and omissions can be legal causes.

B. COMMON LAW APPROACH TO ISSUES OF CAUSATION

Courts use a similar vocabulary in discussing causation. The basic approach to determine causation is:

Step #1: Actual Cause (But-for Cause)
- Was the defendant a link in the chain of causation?

Step #2: Proximate Cause (Legal Cause)
- Were the defendant's actions a sufficiently direct cause of the harm to warrant imposing criminal liability?

1. Actual Cause

The first step in determining causation is to establish whether defendant's conduct was a link in the chain of events that led to the harmful result. Actual cause is also referred to as cause in fact, or but-for cause.

a. **Test for actual cause.** Traditionally, courts have determined actual cause by asking, "But for" defendant's conduct, would the harmful result have occurred? If the answer is "no," there is actual cause.

EXAMPLE AND ANALYSIS

In People v. Acosta, 284 Cal. Rep. 117 (1991), while police were chasing the defendant, two helicopters involved in the pursuit collided. Three of the occupants in one of the helicopters died. The threshold question for the court was whether defendant's act of fleeing from the police was the "actual cause" of the deaths. But for the defendant's act (fleeing the police), would the injury have occurred? The court found that "but for Acosta's conduct of fleeing the police, the helicopters would never have been in position for the crash." Therefore, Acosta's actions were an actual cause of the crash.

---

b. **Alternative test.** Defendant's conduct need not be the sole and exclusive factor in the victim's death. It only needs to be a link in the chain of causation. Accordingly, it is more precise to ask whether defendant's conduct played any role in causing the harmful result instead of whether defendant was the "but-for" cause.

i. **Concurrent causes.** In some cases, there are concurrent causes for an injury involving more than one actor. The conduct of either actor may be a "cause in fact" of the result, even though "but for" one defendant's conduct, the harmful result still would have occurred.

(a) **Example.** Defendant A puts poison in the victim's food. While the victim is swallowing the food, defendant B shoots him. Both defendants are "causes in fact" of the victim's death even though death would have occurred even without either one of the defendants' conduct.

(b) **Acceleration theory.** Where two actors cause a death, the prosecution may argue cause-in-fact against the second actor on the theory that his or her acts accelerated the victim's death. This theory is valid as long as the evidence supports it. See Oxendine v. State, 528 A.2d 870 (1987) (evidence insufficient to prove defendant's blows to child who had already been beaten by a codefendant accelerated the child's death.)

2. Proximate Cause

After the defendant's conduct is established as an actual cause of the required result, the next step is to decide whether it is a sufficiently direct cause to warrant imposing criminal liability. "Proximate cause" is the term historically used to designate those results for which a defendant will be held responsible.

a. **Test for proximate cause.** No specific legal formula exists to determine proximate cause. *People v. Acosta*, supra. Causation is viewed as a matter of common sense. However, courts generally consider some basic factors to determine whether proximate cause exists:

- Was the harm foreseeable?
- How should the courts treat any intervening acts?

b. **Foreseeability.** The most important factor in determining proximate cause is whether the resulting harm was foreseeable. A foreseeable harm means proximate cause exists.

EXAMPLE AND ANALYSIS

In *People v. Acosta*, supra, helicopters collided while the police were chasing the defendant. Defendant claimed there was no proximate cause because such a crash had never occurred before. However, the court held that the probability of a two-helicopter collision was not so extraordinary as to be unforeseeable.

Note: The court reversed the defendant's conviction in *Acosta* anyway because there was insufficient evidence of malice.

i. **Deference to the jury.** In general, the court gives great deference to the trier of fact's determination of whether a defendant was the cause of a harmful result.

ii. **Sufficiently dangerous activity to warrant criminal responsibility.** If the defendant is engaged in dangerous activities, the court is more inclined to find the harm foreseeable, even if the specific manner of the harm could not have been foreseen.

EXAMPLES AND ANALYSIS

In People v. Arzon, 92 Misc. 2d 739 (1978), the defendant set a fire on the fifth floor of a building. A separate fire broke out on the second floor and trapped the responding firefighters. One firefighter died. The court found both actual cause and proximate cause.

- *Actual Cause*: Defendant's fire was a link in the chain of events that resulted in the firefighter's death. Had the defendant not set the fire, the firefighters would not have been at the building.
- *Proximate Cause*: It was foreseeable that firefighters would respond, exposing them to a life-threatening situation. Although technically a second fire led to the firefighter's death, defendant should have foreseen the possibility of the harm. Defendant's behavior was sufficiently dangerous to impose criminal responsibility.
- *Note*: As the *Arzon* case illustrates, a defendant does not ordinarily have to foresee the manner in which harm will result, only that there is likely to be such harm. In *Arzon*, it was not foreseeable that there would be a second fire, but injury from any fire was foreseeable.

In People v. Kibbe, 35 N.Y.2d 407 (1974), defendants robbed an intoxicated victim and left him, with his clothing half-removed, by the side of a dark road in subfreezing temperatures. A passing truck struck and killed the victim.

- *Actual Cause*. "But for" defendants' acts, the victim would not have been in a position to be struck by the passing truck.
- *Proximate Cause*. Because it was easily foreseeable that the victim would die by the side of the road, it was not necessary that the exact manner of death (being struck by a truck) be foreseeable. Defendant's conduct need not be the sole and exclusive factor in the victim's death.
- *Note*. Ordinarily, it is sufficient if the defendant should have foreseen the ultimate harm that could occur. Defendant need not foresee exactly how that harm will occur.

iii. **Warning.** Because there are no fixed rules to determine when causation exists, courts can use the doctrine to preclude liability even in those situations where dangerous conditions exist. Dangerous conditions *alone* are insufficient to prove causation. The court must be satisfied that defendant's acts caused the harmful results in a way that justifies imposing criminal liability.

Example and Analysis

In People v. Warner-Lambert Co., 51 N.Y.2d 295 (1980), defendant corporation and several of its officers were indicted for manslaughter when a massive explosion at one of its factories killed an employee. Although their insurance carrier had warned defendants that dangerous conditions existed in the factory, the court found insufficient evidence that an act by the defendants or their machinery triggered the deadly explosion. No one could prove how the explosion occurred.

---

iv. **Foreseeable harm vs. foreseeable manner of harm.** Ordinarily, defendants need not foresee the actual manner in which harm will occur, only the fact that such harm is likely to occur. However, when a defendant's otherwise socially useful conduct leads to a harmful result, the court may require that the actual manner of the harm be foreseeable and preventable.

(a) No requirement that defendant foresee manner of harm

- **Example**. In the *Twilight Zone* movie case, three actors were killed on a movie set when a special effects explosion caused a helicopter to explode and fall on them. The judge ruled that the precise cause of a crash that killed three actors was irrelevant as long as the risk of death was "reasonably foreseeable."
- **Example**. In People v. Deitsch, 97 A.D.2d 327 (1983), the court held the prosecution need not show the exact cause of a deadly fire if it proved defendants controlled the building and were aware of its dangerous conditions.

(b) **Foreseeing manner of harm required in unusual cases.** In People v. Warner-Lambert Co., 51 N.Y.2d 295 (1980), the court dismissed an indictment because the prosecution could show only that defendants knew they had dangerous conditions in their warehouse but could not prove exact cause of a deadly explosion. The courts opinion suggests that where the defendant is engaged in socially useful conduct, courts will be more strict in requiring not only proof that the harmful result was foreseeable, but also proof that the defendants could have foreseen the manner in which the harm occurred.

v. **Vulnerability of the victim.** Generally, a defendant "takes his victim as he finds him." Thus, a defendant need not foresee a victim's peculiar frailties or vulnerabilities that may aggravate the harm in order to be criminally responsible for the result.

(a) **Example.** In People v. Brackett, 117 Ill. 2d 170 (1987), defendant beat an 85-year-old woman. Although her wounds healed, she later became depressed and died when she needed to be tube fed. The court held defendant was responsible for the death.

(b) **Example.** In State v. Cummings, 46 N.C. App. 680 (1980), defendant beat a victim who died of asphyxiation due to an impaired gag reflex. Because the vomit that choked the victim resulted from the beating, defendant was held responsible for the death regardless of the victim's impaired condition.

(c) **Victim refuses treatment.** If a victim refuses medical treatment because of religious beliefs, defendant still bears responsibility for the ultimate harm caused because the defendant must "take the victim as he finds him." See Regina v. Blaue, (1975) 1 W.L.R. 1411 (victim refused blood transfusion based on her religious beliefs; defendant's attack constituted proximate cause).

vi. **Transferred intent.** If the defendant intends to harm victim A but accidentally harms victim B, proximate cause exists. As long as the defendant intends to injure, the defendant need not foresee who the actual victim may be.

Example. D shoots X intending to kill her. D misses and hits Y instead, killing her. D is guilty of murdering Y.

vii. **Additional harm.** If the defendant intends to harm one victim but accidentally harms another more seriously, common law holds the defendant responsible for the more serious harm committed.

Example. D attempts to strike his wife but accidentally hits their baby. D is responsible for intentionally striking the child, even if that is a more serious offense. State v. Contra-Ramirez, 149 Ariz. 377 (1986).

3. Intervening Acts

The second part of the proximate cause analysis is determining whether any intervening acts broke the chain of causation and therefore make it unjust to punish the defendant.

a. **Terminology.** An intervening act that breaks the chain of causation is called a "superseding intervening act" or an "independent intervening act." If the intervening act does not break the chain of causation, it is a "dependent intervening act."

b. **Warning.** No set rules govern when an intervening act breaks the chain of causation. The issue is whether the original actor should be relieved of responsibility because of a natural occurrence or another person's intervening action.

c. **General approaches to intervening acts.** Although there are no set rules to determine when an intervening act breaks the chain of causation, courts generally analyze:

- whether the intervening act was foreseeable;
- what type of intervening act was involved.

i. **Foreseeable intervening acts.** If the intervening act is foreseeable, then it is unlikely to be considered a superseding intervening act. If the intervening act is unforeseeable, defendant has a better chance of successfully arguing that the intervening act broke the chain of causation.

ii. **Type of intervening acts.** The courts also examine the type of intervening act that occurred.

(a) **Acts of nature.** Acts of nature, such as inclement weather, do not ordinarily break the chain of causation. See *Kibbe*, supra. However, unforeseeable freak acts of nature, like earthquakes, may be sufficient to break the chain of causation.

(b) **Medical maltreatment.** Unless intentional, or grossly incompetent, bad medical treatment does *not* break the chain of causation. In general, "ordinary" medical malpractice does not constitute a superseding, intervening cause. Hall v. State, 199 Ind. 592 (1927). But see Regina v. Jordan, 40 Crim. App. 152 (1956) (rare case finding gross medical negligence sufficient to break chain of causation).

- **Example.** Defendant stabs the victim. Although the wound is not life-threatening, incompetent medical care permits an infection to develop and the victim dies. The incompetent medical care does *not* break the chain of causation.
- **Example.** Defendant stabs the victim. A doctor who doesn't like the victim intentionally uses the wrong medicine in treating the victim who later dies. The doctor's acts may break the chain of causation.

(c) **Intervening disease.** Diseases contracted by victims during medical treatment ordinarily do *not* break the chain of causation because disease and infection are foreseeable. However, a particularly rare disease, such as scarlet fever, contracted directly from the doctor, may relieve the defendant of responsibility. See Bush v. Commonwealth, 78 Ky. 268 (1880).

EXAMPLE AND ANALYSIS

What would happen if the victim contracted HIV from a blood transfusion after being wounded by the defendant? If the victim subsequently died of AIDS, the case could be argued both ways. The prosecution would assert that defendant who caused the need for the transfusion bears responsibility because it is foreseeable that the victim might receive tainted blood. The defense would claim that tainted blood is not foreseeable and is an independent, superseding cause of death. Also, the "year-and-a-Day" rule might absolve defendant from responsibility, depending on the length of time the victim suffered from the disease before dying. See Ch. 5(B)(1)(b) supra.

(d) Acts of the victim

- **Victim's Voluntary Acts.** A victim who voluntarily brings harm upon herself may relieve the defendant of responsibility, even if the defendant provided an opportunity for that harm.
  - **Assisted Suicide.** Jurisdictions differ on how to treat assisted suicide. In most jurisdictions, the defendant will not be guilty of homicide because the victim's acts of committing suicide break the chain of causation. Instead, the defendant may be guilty of a separate crime of "assisting a suicide." People v. Campbell, 124 Mich. App. 333 (1983); People v. Kevorkian, 205 Mich. App. 180 (1994).
- **Involuntary Acts of Victim.** Generally, when a victim acts in response to the defendant's wrongful acts, the victim's action is not a superseding intervening cause. A victim in this situation does not voluntarily choose her actions.
- **Victim's Escape Attempts.** A victim's attempts to escape are often viewed as involuntary and do not break the chain of causation. When the victim engages in desperate acts of escape, defendant's acts have deprived the victim of her ability to make independent, autonomous decisions. See Stephenson v. State, 205 Ind. 141 (1932) (victim tried to escape abduction and sexual attacks by taking poison;

defendant responsible for murder); Rex v. Beech, 23 Cox Crim. Cas. 181 (1912) (victim tried to escape by jumping out of window; defendant responsible for murder).

- **Victim's Attempts to Elude Captor.** In People v. Kern, 545 N.Y.S.2d 4 (App. Div. 1989) [''Howard Beach Incident''], three white youths, wielding bats and clubs, chased two black youths. The black youths ran onto the highway to escape the attack where a passing car struck and killed them. The white youths proximately caused the deaths.

(e) **Additional Perpetrators.** Courts have taken two approaches to evaluate acts of subsequent, intervening perpetrators. Under one theory, if either defendant's act is sufficient to cause death, both will be held responsible for the ultimate harm. Alternatively, courts have held the first perpetrator responsible for an attempt and the second perpetrator responsible for the completed crime.

Example and Analysis

Defendant A stabs victim X. Before X bleeds to death, defendant B shoots X. Because there are strong reasons to punish both A and B, some courts will hold both A and B responsible for murder. Other courts will hold A responsible for attempt and B responsible for murder.

(f) **Omissions.** Failure to act, when there is a legal duty to do so, is sufficient to cause a criminal result. For example, if a baby sitter fails to rescue a drowning child, the babysitter is liable for the drowning. Courts are reluctant, however, to recognize omissions as intervening causes breaking the chain of causation. The person who initially set the harmful events into motion will still be liable, even if the person who failed to intervene may also have some responsibility.

Example and Analysis

A robber shoots and injures a victim. An ambulance driver is called and can easily provide treatment to the victim. However, because the ambulance driver hates the victim, he refuses to treat the victim and the victim dies. The ambulance driver's omission does not absolve the robber of liability for the victim's death. People v. McGee, 31 Cal. 2d 243, 187 P.2d 706 (1947) (wrongful failure to provide proper medical attention not intervening, superseding cause).

(g) **Concurrent causes.** Courts differ on how to punish two individuals whose reckless conduct leads to a harmful result. In some jurisdictions, only the defendant who most directly caused the result is held responsible. In other jurisdictions, all defendants who jointly participate in the enterprise are responsible.

Examples and Analysis

A and B drag-race. B loses control and is killed trying to pass A's car. In some jurisdictions, A is not responsible because the victim voluntarily created the risk of his own injury. Commonwealth v. Root, 403 Pa. 571 (1961). However, other jurisdictions will hold A responsible because A directly participated in the series of acts that led to B's death. State v. McFadden, 320 N.W.2d 608 (1982).

In Commonwealth v. Atencio, 345 Mass. 627 (1963), defendant played Russian roulette with the victim. The court held that defendant's mutual encouragement in a joint enterprise was sufficient to prove proximate cause. But see Lewis v. State, 474 So. 2d 766 (Ala. Crim. App. 1985) (holding no criminal liability for surviving Russian roulette player).

---

4. Summary of Common Law Causation

Courts are not always consistent in analyzing causation. Causation involves a determination of whether the defendant's acts are sufficiently connected to a harmful result to deserve punishment. In making this determination, courts generally look at:

Step 1: Actual Cause
- Were defendant's acts a link in the chain of causation?

Step 2: Proximate Cause
- Was the harm foreseeable?

Step 3: Intervening Acts
- Should any intervening acts excuse defendant from responsibility for the harm?

STUDY TIP

In most cases, the issue of how to treat intervening acts is subsumed within the discussion of "proximate cause." If an act breaks the chain of causation, there is no proximate cause. If the intervening act is foreseeable and sufficiently related to the defendant's acts, proximate cause exists.

EXAM TIP

There is ordinarily no definitive answer as to whether causation is satisfied. In answering a causation issue, students should apply the proper vocabulary of actual cause, proximate cause, foreseeability, and intervening acts in discussing why or why not the defendant should be held culpable. It may be helpful to consider whether the purposes of punishment are served by finding the defendant to be the cause of the harm. Are the defendant's acts sufficiently culpable to deserve punishment? Was the harm sufficiently foreseeable so that punishing the defendant will deter him and others from committing similar acts in the future?

C. MODEL PENAL CODE APPROACH

Very few states have adopted a statutory approach to define causation. Accordingly, the Model Penal Code is not as influential in causation issues as it is in other areas.

1. General Approach of MPC §2.03

As at common law, the Model Penal Code addresses the key issues of whether there was: a. "cause in fact," MPC §2.03(1)(a), and b. "proximate cause." MPC §§2.03(2),(3).

a. **Cause in fact.** The MPC requires that the defendant's conduct be "an antecedent but for which the result in question would not have occurred." **Note.** The MPC does not explicitly address the issue of "concurrent causes."

b. **Proximate cause.** Rather than use common law terminology, the MPC addresses directly the question of how to treat results that differ from those designed or contemplated by the defendant. Whether there is causation from these differing results may depend on the level of mens rea required for the crime.

   i. **Different victim.** Principles of "transferred intent" apply under the MPC. If the defendant intends to harm A and accidentally injures B, the defendant is still culpable. MPC §§2.03(2),(3).

   ii. **Lesser level of harm.** If the defendant causes less harm than intended, under the MPC the defendant is only responsible for that harm that resulted. MPC §211.1(2)(a).

   iii. **Greater or different harm.** If the defendant causes more harm than intended, the MPC requires the trier of fact to determine "whether the harm is too remote or accidental in its occurrence to have a [just] bearing on the actor's liability or gravity of his offense." MPC §§2.03(2)(b),(3)(b). This approach allows for a case-by-case determination of whether the defendant's acts were dangerous enough and intent culpable enough to deserve punishment.

   iv. **Strict liability crimes.** A strict liability crime still requires a causation analysis. The Model Penal Code requires proof that the actual result is "a probable consequence of the actor's conduct." MPC §2.03(4).

EXAMPLE AND ANALYSIS

Defendant is charged with felony murder. The prosecution need not establish that defendant intended the death, but it still must prove that the death resulted from the felonious conduct. Thus, if a bank teller is electrocuted when she pushes an emergency button during a robbery, the robber would not be liable for the teller's death.

FIGURE 7-1

CAUSATION	
Step 1	Actual Cause • "But-for" • Link in chain of causation
Step 2	Proximate Cause • Harm foreseeable enough to hold defendant culpable?
Step 3	Intervening Acts • Foreseeable? • Should intervening acts excuse the defendant from responsibility for harm?

REVIEW QUESTION AND ANSWER

Question: Zack was irate after Taylor fired him from his job. Zack grabbed a gun, jumped in his car and raced toward Taylor's home. At one point, Zack made an illegal right turn from the far left lane. The car behind Zack swerved to miss him and killed a bystander.

When Zack arrived at Taylor's home, Taylor was in the front yard talking to a neighbor. Zack pulled out his gun and ran screaming toward Taylor. Zack fired a shot at Taylor, but it accidentally hit a mail carrier across the street who immediately died. Fearing for her own life, Taylor ran into the street to summon help. A sudden gust of wind caused a pole to fall on Taylor, trapping her. Unable to move or alert traffic, Taylor was hit by a passing car.

Taylor was rushed to the hospital. The doctor on duty told Taylor that he could save her life but that Taylor would probably be a paraplegic after the operation. Taylor said she would rather die than be paralyzed. The doctor then tried an experimental treatment, but it failed and Taylor died. An autopsy revealed that the doctor had not properly administered the experimental treatment.

If Zack is charged with the homicides of the bystander, mail carrier, and Taylor, is the causation element for each crime satisfied?

Answer: This hypothetical raises several causation issues.
A. *Causation for the Death of Bystander*
1. *Actual Cause.* Even though the bystander was hit by another car, "but for" Zack's reckless driving, the accident would not have occurred. Thus, the first requirement for causation is satisfied.

2. *Proximate Cause.* The prosecution will argue that it was *foreseeable* that a person would be injured or killed by Zack's reckless driving and that it is irrelevant that Zack did not foresee the exact manner of the killing. As for the *intervening act* of another driver, the prosecution will argue that the driver did not act independently and there is no reason to punish him and relieve Zack of responsibility. Zack should have foreseen that he could cause someone else to have an accident, and he should be held responsible for his dangerous activities. Accordingly, the other driver is not a "superseding intervening act."

B. *Death of Mail Carrier.*
The doctrine of "transferred intent" applies to the death of the mail carrier. Zack intended to kill Taylor but accidentally shot the mail carrier. Under both common law and the Model Penal Code, Zack is responsible for the killing, even though he shot the wrong victim.

C. *Death of Taylor*
1. *Actual Cause.* The prosecution would argue that "but for" Zack attacking Taylor, Taylor would never have set into motion the series of acts that led to her death. Zack's acts were, at minimum, a link in the chain of causation.
2. *Proximate Cause.* The more difficult issue is whether Zack is the "proximate cause" of Taylor's death. Although Taylor's death was foreseeable once Zack decided to attack her with a gun, the manner of death was so far removed from that intended, and there were so many intervening acts, the courts and juries may believe that "the harm is too remote or accidental in its occurrence to have a just bearing on the actor's liability or gravity of his offense." MPC §2.03(2)(b).

To determine whether Zack would be held responsible, one must analyze the effects of the many intervening acts that occurred. First, Taylor chose to run in the street rather than be shot by Zack. This act by a victim is both foreseeable and involuntary. When a victim is injured trying to escape, the court ordinarily does not view the victim's acts as superseding.

Second, an act of nature caused Taylor to be trapped and hit by a car. Ordinarily, acts of nature do not break the chain of causation unless they are so unforeseeable that they are not part of the ordinary risk of life. Depending on other facts, a gust of wind may not qualify as a "freak" act of nature.

Third, the intervening act of Taylor being hit by a passing car is similar to the *Kibbe* situation in which a robbery victim was left in a weakened condition by the side of the road. When a passing truck struck and killed the victim, the court found that there was still proximate cause because the defendant should have foreseen the risk of danger and nothing about the intervening act argued in favor of relieving the defendant of culpability. Alternately, one may analogize Taylor's situation to the facts in the "Howard Beach" incident in which the victims were killed while attempting to escape the defendant's attack.

Fourth, Taylor's decision to refuse surgery may constitute a victim's intervening act. However, unless a victim is able to make a fully voluntary, autonomous decision, acts by the victim are not seen as breaking the chain of causation.

Finally, the doctor's maltreatment of Taylor would not ordinarily break the chain of causation because it was not intentional, and all medical treatment involves a certain amount of risk.

Despite all of these intervening acts, a court is likely to find that Zack proximately caused Taylor's death because he was trying to kill Taylor and is therefore criminally culpable for the resulting death.

ATTEMPT

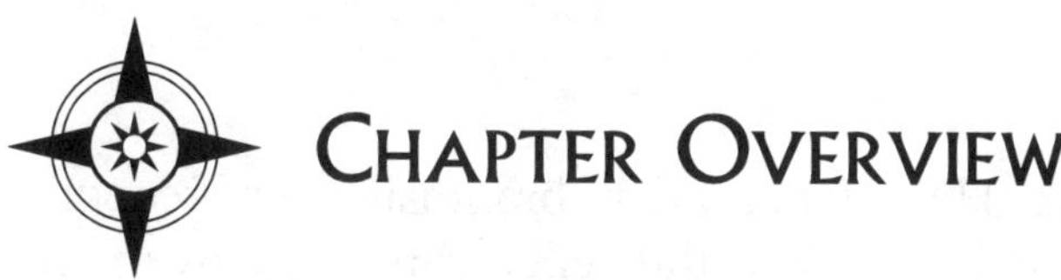

CHAPTER OVERVIEW

A defendant who is unsuccessful in causing a harmful result may still be responsible for attempting to commit a crime. "Attempt" is the crime of trying to commit another crime. It is an "inchoate crime" because of the criminal responsibility it attaches prior to completion of the substantive offense. However, if a defendant successfully completes a substantive offense, there is no separate crime of attempt because it merges into the completed offense.

Attempt is designed to punish defendants who have clearly shown intent to violate the law and who have taken enough steps toward that goal to justify law enforcement stepping in to protect society. The prosecution must prove two elements for the crime of attempt: mens rea and actus reus. Because the crime is never completed, the prosecution need not prove a result or causation.

Chapter 8 addresses the following issues relating to the crime of attempt:

- Background of the Crime of Attempt
  - Theories of punishment
  - Inchoate crimes
- Elements of the Crime of Attempt
  - Mens rea
    - Common law standard
    - Model Penal Code standard
  - Actus reus
    - Common law standard
    - Model Penal Code standard
- Defenses to the Crime of Attempt
  - Abandonment
  - Impossibility

- Related Crimes
  - Stalking
  - Solicitation

A. INTRODUCTION

Attempt is a separate crime. It punishes a defendant who tries to commit an offense but never completes it. To prove an attempt, the prosecution must establish that the defendant met the mens rea and actus reus requirements. The key issues are: 1. Did the defendant have sufficient intent to commit the crime?, and 2. Did the defendant take enough steps to justify punishment?

1. Example

Defendant wants to rob a bank. He enters a bank, brandishes his weapon, and demands money from a teller. Before the teller can hand over the money, the security guard apprehends the defendant. Defendant is guilty of attempted robbery.

2. General Requirements

The general rule is that a defendant must have the purpose to commit the crime and have taken a substantial step toward that goal to be guilty of attempt.

Mens Rea	Purposeful or specific intent
Actus Reus	Substantial step toward completion of the crime

B. HISTORICAL BACKGROUND

Common law first recognized the crime of attempt as a misdemeanor. Today, all American jurisdictions prohibit the crime of attempt. Statutory definitions rely heavily on both common law and Model Penal Code concepts of attempt.

1. Punishment for Attempt

Initially, attempt was only punishable as a misdemeanor. Today, attempt may be charged as a felony, although most jurisdictions punish it less severely than the completed crime.

a. **Majority approach.** In most jurisdictions, an attempt carries lesser punishment than the completed crime.

i. **Examples.** In California, attempt carries a maximum sentence of not more than 1/2 of the maximum term authorized for the completed offense. Cal. Penal Code §664. Similarly, in New

York, the sentence for an attempt is one classification below that for the completed crime. N.Y. Penal Law §110.05.

ii. **Rationale.** Because the defendant's acts caused less harm to society than completion of the substantive crime would have, there is less demand for retribution. If deterrence is the goal of punishment, one must be wary of punishing a defendant equally for unsuccessful and successful efforts. By doing so, the punishment eliminates any incentive for a defendant to abandon the criminal acts prior to completion.

b. **Minority/Model Penal Code approach.** A substantial minority of states as well as federal law follow the Model Penal Code approach, making attempt punishable to the same extent as the completed crime, except for crimes punishable by death or life imprisonment. MPC §5.05(1).

i. **Rationale.** Retribution (i.e., blameworthiness) ordinarily focuses on the defendant's intent, not on the success of the defendant's effort. The defendant who attempts a crime intends the same amount of harm as one who is successful in his or her efforts and should receive equal punishment. A defendant's punishment should not depend on good or bad luck in completing the plan. Additionally, the defendant who attempts a crime must be deterred. That person also poses a danger to society. See H.L.A. Hart, Punishment, and Responsibility 129-131 (1968).

ii. **Example.** In Pennsylvania, a defendant who attempts a crime faces the same punishment as the defendant who completes the crime. Pa. Stat. Ann. tit. 18, §905.

iii. **Note.** The mere fact that an attempt is "punishable" to the same degree as a completed crime does not mean that the defendant will receive the same punishment. To the extent its discretion allows, the court may consider the amount of harm inflicted or not inflicted on society in deciding what sentence to impose.

C. POLICY CONSIDERATIONS

A variety of policy considerations guide the courts in determining the elements of attempt

1. Police Intervention

At what point does it make sense for the police to intervene? If an attempt is not completed until a crime is nearly accomplished, it may be too late for the police to prevent harm. However, if an attempt is completed as soon as a defendant takes a step toward committing a crime, innocent people engaged in equivocal behavior may face punishment.

2. Not Punishing for Bad Thoughts

In general, the law does not punish bad thoughts. Rather, a crime requires criminal intent and a criminal act. Attempt law must require sufficient acts to prevent punishing merely bad thoughts.

3. Chance for Abandonment

Punishment of conduct at too early a stage offers the defendant little reason or opportunity to change his or her conduct to avoid completing the crime.

4. Certainty that Defendant Intended to Commit a Crime

Because there is no harm by which to gauge the defendant's culpability, problems of proof support setting the mens rea requirement for attempt at a high level to ensure that punishment is merited.

D. ELEMENTS OF ATTEMPT

As a separate crime, attempt includes its own elements. The prosecution must establish a mens rea and actus reus for the crime.

1. Mens Rea

Attempt is a specific intent crime that traditionally requires the highest level of mens rea; i.e., purposefulness.

a. **Majority approach purpose/specific intent required.** Under the traditional majority rule, a defendant must have the purpose to commit the crime to be found guilty of attempt, even when recklessness or some lesser mens rea would suffice for conviction of the completed offense.

Example and Analysis

Defendant is charged with attempting to murder another driver by shooting a gun at the victim's car. Defendant claims that he was only trying to scare the victim and didn't intend to kill him. If the jury believes this defense, defendant will *not* be guilty of attempted murder because his purpose was not to kill the victim. This rule applies even though defendant would be guilty of murder if he knew it was virtually certain he would kill his victim or he acted with gross recklessness. See People v. Kraft, 133 Ill. App. 3d 294 (1985).

---

i. **Rationale.** Because attempt crimes do not require a showing of actual harm, courts want to be absolutely certain that, given the defendant's intent, it would only be a matter of time or luck before defendant would cause serious harm. Accordingly, courts require the highest level of intent — purpose or specific intent — to prove attempt.

ii. **Knowledge vs. purpose.** In most jurisdictions, knowledge of the likely consequences of one's act is insufficient to prove the mens rea for attempt. People v. Kraft, supra. The defendant must act with the purpose to cause the harmful result.

   (a) **Example.** In a suicidal fit, defendant shoots directly at police officers to encourage them to shoot back at and kill him. Even though defendant may know that he will likely kill an officer, if he does not have the purpose to kill, there is no attempted murder. People v. Kraft, supra.

   (b) **Example.** Defendant uses a barbecue inside his friend's living room. Although he knows that it is extremely likely that he will ignite the house, his purpose is to cook dinner. The house is not ignited. Because the defendant did not have the purpose to burn the home, he is not guilty of attempted arson.

iii. **Using knowledge to prove purpose.** Even in jurisdictions requiring purpose as the mens rea for attempt, a defendant's knowledge of the likely consequences of his act may be used to prove purpose.

   Example. Defendant throws a hand grenade into a crowd, knowing that people might be killed but allegedly intending only to disperse the crowd. Jurors may nonetheless infer that defendant had a purpose to kill, even though it was not the primary purpose of his actions.

iv. **Model Penal Code approach/purpose or belief.** Under MPC §5.01(1)(b), a defendant who acts "with the purpose of causing or with the belief that [his conduct] will cause'' the prohibited result satisfies the required mens rea for attempt. This standard is more flexible than the common law standard.

Example. To destroy a competitor's experimental aircraft, a defendant plants a bomb on the plane and sets it to explode in midair, knowing that the pilot will be killed. The bomb fails to explode. Because defendant believed his conduct would cause death, it is not controlling that he may have had a different purpose for bombing the plane.

Exam Tip

If the defendant just wants to scare the victim or play a practical joke, there is no attempt even if the defendant comes dangerously close to harming the victim. Under the common law, the defendant must have the purpose (specific intent) to accomplish the crime. Under the Model Penal Code, knowledge of the likely harmful result is sufficient.

b. **Minority approach.** A few jurisdictions uphold attempt convictions even in the absence of an intent to achieve the prohibited result. These jurisdictions mandate only that the defendant have the same mens rea required for commission of the completed offense.

Examples and Analysis

Defendant fires three shots at a man he believes is a fleeing rapist. Two of the shots strike but do not kill the man. Defendant claims that the shots were fired accidentally as warning shots. Because manslaughter only requires that a defendant act recklessly, under the minority approach, the defendant can be convicted of attempted manslaughter even though he lacked the purpose to kill. The prosecution need only prove that defendant acted with gross recklessness. People v. Thomas, 729 P.2d 972 (Colo. 1986).

Defendant has intercourse with a woman and is reckless as to whether she agrees to the act. If the mens rea requirement in that jurisdiction for the completed crime of rape is proof that the defendant knew or was reckless as to whether the victim consented, the same mens rea requirement would apply to a charge of attempted rape. See Regina v. Khan, 1990 1 W.L.R. 813.

---

c. **Reckless endangerment.** Given the high mens rea standard for attempt, some jurisdictions have enacted lesser crimes with which to charge a defendant who lacks the mens rea of purposefulness for attempt. MPC §211.2 charges a defendant who "recklessly engages in conduct which places or may place another person in danger of death or serious bodily injury" with "reckless endangerment." Unlike attempted murder, reckless endangerment is a misdemeanor.

d. **Attempted felony murder.** A majority of states do *not* recognize "attempted felony murder." See, e.g., Bruce v. State, 317 Md. 642 (1989). Attempted felony murder applies when the defendant intends to commit the underlying felony but not a death that almost occurs during that felony. Only a few courts have recognized attempted felony murder.

EXAMPLE AND ANALYSIS

Defendant participates in a bank robbery. During the robbery, a cofelon shoots a guard who survives. The evidence suggests that the robbers only intended to frighten the guard, not kill him. If attempted felony murder applied, defendants would be guilty of the attempted murder even though there was no purpose to kill. Amlotte v. State, 456 So. 2d 448 (Fla. 1984).

---

e. **Mens rea requirement for attendant circumstances.** Courts are split as to whether attempt requires that the defendant purposely act with regard to all of the attendant circumstances of a crime, even those that may be covered by the strict liability standard for the completed crime.

   i. **Majority approach.** Most courts do not require that the defendant act with purpose as to circumstances of a crime that the defendant would not need to know to be guilty of the complete crime.

Example and Analysis

Defendant is charged with statutory rape. Although defendant intends to have sexual intercourse with the girl, he does not know or have the purpose to have sex with a girl under the legal age of consent. Defendant is still guilty of attempted statutory rape. Commonwealth v. Dunne, 394 Mass. 10, 474 N.E.2d 538 (1985) (defendant convicted of assault with intent to commit statutory rape even though there was no allegation defendant knew or should have known the victim was underage).

(a) **Recklessness sufficient.** In some jurisdictions, the courts require that the defendant act at least recklessly as to any attendant circumstance of the crime. Thus, a defendant charged with attempted statutory rape would be guilty if he knew there was a substantial risk that the girl was underage.

ii. **Minority approach.** In very few jurisdictions, the defendant must act with purposefulness concerning all elements of the crime.

Example and Analysis

Defendant attempts consensual sexual intercourse with a girl who he believes is over 18. In fact, the girl is a minor. If the minority approach were to be applied, defendant would not be guilty of attempted statutory rape because he did not purposely try to have sex with an underaged girl.

iii. **Model Penal Code approach.** MPC §5.01 adopts the majority approach and does not require that a defendant act with intent concerning all of the attendant circumstances to be guilty of attempt.

Example and Analysis

Defendant faces charges of attempting to kill a federal agent. Under the statute, the agent's status as a member of a federal agency is a jurisdictional ingredient that does not require defendant's intent. If a defendant shoots at a person who turns out to be a federal agent, that defendant is guilty of an attempted violation of the federal offense even if the defendant was unaware of the victim's status.

---

2. Actus Reus

There are several approaches to determine whether a defendant's actions are sufficient to warrant punishment for attempting a crime

- First Step
- Last Step
- Dangerous Proximity Approach
- Unequivocality Test
- Indispensable Element Test
- Abnormal Step Test
- Probable Desistance Test
- Substantial Step Strongly Corroborative of Intent (MPC Standard)

These tests aim to establish whether the defendant engaged in mere preparation or crossed the line into criminal attempt. A majority of courts now apply either the common law "dangerous proximity" test or the Model Penal Code "substantial step" standard.

a. **Rationale of actus reus requirement.** Sinful thoughts alone are not punishable. A defendant's conduct must justify using law enforcement resources for deterrence and prevention. Accordingly, attempt requires that a defendant engage in more than mere preparation to commit a crime. However, no firm line specifies how much more conduct is needed. King v. Barker, N.Z.L.R. 865 (1924). Several tests were developed at common law to establish the line between lawful and unlawful conduct.

b. **Common law standards.** Courts have used several tests to determine how much conduct constitutes an attempt. The principal tests among these are:

i. **First step test.** Ordinarily, a defendant's first step toward committing a crime is insufficient to establish an attempt. Rather, such acts constitute mere preparation.

(a) **Example.** Defendant plans to rob a bank. She calls the bank to find out the bank's hours. Although the defendant has taken a first step toward completing the crime, it is mere preparation.

(b) **Exception.** The first administration of poison may be sufficient to constitute attempted murder if the defendant has the purpose to kill. See R. v. White, 2 K.B. 124 (1910).

(c) **Criticisms of the first step approach.** Most courts have rejected the first step approach because it requires that law enforcement invest resources long before the defendant poses an actual harm and usually before it is clear that the defendant intends to do harm. The first step also infringes on personal liberty by allowing government interference in people's lives at stages often involving innocent behavior. Under the first step approach, the police could arrest a defendant for buying matches even though she has done nothing else to cause an arson.

ii. **Last step *Eagleton* test.** Under early common law, a defendant was not guilty unless he had done all he could do to commit a crime and external forces prevented him from causing a harmful result. Regina v. Eagleton, 6 Cox. C.C. 559 (1855).

(a) **Example.** Defendant pulls the trigger, but the gun jams or the bullet misses the victim. The defendant has taken the last step toward completing the crime of homicide.

(b) **Example.** Defendant tries to pick a pocket which turns out to be empty. Defendant has taken the last step toward completing the crime of theft.

(c) **Criticisms of the last step test.** The last step test delays law enforcement involvement until long after manifestation of the defendant's intent and ability to harm, thus putting victims at undue risk. The need to deter and punish the defendant are often apparent before he commits the last act toward completion of the crime.

iii. **Traditional proximity approach.** The traditional dangerous proximity test addresses how close the defendant has physically come to completing the criminal act. The test focuses both on how much defendant has done to complete the crime and how much is left to be completed. Some courts seek to clarify the standard by stating that the act must be "very near" or "dangerously near" to completion. However, the standard remains vague and simply requires that the defendant go beyond the first act but not as far as the last act of completing a crime.

(a) **Criticisms of proximity approach.** The proximity approach gives relatively little guidance concerning when a defendant's conduct sufficiently constitutes an attempt. As a result, court decisions may appear arbitrary or contradictory.

EXAMPLES AND ANALYSIS

In Commonwealth v. Peaslee, 177 Mass. 267 (1901), defendant was charged with attempting to burn a building. Defendant constructed and arranged combustibles in the building so that they were ready to be lighted. However, the closest he got to lighting the materials was driving a prospective accomplice within 1/4 mile of the building. The court suggested such conduct passed the level of preparation and could constitute sufficient actus reus for attempted arson because the defendant was dangerously close to completing the crime.

In Hope v. Brown, 1 All E.R. 330 (1954), defendant butcher prepared tags with prices exceeding those permitted by law but never affixed them to the product. The court held that defendant's actions were too remote to constitute attempt.

In People v. Rizzo, 246 N.Y. 334 (1927), defendant drove around looking for a particular payroll clerk to rob. He was armed and prepared to commit the robbery. However, because police apprehended him before he could find his prospective victim, the court found that his acts were "mere preparation."

STUDY TIP

To determine whether the defendant's actions fall within "dangerous proximity" of completing the crime, students should focus on: 1. how many steps defendant has taken, 2. how much more action would be required to complete the act, 3. why the harm never occurred, 4. the amount of harm likely to result, 5. the seriousness of the prospective harm, and 6. the appropriateness of law enforcement interference with defendant's acts.

iv. **Unequivocality test.** Instead of assessing on how far defendant's conduct has proceeded, the unequivocality test examines whether defendant's actions, viewed in the abstract, demonstrate an unequivocal intent to commit a crime. The jury is instructed to focus on the defendant's acts alone to determine whether there is some other, lawful, explanation for defendant's conduct. In making this assessment, the jury should not focus on any statements defendant made regarding his intent.

(a) **Res ipsa loquitor test.** The unequivocality test is also called the Res Ipsa Loquitor test because it assumes that the defendant's acts "speak for themselves." King v. Barker, N.Z.L.R. 865 (1924).

EXAMPLES AND ANALYSIS

Defendant buys a box of matches, intending to burn a haystack. There are many lawful explanations for buying matches. The act is equivocal. Accordingly, it is insufficient to convict defendant of attempted arson, even if the defendant admits he purchased the matches to set an illegal fire. King v. Barker, N.Z.L.R. 865 (1924).

In People v. Miller, 2 Cal. 2d 527 (1925), defendant, who threatened to kill the victim, approached him with a loaded gun. The court found that because defendant had not yet aimed the gun at the victim, his acts were equivocal and did not prove attempt.

(b) **Criticisms of unequivocality test.** The unequivocality test is often criticized as setting too high a barrier to conviction. As long as the defendant's act is ambiguous, the defendant cannot be convicted even with conclusive proof of mens rea. Conversely, the unequivocality test also allows prejudicial assumptions about the way people act to lead to attempt convictions in situations where a defendant's acts clearly have not passed the preparation stage.

EXAMPLE AND ANALYSIS

In McQuirter v. State, 36 Ala. App. 707 (1953), the defendant was charged with attempt to commit an assault with intent to rape. Defendant, an African-American man, had simply followed a white woman down the street. Using racial stereotypes, the court believed that defendant's actions sufficiently demonstrated a clear intent to attack the woman and supported the jury's conviction of defendant for attempted assault.

---

v. **Other common law tests.** In United States v. Mandujano, 499 F.2d 370, 373 n.5 (5th Cir. 1974), the court mentioned several other lesser-used tests, including:

(a) **Indispensable element test.** This variation of the proximity test analyzes whether any indispensable element of the crime still remains to be completed. If one does exist, defendant is not guilty of attempt. If all indispensable elements of the crime have been completed, the defendant is guilty of attempt.

(b) **Probable desistance test.** If the defendant goes beyond that point where someone who wanted to stop would have stopped, the defendant has met the actus reus standard for attempt. Therefore, if defendant's conduct would have ordinarily caused the harmful result but for an interruption from an external source, there is an attempt.

c. **Model Penal Code approach.** More than half of the courts have adopted the Model Penal Code's standard for the actus reus of attempt. MPC §5.01(2) provides that the defendant must take "a substantial step strongly corroborative of the actor's criminal purpose." The Model Penal Code also lists certain acts that per se satisfy attempt's actus reus requirement. These include, for example, lying in wait and possessing materials specially designed to commit the crime. MPC §5.01(2).

i. **Note.** The Model Penal Code test focuses on what the defendant has done toward completing the crime, not what he still has left to do. The MPC test directs that defendant's actions be viewed in the context of other evidence that might show whether the defendant had the purpose of completing the crime. If the defendant's acts corroborate that evidence of intent, they may be sufficient to prove attempt.

Examples and Analysis

In United States v. Jackson, 560 F.2d 112 (1977), defendant was charged with armed robbery. Planning to rob a bank, he and his co-conspirators drove to the bank location; removed their license plates; and possessed a gun, tools, and disguises with which to commit the robbery. At that point, they were apprehended. The court held that defendant's acts showed "a substantial step" taken toward committing the crime and corroborated defendants' criminal intent as proven by the testimony of a cooperating co-conspirator.

Compare. In United States v. Buffington, 815 F.2d 1292 (9th Cir. 1987), defendants planned to rob a bank, drove to the location of the bank, and started to disguise themselves. When they were apprehended, the police found a gun they planned to use in the robbery. Here the court found the defendants' conduct fell short of constituting a substantial step toward bank robbery.

Note. The court's reluctance to find an attempt in *Buffington* may have been the result of the status of the two banks in the defendants' general vicinity, only one of which—the federally insured institution—would fall within the jurisdiction of federal criminal laws.

In United States v. Mandujano, 499 F.2d 370 (5th Cir. 1974), defendant was convicted of attempting to distribute narcotics because he originally agreed to locate a source for an undercover agent and informant to buy heroin. Even though the defendant was never able to locate his contact and returned the advanced money, he had still taken a "substantial step strongly corroborative of intent" by making several calls to his contacts. Defendant's calls corroborated the informant's claims that defendant was in the practice of distributing narcotics.

In United States v. Joyce, 693 F.2d 838 (8th Cir. 1982), defendant met with an undercover agent to purchase cocaine. The deal fell through when the agent would not open the cocaine package for the defendant to inspect unless the defendant delivered his money. Defendant then left with no apparent purpose of returning to complete the transaction. The court held that defendant was involved in "mere preparation" to purchase the cocaine and whatever intention defendant had to commit the crime had been abandoned.

In People v. Acosta, 80 N.Y.2d 665 (1993), the court reinstated defendant's conviction for attempting to possess cocaine because the evidence showed defendant admitted a drug courier into his home, inspected the drugs, and ultimately rejected them because of perceived defects in their quality.

---

ii. **Criticisms of Model Penal Code test.** While an improvement over most common law tests, the MPC standard still can lead to arbitrary decisions and allows a defendant's intent to establish both the mens rea and actus reus for attempt.

iii. **Model Penal Code vs. common law tests.** The Model Penal Code approach attaches liability earlier in the sequence of events than most common law approaches, but mitigates its harshness by recognizing an abandonment defense. See p. 16 infra.

STUDY TIP

The prevailing standard for the actus reus for attempt is the "substantial step strongly corroborative of intent" test set forth in the Model Penal Code. A good answer will focus on what acts the defendant has already done (even if legal), not what remains to be done. Those acts should then be analyzed in the context of any other evidence that shows the defendant's purpose in doing those acts. Even a small step can be a substantial step when combined with other evidence of intent.

d. **Impact of actus reus requirement.** Regardless of the standard selected, the actus reus requirement excludes "merely preparatory" acts. Consequently, the law of attempt may frustrate the need for early police intervention in some cases. The law has compensated through: 1. relaxation of criminal procedure laws, and 2. recognition of substantive crimes of preparation. See Ch. 8(D) infra.

i. **Adjustments in criminal procedure law.** Allowing the police to stop and detain a suspect in circumstances short of those justifying arrest is a procedural response to the actus reus requirement for attempt. Terry v. Ohio, 392 U.S. 1 (1968).

ii. **Making preparatory behavior criminal.** Criminal law has always recognized some crimes involving preparatory behavior. Burglary punishes breaking and entering a dwelling of another with "an intent to commit a felony." Assault punishes an attempt to commit a battery. Likewise, vagrancy and stalking statutes are preparatory crimes. Ch. 8(D) infra.

(a) **Note.** Convicting a defendant of an attempt to commit an assault may push back the point of criminality too far. Courts divide over whether an attempt to commit an assault is a recognizable offense. Compare Wilson v. State, 53 Ga. 205 (1874) (refusing to recognize an attempt to assault) with State v. Wilson, 218 Or. 575 (1959) (recognizing an attempted assault).

(b) **Stalking statutes.** Strict actus reus requirements for attempt have led to statutory crimes outlawing harassment that has not yet reached the point of an actual physical attack. California enacted the nation's first stalking statute in 1990. Since then, 30 other states have adopted similar laws. Typically, they prohibit a person from intentionally harassing another and placing that person in immediate and reasonable fear for her safety. See Cal. Penal Code, §646.9 (Supp. 1994).

E. DEFENSES TO ATTEMPT

In addition to arguing that the elements of the crime have not been proven, there are two other key defenses to attempt: 1. abandonment/renunciation, and 2. impossibility. The Model Penal Code refers to "abandonment" as "renunciation." MPC §5.01(4).

1. Abandonment

A defendant who repents and deserts efforts to commit a crime may try to raise the defense of abandonment.

a. **Common law.** Common law did not recognize abandonment as a defense. At common law, a person was not guilty of attempt until he had almost completed the crime; therefore, it was unlikely that at that point the defendant would undergo a sincere change of heart and be able to take meaningful steps to correct his or her actions.

EXAMPLES AND ANALYSIS

Defendant decides to rob a store. He enters the store and starts to check out its security. Just as defendant begins to point a gun at the teller, he sees the store's video camera recording his actions. Defendant then tries to exit the store but is arrested before he can leave. Even though defendant did not leave the store with any merchandise, he has completed enough acts to be guilty of attempt.

In People v. Staples, 6 Cal. App. 3d 61 (1970), defendant rented a room and started to drill into a bank vault next door. While defendant debated whether to follow through with his plans, his landlord turned over his tools to the police. Because defendant had crossed the line from preparation to attempt, the court rejected any defense of abandonment.

---

b. **Modern laws and Model Penal Code.** Some jurisdictions with lower threshold standards for the actus reus requirement of attempt have recognized abandonment as a defense. They usually pattern their defenses after MPC §5.01(4), requiring "a complete and voluntary renunciation of the defendant's criminal purpose."

i. **Complete renunciation.** Defendant must not be motivated by a decision to postpone the criminal conduct until a more advantageous time or to transfer the criminal effort to another prospective victim.

ii. **Voluntary.** A fear of getting caught cannot, in whole or in part, motivate the defendant. It is also not voluntary renunciation if someone else prevents the defendant from completing the crime. To be voluntary, defendant must have experienced a sincere change of heart.

STUDY TIP

To constitute abandonment, defendant must "CAV" in:

"C"	=	Complete renunciation
"A"	=	Abandon efforts before the crime is completed
"V"	=	Voluntary renunciation

EXAMPLE AND ANALYSIS

Courts apply the abandonment defense inconsistently. Consider the situation in which a defendant accosts a woman, intending to rape her. However, he chooses not to do so after the woman talks him out of it. Some courts find that the renunciation was not voluntary because it depended on the victim's resistance. See, e.g.,

People v. McNeal, 152 Mich. App. 404 (1986). Other courts allow the abandonment defense. See, e.g., Ross v. State, 601 So. 2d 872 (Miss. 1992). The lower the threshold for proving attempt, the more likely the jurisdiction is to allow an abandonment defense.

2. **Impossibility**

The defense of impossibility arises when a defendant has done everything possible to commit a crime, but unexpected factual or legal circumstances prevent the crime from occurring.

a. **Example.** Defendant purchases property she believes is stolen. Unbeknownst to the defendant, the property is not stolen. Defendant will claim it was impossible for her to receive stolen property because the property purchased was not stolen. People v. Jaffe, 185 N.Y. 497 (1906).

b. **General rule.** There is an old saying, "Legal impossibility is a defense, factual impossibility is not." This statement is not particularly helpful given that many situations can be arbitrarily labeled as either factual or legal impossibility.

EXAMPLES AND ANALYSIS

In People v. Jaffe, 185 N.Y. 497 (1906), defendant was charged with receiving stolen property. In fact, the property was not stolen. Because it was legally impossible for defendant to commit the crime, the court reversed defendant's conviction. However, this case may also be characterized as one of "factual impossibility." The fact that the property was not stolen made it impossible for defendant to complete the crime. See People v. Rojas, 55 Cal. 2d 252 (1961) (reaching opposite result from Jaffe).

In People v. Dlugash, 41 N.Y.2d 725 (1977), defendant was charged with attempted murder when he shot a victim who, according to the medical experts, was probably already dead. Even though it is not attempted murder to try to kill a dead person (i.e., legal impossibility), the court found that the case posed an issue of "factual impossibility" because it was factually impossible to try to kill someone who is already dead. Therefore, the defendant could be charged with attempt.

c. **Typical factual impossibility situations.** Even though most cases can be categorized as either factual or legal impossibility, typically the following situations are treated as factual impossibility and no defense is allowed:

- pickpocket trying to pick an empty pocket;
- shooting a weapon that is defective and incapable of firing;
- trying to infect another with a disease even though it turns out the defendant is not infected, State v. Smith, 262 N.J. Super. 487 (1993);
- shooting at a victim's home when the victim is not present;
- having sexual intercourse with a woman who, unbeknownst to the defendant, is already deceased.

In these cases, the court asks the question "Had the circumstances been as defendant believed them to be, would there have been a crime?" If the answer is yes, defendant is guilty of attempt and impossibility is NOT a defense.

d. **Legal impossibility situations.** In situations where the court does not want to impose criminal liability, it may label the situation as "legal impossibility." In reality, there are two types of legal impossibility: 1. "True legal impossibility" arises when defendant consciously tries to violate the law but there is no law prohibiting his behavior; and 2. "Hybrid legal impossibility" arises when a defendant's conduct might otherwise violate the law, but he makes a mistake as to the legal status of some aspect of his conduct.

i. **True legal impossibility situations.** Very few true legal impossibility situations arise. In these cases, a full defense is provided because even if defendant wanted to do something bad, there is no law prohibiting his behavior. The principle of legality bars people from being convicted of conduct that would never constitute a crime in that jurisdiction. Example of "true legal impossibility" cases include:

- Defendant performs an abortion she believes to be unlawful. In fact, abortion is legal in that jurisdiction.
- Defendant tries to smoke marijuana believing it is illegal to do so. In fact, there is no law against smoking marijuana.
- Defendant takes a tax deduction that she believes is illegal, however, the deduction is legal.
- Defendant has sex with a minor believing it is statutory rape. In fact, that jurisdiction has no prohibition against statutory rape.

Because the law does not prohibit that which the defendant believed he or she was doing, legal impossibility applies as a defense to attempt.

ii. **Hybrid legal impossibility situations.** In most situations, legal impossibility situations may fall under either factual or legal impossibility. Once again, the courts ask "even if the facts were as defendant believed them to be, would he be guilty of a crime?" However, the "fact" the defendant got wrong was the legal status of some of the circumstances related to his conduct. In these situations, courts tend to select the label of "legal impossibility," thereby giving the defendant a full defense to attempt.

(a) **Examples.** Classic examples of hybrid legal impossibility that could as easily be interpreted by the court as factual impossibility include:

- Receiving unstolen property the defendant mistakenly believes to have been stolen. People v. Rojas, 55 Cal. 2d 252 (1961).
- Shooting at a corpse defendant mistakenly believes to be alive. In order for there to be the crime of murder, there must have been a live human being who was killed. Defendant's mistake as to the legal status of his victim makes it impossible for him to complete the crime.
- Trying to hunt a deer out of season but mistakenly shooting a stuffed deer. It is out of season but shooting a dead deer does not fall under the prohibition of the law.

e. **Confusion in applying factual impossibility and legal impossibility labels.** For all of the above situations, courts use the label of "legal impossibility" because defendant's behavior is not dangerous enough to punish. However, in theory these situations could as easily be labeled as "factual impossibility" and the defendants could be convicted of attempt.

EXAMPLE AND ANALYSIS

In United States v. Berrigan, 482 F.2d 171 (3d Cir. 1973), an imprisoned Vietnam War resister was convicted of attempting to send letters contrary to prison regulations. Regulations required that such letters be sent only with the "knowledge and consent" of the warden. Unbeknownst to the defendant, the warden had been monitoring defendant's letters. The appellate court labeled the case as one of "legal impossibility" and reversed defendant's conviction, stating "[A]ttempting to do that which is not a crime is not attempting to commit a crime." Of course, it would have been just as easy for the court to label the situation as "factual impossibility" because if the facts had been as defendant believed them to be (i.e., the warden was unaware of his correspondence), he would have been guilty of the crime.

Compare. In United States v. Everett, 700 F.2d 900 (3d Cir. 1983), the court distinguished the *Berrigan* decision and found "factual impossibility" when the defendant sold a substance that he believed was a dangerous narcotic but turned out not to be a controlled substance. In imposing the label "factual impossibility" and upholding the attempt conviction, the court noted the "all-out effort" to end drug trafficking. However, in a similar situation, a court rejected the factual vs. legal impossibility distinction and allowed a defense to attempt. See United States v. Oviedo, 525 F.2d 881 (5th Cir. 1976).

---

f. **Alternative approaches to the impossibility issue.** Several alternative approaches exist to the "factual" vs. "legal" impossibility distinction.

   i. **Primary vs. secondary intent.** Some commentators suggest that courts focus only on a defendant's primary purpose for her actions as demonstrated by defendant's objective acts. For example, in *The Case of Lady Eldon's French Lace*, Lady Eldon took dutiable lace out of the country. On its face, this objective act does not seem to warrant punishment. However, Lady Eldon believed there was a duty on the lace and that she was smuggling it out illegally. In fact, the lace turned out not to be subject to duty. Because Lady Eldon's "primary intent" was simply to take out the lace, she would not be guilty of attempt. It was only her secondary intent, to smuggle dutiable lace that was improper. This approach of focusing only on the objective act is not helpful given that it ignores defendant's subjective intent to violate the law, an intent that warrants punishment.

   ii. **Dangerous proximity test.** Some courts have abandoned the factual vs. legal impossibility distinction and simply try to determine how close the defendant came to doing actual harm. If a defendant shoots at the victim's window, even if the victim is not home, defendant has come within dangerous proximity of causing substantial harm.

iii. **Inherent impossibility test.** If it is "inherently impossible" for the defendant to commit the crime, courts are more apt to recognize an impossibility defense. What if a defendant attempts to kill another with voodoo? Because voodoo does not pose a real threat of harm, impossibility would be a defense, even though the defendant had a firm intent to kill.

g. **Model Penal Code approach.** The Model Penal Code sets forth the best approach to the impossibility situation. See United States v. Thomas, 13 U.S.C.M.A. 278 (1962).

i. **General rule.** MPC §5.01 does not recognize impossibility as a defense.

ii. **Exception.** Under MPC §5.05, in situations where an attempt is "so inherently unlikely to result or culminate in the commission of a crime that neither such conduct nor the actor presents a public danger," the court has the discretion to mitigate the level of the crime or dismiss the prosecution.

iii. **Example.** Believing that it is a crime to fish off the local pier, defendant fishes there. In fact, it is legal to fish off the pier. Defendant's acts are not inherently dangerous and the court may allow the equivalent of an "impossibility" defense.

iv. **Note.** The Model Penal Code does not expressly abolish the defense of pure legal impossibility. In fact, the Commentary recognizes that a defendant should not be punished unless the result he desires or intends constitutes a crime. Comment to MPC §5.01, at 318.

Study Tip

The best approach to impossibility situations is to analyze the facts according to this formula:

Step 1: Determine whether the elements of attempt have been met.

- Did the defendant have the purpose to commit a crime?
- Did the defendant take a "substantial step" toward committing that crime?

Step 2: Were there facts that were "unbeknownst" to the defendant that made it impossible for the defendant to complete the crime?

- If the facts were as defendant believed them to be, would defendant have been guilty of a crime?
  - If no law exists prohibiting defendant's behavior, defendant may be excused under the doctrine of "true legal impossibility."
  - If defendant made a mistake as to the legal status of some of his conduct, but without such a mistake defendant would be violating the law, defendant's "legal impossibility" should be treated more like factual impossibility and no defense provided. Defendant is guilty of attempt.
  - Under the Model Penal Code
    - Impossibility is generally not a defense. MPC §5.01;
    - Defendant's case may be mitigated if defendant's actions are not dangerous on their face and do not need to be punished. MPC §5.05.

h. Warning. Do not confuse mistake of law and mistake of fact with factual impossibility and legal impossibility.

Mistake of Fact	=	defense
Factual Impossibility	=	no defense
Mistake of Law	=	generally, no defense
Legal Impossibility	=	defense

3. Merger

If an attempt succeeds, the defendant is only guilty of the completed substantive crime. Attempt merges with the substantive crime.

Example. Defendant tries to steal a watch from the victim's pocket. After several tries, defendant removes the wallet. Defendant is guilty of theft only, not theft and attempted theft.

F. SUMMARY

Figure 8-1 presents a summary of the elements of attempt and key defenses to the crime.

FIGURE 8-1

ATTEMPT	
Mens Rea	Purpose to commit crime • Knowledge insufficient • MPC (purpose or belief)
Actus Reus	Major Common Law tests • Last step • Proximity approach • Unequivocality MPC test • Substantial step strongly corroborative of intent
Defenses	Abandonment • Not defense at common law Renunciation [MPC §5.01(4)] • Complete and voluntary Impossibility • Factual vs. legal • MPC approach

G. SOLICITATION

Solicitation is a separate crime from attempt. Solicitation consists of recruiting, encouraging, directing, counseling, or inducing another person to commit a crime. Even if no further steps are taken toward the commission of that crime, purposely promoting the commission of the crime is enough to constitute solicitation.

EXAMPLES AND ANALYSIS

After years of fighting with his wife, defendant asks his neighbor to kill her. The neighbor never agrees to the plan. If defendant made the request with the purpose of enlisting his neighbor to kill defendant's wife, he committed the crime of solicitation.

Defendant approaches a woman he believes to be a prostitute and offers her money in exchange for sex. Unbeknownst to the defendant, the woman is an undercover policewoman. Defendant can be prosecuted for solicitation. See People v. Leffel, 54 Cal. App. 3d 569 (1976).

1. Common Law vs. Modern Statutes

At common law, solicitation was a misdemeanor even if the defendant sought to solicit a felony crime. There was no general crime of solicitation. Instead, the solicitation of specific types of felonies and serious misdemeanors, like murder and prostitution, was prohibited. Today, most state statutes contain a general criminal solicitation statute that make it unlawful to solicit any crime.

2. Elements of the Crime

Solicitation requires both an actus reus and mens rea.

a. **Actus reus.** The actus reus of solicitation may be purely verbal. It includes any command, request, or encouragement to another to commit a crime.

b. **Mens rea.** Solicitation is a specific intent crime. The defendant must have the purpose to promote or facilitate the commission of a crime.

3. Solicitation vs. Attempt

The key differences between solicitation and attempt are: 1. Attempt requires the performance of some act toward the commission of the crime. Usually, that act must be a "substantial step" toward completion of the crime. Solicitation can occur at a much earlier stage when a plan to commit a crime is just beginning. 2. Solicitation involves a third party who is recruited to participate in a crime. Attempt may be done by the defendant alone. 3. Attempt generally carries a heavier sentence than solicitation.

Example and Analysis

In State v. Davis, 319 Mo. 1222 (1928), defendant planned to have a friend's husband killed in order to collect his life insurance. Defendant approached a possible "hit man" for the job, but aborted the plan when the hit man contacted the police. The court held that mere solicitation of the hit man was not enough of a step to constitute attempted murder. It may have been sufficient to support a charge of "solicitation to commit murder."

4. Solicitation as Attempt

Solicitation can constitute a punishable attempt if it represents a "substantial step" toward commission of the crime.

Example and Analysis

In United States v. Church, 29 M.J. Rptr. 679 (C.M.R. 1989), defendant was found guilty of the attempted premeditated murder of his wife. Defendant recruited and paid a person to kill defendant's wife. Unbeknownst to defendant, he had recruited an undercover police officer who feigned the crime. Contracting an agent for the killing and paying him when he believed the job would actually be performed constituted "a substantial step toward commission of the crime." As the court stated, it was as if defendant armed a missile (the hired assassin) and fired it toward his intended victim.

Opposing view. Many states adhere to the view expressed in the Model Penal Code commentaries that "no matter what acts the solicitor commits, he cannot be guilty of an attempt because it is not his purpose to commit the offense personally." MPC and Commentaries, Comment to §5.02.

5. Defenses to Solicitation

Very few defenses exist to a charge of solicitation:

a. **Abandonment.** Because solicitation is completed after the defendant makes initial contact, the defense of abandonment is generally not available.

b. **Renunciation.** The Model Penal Code recognizes an affirmative defense that the defendant, after soliciting another person to commit a crime, persuades that person to abort the plan or otherwise prevents the commission of the crime. MPC §5.02(3).

c. **First Amendment.** Under the Supreme Court's *Brandenburg* rule, public advocacy of violent acts may be constitutionally protected when the advocacy is not intended or likely to produce imminent lawless action. NAACP v. Claiborne Hardware Co., 458 U.S. 886 (1982). Accordingly, unless the defendant's acts of solicitation threaten imminent harm, the defendant may have a first amendment defense. See People v. Rubin, 96 Cal. App. 3d 968 (1979) (first amendment defense rejected because defendant's offer to "pay anyone who kills a member of the American Nazi party" had a likelihood of inciting imminent lawless action).

6. Model Penal Code

The Model Penal Code has had a great influence on modern day solicitation statutes. Under the Model Penal Code §5.02(1), the crime of solicitation exists if:

- the actor's purpose is to promote or facilitate the commission of a substantive offense (Mens Rea);
- with such purpose, [the defendant] commands, encourages, or requests another person to engage in conduct that would constitute the crime, an attempt to commit it, or would establish the other person's complicity in its commission or attempted commission.

7. Model Penal Code vs. Traditional Common Law

The Model Penal Code expanded the definition of the traditional crime of solicitation by:

- applying the crime of solicitation to all crimes, not just specified felonies and serious misdemeanors;
- recognizing as solicitation a request that another commit an attempt (e.g., asking another to shoot at the victim even though the defendant knew the gun to be unloaded);
- applying the crime of solicitation to defendants who ask others to help them commit a crime, even though the soliciting defendant still plans to be the actual perpetrator of the offense; and
- recognizing as a solicitation uncommunicated requests for assistance with a crime (e.g., writing to another for assistance in committing a crime but never having the request delivered).

Review Question and Answer

Question: Jill decides to kidnap a child and hold the child for ransom. In preparation for her crime, she asks her neighbor, Kenny, to find out what time the children at the neighborhood school get out at the end of the day. Jill also says to Kenny, "Think about joining me with this harmless, little scheme. No one will get hurt and we'll make plenty of money." Kenny just shakes his head and walks away.

The next day, Jill drives to the neighborhood school. In her car, she has placed coloring books and candy. Even though she believes it is illegal to do so, Jill removes the front license plate from her car. As the children are excused, Jill spots the child she wants to kidnap. However, before she can get out of the car, Jill sees a rush of parents running to greet their children. Jill decides to wait until another day to decide whether or not to go through with her plan. As it turns out, it is not illegal in the jurisdiction to drive without a front license plate. What crimes, if any, has Jill committed?

Answer: Jill has potentially committed the anticipatory ("inchoate crimes") of solicitation, stalking, and attempted kidnapping.

1. *Solicitation.* The crime of solicitation is completed when the defendant commands, requests, or encourages another person's participation in a crime. In this case, Jill asked her neighbor to help with the plan. If, as it appears, Jill made this request with the purpose of having the neighbor facilitate the commission of the crime, she is guilty of solicitation. It is irrelevant that Kenny declines her offer.

2. *Stalking.* In some jurisdictions, stalking statutes prohibit intentionally harassing another and placing that person in immediate and reasonable fear for his or her safety. However, stalking does not seem to apply in this case because the child who was the target of Jill's scheme was unaware of any acts by the defendant. Therefore, the child could not have been placed in fear for his or her safety.

3. *Attempted Kidnapping.* Jill is guilty of attempted kidnapping if she had the purpose to kidnap the child and took a "substantial step" toward completion of that crime.

Mens Rea. Until she sees the parents greeting their children, Jill's intent seems clear. She has told another person she wants to kidnap a child and has taken steps toward doing so. She also had a motive for the kidnap; i.e., to obtain ransom money. There is no indication in the facts that Jill intended only to scare the child or play a mean trick.

Actus Reus. There are many tests for determining whether the defendant has moved beyond "mere preparation" into the actual commission of an offense. Jill took several steps toward the kidnapping. She found out the time the children were excused from school, got coloring books and candy to lure her victim into the car, and went to the school. Depending on which test is applied, a court may find that Jill had done enough to constitute an attempt.

First Step. The first step test is not used by most jurisdictions. If it were applied, Jill would be guilty of attempt because she took a first step when she asked her neighbor to assist with the kidnapping.

Last Step. Jill did not complete the last step toward the kidnapping. For example, she had not yet approached a particular child or started leading that child toward her car. Thus, if the last step test is applied, Jill would not be guilty of attempt.

Dangerous Proximity. Whether Jill was within dangerous proximity of completing her crime is debatable. Prosecutors would argue that there was very little left for Jill to do other than physically approach the child. She was at the location, had the means to take the child, and had taken precautions to hide her identity by removing her license plate. On the other hand, Jill never approached the child and quit her endeavor before making any contact.

Unequivocality. If the unequivocality test is applied, Jill can argue there are many legitimate explanations for driving near a school with candy and coloring books. Those facts alone do not show criminal intent.

Substantial Step Strongly Corroborative of Intent. If the Model Penal Code approach is applied, the parties will argue whether Jill took a substantial step strongly corroborative of her intent to kidnap. Her many preparations for the kidnap, as well as her physical location strongly corroborate her stated intent to Kenny and provide the prosecution with a strong argument that Jill committed an attempt. On the other hand, Jill can argue that she never was sure that she would go through with the plan and that is why she gave herself more time to think about the issue.

Defense to Attempted Kidnapping

Abandonment. The majority rule is that abandonment is not a defense to attempt. Thus, if Jill did commit a substantial step toward the perpetration of the crime with the purpose that the crime succeed, she is still guilty even if she later changes her mind.

Under the Model Penal Code and some modern laws, renunciation (abandonment) is a defense but Jill must demonstrate that it is complete and voluntary. Jill's abandonment is not complete because she is just postponing the kidnap until another day. The abandonment also may not be voluntary because she appears to have been motivated, in whole or in part, by the fear of being apprehended by the other parents who were there picking up their children.

4. *Removing Front License Plate and Legal Impossibility.* If Jill is charged with removing her front license plate, or attempting to do so, she will argue legal impossibility because it was impossible for her to commit a crime that does not exist. Under the Model Penal, the general rule is that impossibility is not a defense. However, in this case, the violation poses little or no danger to society. Jill may, therefore, be able to argue that she should not be charged with attempt because the prosecution has the discretion to mitigate the crime or dismiss the prosecution.

9 ACCOMPLICE LIABILITY

CHAPTER OVERVIEW

Under both common law and statute, a defendant may be accountable for committing a crime even if he or she simply helps another in its commission. Under common law, there were distinct categories to identify the roles of individuals participating in a crime. Today, all individuals who assist in the commission of a crime are accomplices and are jointly responsible for the offense committed.

For the most part, the terms "accomplice" and "aider and abettor" are now interchangeable. These terms are used to refer to those individuals who assist in the commission of a crime.

Chapter 9 outlines those elements that must be proven to establish accomplice liability. Namely, the defendant must do something to assist a crime and do so with the purpose of having the crime succeed. Slightly different mens rea requirements may apply when the crime requires negligence or strict liability.

In discussing the operation and scope of accomplice liability, this chapter will address the following topics:

- Background of Accomplice Liability
  - Common law vs. statutory law
  - Punishment
- Requirements for Accomplice Liability
  - Mens rea
    - Mens rea as to actions of the principal
    - Departures from common scheme
    - Mens rea as to attendant circumstances
    - Mens rea as to result
  - Actus reus
- Relationship Among the Parties

Accomplice liability is not a separate crime; it is a theory by which a defendant is guilty for a specific substantive crime. In other words, one is *not* "guilty of being an accomplice." Rather, an accomplice is guilty of the crime he or she helped to commit. For example, a person who helps with a murder is guilty of murder. There is no separate crime of being an "accomplice."

A. INTRODUCTION

Accomplice liability is based on the premise that all persons who assist in the commission of a crime should be held accountable, to some degree, for that offense. Whereas the law normally regards a person's acts as the products of his or her own choice, accomplice liability is based on the doctrine of complicity. Complicity recognizes that one individual's actions may influence whether or how another person acts. The involvement of more than one person in the criminal activity means there is more danger and more likelihood of the participants achieving their goal.

1. Common Law Distinctions

At the common law, there were distinct categories and labels that applied to participants in crimes.

a. **Principal in the first degree.** This was the actual perpetrator of the crime. For example, in a bank robbery, the principal in the first degree was the defendant who actually entered the bank and demanded the money from the teller.

b. **Principal in the second degree.** This was the person who aided and abetted the principal by being present, or nearby. For example, in a bank robbery, the lookout or getaway driver was the classic principal in the second degree.

c. **Accessory before the fact.** This was the person who helped prepare for the crime. For example, in a bank robbery, the person who cased the bank or purchased the disguises, but did not participate in the actual robbery, was considered an accessory before the fact.

d. **Accessory after the fact.** This was the person who, knowing that a felony had been committed, received, relieved, comforted, or assisted the felon. For example, in a bank robbery, a person who learned that her friend had just committed a robbery but offered to hide the defendant and her loot until the police had called off their search was considered an accessory after the fact.

2. Modern Approach

Most modern statutes have eliminated the first three common law categories and hold that all participants in a crime, apart from the accessory after the fact, are subject to the same punishment. All those who assist the principal either before or during the commission of a crime are considered accomplices or aiders and abettors.

a. **Same punishment for all except accessory after the fact.** Generally, punishment is the same for the principal and all accessories, except for an accessory after the fact. For example, in a bank robbery, the robber, getaway driver, and planner of the robbery would all be subject to the same punishment.

   i. **Rationale.** The person who plans a crime may be as culpable or more culpable than the less sophisticated individual who puts the plan into action. That person should not be rewarded because he or she hid behind the scenes and convinced another to take the risks of the actual perpetration of the crime. Moreover, when a crime is the combination of more than one person's efforts, each defendant is contributing to the overall commission of the crime.

   ii. **Note.** Although all who commit a crime are subject to the same punishment, the court will not necessarily impose the same punishment on all defendants. Where there is discretion in sentencing, the court may take into consideration each defendant's role in the crime and impose individualized sentences. In fact, the movement to eliminate the strict classifications of participants in a crime is largely an effort to eliminate formalism and to give judges more discretion to sentence according to actual culpability.

b. **Principals need not be convicted.** Under modern statutes, the prosecution need only prove that a crime was actually committed and the accomplice participated before or during its commission.

   Example. Three persons participate in a bank robbery: the robber, lookout, and planner. Only the lookout is apprehended. As long as the prosecution proves that the robbery occurred, and that the lookout played a role in the robbery, the lookout can be convicted even if her coparticipants are never apprehended.

c. **No need to charge specific form of complicity.** Instead of charging defendants under a specific common law label, all defendants, other than accessories after the fact, may now be charged directly with the substantive crime committed.

Example. The planner of a bank robbery need not be charged as an "accessory before the fact." Rather, that individual can simply be charged with bank robbery.

i. **Sample statutes**

(a) **California law.** "All persons concerned in the commission of a crime, whether it be felony or misdemeanor, and whether they directly commit the act constituting the offense, or aid and abet in its commission, or, not being present, have advised and encouraged its commission . . . are principals in any crime so committed." Cal. Penal Code, §31.

(b) **Federal law.** "Whoever commits an offense against the United States or aids, abets, counsels, commands, induces or procures its commission is punishable as a principal." 18 U.S.C. §2(a).

(c) **Model Penal Code.** "A person is guilty of an offense if it is committed by his own conduct or by the conduct of another person for which he is legally accountable, or both." MPC §2.06 sets forth the conditions under which a person is legally accountable for the conduct of another.

d. **Accessory after the fact.** Under both common law and modern statutes, accessories after the fact are treated as less culpable than principals or accessories before the fact.

i. **Example.** After a bank robbery is committed, the accessory after the fact offers to conceal the robber and hide the loot. Typically, if the accessory had no role in the robbery prior to its commission, that defendant would be subject to a lesser punishment.

ii. **Excluded persons.** At common law, a spouse could not be charged as an accessory after the fact.

e. **Using another as an instrument to commit a crime.** If a person unknowingly or unwittingly participates in a crime, that person is not an accomplice but is considered a mere instrument by which the actual perpetrator committed the offense.

i. **Example.** A asks B to deliver a sealed envelope to a bank teller. Inside the envelope is a note demanding the bank's money and threatening harm if it is not produced. B is an innocent agent and not an accomplice to the crime.

ii. **Other types of instruments.** Animals and objects may also be used as instruments. For example, a defendant may train a dog to enter another person's house to steal an item or use a remote control device to accomplish the same. In these situations, the defendant is still responsible for the crime.

iii. **Statutory authority.** Federal law and some state statutes expressly provide, "Whoever willfully causes an act to be done which if directly performed by him or another would be an offense against the United States is punishable as a principal." 18 U.S.C. §2(b).

iv. **Nonproxyable offenses.** Laws criminalizing the "causing of another to commit a crime" are especially important in the area of nonproxyable offenses. For example, traditionally one could not be guilty of perjury as an accomplice because perjury requires that the convicted person be the one who actually testified falsely. An accomplice may encourage or dupe another into testifying falsely, but that person is still not lying under oath. Modern statutes, however, would hold a defendant responsible for "causing" an act which, if done by the defendant, would constitute a crime.

B. REQUIREMENTS FOR ACCOMPLICE LIABILITY

Accomplice liability requires mens rea and actus reus. If the defendant meets both of these requirements, he is guilty of the underlying substantive crime.

Actus Reus	—	Act of encouragement
Mens Rea	—	Purpose to have crime succeed

1. Mens Rea Rule

For accomplice liability, the defendant must help or encourage another in the commission of the crime and with the purpose of having the crime succeed.

- Purpose to help
- Purpose that the crime succeed

a. **Hicks v. United States.** This case is standardly used to demonstrate the principles of accessory liability. 150 U.S. 442 (1893).

i. **Facts.** In *Hicks*, the defendant was accused of murder for allegedly encouraging his friend, Stand Rowe, to kill the victim, Andrew Colvard. In the version of the facts adopted by the Court, Rowe and Hicks had a confrontation with the victim. At some point during their conversation, Colvard said something that led Hicks to laugh and caused Rowe to direct his rifle at Colvard. Hicks then took off his hat and hit his horse with it. He stated to Colvard, "Take off your hat and die like a man." At that point, Rowe shot and killed Colvard. Hicks then rode off with Rowe. Later, Hicks testified that he left with Rowe because he feared him and separated from Rowe as soon as he could. The judge instructed the jury that "[i]f the deliberate and intentional use of words [had] the effect to encourage one man to kill another, he who uttered the words is presumed by law to have intended that effect, and is responsible therefore."

ii. **Issue.** Defendant raised two errors in the jury instructions:

- They did not require a finding that Hicks intended his words to encourage Rowe's killing of Colvard; and
- They allowed the jury to find accomplice liability based upon Hicks' mere presence at the scene of the crime.

iii. **Ruling.** The Court reversed Hicks' conviction because the jury instructions misstated the law. To be guilty of aiding and abetting a murder, a defendant must speak or act with the purpose to encourage or assist another in the commission of a crime. The focus must be on the defendant's purpose when uttering the words, not on the effect of defendant's conduct on the principal.

b. **Mere presence.** As established in *Hicks*, mere presence at the commission of a crime is ordinarily insufficient to constitute aiding and abetting. However, if a defendant agrees in advance to be present in order to provide moral support or assistance to the principal, accomplice liability is established.

c. **Sample applications of mens rea requirement.** Consider the following hypotheticals in Kadish and Schulhofer, Criminal Law, at 647:

i. Hicks hears that Rowe has set out to kill his old enemy, Colvard, and goes along to enjoy the spectacle.

- Hicks is not guilty of aiding and abetting because his intention was to enjoy the spectacle, not assist or encourage

Rowe in the commission of his crime. Mere presence is ordinarily insufficient to trigger accomplice liability.

ii. Same situation, except that while watching Rowe's assault on Colvard with satisfaction, Hicks shouts such words of encouragement to Rowe as "Go get him!" and "Attaboy!"

- Hicks is guilty of aiding and abetting if he shouts to Rowe with the purpose of encouraging him to commit the crime.
- Note: Unlike in *Hicks*, the alleged words of encouragement in this hypothetical are directed at the perpetrator, not the victim.

iii. Same situation, except that Hicks resolves to make certain Rowe succeeds — by helping him if necessary.

- Hicks has the mens rea to help Rowe but he has not done any act to assist him. Therefore, Hicks is not guilty of aiding and abetting unless he communicates to Rowe his intent to assist.

iv. Same situation, except that Hicks tells Rowe on the way that he will help him if it seems necessary.

- Hicks is guilty of aiding and abetting because he has the purpose to help Rowe as demonstrated by his prior agreement to be present.

d. Purpose vs. knowledge. To be guilty as an accomplice, a defendant must not only know that his acts may assist the commission of a crime, but must also have the specific purpose of having the crime succeed. United States v. Peoni, 100 F.2d 401 (2d Cir. 1938) (Learned Hand, J.).

EXAMPLE AND ANALYSIS

In State v. Gladstone, 78 Wash. 2d 306 (1980), Gladstone was charged with aiding and abetting the unlawful sale of marijuana. A police informant, Thompson, had approached Gladstone and asked him to sell some marijuana. Gladstone answered that he did not have enough to sell but volunteered the name of another person,

Kent, who might be willing to sell. Gladstone then gave Thompson Kent's address and drew a map to his residence. The court reversed Gladstone's conviction for aiding and abetting Kent's unlawful sale of marijuana. Even though Gladstone knew that Kent would probably sell marijuana to Thompson, the court found the evidence insufficient to show that he had a "purposive attitude" toward the sale.

Note. In *Gladstone,* the court emphasizes that the defendant was not charged with aiding and abetting the purchase of marijuana, but with Kent's sale of it. But, charging the case differently would really have made no difference. In either case, the key question was whether Gladstone indifferently provided information that helped a crime or whether he did so with the purpose of promoting or facilitating its commission.

---

i. **Establishing purpose to aid and abet.** Courts use a variety of approaches and terms to determine whether the defendant has sufficient purpose for accomplice liability. The goal of these tests is to draw a line between those who incidentally assist in the commission of a crime and those who act with the specific purpose of having a crime succeed.

(a) **Examples.** There are many examples of situations in which a person knowingly helps another commit a crime without the purpose of seeing the crime actually occur.

- A doctor counsels against a late-term abortion but gives the patient the name of an available abortionist.
- A utility provides telephone service to a business it knows is engaged in bookmaking.

e. **Tests for determining purpose.** The following approaches are used to determine whether an act of assistance is provided with the "purpose" of committing a crime.

i. **Nexus.** This approach is not very helpful, but the label is used by many courts. Courts look for a connection or relation between the accomplice and principal that shows that the accomplice had the purpose of aiding the principal's commission of the crime. The label ascribed to this connection is "nexus," although there is no specific test for determining when a sufficient connection exists.

Example. Gladstone gives Thompson directions to Kent's house so Kent can sell him some marijuana. Gladstone and Kent have an informal working partnership. On a repeated basis, Gladstone refers customers to Kent and vice versa. A "nexus" exists between the two of them and therefore, it is more likely that Gladstone is acting with the *purpose* of having the sale occur.

ii. **Stake in the venture.** Somewhat more helpful is the "stake in the venture" test. To draw the line between whether the accomplice just knowingly aided, or did so purposely, courts look to how much of a stake the accomplice has in the principal's commission of the crime. People v. Lauria, 251 Cal. App. 2d 471 (1967).

(a) **Example.** Gladstone refers potential marijuana customers to Kent in exchange for kickbacks.

(b) **Example.** A manufactures and sells a chemical that can be used for the manufacture of a variety of substances. A's only customer for the last five years has been B who uses it with A's knowledge to manufacture an illegal narcotic. A has a stake in B's illegal venture because B is A's only customer.

f. **Model Penal Code approach.** Originally, the MPC was drafted to allow accomplice liability to be proven with knowing participation in a crime. However, the final draft of the MPC now requires that the actor have "the purpose of promoting or facilitating" the commission of the crime. MPC §2.06(3)(a).

g. **Rationale for purpose requirement.** Both the Model Penal Code and common law set the mens rea requirement at purpose in order to ensure the maximum autonomy for individuals in a laissez-faire society.

h. **Criminal facilitation.** In some jurisdictions that require proof of purpose for accomplice liability, knowingly providing aid is recognized as a separate, lesser crime. See, e.g., N.Y. Penal Code, §115.

EXAMPLE AND ANALYSIS

Defendant works as a gasoline attendant. There have been a rash of late afternoon bank robberies in the area. At 4:30 p.m., a car with no license plates and a driver dressed suspiciously pull into the station. Although defendant is fairly sure that the driver is the serial bank robber, she fills up the car with gas. The driver then proceeds to rob another bank. Because the defendant does not have the purpose to aid a bank robbery, she is not guilty of being an accomplice to the robbery. However, her aid may constitute the lesser crime of "criminal facilitation."

---

i. **Alternative approaches.** In some jurisdictions, the purposeful requirement is relaxed depending on the circumstances and the nature of the crime.

   i. **Knowledge sufficient for serious crimes.** In a minority of jurisdictions, although purpose is required to convict lesser offenses, knowledge suffices to establish accomplice liability for major crimes.

EXAMPLES AND ANALYSIS

In United States v. Fountain, 768 F.2d 790 (7th Cir. 1985), defendant lifted his shirt to reveal a knife which another inmate then seized and used to stab a guard. Because of the seriousness of the crime, knowing assistance was sufficient to prove accomplice liability.

Defendant is charged with aiding and abetting the less serious crime of prostitution by renting motel rooms by the hour. Defendant may know that some rooms are rented for prostitution, but most courts would not find accomplice liability unless the defendant had the purpose of aiding the relatively minor criminal act.

---

   ii. **Liability for all reasonably foreseeable offenses.** Ordinarily, an accomplice is only responsible for those crimes he or she purposefully helps to succeed. However, a majority of jurisdictions now extend accomplice liability to both intended crimes and those criminal harms that are "*reasonably* foreseeable" or "the natural and probable consequence" of the defendant's acts.

EXAMPLES AND ANALYSIS

In People v. Luparello, 187 Cal. App. 3d 410 (1987), the defendant asked friends to help him obtain information regarding his former lover "at any cost." The friends ended up killing a person in an effort to obtain the information. Defendant was convicted of murder because the killing was reasonably foreseeable given defendant's request.

In People v. Brigham, 216 Cal. App. 3d 1039 (1990), the defendant set out with a friend to kill X. The friend mistook Y for X and prepared to kill him. Although the defendant protested that Y was the wrong person, his friend killed him anyway. Because the defendant knew of his friend's hot-headed, erratic nature, the killing was foreseeable and defendant was guilty as an accomplice to the murder of Y.

---

iii. **Criticism of natural and probable consequence doctrine.** The "natural and probable consequence" rule of accomplice liability is inconsistent with fundamental principles of criminal law because it allows a conviction even when the defendant does not have the required mens rea for that crime. For example, although it may be correct to say the defendant in *Luparello* is guilty of involuntary manslaughter for enlisting the help of his friends in committing negligent acts, imposing accomplice liability makes him guilty of premeditated, first degree murder.

iv. **Separate frolic.** If the principal engages in a "separate frolic" during the commission of a crime, the accomplice may be able to escape liability by arguing the separate crime was not foreseeable. For example, in State v. Lucas, 55 Iowa 321 (1880), defendants robbed a safe at a mill. While defendant was busy with the safe, his accomplices stole silver dollars from the watchman's pocket. The court found that the robbery of the watchman was a separate and unforeseeable crime. See also Regina v. Anderson & Morris [1996] 2 W.L.R. 1195 (killing was a departure from the common scheme agreed upon by defendants).

j. **Accomplice mens rea for strict liability crimes.** Different mens rea standards apply to accomplices and principals in strict liability crimes. To be guilty of strict liability crimes, the principal need not have any mens rea as to attendant circumstances. An accomplice, however, must at least know the essential matters which constitute the offense.

EXAMPLE AND ANALYSIS

In Johnson v. Youden, 1 K.B. 544 (1950), defendants were charged with aiding and abetting a builder to sell a house at a price in excess of that permitted by law. Selling a house at an unlawful price is a strict liability crime. Although the builder could be convicted of the unlawful sale, even if he did not know he was charging an unlawful price, the defendants (lawyers for the builder) could not be convicted as accomplices unless they knew the builder was charging an excessive price.

---

i. **Willful blindness sufficient.** When it is required that the accomplice know a circumstance of the crime, a defendant who is willfully blind to the situation is deemed to have sufficient knowledge for conviction.

EXAMPLE AND ANALYSIS

Defendant was charged with aiding and abetting the improper disposal of hazardous waste which is a strict liability crime. The evidence shows that defendant suspected that his workers were handling drums of hazardous waste, but he intentionally told his workers not to discuss what was in the drums with anyone, including himself. Defendant had sufficient mens rea to be an accomplice to the crime.

---

ii. **Model Penal Code ambiguity.** The MPC requires that the defendant act with purpose as to the "commission of the offense." MPC §2.06(3)(a). This clause is intentionally ambiguous as to whether the accomplice must have knowledge or purpose as to the elements of a crime for which the principal is strictly liable. However, unless the crime is a strict liability offense, most courts will impose a mens rea requirement for the attendant circumstance.

EXAMPLE AND ANALYSIS

In Bowell v. State, 728 P.2d 1220 (Alaska 1986), defendant was convicted as an accomplice to first-degree sexual assault. The Alaska statute was based upon the Model Penal Code and held a person responsible as an accomplice if "with intent to promote or facilitate the commission of the offense," the person aids in the crime. Rape is not a strict liability offense. Accordingly, as an accomplice, defendant was required to know that he was helping his friend engage in sexual intercourse with the victim and that at the time he aided his friend, he recklessly disregarded the victim's lack of consent.

Note. If defendant had been charged with being an accomplice to statutory rape, the MPC would leave to the courts whether the defendant needed to know the girl was a minor. Statutory rape is a "strict liability" crime and a court would therefore be free to find that defendant need not have a mens rea as to the attendant circumstance of the victim's age.

---

k. **Accomplice mens rea for reckless or negligent crimes.** It is impossible, by definition, to intend a negligent result. If the defendant intended the harm, the result would have been purposeful, not negligent. Therefore, accomplice liability for negligent crimes requires that the defendant: 1. had the purpose to assist the principal; and 2. was negligent regarding the results.

Examples and Analysis

In State v. McVay, 47 R.I. 292 (1926), the defendants were the captain and engineer of a steamer. When the boilers to the steamer burst and killed passengers, defendants were charged as accomplices to involuntary manslaughter because they fired up the boilers. Even though defendants did not intend to kill anyone, they were guilty of the negligent homicides that resulted, because they had the purpose to assist the ship's operation and design and, like the principal, acted negligently in doing so.

In People v. Abbott, 84 A.D.2d 11 (1981), defendant participated in drag racing. His opponent careened out of control and killed passengers in another car. Both defendant and his opponent were guilty of criminally negligent homicide. Defendant was an aider and abettor to the crime because he purposely encouraged and participated in the activity and was negligent as to the resulting deaths.

In State v. Foster, 202 Conn. 520 (Conn. 1987), the defendant, Michael Foster, tracked down the man he thought raped his girlfriend. After subduing the man, Foster gave a knife to his friend, Cannon, and asked him to watch the suspect while Foster went to retrieve his girlfriend to make a positive identification. While Foster was gone, the suspect charged at Cannon, who held out the knife and fatally stabbed him. Foster was found guilty of aiding criminally negligent homicide. The mental state required for aiding a negligent crime does *not* include intending to cause the result of the negligent conduct. It is sufficient if a defendant intentionally aids another in an act and is negligent as to the resulting death.

Defendant gives his car keys to a person he knows to be drunk. That person drives the car, has an accident, and kills somebody. Although courts are split, many courts have found accomplice liability in this situation. But see People v. Marshall, 106 N.W.2d 842 (Mich. 1961) (finding no accomplice liability because defendant was not with the driver at the time he drove drunk; defendant could be guilty, however, as principal to misdemeanor-manslaughter for providing car keys to a drunken person).

EXAM TIP

Involuntary manslaughter is the crime most frequently used to test whether a student understands the mens rea required for accomplice liability for negligent crimes.

i. **Model Penal Code.** A similar approach is taken by the MPC in defining accomplice liability for negligent crimes. The defendant need only act with the kind of culpability that is sufficient for commission of the offense; i.e., negligence, not purposefulness. MPC §2.06(4). Accomplice liability for negligent crimes raises two important issues that should be addressed separately: causation and the mens rea for complicity in a negligent crime.

EXAMPLE AND ANALYSIS

In State v. Ayers, 478 N.W.2d 606 (Iowa 1991), defendant was charged with aiding and abetting involuntary manslaughter after he sold a handgun to a minor who accidentally shot and killed a friend while displaying the gun. This raises two issues: 1. Were defendant's actions a cause of the death? and 2. Did the defendant have the requisite purpose to assist and was there negligence as to the result?

Note. The closer the accomplice is physically to the action, the more likely the court will find that reckless and negligent conduct satisfy the mens rea requirement for accomplice liability. See State v. Travis, 497 N.W.2d 905 (Iowa App. 1993).

---

2. Actus Reus

To be an accomplice, the defendant must provide an act of assistance. The actus reus for accomplice liability may be either a positive act or an omission when there is a duty to act.

Actus Reus — Any aid or encouragement

a. **Examples of positive acts.** There are an infinite number of ways an accomplice may help the principal in the commission of a crime. For example, in a bank robbery an accomplice can devise a plan for the robbery, survey the bank, serve as a lookout, drive the getaway car, or provide encouragement to the principal robber.

b. **Examples of omissions.** A failure to act can constitute the actus reus for accomplice liability if the defendant has a legal duty to intervene but fails to do so. For example, if a police officer, realizing that a robbery is occurring, purposely turns the other way and allows the robbery to occur, the officer is an accomplice. See also MPC §2.06(3)(a)(iii).

c. **Mere presence and acts of encouragement.** Mere presence at the scene of a crime ordinarily is *not* enough to constitute an actus reus for accomplice liability unless the defendant's presence is offered as a form of encouragement.

EXAMPLES AND ANALYSIS

In Pace v. State, 248 Ind. 146 (1967), defendant was driving a car with his family and a friend, Rootes, in the back seat. They stopped to pick up a hitchhiker. Rootes then robbed the hitchhiker. Defendant said nothing and continued to drive. The court held that defendant was "merely present" and not an accomplice to the robbery.

In Evans v. State, 643 So. 2d 1204 (1994), defendant was riding in a truck when one of his co-passengers shot out the window at a building. Although defendant knew his fellow passenger was likely to engage in such conduct, he did nothing to help and was therefore not guilty as an accomplice.

Compare. In Wilcox v. Jeffery, 1 All E.R. 464 (1951), the defendant was a jazz magazine publisher who attended the concert of a foreign saxophonist illegally performing in England. The court upheld defendant's conviction for aiding and abetting the saxophonist's violation of immigration labor laws because defendant's presence at the concert, together with his positive act of buying a ticket, served as a form of encouragement.

---

d. **Help need not contribute to the criminal result.** A person is guilty of aiding and abetting even if the criminal result would have occurred anyway and defendant's actions had no actual impact on the outcome.

   Example. In State v. Tally, 102 Ala. 25 (1894), a group of men set out to kill the victim. The defendant took steps to prevent the victim from receiving warning of the attack. Even though it is likely that the victim would have been killed even if there had been a warning, the defendant was an aider and abettor because he performed an act of assistance which made it more likely that the crime would succeed.

e. **Principal need not be aware of accomplice's acts.** A person can aid and abet a crime even though the principal is unaware of the accomplice's help.

   Example. Principal decides to rob a store. While the principal is taking money from the store owner, accomplice, who dislikes the owner but does not know the principal, cuts the wires of the store's security system. Even though principal and accomplice do not know each other and had not coordinated their efforts, accomplice is guilty of aiding and abetting the robbery.

f. **Attempted complicity.** An accomplice's acts must constitute some type of aid to qualify as aiding and abetting. If the would-be accomplice's acts cannot actually help, given the circumstances of the case, then under traditional common law there is no accomplice liability.

   i. **Example.** Defendant sees the principal about to kill the victim. Defendant yells words of encouragement to him but the principal is deaf and unaware of defendant's presence. Under traditional common law, there is no accomplice liability.

   ii. **Compare Model Penal Code approach.** Under the Model Penal Code, there is accomplice liability if a person aids, or attempts to aid, another's commission of a crime. MPC §2.06(3).

The MPC focuses on the defendant's actual blameworthiness, not the fortuity of success.

Example and Analysis

In People v. Genoa, 188 Mich. App. 461 (1991), defendant gave an undercover agent $10,000 toward the purchase of cocaine. The agent did not use the money to purchase the cocaine, but instead arrested defendant. Under common law, defendant could not be convicted of attempting to aid the possession of cocaine because the underlying crime of possession could never have been committed. However, under the Model Penal Code approach, defendant would be guilty.

g. **Accomplice liability for failure to protect victim.** Accomplice liability may be established by proof that the defendant failed to protect the victim from harm if: 1. there was a duty for the defendant to intervene; and 2. defendant's purpose in not intervening was to allow the principal to inflict harm.

Example. A mother stands by while her boyfriend abuses her young child. The mother is an accomplice to the abuse if her purpose in not acting was to allow the abuse.

Note. Some jurisdictions expand culpability in the above situation to cases where the parent knows, but does not have the purpose for the abuse to occur. See People v. Stanciel, 606 N.E.2d 1201 (Ill. 1992). However, the Model Penal Code requires purpose.

C. RELATIONSHIP BETWEEN THE LIABILITY OF THE PARTIES

In general, an accomplice is liable if the principal committed the crime, even if the principal is not convicted.

1. Situations in which the Liability of the Accomplice and Principal Do Not Depend upon Each Other

The general rule is that an accomplice is guilty when he or she helps another commit a crime. The status of an accomplice, however, may excuse that person from liability.

a. **Feigned accomplice.** A person who acts as an accomplice in an effort to apprehend the principal during the commission of a crime is not guilty of aiding and abetting the offense. The person does not act with the purpose of having the crime succeed, but with the purpose of stopping the criminal activity.

i. **Example.** In State v. Hayes, 105 Mo. 76 (1891), the defendant heard the principal to the crime was planning to commit a burglary of a store and offered to help him. Defendant stood outside the window of the store as the principal entered and handed out a side of bacon. Defendant was not guilty of aiding and abetting the burglary because his purpose in being present was to capture the principal during the commission of the crime, not to actually help the burglary succeed.

ii. **Undercover agents.** Similarly, an undercover agent or informant who participates in the commission of a crime in an attempt to apprehend the principals, is not guilty of aiding and abetting the offense.

Example. Hearing that inmates will attempt a prison break, an undercover officer poses as one of the inmates and helps the prisoners escape. As the inmates are leaving the jail, they are apprehended. The officer is not guilty as an accomplice to escape.

b. **Excused principal.** Accomplice liability depends on proof that a crime was committed and the defendant assisted in the commission of the crime. Liability does *not* depend on the prosecution and conviction of the principal. Principals may be excused from crimes for many reasons.

i. **Public authority justification defense.** There can be accomplice liability even though the principal cannot be prosecuted because he was working for law enforcement.

(a) **Example.** In Vaden v. State, 768 P.2d 1102 (Alaska 1989), defendant was charged with aiding and abetting the illegal hunting of foxes after he piloted a plane used by an undercover agent to hunt. The officer's actions were justified under the "public authority justification defense," but that defense did not provide any immunity to the aider and abettor.

- **Note.** An accomplice who participates in a crime with an undercover agent is not made immune from liability by the agent's status. However, the accomplice can raise a defense of entrapment. See Ch. 12 (F) infra.

(b) **Model Penal Code.** The Model Penal Code also imposes liability on an accomplice when he or she helps an innocent or irresponsible party engage in criminal conduct. MPC §2.06(2)(a).

ii. **Protected class of persons.** If a statute is designed to protect a certain class of persons, those persons may not be charged with aiding and abetting the offense. MPC §2.06(6)(a) (victims not liable as accomplices).

(a) **Example.** Child labor laws are designed to protect children. Accordingly, children who contract their services in violation of those laws are not accomplices.

(b) **Example.** An underaged girl cannot be charged with aiding and abetting statutory rape because the statutory rape laws are designed to protect her.

iii. **Using another as an instrument.** When the principal is not in control of his or her actions or has no culpability for his or her acts, it is more appropriate to charge the defendant with causing a crime by using another as an instrumentality rather than to charge him or her with aiding and abetting of an offense.

Example. Defendant causes a married person to marry another by falsely leading the married person to believe her prior marriage was legally terminated. Defendant has caused another to commit bigamy, even though the principal is innocent of the crime. 18 U.S.C. §2(b).

iv. **Culpable-but-unconvictable principal.** An accomplice may be guilty of aiding and abetting even though the principal has a policy-based defense to the crime. These include:

- diplomatic immunity
- entrapment
- immunity from state prosecution

Example. Defendant helps the ambassador from another country defraud a bank. Although the ambassador may not be convictable of the fraud, defendant is still guilty of aiding and abetting the offense.

c. **Acquitted principal.** If the principal and defendant are tried in separate proceedings, the acquittal of the principal does not preclude the conviction of the accomplice. Inconsistent verdicts are permitted. United States v. Standefer, 447 U.S. 10 (1980).

2. Differences in Degree of Culpability

Accomplice liability is usually viewed as derivative liability. The accomplice is guilty to the same degree as the principal. Some courts, however, gauge the relative culpability of the parties based upon their individual mens rea.

Example. In a rage, defendant hires a killer to murder her husband. Because she was acting under the heat of passion, defendant may be guilty of manslaughter, but the hired killer is guilty of murder because the killer acted with the purpose to kill.

D. ABANDONMENT/WITHDRAWAL DEFENSE

Under rare circumstances, a defendant can claim an abandonment as a defense to accomplice liability if the defendant withdraws from involvement before the principal completes the crime.

1. Common Law

At common law, a majority of jurisdictions did not recognize an abandonment defense to accomplice liability. Some jurisdictions, however, have added a statutory defense when a defendant voluntarily and completely renounces involvement in a crime and makes substantial efforts to prevent it. N.Y. Penal Code §40.10(1).

2. Model Penal Code

MPC §2.06 recognizes an abandonment defense if the defendant terminates his or her complicity prior to the commission of the offense; and either 1. wholly deprives it of effectiveness; or 2. gives timely warning to law enforcement authorities or otherwise makes proper efforts to prevent the crime.

3. Example

In People v. Cooper, 332 N.E.2d 453 (Ill. App. 1975), defendant broke into a woman's home with two accomplices and helped gag and bind her. He then changed his mind and left her house without taking anything. After he left, one of his accomplices killed the woman. Defendant was still guilty of the murder because he had not done anything to withdraw his aid or thwart the crime.

EXAM TIPS

When there are two or more actors in a factual scenario, consider both accomplice liability and conspiracy theories. Additionally, it can be helpful to start analysis with the principal actor and then analyze all of the remaining actors for accomplice liability.

FIGURE 9-1

ACCOMPLICE LIABILITY	
Theory of Liability	Accomplice liability is not a separate crime; it is a theory of liability for committed offense.
Requirements: Mens Rea Actus Reus	 Purpose to help; Purpose for crime to succeed Slightest assistance or encouragement
Relationship with Principal	Accomplice and Principal liability do not depend on each other.
Defenses	Abandonment/Withdrawal • C/L: No • MPC: Yes

REVIEW QUESTION AND ANSWER

ACCOMPLICE LIABILITY

Question: Kevin and Nancie are a young couple in the Midwest, looking to add some cash to their coffers so they can start a family. They decide to hit the road to "rob banks and raise heck just like Bonnie and Clyde." They call up their friends Hank and Petunia, who agree to join them on their spree. That night, Nancie, who worked in a bank for several years, carefully plans the first job to avoid silent alarms and other security devices. Kevin will drive the getaway car;

Hank will stand immediately outside the bank to keep lookout; and Petunia will enter the bank and hold up the first teller with a small toy pistol. (None of them wants anyone in the bank to get hurt.) Meanwhile, Nancie will go shopping at the local grocery store. She has assigned herself the duty of cooking the celebratory meal after it is all over.

The following day, Nancie, Kevin, Petunia, and Hank drive to a nearby town to do the job. At first everything goes according to plan. They drop Nancie off at the store, drive to the bank, and take their positions. But once Petunia is inside, Hank begins to get cold feet. He begins to think of his future and cannot bear the thought of going to jail. Suddenly, he sees a police officer approaching the bank. Hank sees this as his perfect opportunity to get out of the whole mess and walks quickly down the street away from the bank.

Meanwhile, inside the bank Petunia realizes that she forgot the hold-up note in the car, so she stops to ask a young man, Clark, if she can use his pen for a minute. Clark sees the gun Petunia is carrying and the paper money sack, but he lends her a pen anyway. Petunia uses the pen to write a hold-up note and approaches the teller. Just as the teller is giving Petunia the money, the police officer enters the bank, but Petunia is able to slip out the door before he notices that anything is wrong.

Kevin and Petunia leave the bank and pick up Nancie with the groceries. Before they leave the store, Kevin decides to let Petunia drive home because he is tired. On the way, Nancie exhorts Petunia to drive faster and run all the lights because "that's the way Bonnie and Clyde would do it!" Kevin enjoys the wild ride and is glad to get out of town quickly, but he just sits quietly in the back seat. Petunia careens down the highway at over 120 miles per hour and accidentally runs another car off the road and down a steep embankment. Unfortunately, the driver of the car is killed.

Several witnesses to the robbery and the road accident are able to make out the license number on Kevin's car. That evening, the police arrive at Kevin and Nancie's house just as they are sitting down to dinner with Petunia and dividing the loot. (They have just decided that Hank should not get a full share.)

What crimes, if any, have Petunia, Nancie, Kevin, Hank, and Clark committed?

Answer:

1. *Crimes Committed by Petunia.* It is always easiest to start analysis with the primary actor. Petunia is guilty of bank robbery and reckless homicide.

2. *Crimes Committed by Nancie.* Nancie is potentially guilty as an accomplice to bank robbery and an accomplice to reckless homicide.

Accomplice to Bank Robbery. To be guilty as an accomplice to bank robbery, a defendant must have the purpose to assist Petunia in robbing the bank and commit an act of assistance. Nancie certainly had the purpose to assist. She was the actual mastermind of the plan and told Petunia what to do; i.e., there was a suitable nexus or connection between them. Nancie also had a clear stake in the venture. She was going to get enough money to settle down and raise a family.

Nancie also meets the actus reus requirement because she planned the crime to facilitate the robbery and help Petunia avoid detection by security. Without Nancie's planning, it is likely that the crime would never have occurred.

Accomplice to Reckless Homicide. An accomplice to a reckless offense must have the purpose to aid the primary actor in a reckless activity and commit an act of assistance or encouragement. The accomplice need only be negligent as to the result of the crime. Nancie showed her purpose to encourage Petunia's reckless driving by telling her to drive faster and run all the lights. Similarly, Nancie had a stake in Petunia's driving because she was in the car and wanted to be like Bonnie and Clyde. Finally, Nancie was reckless as to the death of the motorist. She knew of a substantial and unjustifiable risk in encouraging Petunia and took the risk anyway.

Encouraging words also meet the actus reus requirement. Therefore, Nancie is guilty as an accomplice to reckless homicide.

3. *Crimes Committed by Kevin.* Kevin is potentially guilty as an accomplice to bank robbery and reckless homicide.

Accomplice to Bank Robbery. Kevin meets both the mens rea and actus reus requirements for accomplice liability even though he never entered the bank. The fact that he met with Nancie, Petunia, and Hank to plan the crime shows a direct connection or nexus between himself and Petunia, the principal actor. Like Nancie, he had a direct stake in the venture because he would receive a share of the loot. Therefore, Kevin had purpose to assist Petunia in her endeavor.

Kevin met the actus reus requirement because he drove Petunia to the bank and drove her away after the robbery. These acts clearly helped Petunia avoid detection and encouraged her to go through with the plan. Therefore, Kevin is guilty as an accomplice to bank robbery.

Accomplice to Reckless Homicide. The mens rea requirement for accomplice liability to a reckless or negligent crime is intent to assist or encourage the primary actor in the negligent or reckless conduct, and recklessness or negligence as to the result is not required. Kevin meets the mens rea requirement. He was riding in the car, enjoying the wild ride, and like Petunia and Nancie, wanted to get out of town and away from the police quickly. In this way, he had a sufficient connection to Petunia's actions and a stake in her driving.

Kevin might not meet the actus reus requirement for accomplice to reckless homicide. Mere presence at the scene of a crime is generally not enough to constitute actus reus unless the presence is offered as a form of encouragement. Unlike the defendant in *Wilcox v. Jeffrey*, Kevin took no affirmative act such as buying a ticket that would serve as a form of encouragement. He was merely in the car because the three of them were riding home together. He did allow Petunia to drive, but he in no way participated in or encouraged the criminal act which was driving *recklessly*.

On the other hand, prosecutors could argue that the robbery and homicide were part of one criminal activity—"robbing banks and raising heck." If this is true, then Kevin acted to encourage Petunia in both the robbing and the driving by taking part in the planning the night before. In addition, a majority of jurisdictions extend accomplice liability to criminal actions that are reasonably foreseeable or the natural and probable consequence of the defendant's acts. The prosecution would argue that a high-speed reckless get away is a reasonably foreseeable and a natural and probable consequence of any bank robbery. This is an especially convincing argument because the homicide offense only requires a reckless mental state. It would be hard for Kevin's defense to argue that he was not reckless in deciding to join the robbery in the first place. Instead, the defense would try to separate the robbery from the driving, arguing that there was no police pursuit and that only Petunia and Nancie were responsible for the reckless driving. Ultimately, however, Kevin is probably guilty as an accomplice to the homicide.

4. *Crimes Committed by Hank.* Hank is potentially guilty as an accomplice to bank robbery and reckless homicide.

Accomplice to Bank Robbery

Elements of Accomplice Liability. Hank, like Kevin and Nancie, meets the requirements for accomplice liability. He had a clear stake in the venture (his share of the loot) and a connection to the other culprits that show his purpose to aid and encourage the robbery. His actions of planning the crime and being present to lend moral support and warning if necessary were designed to encourage Petunia. It is important to note that the act performed need not actually contribute to the criminal result. Even though Hank did not successfully warn Petunia about the police, he did initially act to encourage and assist. Therefore, Hank has the requisite mens rea and actus reus for accomplice to bank robbery.

Abandonment Defense. The more important issue regarding Hank, however, is whether he can successfully claim an abandonment defense. There are two basic approaches to this defense.

- *Common Law/Majority Statutes.* In general, common law does not recognize an abandonment defense to accomplice liability, but most state statutes allow the defense if the defendant voluntarily and completely renounces involvement in the crime and takes substantial steps to prevent it. Hank ended his involvement before Petunia completed the robbery, but he did not renounce his involvement to the other members of the gang. He also took no affirmative steps to prevent the crime such as warning the police officer. Hank would argue that he assumed the officer would stop Petunia and that he acted to stop the robbery by not fulfilling his duties as a lookout. This argument, however, is likely to fail under the statutes because his renunciation was too passive and may have been simply an effort to escape capture by the police.
- *Model Penal Code.* The MPC recognizes an abandonment defense if the defendant terminates his or her complicity prior to the commission of the offense and either wholly deprives it of effectiveness or gives timely warning to law enforcement authorities. Hank has a better abandonment argument under the MPC because he made his participation as a lookout wholly ineffective by failing to warn Petunia. Hank might successfully claim abandonment under the MPC.

5. *Crimes Committed by Clark.* Clark is potentially guilty as an accomplice to bank robbery or criminal facilitation.

Accomplice to Bank Robbery. Even though Clark may have acted with knowledge of Petunia's crime, Clark did not have the purpose to assist required for ordinary accomplice liability. He simply loaned Petunia a pen. There was no nexus or connection between Clark and Petunia either before or after that act and he had no stake whatsoever in the success of the bank robbery.

Some jurisdictions, however, relax the purpose requirement depending on the seriousness and nature of the crime. In some cases mere knowledge establishes accomplice liability for major crimes. Bank robbery is definitely a major crime, but Clark did little to assist Petunia. Unlike the knowing accomplice in *United States v. Fountain*, Clark's assistance was not necessary to the commission of the crime. Petunia could have easily borrowed a pen from someone else or just spoken her request. However, any help may suffice if done with the required mens rea.

Criminal Facilitation. Some state statutes provide for a separate lesser crime that requires only that the defendant knowingly facilitates a crime. Clark knew that Petunia would rob the bank or at least had a strong suspicion, but he loaned her the pen anyway. Clark is guilty of criminal facilitation.

CORPORATE LIABILITY

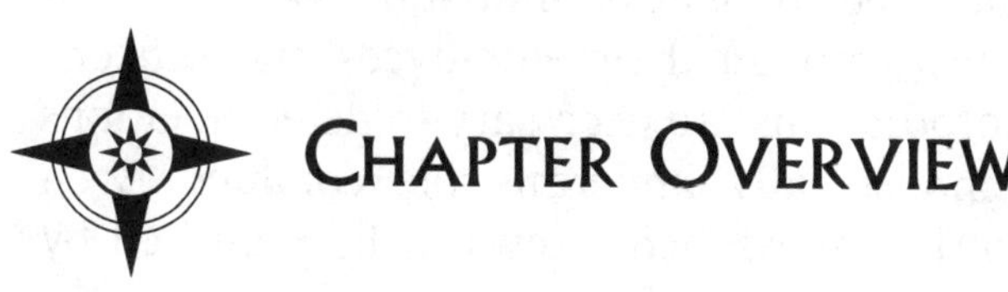

CHAPTER OVERVIEW

Corporate criminality provides unique problems for the application of criminal law. Although corporations are legal "persons," they can only act through their individual employees and officials. Corporate criminal liability raises two key issues: 1. What acts create criminal liability for a corporation? 2. What corporate acts create criminal liability for individuals in a corporation?

Accordingly, Chapter 10 reviews two key concepts in corporate liability:

- Liability of the Corporate Entity
- Liability of Corporate Agents

A. LIABILITY OF THE CORPORATE ENTITY

At early common law, courts and commentators believed that corporations could not commit a crime. Modern authorities universally recognize corporate criminal liability, even for crimes that require purposeful conduct. State v. Christy Pontiac-GMC, Inc., 354 N.W.2d 17 (1984).

1. Should There Be Corporate Criminal Liability?

There are policy arguments for and against the recognition of corporate criminal liability.

a. **Arguments against corporate liability.** Criminal liability depends on the culpability of individuals. Because a corporation is a fictitious entity, it cannot form the mens rea that traditionally triggers criminal liability for individuals. Moreover, traditional modes of punishment, such as imprisonment, cannot deter corporations from criminal conduct. Rather, criminally prosecuting a corporation ordinarily yields no greater sanction than civil prosecution with punitive damages. Criminal sanctions against corporations also punish innocent stockholders who may have been unaware of the criminal behavior. Finally, corporate criminal liability encourages erratic jury behavior because jurors may simply impose liability on the corporate entity when it is difficult to identify criminal liability by any specific individuals.

b. **Arguments in favor of corporate liability.** Corporations are legal entities that receive the benefits of the law and should be responsible for compliance with the law, including criminal law. Although corporations cannot act in the same manner as individual persons, corporations can commit crimes through their employees and officers. Criminal prosecutions of corporations are necessary to deter violations of the law and to condemn socially impermissible conduct. Even though corporations cannot be imprisoned, they can be punished by other methods, such as fines, administrative sanctions, injunctive orders, and public opprobrium. Corporate criminal liability does not unfairly punish shareholders because their losses are limited to the equity of the corporation, and no personal stigma attaches to a shareholder when the corporation is guilty of a crime.

2. Constitutionality of Corporate Criminal Liability

The Supreme Court has held that corporate criminal liability is constitutional. New York Central & Hudson River Railroad Co. v. United States, 212 U.S. 481 (1909).

3. Requirements for Corporate Liability

Traditional law holds a corporation liable for the acts of its agents which occur in the scope of the employment, even if the acts are contrary to corporate policy or express instructions. United States v. Hilton Hotels Corp., 467 F.2d 1000 (9th Cir. 1972). Corporate criminal liability is a form of vicarious liability. There are four basic approaches to corporate criminal liability.

a. **Respondeat superior approach.** This approach governs corporate criminal liability through the tort doctrine of respondeat superior. Under this doctrine, a corporation is criminally liable for the acts of its agent if the agent:

- commits a crime
- while acting within the scope of employment
- with the intent to benefit the corporation

i. **Warning.** Any job-related act is considered "within the scope of employment," even if a superior or the corporation specifically forbids the act and makes good faith efforts to prevent it.

Example and Analysis

The manager of a hotel joins in an illegal boycott of a supplier even though his act is contrary to the policy and instructions of corporate officers. Because it is within a manager's job responsibilities to decide from whom to purchase hotel supplies, the corporation is responsible for the criminal conduct. United States v. Hilton Hotels Corp., 467 F.2d 1000 (9th Cir. 1972).

ii. **Rationale.** Given the profit motive pressures on employees in a corporate structure, generalized instructions to obey the law are often not taken seriously, especially if a violation earns additional profits.

b. **The Model Penal Code alternative.** The MPC approach cuts back the traditional scope of corporate liability based on the acts of the corporation's officers and employees. Under MPC §2.07, there are three rules that govern corporate liability:

i. **Minor infractions and nonpenal offenses.** Corporations are liable if a corporate agent commits the offense while acting within the scope of his employment and on behalf of the corporation. The corporation is not liable, however, if it meets the "due diligence defense." The due diligence defense requires proof that "the high managerial agent having supervisory responsibility over the subject matter of the offense employed due diligence to prevent its commission." MPC §2.07(1)(a).

ii. **Omissions.** A corporation is accountable for failure to discharge specific duties imposed on corporations by law. MPC §2.07(1)(b).

iii. **True crimes.** A corporation is guilty of serious crimes only if the conduct constituting the offense is authorized, commanded, solicited, performed, or recklessly tolerated by the board of directors or a "high managerial agent" whose acquiescence to the wrongdoing reflects corporate policy. MPC §2.07(1)(c).

c. **Particular responsibility approach.** Some courts use an intermediate position in imposing corporate criminal liability. Rather than adopting either the respondeat superior or MPC approach, these courts require proof that the agent committing the unlawful act had particular responsibility or authority for that aspect of the corporation's business. If the corporation made that agent responsible for a particular aspect of the business, then it should face corporate liability for the agent's decision. See Commonwealth v. Beneficial Finance Co., 360 Mass. 188 (1971).

d. **Corporate character theory.** Under this theory, a corporation is guilty if the prosecution proves a "corporate ethos" that encourages agents of the corporation to commit criminal acts. To determine the corporate ethos, the trier of fact must examine the corporation's internal structure, supervision of personnel, goals, steps to educate employees, reaction to past violations, and general attitude toward complying with the law.

EXAMPLE AND ANALYSIS

An oil corporation has been drilling for years under a local dam gradually making it structurally unsound. Company officers are known for their policy of "blaming the messenger" when any manager brings them bad news. The company regularly fires officers who report low profits or unfavorable government regulation in their divisions. The engineers in charge of monitoring structural stability at the dam follow this corporate ethos by hiding their test results until the dam finally breaks causing heavy property damage and several deaths. The corporation is liable for the engineers' actions under corporate character theory.

4. Corporate Homicide

Recently, some prosecutors have charged corporations with common law crimes, including homicide. Courts and juries, however, remain uncomfortable with imposing criminal liability on fictional entities for such crimes.

Example. In State v. Ford Motor Co., Ind. Super. Ct. (1979), the Ford corporation was charged with reckless homicide for designing and manufacturing the Pinto automobile with a gas tank that exploded upon rear-end impact. The corporation successfully limited much of the evidence presented at trial, and the jury returned acquittals to the charges.

5. Alternatives to Corporate Criminal Liability

Civil judgments may also be used to influence corporate conduct, especially regarding product safety. In fact, some commentators believe that civil liability more accurately measures public willingness to force corporations to invest in safety. Unlike the relatively small fines for criminal convictions, civil judgments may include multimillion dollar awards. However, criminal convictions tend to carry more of a social stigma.

B. LIABILITY OF CORPORATE AGENTS

One of the more difficult issues relating to corporate crime is whether individuals working in the corporate setting should have responsibility not only for their own criminal acts, but also for the actions of those working under their supervision. When imposed, this indirect culpability is called vicarious liability.

1. Traditional View

Under both the Model Penal Code and prevailing case law, a person operating in the corporate setting is responsible for:

a. any crimes that person personally commits;
and
b. reckless failure to discharge a duty for which the corporate agent has primary responsibility.

See MPC §2.07(6).

2. Vicarious Liability

Some courts have been willing to impute to partners knowledge of the illegal acts of their agents, especially for public welfare offenses. Using this approach, a partnership is vicariously liable for illegal conduct committed by its employees at the corporation, whether or not the other partners were directly involved in that conduct.

EXAMPLE AND ANALYSIS

In Gordon v. United States, 203 F.2d 248 (10th Cir. 1953), *rev'd*, 347 U.S. 909 (1954), appliance business partners were convicted of selling sewing machines on illegal credit terms. Although the employers denied knowledge of the practice, the court imputed to them knowledge of the actions of their salespeople and upheld the partners' convictions for "willfully" violating the law. The Supreme Court later rejected the vicarious liability theory and reversed the conviction. Subsequent cases, however, have permitted the vicarious liability theory to be applied to the partnership entity. See, e.g., United States v. A&P Trucking Co., 358 U.S. 121, 126 (1958).

---

3. Responsible Relationship Doctrine

In order to avoid controversy surrounding vicarious liability, some courts have chosen an alternative standard for corporate agent liability. These courts hold corporate officials responsible for causing strict liability violations based upon their own failure to exercise the quality of care in supervision necessary to prevent such violations. In such cases, the prosecution must show a responsible relationship between the defendant and the subordinates' acts or omissions that resulted in the crime.

a. **Example.** In United States v. Park, 421 U.S. 658 (1975), the chief executive officer of a corporation selling rat-infested, contaminated food was held personally responsible for the acts of his subordinates when he admitted that their work fell under his supervision at the company, and he had prior notice of an ongoing problem with sanitation.

b. **Note.** Most courts have rejected the "responsible relationship" doctrine for crimes that require actual knowledge. Thus, in United States v. MacDonald & Watson Waste Oil Co., 933 F.2d 35 (1991), the court reversed a conviction for knowing illegal transportation of hazardous waste where the government conceded that there was no direct evidence that the defendant knew of the violation. The prosecution had argued he was guilty simply because he was the supervisor of that part of the corporation's activities.

4. Impossibility Defense

Even where courts recognize vicarious liability, they ordinarily allow a defense if the corporate agents show it was "objectively impossible" to avoid the harm.

Example. In United States v. New England Grocers Supply Co., 488 F. Supp. 230 (D. Mass. 1980), the court allowed the corporate officer to establish an affirmative defense that he exercised extraordinary care and still could not prevent the violations of the law.

5. Future of Corporate Criminal Liability?

There are ongoing proposals to expand vicarious liability to the directors and officers of corporations who have the power to prevent criminal violations. Such rules would impose vicarious liability on directors and officers for offenses within their "sphere of authority." Other proposals would impose such liability only if the defendant's reckless supervision resulted in criminal behavior.

a. **Strict liability crimes.** The crimes most commonly charged against corporations are those involving strict liability. See Chapter 3 supra for general discussion of strict liability. Strict liability crimes raise none of the complications of proving mens rea by a fictional entity. The entity is guilty once it has engaged in the lawful act. Corporations are often engaged in those high-risk activities that are likely to be regulated under a strict liability theory. Both a corporation and its individual officers or directors may be charged with violations of strict liability laws.

FIGURE 10-1

CORPORATE CRIMINAL LIABILITY	
Corporation's Criminal Liability	
Respondeat Superior Approach	Corporation is criminally liable if its agent: 1. commits a crime, 2. while acting within the scope of employment, 3. with the intent to benefit the corporation.
Model Penal Code Approach	Respondeat Superior liability only for minor infractions Serious crimes require board of directors or management involvement
Liability of Individuals for Acts of Corporation	
Traditional View	Individual responsible for: 1. crimes personally committed; 2. reckless failure to discharge duty.
Responsible Relationship Doctrine	Vicarious liability if there is a "responsible relationship" between the defendant and subordinate's acts or omissions

Review Question and Answer

CORPORATE LIABILITY

Question: HUGE Aircraft Corporation of Southern California designs and manufactures the finest helicopters and airplanes in the world. Recently HUGE decided to expand its large defense contracting operation by manufacturing high-tech household goods for use on U.S. military bases. In a corporate coup HUGE has been able to hire Betty Brawn, a hard-charging young executive from rival Boing! corporation, to head up its Thermonuclear Coffeemaker division and go after the government contract.

During her first day on the job, Betty meets with Derrick Snivel, a lowly lab technician in charge of research and development on the coffeemaker. He tells her that there are huge problems with the project. Although the miniature nuclear generator is an excellent alternative energy source, it has a tendency to melt down and release toxic levels of radiation whenever the machine is used to brew more than six cups of coffee. Derrick is currently writing his final report on the project, which must be submitted to the Defense Department for evaluation by the end of the month. Betty tells Derrick that despite her desire for the contract and the promotion she would likely get, she wants to see everything in her division done above board and according to the law. Knowingly submitting false documents for government contract review is a criminal offense. Betty tells Derrick she can always find a job elsewhere if the project does not turn out well, and integrity means a lot to her. She wants Derrick to do his best to fix the problems before the deadline and turn in an honest report to the government. Derrick has also read the HUGE corporate manual, which admonishes all employees always to obey the law in their duties for the company.

Unfortunately, integrity is not very important to Derrick, and he is likely to lose his job at HUGE if the project fails. Unable to fix the problems with the coffeemaker, he gives Betty a report rating the machine as A-1 for both performance and safety. Betty is amazed and slightly suspicious when she learns that Derrick was able to fix the problem so quickly. She is a busy woman, however, and does not have time to look into the matter further. Betty stamps "Approved" on the report and returns it to Derrick for submission to the Defense Department. Two years later with the coffeemakers installed in military bases throughout the eastern seaboard, the meltdowns begin and 63 people are killed.

1. For what crimes, if any, is HUGE Corporation liable?
2. For what crimes, if any, is Betty liable?

Answer:

1. *HUGE Corporate Liability*. HUGE is potentially liable for the crime of falsifying documents related to a government contract and may even be charged with reckless or negligent homicide for the deaths.

Respondeat Superior Approach. Under this approach, HUGE is liable if an employee: a. commits a crime; b. within the scope of employment; c. with the intent to benefit the corporation. In this case, Derrick's actions were definitely job-related, which is usually enough to be considered within the scope of employment. Derrick knew he would lose his job if the project failed. He acted with the intent to benefit the company and thereby save his job and get a promotion. HUGE is liable for Derrick's crime despite admonishments to obey the law by Betty and the HUGE corporate manual.

The Model Penal Code Alternative. The MPC approach cuts back on the traditional scope of corporate liability based on respondeat superior.

Minor Infractions and Nonpenal Offenses. If falsifying documents is a minor or nonpenal offense, HUGE is liable because Derrick was acting within the scope of employment on behalf of the corporation. However, HUGE is not liable if it can show that "The high managerial agent having supervisory responsibility over the subject matter of the offense employed due diligence to prevent its commission." MPC §2.07(1)(b). Betty, as supervisor of the project, did warn Derrick to obey the law, but she probably did not exercise due diligence to prevent the infraction. When Derrick's report crossed her desk, she suspected or had reason to suspect that Derrick could not have fixed all the coffeepot problems in the time allotted, and submitted the report anyway. HUGE is liable for Derrick's actions.

Omissions. Corporate omission theory does not apply because in this instance there was an affirmative action (submitting false documents to the government), not a failure to act.

True Crimes. Under the MPC, HUGE is liable for a serious crime if the offense was authorized, commanded, solicited, performed, or recklessly tolerated by the board of directors or a high managerial agent whose acquiescence to the wrongdoing reflects corporate policy. MPC §2.07(1)(c). In this case, Betty was negligent or reckless in not finding out more when she suspected the report might be false, especially when she knew that the coffeemaker glitch could kill someone. However, there is no evidence that tolerating the submission of false reports reflects HUGE corporate policy. In fact, their corporate manual states the contrary. HUGE is not criminally liable if falsifying documents is considered a serious federal offense unless the prosecution can show an unwritten policy to disobey the law.

Particular Responsibility Approach. Under this theory, the corporation is liable if the employee committing the unlawful act had particular responsibility for that aspect of the corporation's business. Derrick is a scientist in charge of all research and development on the coffeemaker project. It is very likely that he is the only person at HUGE who understands the technical aspects of the project well enough to write detailed government report. In this way, he is particularly responsible for that report and HUGE is liable for his actions because the corporation put him in an important decision-making position.
Corporate Character Theory. Using this approach, a corporation is liable if the prosecution proves a "corporate ethos" that encourages the criminal act. HUGE does not seem to have such an ethos. The corporate manual tells employees to obey the law, and HUGE hired Betty, an executive with a great deal of integrity. On the other hand, the corporation has created a work environment where Derrick feels that he will be fired if HUGE does not get the contract he is working on, which may encourage illegal actions. More evidence would be needed to determine if the manual and Betty's instructions represent the true corporate ethos or are mere lip service to legality.
Corporate Homicide. The prosecution may try to charge HUGE with a reckless or negligent homicide offense, but the courts and juries are generally uncomfortable imposing such liability on corporations. See State v. Ford Motor Co., supra.
Alternatives to Criminal Liability. It is important to note that those injured or killed by the coffeemakers and their families are likely to bring large civil suits against HUGE. Large punitive damages against the corporation may have a great deterrent effect to prevent such practices at HUGE and other corporations in the future.

2. *Betty Brawn Personal Criminal Liability.* Betty is potentially personally liable for falsifying documents and reckless or negligent homicide.
Traditional View. Under both the MPC and prevailing case law Betty is responsible for any crimes she personally commits and reckless failure to discharge a duty for which she has primary responsibility.

Technically speaking Betty did not herself submit a false report to the Defense Department, but she may be guilty of using Derrick as an instrument to perform a criminal act because she ordered him to submit the report. Betty also approved Derrick's report without checking its accuracy. Her order to submit the report and failure to oversee the project were probably reckless because she knew of the substantial and unjustifiable risk that a coffeemaker meltdown posed and suspected that Derrick could not have fixed the problem in only a month. Therefore, Betty is personally liable for the submission of false documents.

Similarly, Betty is probably liable for the homicide charge. Her own reckless approval of the report was a direct and proximate cause of death. She is also the person primarily responsible for the report and the entire coffeemaker project.

Vicarious Liability. According to this theory, managers and supervisors have constructive knowledge of the actions of their workers. This theory definitely makes Betty liable for both the false documents and homicide charges, even if she had no reason at all to suspect that the report might be false.

Responsible Relationship Doctrine. This approach holds corporate officials responsible for their own failure to exercise the quality of care necessary to prevent the violation. Betty was personally responsible for the project, and she knew of an ongoing problem with the coffeemaker, but the offense requires that the defendant knowingly submit false documents and most courts reject the "responsible relationship" doctrine when the crime requires actual knowledge. Betty did not actually know that the report was false.

However, Betty may still be liable under this doctrine for reckless or negligent homicide because she failed to exercise the proper care in supervising Derrick's actions.

Objective Impossibility Defense. Betty would not be able to prove that it was impossible for her to avoid Derrick's illegal action. A simple check of the accuracy of his report would have changed everything; Betty had every reason to make such a check and she did not.

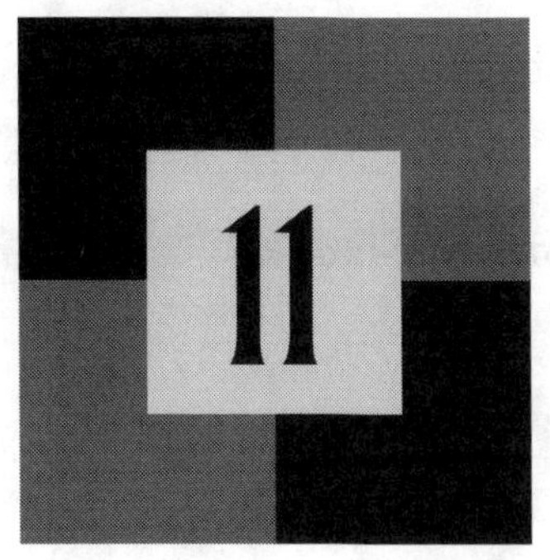

CONSPIRACY

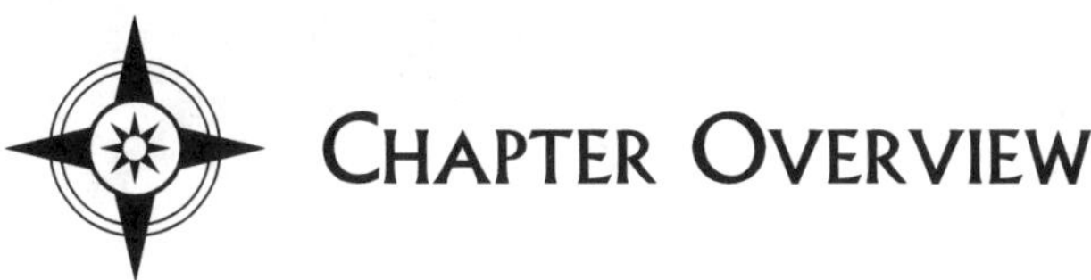

CHAPTER OVERVIEW

Conspiracy is a unique and controversial crime. Like attempt, it is an *inchoate* crime. It punishes behavior before it has harmful effects. However, unlike attempt, it does not require a substantial step toward completing the crime. The gist of the offense of conspiracy lies in the unlawful agreement. A mere agreement to commit a crime is conspiracy. Conspiracy laws allow prosecutors to strike at the special danger posed when groups of people come together to commit crimes.

Conspiracy is a crime separate from the underlying offense. It does not merge with any completed offense. Thus, if conspirators are successful in their plans, they face at least two charges: one for conspiracy and the other for the completed offense.

Prosecutors favor conspiracy charges for several reasons: 1. It is a separate crime carrying its own penalties; 2. It allows the apprehension of potential criminal conduct at an earlier stage than attempt; 3. Members of a conspiracy are vicariously responsible for the criminal acts of their co-conspirators, even without proof of accomplice liability; 4. Conspiracy allows the apprehension and prosecution of large groups of individuals; 5. Conspiracy is a continuing offense which gives a longer time period for prosecutors to file charges; 6. Venue for conspiracy charges may be brought in any jurisdiction in which an act of the conspiracy occurred; and 7. Hearsay exceptions allow admission of co-conspirators' statements.

A conspiracy is defined as "an agreement by two or more persons to commit a crime." To be guilty of conspiracy, a defendant must have: 1. agreed to commit a crime; 2. with the intent to have the crime succeed. In some jurisdictions, there is a third requirement: 3. one of the conspirators must have committed an "overt act" toward the commission of the crime.

Chapter 11 reviews the law of conspiracy and special types of conspiracy charges brought against ongoing criminal organizations. The Racketeer Influenced and Corrupt Organizations Act (RICO) is one of the tools used to combat such organizations. Chapter 11 includes a discussion of the following topics:

- Overview: The Nature and Consequences of a Conspiracy Charge
  - Impact of conspiracy liability
  - Substantive consequences
  - Procedural advantages
- Conspiracy as a Form of Accessorial Liability
  - Pinkerton liability
- Elements of Conspiracy
  - Actus reus
  - Overt act
  - Mens rea
- Scope of the Agreement
  - Chain vs. wheel conspiracies
- Parties to Conspiracies
- Summary of Conspiracy Law
- Criminal Enterprises and RICO

A. INTRODUCTION

Conspiracy law is premised on the assumption that group crimes pose an extra risk to safety and compliance with the laws. The more people involved in the planning and execution of a crime, the more likely the crime will succeed. Conspiracy allows for more complex crimes, and the group's moral support and peer pressure add to each member's perseverance in the assigned task. Because of these added dangers, conspiracy is treated as a separate crime with serious consequences.

1. Definition of "Conspiracy"

A conspiracy is an agreement by two or more persons to commit a crime.

2. Objective of the Conspiracy

In most jurisdictions, the objective (goal) of a conspiracy must be to commit a crime. The law no longer recognizes conspiracies "to offend public morals." Compare Shaw v. Director of Public Prosecutions, (1962) A.C. 220. However, some jurisdictions still recognize a conspiracy to pursue some noncriminal but harmful objective, such as a conspiracy "to cheat or defraud another person." See, e.g., Cal. Penal Code, §182(a)(4); 18 U.S.C. §371 (recognizing conspiracy to defraud the United States).

3. Punishment

Conspiracy is punished as a separate crime, but in some jurisdictions the level of punishment depends on the seriousness of the crime defendants conspired to commit. In federal court, the punishment for all conspiracies is a maximum of five years imprisonment. 18 U.S.C. §371. Under the MPC, the punishment for conspiracy is the same as provided for the most serious offense which the parties conspired to commit. MPC §5.05(1).

B. CONSEQUENCES OF A CONSPIRACY CHARGE

"A conspiracy is a partnership in crime." Pinkerton v. United States, 328 U.S. 640, 644 (1946). As such, it has some unique substantive and procedural consequences.

1. Substantive Consequences

a. **Conspiracy is a separate crime.** Conspiracy is an offense that carries its own penalty. Thus, if two or more persons agree to commit a crime and then commit the crime, each person is guilty of at least two crimes: conspiracy and the completed substantive offense.

i. **Example.** A and B agree to rob a bank. They then rob the bank. A and B are guilty of both conspiracy and robbery.

ii. **Model Penal Code.** The Model Penal Code diverges from common law. Under the Model Penal Code, the crime of conspiracy merges with the completed target offense unless the prosecution proves the conspiracy involved the commission of additional offenses not yet committed or attempted. MPC §1.07(1)(b); ALI Comment to §1.07, at 109.

b. **Conspiracy punishes preparatory conduct.** The mere act of agreeing to commit a crime is sufficient for the conspiracy even if there is no substantial step toward completing that crime. Conspiracy is an inchoate crime that punishes behavior at the earliest stage of planning.

Example. A and B agree to rob a bank. Assuming there is no overt act requirement, see §D(2) infra, A and B are guilty of conspiracy the moment they agree to commit a crime.

c. **Conspirators have co-conspirator liability.** Once a defendant joins a conspiracy, he or she is responsible for all acts of the co-conspirators done within the scope of the conspiracy, even if there is no evidence of accomplice liability. See §C(1) infra.

Example. A and B agree to rob a bank. Unbeknownst to B, A steals a car to use in the robbery. Because he is a co-conspirator, B is automatically guilty of the car theft.

d. **In federal law, conspiracy aggravates the degree of the crime.** Conspiring to commit a misdemeanor is a felony even though the target offense, when accomplished, would only be a misdemeanor. Conspiracy aggravates the degree of the crime because of the risks accompanying group criminality.

Example. Defendants conspire to work together as prostitutes. Their conspiracy is a felony even though prostitution is only a misdemeanor.

2. Procedural Consequences

a. **A conspiracy charge joins multiple defendants for trial.** A conspiracy charge allows the prosecution to join a large group of defendants for trial and thereby present a broad view of their criminal activities for the jurors' considerations. Seeing a group of defendants sitting together for trial, jurors are more likely to believe that "birds of a feather flock together," i.e., all the defendants were jointly involved in criminal activity.

b. **A conspiracy charge can extend the statute of limitations.** Conspiracy is a continuing offense that does not end until the objectives of the conspiracy have succeeded or failed. Accordingly, the statute of limitations for conspiracy does not begin to run until the last act of the conspiracy. By charging conspiracy, prosecutors can extend the statute of limitations beyond that which would apply if the focus was on a specific act by a specific defendant.

Example. Defendants A and B agree to rob a series of banks. The statute of limitations for the first bank they rob has run out, but because their conspiracy has continued, that first robbery can be charged as part of the conspiracy.

c. **Venue for a conspiracy charge is proper anywhere acts of the conspiracy occurred.** A conspiracy charge allows prosecutors greater latitude in selecting the venue. Venue is proper anywhere a conspiratorial act occurred.

Example. Defendants A and B agree to bribe a popular local politician. Defendant A, who lives in a different state, arranges for the bribe money. Prosecutors may charge the conspiracy in A's jurisdiction where there will be less popular support for the politician and the defendants.

d. **Admissibility of co-conspirator statements.** A major procedural benefit of charging a conspiracy is that the prosecution can introduce hearsay statements of co-conspirators made during the course of the conspiracy. Fed. Reg. Evid. §801(d)(2)(E). The statement of one conspirator is deemed to be a vicarious admission by an agent of the other partners to the conspiracy. In order to introduce a co-conspirator's statement, there must be independent proof that a conspiracy existed and the defendant was connected with it. However, the co-conspirator's statement may be used in making this determination. Bourjaily v. United States, 483 U.S. 171 (1987).

i. **Example.** Defendants A and B are charged with conspiring to rob a bank. As part of their case against B, prosecutors are allowed to introduce a hearsay statement by A to a friend, C, that A and B planned to rob the bank and would love to have C join their venture.

ii. **Note.** One key limitation on the admissibility of co-conspirators' statements is that the hearsay statement must have been made *during the course of* the conspiracy. If the co-conspirator makes the statement after the conspiracy is concluded, it is not admissible. Krulewitch v. United States, 336 U.S. 440 (1949).

3. Duration of a Conspiracy

A conspiracy remains in effect until it has been abandoned or until its objectives have been achieved.

a. **Efforts to conceal offense.** Unless the parties originally agreed prior to the commission of the offense that they jointly would make efforts to conceal their criminal activity, an act of concealment is *not* considered part of the conspiracy. Grunewald v. United States, 353 U.S. 391 (1957).

b. **Abandonment.** A conspiracy is generally considered to be abandoned when none of the conspirators is engaging in any action to further the conspiratorial objectives.

c. **Withdrawal/renunciation.** A single conspirator can limit his criminal liability to some degree by renouncing his involvement and withdrawing from the group. There are two basic approaches to renunciation.

i. **Common law approach.** Under common law, a co-conspirator can end his responsibility for later acts and statements of his co-conspirators by withdrawing from the conspiracy. However, the defendant is still guilty for the initial act of conspiracy. Once committed, a conspiracy could not be "uncommitted." To withdraw from a conspiracy, a defendant must take "affirmative action" to announce his withdrawal to all the other conspirators. In some jurisdictions, the defendant must also notify law enforcement or otherwise thwart the plot.

ii. **Model Penal Code approach.** There are two differences in how the MPC approaches renunciation.

(a) **Withdrawal.** Under MPC §5.03(7)(c), an individual can either inform his co-conspirators or notify the authorities that he is terminating his association with the conspiracy. Once this is done, the defendant is no longer a member of the conspiracy and is not responsible for his co-conspirators' acts.

(b) **Renunciation.** MPC §5.03(6) recognizes an affirmative defense to the crime of conspiracy if the defendant successfully thwarts the success of the conspiracy, under circumstances manifesting a complete and voluntary renunciation of his criminal purpose. If a defendant actually thwarts the criminal acts of the conspiracy, he can avoid liability for even the initial conspiracy he joined.

C. CONSPIRACY AS A FORM OF ACCESSORIAL LIABILITY

One of the important consequences of belonging to a conspiracy is that a conspirator is responsible for all acts of his or her co-conspirators during the course of and in furtherance of the conspiracy, even if the conspirator is unaware that these acts are being committed.

1. Pinkerton Liability

In 1946, the Supreme Court decided a pair of cases establishing the rule of co-conspirator liability. In the first of these cases, Pinkerton v. United States, 328 U.S. 640 (1946), the Court recognized that conspirators are responsible for each other's criminal acts even if they don't directly participate in them. In the second case, the Court narrowly defined what constitutes one conspiracy and thereby limited the impact of the *Pinkerton* co-conspirator liability rule. See Kotteakos v. United States, 328 U.S. 750 (1946) infra.

EXAMPLE AND ANALYSIS

In *Pinkerton*, Daniel Pinkerton was charged with conspiring with his brother, Walter, to commit tax violations by not reporting income they made from manufacturing and selling whiskey. Daniel was also charged with the substantive tax counts relating to the conspiracy, even though he was in prison when his brother committed these offenses. Because the tax offenses were during the course of and in furtherance of their conspiracy, Daniel was liable for the substantive criminal acts of his brother, even though he could not be charged as an aider and abettor.

Conspirators are responsible for all substantive offenses committed by one of the conspirators in furtherance of the conspiracy, regardless of whether they assisted in the commission of those offenses. Conspirators are agents of each other in the commission of crimes.

Co-conspirator liability is *broader* than accomplice liability because it applies even if the co-conspirator is unaware that the crime is being committed or participates in the crime.

STUDY TIP

Whenever a fact pattern includes two individuals participating in criminal activity, students should analyze the problem for *both* accomplice liability and possible co-conspirator liability.

2. In Furtherance of Conspiracy

Crimes "in furtherance of the conspiracy" include more than those crimes the co-conspirator contemplated when he entered into the unlawful agreement. They also include any crimes that are "reasonably foreseeable as the necessary or natural consequences of the conspiracy."

EXAMPLE AND ANALYSIS

In State v. Bridges, 133 N.J. 447 (1993), defendant asked two friends to accompany him to a fight, where they would hold his opponents' supporters at bay. At the fight, defendant's friends ended up shooting an onlooker after they were attacked. Although their conspiracy did not have as its object the purposeful killing of another person, it contemplated bringing loaded guns to the fight location. Accordingly, it was a *reasonably foreseeable* and a *natural consequence of the conspiracy* that one of the conspirators would shoot someone. As a co-conspirator, defendant was vicariously liable for the murder (not just negligent homicide).

---

3. Pinkerton Liability is Not Retroactive

A conspirator is *not* responsible for substantive offenses committed prior to his joining the conspiracy, but acts by the defendant's co-conspirators before he joined the conspiracy can be used as evidence for general conspiracy charges. United States v. Blackmon, 839 F.2d 900, 908-909 (2d Cir. 1988); Levine v. United States, 383 U.S. 265, 266 (1965).

Example. Defendant joins an ongoing conspiracy to distribute narcotics. Prior to his entry into the conspiracy, one of the co-conspirators killed an undercover agent who was trying to infiltrate their operation. The killing may be used as evidence of the conspiracy the defendant joined, but the defendant is not vicariously liable for the murder.

4. Co-conspirator Liability vs. Accomplice Liability

Co-conspirator liability is broader than accomplice liability. Accomplice liability requires purpose to assist in a particular crime and an act of assistance. Co-conspirator liability occurs when a co-conspirator commits a crime that is reasonably foreseeable given the nature of the conspiracy.

Example and Analysis

In United States v. Alvarez, 755 F.2d 830 (11th Cir. 1985), defendants arranged for the sale of narcotics. A shootout started at the location and the defendants' co-conspirators killed a law enforcement officer. Defendants did not intend to kill anyone when they joined the conspiracy, and they in no way assisted in the killing. Nonetheless, defendants were guilty as co-conspirators to the murders that were "reasonably foreseeable" given the nature of a drug conspiracy.

Note. Some courts will only extend *Pinkerton* liability to serious crimes when the co-conspirators being charged with the substantive offense play more than a "minor" role in the conspiracy.

---

5. Rationale for Pinkerton Liability

Conspirators act as one another's agents and therefore should be responsible for one another's crimes. Moreover, without co-conspirator liability, a conspirator behind the scenes could insulate himself from liability for those acts that help the conspiracy succeed.

6. Criticisms of Pinkerton Liability

Generally, criminal law requires that the defendant be *personally* culpable. *Pinkerton* liability is imposed even when the defendant is not personally responsible for the substantive crime.

7. Model Penal Code

The MPC has rejected the *Pinkerton* doctrine. A conspirator is only guilty of the substantive crime of a co-conspirator if there is evidence of accomplice liability.

D. ELEMENTS OF CONSPIRACY

Conspiracy requires "an agreement by two or more persons to commit a crime." Depending on the jurisdiction, there are two or three elements of conspiracy. They are:

1. Actus Reus	—	Agreement
2. Overt Act	—	(some jurisdictions)
3. Mens Rea	—	Purpose

1. Actus Reus of Conspiracy

The actus reus of conspiring is an "agreement" to commit a crime.

a. **Expressed or implied agreement.** An agreement to commit a crime may be expressed or implied. It is relatively rare for conspirators to openly agree to commit a crime. Accordingly, one must look to circumstantial evidence to determine whether there has been such an agreement.

> **STUDY TIP**
>
> Agreement may be demonstrated by words, actions, similar motives, or gestures, like a nod, wink, or handshake.

b. **Concerted action.** In order to establish agreement, one can draw inferences from the course of conduct of the alleged conspirators. If conspirators act in a concerted manner to achieve a common object, an agreement may be inferred.

EXAMPLES AND ANALYSIS

In Interstate Circuit, Inc. v. United States, 306 U.S. 208 (1939), film distributors simultaneously adopted proposals restricting the use of distributed films. Although there was no evidence that the distributors had directly agreed with each other to restrain business, their simultaneous action with similar motives established a conspiracy.

In United States v. Alvarez, 625 F.2d 1196 (1981), a defendant was charged with being part of a conspiracy to import marijuana. Although the defendant never said he was part of the conspiracy, his willingness to help off-load the shipment was sufficient proof that he agreed to take part in the scheme.

In United States v. Brown, 776 F.2d 397 (2d Cir. 1985), defendants were charged with conspiracy to distribute heroin. Defendant's sole role in the conspiracy was to indicate that the potential buyer was "all right," meaning that the co-conspirator should make the sale. Defendant's remark was sufficient to prove that he had joined the conspiracy.

---

c. **Parallel actions vs. common design.** Two defendants coincidentally engaged in parallel action to commit a crime are not guilty of conspiracy. The evidence must indicate a tacit agreement between them.

EXAMPLES AND ANALYSIS

On the same day, A and B independently decide to rob a store. A enters through the front door; B enters through the back door. They rob the store at the same time. Although they are involved in parallel actions, there is no evidence that A and B agreed with each other to commit a crime. Accordingly, there is no conspiracy.

In People v. McChristian, 18 Ill. App. 3d 87 (1974), members of a gang began shooting simultaneously at a rival gang member. Because there was no evidence that the participants planned the meeting or the shooting, the court reversed the conviction for conspiracy to murder.

---

d. **Agreement with unknown parties.** It is not necessary that all parties know each other or even have contact with one another. It is sufficient if the defendant knows he is agreeing with others to commit a crime.

Example. A agrees to help unload a box of narcotics from a plane. Even though A might not know the pilot of the plane or the sender who loaded the shipment for delivery, A is still involved in a conspiracy with them to import narcotics.

e. **Presence at crime scene.** Mere presence at a crime scene is not enough to establish agreement to participate in a crime. However, given the unlikelihood that conspirators would invite an innocent party to witness their acts, presence at a crime scene provides some evidence of an illegal agreement, especially if coupled with any acts by the defendant to help the crime occur.

f. **Joining ongoing conspiracy.** Not all conspirators must join the conspiracy at the same time. When a defendant joins an ongoing criminal conspiracy, prosecutors may use actions by co-conspirators prior to defendant's joining as evidence for a conspiracy charge against him.

2. Overt Act Requirement

At common law, the sole actus reus requirement was the agreement itself. Most modern conspiracy statutes now have added a general overt act requirement, but do not require it for conspiracies to commit the most serious offenses. Compare 18 U.S.C. §371 (general federal conspiracy statute requires overt act); 21 U.S.C. §846 (omits overt act requirement for conspiracies to distribute illegal drugs). See also MPC §5.03(5) (general requirement of an overt act but no overt act requirement for most serious crimes).

a. **Definition of "overt act".** An overt act is any legal or illegal act done by any of the conspirators to set the conspiracy into motion.

i. **Example.** A and B decide to rob a bank. A calls the bank to see what time it opens. A's act is sufficient to be an overt act for both A and B.

ii. **Example.** Defendants conspire to overthrow the government. Pursuant to that conspiracy, they hold public meetings advocating their position. Assuming no First Amendment defense, these meetings are sufficient to satisfy the overt act requirement for conspiracy. Yates v. United States, 354 U.S. 298 (1950).

b. **Only one conspirator needs to commit an overt act.** When one conspirator commits an overt act, all members of the conspiracy are guilty.

Example. Seven defendants agree to steal a shipment of cars. One of the defendants rents a truck for the hijack. At that point, all seven of the defendants are guilty of conspiracy.

c. **Innocuous acts.** Overt acts may be innocent in themselves and need not be a substantial step toward committing a crime. The sole purpose of an overt act is to show "that the conspiracy is at work."

Example. A and B agree to kill the president. A buys a newspaper to see when the president will be visiting their town. The purchase of the newspaper, an otherwise innocuous act, is sufficient to meet the overt act requirement.

Note. Some states have required a more substantial overt act that demonstrates a clear purpose by the actor to accomplish the crime. See, e.g., Ohio Rev. Code Ann. tit. 29, §2923.01(b).

d. **Rationale for overt act requirement.** An overt act requirement shows that the conspiracy has moved from the mere idea stage to action. Even though the overt act requirement may be satisfied by an otherwise innocuous act, the mens rea requirement for conspiracy ensures that innocent persons will not be convicted.

3. Mens Rea of Conspiracy

Conspiracy requires two mens rea: a. an intent to agree; i.e., an intent to join the conspiracy; and b. with the purpose to commit a crime.

a. **Intent to agree.** It is essential that the defendant know he is agreeing to join a conspiracy. For example, if a defendant nods to another simply as a greeting, there is no intent to agree to join a conspiracy.

b. **Purpose to commit crime.** Most jurisdictions require the same level of mens rea for conspiracy and accomplice liability—purpose to commit a crime.

i. **Example.** A asks B and C to help him package white powder that A knows to be cocaine and plans to sell on the streets. B and C are only guilty of conspiracy to distribute if their purpose is to assist in the crime of drug distribution. They are not guilty if they simply believe A is storing the powder for his own use.

ii. **Example.** A asks his friend B to help burn down City Hall. B thinks A is kidding and answers, "sure." There is no conspiracy because B did not have the purpose to commit the crime.

iii. **Knowledge vs. purpose.** When purpose is required, knowledge alone is insufficient to establish the mens rea for conspiracy.

EXAMPLE AND ANALYSIS

In People v. Lauria, 251 Cal. App. 2d 471 (1967), defendant ran a telephone answering service used by prostitutes. Defendant knew that prostitutes used the service because he engaged one of their services. The court held that knowledge alone was insufficient to establish the mens rea for conspiracy. Rather, prosecutors needed to prove defendant had a stake in the venture or otherwise had the purpose to facilitate prostitution.

---

iv. **Rationale for purpose requirement.** The distinction between purpose and knowledge safeguards against conspiracy charges being used as dragnets to charge all those who have been associated with illegal activities to any slight degree. For example, condom manufacturers, mattress salesmen, and negligee outlets know that some of their customers are prostitutes, but many would view it as unjust to charge these legitimate businesses with conspiracy to commit prostitution.

v. **Inferring purpose.** In *Lauria*, the court held that a manufacturer or service provider's purpose may be inferred when:

- The purveyor of legal goods used for illegal purposes has a stake in the venture. A stake in the venture may be shown by the inflation of rates charged for the illegal use of the business.
- The defendant's goods or services serve no legitimate use.
- The volume of business with buyers engaged in illegitimate business is grossly disproportionate to any legitimate demand, or sales for illegal use amount to a high proportion of the defendant's business.

vi. **Knowledge sufficient for more serious crimes.** In some jurisdictions, knowledge that one's goods or services will be used for criminal purposes may be enough to establish the mens rea for conspiracy, when the crime involved is a serious one and the substances being provided are themselves dangerous.

EXAMPLES AND ANALYSIS

In Direct Sales v. United States, 319 U.S. 703 (1943), a wholesaler of drugs was convicted of conspiracy for selling dangerous drugs in large quantity to a physician who supplied them to addicts. The wholesaler's knowledge that the drugs would be resold illegally was sufficient to prove conspiracy.

In United States v. Falcone, 311 U.S. 205 (1940), defendant provided large quantities of sugar and yeast that were used for a moonshining conspiracy. Given the innocuous nature of substances like sugar and yeast, and the less serious nature of the crime of moonshining, knowledge was held insufficient to prove conspiracy.

---

vii. ***Powell* doctrine.** In People v. Powell, 63 N.Y. 88 (1875), the court held that a defendant must have a "corrupt motive" to be guilty of conspiracy. Given this requirement, a defense is allowed if the defendant had a good faith belief that the conduct she agreed to was not illegal. Conspiracy defendants are allowed to use this defense even though mistake of law is ordinarily not a defense. Both the Model Penal Code and England have rejected the *Powell* doctrine.

viii. Mens rea requirement for attendant circumstances. If knowledge as to attendant circumstances is not required for the substantive offense, then such knowledge is also not required for conspiracy to commit that offense.

EXAMPLES AND ANALYSIS

In United States v. Feola, 420 U.S. 672 (1975), defendants were charged with assaulting federal officers. The substantive crime of assaulting federal officers does not require that the defendants know that the officers they are attacking are federal agents. The victims' federal status is merely a "jurisdictional fact." See Chapter

3 supra. Likewise, a conspiracy to assault federal officers does not require that the conspirators know that the officers have federal status.

Defendants agree to sell drugs on a particular street corner. As it turns out, the location of the sale is within 1000 feet of a school, a crime which carries a higher penalty. The substantive crime does not require that the defendants know they are within 1000 feet of a school. Similarly, conspiracy to commit the crime does not require such knowledge.

Exception. When defendants agree to do an act that is otherwise "innocent in itself," courts may require proof that the conspirators acted with the purpose to commit an illegal act. For example, if A and B decide to have consensual sex and C drives them to a motel, C is not guilty of conspiracy to commit statutory rape unless C knows B is a minor. There must be an agreement to engage in prohibited conduct.

E. SCOPE OF THE AGREEMENT—SINGLE OR MULTIPLE CONSPIRACIES

When there is group criminality, it can be crucial whether there is one conspiracy or multiple conspiracies. Members of the same conspiracy are liable for each other's co-conspirator acts. They may also be tried together, have their hearsay statements used against one another, and have venue and the statute of limitations for their crime defined by each other's acts. Accordingly, it may be more beneficial for the defense to argue that there are multiple small conspiracies, of which the defendant is a member of only one, than to be dragged into the net of a large conspiracy.

1. Wheel vs. Chain Conspiracies

There are two basic types of conspiracies, although it is rare for a complex conspiracy to be exclusively one or the other. Often conspiracies contain aspects of both.

a. **Wheel conspiracy.** In a wheel conspiracy, all of the conspirators are tied together through the same middleman or "hub." Although the individual conspirators do not know each other, they are all connected to the same conspiracy because they are operating through the same middleman. If the separate spokes of this wheel have a vested interest in the success of one another's illegal conduct, then there is a single wheel conspiracy and each individual member is responsible for the crimes of every other member of the conspiracy. However, if the only connection among the spokes is that they know the same middleman, there are multiple small conspiracies and the spokes of the wheel are not liable for one another's acts.

Example and Analysis

In Kotteakos v. United States, 328 U.S. 750 (1946), the Supreme Court sought to limit the impact of *Pinkerton* liability. Justice Rutledge, who had written the dissent in *Pinkerton*, authored the Court's opinion in *Kotteakos.* The Court held in *Kotteakos* that for members of a wheel conspiracy to be responsible for each other's acts, there must be a rim enclosing the individual spokes involved in a crime through the same middleman.

In *Kotteakos*, 32 defendants used the same loan broker, Brown, to obtain false loans. Other than using the same loan broker, many of the individual borrowers had no other connection. The government sought to try all of the defendants in one conspiracy and charge them with the substantive crimes of one another.

The Court held that the defendants were involved in smaller individual conspiracies and not the one large conspiracy charged by the government.

To create a wheel conspiracy, the individual spokes acting with the same hub must be tied together by common interests in a single venture.

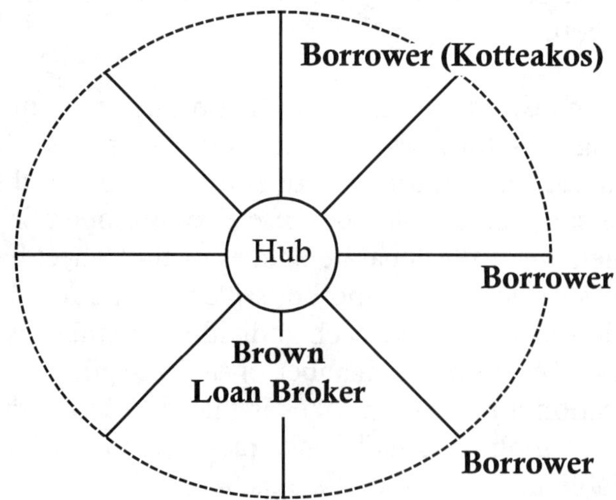

Exam Tip

Another common example of a defective wheel conspiracy that has spokes that are not connected is the "fence" in a receiving stolen property scheme. Several thieves may sell their stolen property to the same person, but they are not all in the same conspiracy. Rather, each thief has his or her own conspiracy with the fence who disposes of the stolen goods.

i. **Connecting the spokes.** One way to show a common interest tying spokes together is to prove that the individual conspirators relied on the success of each other in succeeding at their plan. For example, if the individual borrowers used part of the proceeds obtained by the others' loans as the down payment for their loans, then a common venture would be shown.

Example and Analysis

In Anderson v. Superior Court, 78 Cal. App. 2d 22 (1947), an illegal abortionist paid 17 persons to refer pregnant women to him. Defendant Anderson was one of the persons hired to make referrals. The court found one conspiracy with the abortionist at the hub of the conspiracy. Defendant Anderson was tied to the other spokes of the wheel because they all shared a common interest in keeping the abortionist in business.

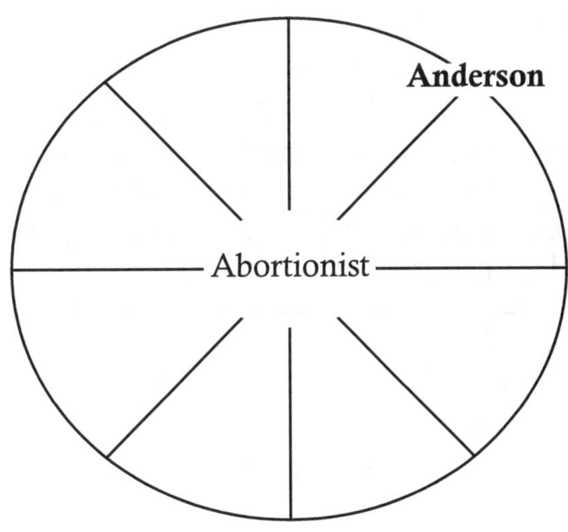

b. **Chain conspiracy.** In a chain conspiracy, conspirators participate in a single conspiracy by performing different roles along a single distribution line. Each conspirator plays a different role at his or her stage of the criminal plan. The classic example is the sale of narcotics. The manufacturer, middleman, and distributor are all on the chain of one conspiracy to distribute drugs. Although they might not know each conspirator's identity, they know that there must be someone at the various stages to ensure that the scheme works.

- Manufacturer
- Wholesaler
- Distributor

Example and Analysis

In Blumenthal v. United States, 332 U.S. 539 (1947), the Supreme Court recognized that a chain conspiracy constitutes a single conspiracy and that each member of the chain is responsible for every other co-conspirator's action.

In *Blumenthal*, the whiskey wholesaler, middlemen, and distributors were engaged in a conspiracy to sell the whiskey at prohibited prices. Each was engaged in a discrete stage of the distribution process and did not know the identity of the other co-conspirators.

Although the parties did not know each other, they were all part of one conspiracy because they knew and relied upon the fact that others would be involved in the distribution plan at various stages.

In fact, *Blumenthal* may be an example of both a chain and wheel conspiracy because there were multiple parties involved at the different stages of distribution who shared in the scheme. The wholesalers had contact with several different middlemen who could be seen as spokes of a wheel. The Court did not make a specific finding of how these unrelated parties benefited from each other's participation, other than to state that they pursued "a common end."

c. **Combined conspiracies.** In reality, many conspiracies have elements of both wheel and chain conspiracies. There may be a line of distribution, but parties along that line may also have multiple customers who operate more like a wheel conspiracy. At minimum, courts look to see whether there is some evidence that suggests that the groups at each level know of the overall scope of the conspiracy and benefit from it. United States v. Borelli, 336 F.2d 376 (2d Cir. 1964) ("extreme links of a chain conspiracy may have elements of the spoke conspiracy"); United States v. Townsend, 924 F.2d 1385 (7th Cir. 1991) (Conspirators at lower end of chain are more likely to be competitors than collaborators).

Example and Analysis

In United States v. Bruno, 105 F.2d 921 (2d Cir. 1939), 88 people were charged in one conspiracy to import, sell, and possess narcotics. The court found that there was one conspiracy because each defendant knew he was working along a chain of individuals engaged in a scheme to distribute drugs. The importers, middlemen, and retailers were tied together in a single chain. However, *Bruno* also shared an aspect of wheel conspiracies. Multiple retailers dealt with individual middlemen. The court failed to analyze how the retailers, as spokes of a mini-wheel conspiracy, had enough of a stake in each other's venture to tie together the rim of their part of the conspiracy.

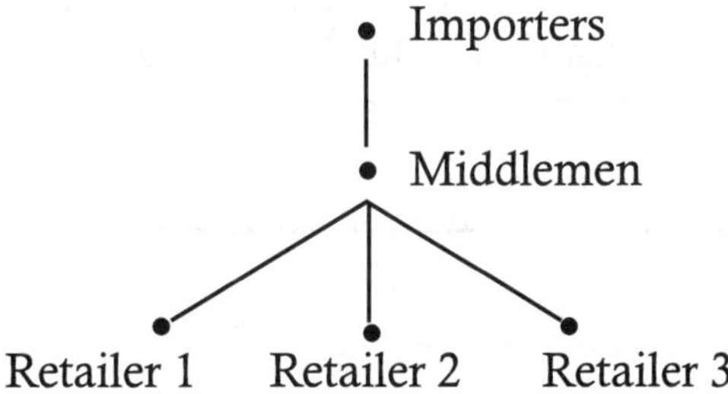

Note. The Model Penal Code would address this case differently. First, the retailers would not be guilty of the importation of drugs by the smugglers because conspirators have to agree to commit a particular crime. Importation and drug distribution are different offenses. MPC §5.03(1). Second, if a retailer did not know that his middleman was selling to other retailers, he would not be responsible as a co-conspirator for the criminal acts of the other retailers. MPC §5.03(2). See generally, Model Penal Code and Commentaries, Comment to §5.03 at 425-431 (1985). See also United States v. Borelli, 336 F.2d 376 (2d Cir. 1964).

2. One Conspiracy with Multiple Objectives

A single conspiracy can have multiple objectives. If a conspiracy has as its goal to commit several crimes, it is still ordinarily viewed as one conspiracy. This is called the "*Braverman* rule."

EXAMPLES AND ANALYSIS

In United States v. Braverman, 317 U.S. 49 (1942), a group of defendants was indicted for conspiring to violate multiple tax laws. Although defendants planned to commit several different violations, their agreement should have been charged as one conspiracy.

In Albernaz v. United States, 450 U.S. 333 (1981), the court permitted the government to charge separate conspiracies for agreeing to distribute drugs and agreeing to use firearms during their distribution. The ruling was based upon a finding that Congress, by enacting two different statutes, intended for the government to be able to charge two different conspiracies.

3. Model Penal Code Approach

Under MPC §5.03, a person is guilty of conspiring with others if he knows that the person with whom he has directly conspired has conspired with other people, even if the defendant does not know their identity. MPC §5.03(2). A conspiracy with multiple criminal objectives is only one conspiracy under the MPC, as long as such multiple crimes are the object of the same agreement or continuous conspiratorial relationship. MPC §5.03(3).

Note. Because the focus of the MPC approach is on whether the defendant knew others have been recruited, the scope of a conspiracy may be different for its parties depending on what they knew about the likelihood of other people's participation.

F. PARTIES

A conspiracy requires an agreement between a minimum of two qualified parties. Depending on the jurisdiction, certain individuals may not qualify as parties to a conspiracy.

1. Gebardi Rule

A person that a particular law is intended to protect cannot be a party to a conspiracy to violate that law.

a. **Example.** In Gebardi v. United States, 287 U.S. 112 (1932), a man and woman were charged with conspiring to violate the Mann Act because they agreed to cross state lines to have sex. The Mann Act was designed to protect women. Accordingly, a woman who consents to cross state lines for sex cannot be charged with conspiring to violate the Act.

b. **Example.** Child labor laws are designed to protect children from improper working conditions. If a child agrees to work in violation of these laws, the child cannot be guilty of conspiracy to violate the law designed to protect her.

2. Wharton Rule

If it is impossible to commit the substantive offense without cooperative action, the preliminary agreement between the parties to commit the offense is not an indictable conspiracy. *Wharton's* Rule prohibits "double-counting" the conspiracy and substantive offense.

a. **Example.** Crimes that necessarily involve at least two people include: dueling, bigamy, adultery, incest, gambling, and buying and selling contraband. Thus, if the only two persons involved are the giver and recipient of a bribe, they are guilty of bribery and cannot also be charged with conspiracy to bribe.

b. **Exception.** If legislative intent clearly intends to allow both a conspiracy charge and a substantive charge for a particular group activity, conspiracy may be charged. See Ianelli v. United States, 420 U.S. 770 (1975) (conspiracy and substantive charge proper for crime of five persons participating in gambling business).

c. **Note.** Because buying and selling drugs would ordinarily be covered by the *Wharton* Rule and thereby not allow a charge of conspiracy, many jurisdictions have rejected the *Wharton* Rule. Other courts interpret the rule narrowly, finding, for example, that one can be guilty of "conspiring to offer" a narcotic for sale, because it only takes one person to make an offer even if it takes another person to accept it. State v. Cavanaugh, 583 A.2d 1311, 1314 (Conn. App. Ct. 1990).

d. **Caution.** If commission of a crime requires at least two people, but more than two are involved, the *Wharton* Rule does not prohibit a conspiracy charge. The *Wharton* Rule only applies when the only two people involved are the two necessary to commit the substantive crime.

e. **Model Penal Code.** The Model Penal Code does not recognize the *Wharton* Rule. Model Penal Code and Commentaries, Comment to §5.04, at 482-483.

3. Bilateral Rule

At traditional common law, a conspiracy requires at least "two guilty minds"; i.e., at least two persons who can actually be prosecuted for conspiracy. This is also called the "plurality requirement." Thus, if one of two persons charged with a conspiracy could not be prosecuted for the crime, there is no conspiracy.

a. **Feigned conspirator.** Under the bilateral rule, a defendant could not be convicted for conspiring with a police informant or undercover officer. The rationale for the bilateral rule is that a conspiracy with a government agent is not likely to create the same risk as those collective actions conspiracy law is designed to prevent. See United States v. Escobar de Bright, 742 F.2d 1196 (9th Cir. 1984).

Note. When the bilateral rule applies, courts do *not* allow convictions for "attempted conspiracy."

b. **Acquittal of all co-conspirators.** The acquittal of all other co-conspirators in the *same* trial is also a basis for alleging that there is no conspiracy because there are not two guilty minds. However, acquittal of co-conspirators in a separate trial does not automatically undermine the defendant's conspiracy conviction.

c. **Diplomatic immunity.** Typically, diplomatic immunity for one of the co-conspirators is not viewed as an acquittal, and there can still be a conspiracy prosecution of the nonimmune co-conspirator.

d. **Insanity.** A finding of insanity for one co-conspirator does not affect the culpability of the noninsane co-conspirator. Regle v. State, 9 Md. App. 346 (1970).

e. **Spouses.** At traditional common law, a husband and wife could not by themselves compose a conspiracy. The modern view has rejected this rule.

f. **Corporations.** A corporation can be a member of a conspiracy but there must be at least two human beings involved in the conspiracy. Additionally, a corporation cannot conspire solely with agents of the same corporation.

g. **Failure to try remaining co-conspirators.** The bilateral rule only requires that there be two or more defendants eligible for prosecution. However, there is no requirement that all these conspirators be tried. The death, absence, or general unavailability of a co-conspirator will not jeopardize the conviction of an apprehended defendant, even if there were only two members of the conspiracy.

4. Model Penal Code Approach

The MPC and many state jurisdictions have adopted the "unilateral" concept of conspiracy. Thus, if the defendant believes he is conspiring with another to commit a crime, he is guilty of conspiracy regardless of whether the other person can be convicted. MPC §5.04(1); Minn. St. 1961, 613.70.

Example. Defendant asks a person she believes to be a "hit man" to kill her husband. Unbeknownst to defendant, the hit man is an undercover police officer. Under the bilateral rule, defendant could not be charged with conspiracy. However, under the MPC unilateral rule, a conspiracy charge would be appropriate. See Garcia v. State, 71 Ind. 366, 394 N.E.2d 106 (1979).

G. SUMMARY OF CONSPIRACY LAW

Figure 11-1 presents a summary of conspiracy law.

FIGURE 11-1

CONSPIRACY	
Elements of Crime	
Actus Reus	Agreement (express or implied)
Mens Rea	Intend to agree Purpose for crime to succeed
Overt Act	Not required at common law; Can be any act by any co-conspirator in furtherance of conspiracy.
Parties	
Gebardi Rule	Persons protected by statute are ineligible
Wharton Rule	If substantive crime requires at least two persons, no conspiracy.
Bilateral Rule	Conspiracy only exists if there are two or more persons eligible for prosecution. • Feigned conspirator? • Acquittal of all co-conspirators?
Unilateral Rule (MPC)	One party intending to commit crime is sufficient

FIGURE 11-1

(CONTINUED)	
Consequences of Joining Conspiracy	
Co-conspirator liability Conspiracy as separate crime	*Pinkerton* liability for all crimes by co-conspirators in furtherance of conspiracy. A defendant may be guilty of conspiracy and the substantive crime that was the object of the conspiracy.
Procedural consequences	Hearsay admissible as co-conspirator statements; extension of statute of limitations; broader venue.
Scope of Conspiracy	
Duration	A conspiracy begins at the time of agreement and continues until either the objects of the conspiracy are accomplished or the conspiracy is abandoned.
Wheel	Individuals connected through a common middleman must be tied together in a common venture to constitute one conspiracy.
Chain	Individuals along a common distribution chain are considered one conspiracy.
Defenses to Conspiracy	
Abandonment	When all conspirators abandon a conspiracy, the conspiracy is over. However, conspirators are still responsible for their original unlawful agreement.
Withdrawal	Common Law • Still responsible for original crime of conspiracy • Ends liability for co-conspirator crimes • Must notify co-conspirators MPC • Ends liability for co-conspirator acts • Must notify co-conspirators or police
Renunciation	MPC • If conspiracy is thwarted, defendant can avoid liability for original conspiracy.

Exam Tips

Conspiracy cases pose an array of complicated issues. The following is the best approach to conspiracy issues:

1. **Elements of the Crime**
   a. **Actus reus.** Are there two or more eligible persons agreeing to commit a crime?
      1. **Express or Implied Agreement.** Is there an express agreement or concerted action demonstrating an implied agreement?
      2. **Eligible Parties.** Sometimes parties are ineligible for conspiracy charges.
         - **Gebardi Rule.** Is the potential defendant a person the substantive law was designed to protect?
         - **Wharton Rule.** Does the crime necessarily involve only two people and are there only two people involved?
         - **Bilateral or Unilateral Jurisdiction.** In a bilateral jurisdiction, are the defendant's co-conspirators not chargeable with the conspiracy?

   b. **Mens rea.** Does the defendant join the conspiracy with intent to commit a particular crime?
      1. **Knowledge vs. Purpose.** In most jurisdictions, the mens rea for conspiracy is purpose, not mere knowledge. Purpose can be inferred from knowledge when the defendant:
         - has a stake in the venture;
         - provides goods or services that serve no legitimate use;
         - commits a grossly disproportionate amount of her business to the illegal endeavor.

   c. **Overt Act.** At common law, no overt act was required. Now, most states require an overt act.
      1. **Any step.** Did any one of the conspirators take any step toward effectuating the conspiracy?

2. **Co-conspirator Liability.** A conspirator is guilty of both conspiracy and all acts of her co-conspirators in furtherance of the conspiracy.
   a. **In furtherance.** Were the crimes of the co-conspirators reasonably foreseeable?
   b. **Scope of the Conspiracy.** How far does the defendant's co-conspirator liability extend? Is this a chain or wheel conspiracy? Is there a rim for the wheel conspiracy?

3. **Abandonment or Renunciation.** At common law, withdrawal from a conspiracy only limits ongoing co-conspirator liability. Under the MPC, withdrawal can also provide a defense to the general conspiracy charge, if the defendant successfully thwarts the conspiracy's criminal act.

H. CRIMINAL ENTERPRISES AND RICO

In 1970, Congress enacted the Racketeer Influenced and Corrupt Organizations Act (RICO) to combat ongoing, sophisticated criminal enterprises. More recently, states also enacted RICO statutes and anti-gang statutes. Both types of statutes are aimed at activities that may not be punishable under traditional conspiracy law. Both types of statutes are also controversial.

1. RICO

The federal RICO law prohibits participation in enterprises through a pattern of racketeering activity. 18 U.S.C. §§1961-1963. Penalties for engaging in these activities are far higher than those that would be imposed if the crimes were not part of a pattern of racketeering. Penalties also include forfeiture. RICO claims may be brought by criminal or civil action.

a. **Enterprise.** The key aspect of RICO is that defendants must be associated with an "enterprise," which is defined as an organization engaged in ongoing activities. Initially, "enterprise" was interpreted as requiring an organization engaged in legal activities that was being infiltrated by criminal interests. However, in United States v. Turkette, 452 U.S. 576 (1981), the Supreme Court held that an "enterprise" can be an exclusively criminal organization. As long as there is evidence of the organization apart from the pattern of criminal acts charged in the case, the "enterprise" requirement is met.

b. **Pattern.** RICO defendants must be engaged in a pattern of racketeering activity. For a pattern to exist, RICO requires at least two acts of racketeering activity. 18 U.S.C. §1961(5). In order to pose a pattern, the criminal activities must be related and pose a threat of continued criminal activity. There is no precise definition of "related." If the criminal acts have the same or similar purpose, result, victims, participants, or methods of commission, or are otherwise interrelated, the requirement is met. Courts often state that they are looking for "continuity plus relationship." H.J. Inc. v. Northwestern Bell Telephone Co., 492 U.S. 229 (1989).

i. **Continuity plus relationship.** The Court has had difficulty in defining what it means by "continuity" plus relationship. It has held that "continuity" is "both a closed- and open-ended concept, referring either to a closed period of repeated conduct, or to past conduct that by its nature projects into the future with a threat of repetition." *H.J. Inc.*, supra at 239. This description is extremely vague. It almost suggests that any period of continued and related predicate acts may satisfy the RICO requirements, even though the Court has stated that its threshold is higher. See *H.J. Inc.*, supra at 252-256 (Scalia, J. concurring).

c. **Racketeering activity.** The prohibited acts of racketeering activity are defined in 18 U.S.C. §1961(1). They include a wide range of state and federal crimes often committed by organized crime: murder, kidnapping, gambling, arson, robbery, bribery, extortion, dealing in obscene manner, interfering with labor organizations, bankruptcy fraud, securities fraud, and narcotics dealing.

d. **Conduct and participation.** In order to be participating in the conduct of an enterprise, an individual must have some role in directing or managing the business of the enterprise. The individual may be involved in either the operation or management of the enterprise. Professionals who merely advise the organization, such as accountants, generally are not participating in the enterprise. Reeves v. Ernst & Young, 113 S. Ct. 1163 (1993).

2. RICO Conspiracies

RICO conspiracies fill a gap left open by traditional conspiracy law. Under traditional conspiracy law, defendants who are charged in the same conspiracy must know of each other or each other's likely role in the conspiracy, and have a stake in each other's crime. Under RICO, the only link that conspirators need have is that they agree to participate, directly and indirectly, in the affairs of the enterprise by committing two or more predicate crimes. Co-conspirators need not know each other, need not participate in similar crimes, and need not have a stake in each other's success, other than having an interest in furthering the enterprise's affairs. Figure 11-2 presents a summary of the elements inherent in RICO conspiracies.

a. **RICO vs. traditional conspiracies.** There is no need under RICO statutes to fit defendants into a wheel or chain conspiracy. Multifaceted, diversified conspiracies are covered by the statutory concept of "the enterprise." It is enough that defendants associate for the purpose of making money through repeated criminal activity. United States v. Elliott, 571 F.2d 880 (5th Cir. 1978). Thus, the two key differences between RICO and traditional conspiracies are:

- Activity that would be viewed as multiple conspiracies under traditional law may be charged together under RICO as a pattern of racketeering activity.

- Evidence of other conspirators' crimes that are unrelated to a defendant's specific racketeering activity are admissible against a RICO defendant.

3. Criticisms of RICO

RICO has been criticized on several grounds:

a. It provides vague standards for charging a large number of people for only tangentially related criminal activities;

b. It threatens federalism by adopting wholesale into federal law large areas of State criminal law;

c. It gives too much discretion to prosecutors in deciding what offenses should be joined for trial;

d. It constitutes "guilt by association," taking the focus off individual criminal acts of individual defendants, and judges individuals by a course of conduct over a potentially lengthy period of time;

e. It affords more lenient rules of admissibility and joinder than traditional conspiracy cases;

f. It opens the door to a large number of civil suits that may affect criminal RICO prosecutions;

g. It allows pretrial seizure of defendant's assets and forfeiture of assets connected to the enterprise.

FIGURE 11-2

RICO ELEMENTS	
Enterprise	Organization, legal or illegal, with ongoing activities
Pattern	Two or more related acts of racketeering activity
Racketeering Activity	Designated state and federal crimes
Conduct and Participation	Role in operating or managing enterprise

4. Antigang Statutes

As well as enacting their own RICO statutes, states have sought to combat ongoing criminal organizations by enacting antigang statutes. These statutes typically enhance the penalty for crimes, if it can be shown that the defendant was a member of a gang. Because limits on gangs affect freedom of association, and gangs are often divided on racial and ethnic lines, antigang statutes raise serious First Amendment questions and questions regarding discriminatory prosecution.

Review Question and Answer

CONSPIRACY

Question: Part I. Bill Branes is a disgruntled young man, who was recently fired from his job at a local McDougal's fast food restaurant for "cussing out the customers." Ray has sworn revenge and decides to blow up the "golden arches" sign at every McDougal's in the greater metropolitan area. Bill does not know much about explosives and realizes that he will need some help if his plan is to be successful.

Bill calls on his friend, Ray Drule, and offers to pay him $500 to build a bomb. Ray is only 17 years old, but he looks much older, and Bill does not know that he is still a minor. Ray is known around the neighborhood as a genius with chemicals, because he was expelled from school in the seventh grade for blowing up the science lab, and for years he has been making and selling his own firecrackers. Ray is excited to join the bombing plot because he thinks it will be "neat" to see a McDougal's sign blow up. Bill tells Ray that he wants a bomb by next Friday, but he leaves the details of the bomb up to Ray. Ray decides to take the bus to nearby Farmdale County to buy fertilizer, the base ingredient for the "really big bomb" he learned how to make on the internet.

Once in Farmdale, Ray goes immediately to Jed's Fertilizer Supply Store, a place known for its "don't ask, don't tell" policy when it comes to selling fertilizer. Jed started up his business a few years ago in response to the increasing number of people in the area who "want to blow stuff up." Jed also sells about 40 percent of his products to farmers who actually use it as fertilizer, but with banks foreclosing on many farms in the region, the legitimate portion of his business is shrinking rapidly. Jed is suspicious that Ray wants to make a bomb, because he wants to take his fertilizer home in a suitcase. The "How to Build a Really Big Bomb" printout in Ray's back pocket only increases those suspicions, but Jed makes the sale anyway.

On Thursday afternoon Jed is contemplating his years of fertilizer selling and "what it all means," and in a fit of remorse he turns over all his credit card receipts to a BATF agent. The bureau immediately begins tracking the purchasers and storms Ray's house in the predawn hours Friday morning. They capture Ray, but Bill has already left for the first job.

At 6:00 a.m., Bill plants the bomb at the base of a McDougal's sign. The explosion is a beauty and, as planned, no one is hurt. However, bombing a nationally franchised fast-food restaurant is a little known federal offense. There is also a local criminal statute against making firecrackers.

What crimes, if any, have Bill, Ray, and Jed committed?

Answer:

1. *Crimes Committed by Bill.* Bill is potentially guilty of bombing a fast-food restaurant and conspiracy to bomb a fast-food restaurant.
Bombing a Fast-Food Restaurant. Bill is guilty of the bombing because it was his conscious object to blow up the sign and he actually planted the bomb and tripped the remote control. The mens rea and actus reus requirements are met; therefore, Jed is guilty of the substantive crime of bombing McDougal's.
Conspiracy to Bomb a Fast-Food Restaurant. Bill is also guilty of a separate conspiracy offense if he agreed with another to commit a criminal act, joined the conspiracy with intent to commit the crime, and committed an overt act toward the commission of the crime.

Bill and Ray expressly agreed to blow up the sign together; it was Bill's conscious object to work with Ray to blow up the sign and Bill actually did blow up the sign. Therefore, Bill is guilty of a separate conspiracy offense.
Making Firecrackers. Ray made the firecrackers before he and Bill entered into the conspiracy, so Bill is not liable as a co-conspirator for this offense. Even if the firecracker-making had occurred during Bill and Ray's conspiracy, Bill would probably not be responsible, because making firecrackers would not be an act in furtherance of the conspiracy to bomb the restaurant.

2. *Crimes Committed by Ray.* Ray has potentially committed the crime of making firecrackers, conspiracy to bomb a fast-food restaurant, and the substantive crime of bombing a fast-food restaurant.
Making Firecrackers. It was Ray's conscious objective to make and sell firecrackers, and he, in fact, made and sold firecrackers. The mens rea and actus reus requirements are therefore met, and Ray is guilty of making firecrackers.
Conspiracy to Bomb a Fast-Food Restaurant. A defendant is guilty of conspiracy if he agreed with another to commit a criminal act, joined the conspiracy with the intent to commit a criminal act, and committed an overt act toward the crime.

Ray expressly agreed with Bill to bomb the restaurant, and it was his conscious objective to see the sign blow up, because it would be neat. Ray also meets the overt act requirement that some jurisdictions require, because he made the bomb for Bill. Therefore, Ray is guilty of conspiracy to bomb McDougal's.
Bombing a Fast-Food Restaurant. A defendant is liable under *Pinkerton* for any act of a co-conspirator "in furtherance" of the crime. Any act that is reasonably foreseeable is in furtherance of the crime. Ray is guilty of the substantive offense of bombing because the whole plot was designed to bomb the sign. Therefore, it was entirely foreseeable that Bill would bomb the sign. Ray is guilty of bombing under co-conspirator liability.

3. *Crimes Committed by Jed.* Jed is potentially guilty of conspiracy to bomb, the substantive offense of bombing a fast-food restaurant, and making firecrackers.
Conspiracy to Bomb a Fast-Food Restaurant. A defendant is guilty of conspiracy if he agreed with another to commit a criminal act, joined the conspiracy with the intent to commit a criminal act, and committed an overt act toward the crime. Jed implicitly agreed to assist and committed an overt act when he sold Ray the fertilizer.

At common law, the major issue regarding Jed's conspiracy liability is whether he had the purpose to bomb the restaurant. Jed probably knew that Ray was going to make a bomb and blow something up. He did not know specifically that it was a McDougal's restaurant, but he likely knew that he was agreeing to a criminal act by selling the fertilizer. For conspiracy, purpose can be inferred from knowledge if the defendant has a stake in the venture; the defendant provides goods or services which serve no legitimate purpose; or the defendant commits a disproportionate amount of his business to the illegal endeavor. Jed has a stake in Bill and Ray's venture because he made a profit from the sale, and the majority of Jed's business comes from bombmakers like them. Jed's goods do serve a legitimate purpose, but he knows that few of his customers use them for that purpose. Finally, devoting a majority of a business to an illegal endeavor is probably enough to infer purpose that Bill and Ray succeed in their plot. Therefore, Jed is guilty of conspiracy to bomb McDougal's.
Bombing a Fast-Food Restaurant. Once we decide that Jed is a conspirator, he is guilty for all actions of his co-conspirators in furtherance of the crime.
Making Firecrackers. Same analysis as for Bill. See §1, supra.

Question: Part II. Farmdale has a local criminal ordinance, which prohibits knowingly or unknowingly selling to a minor any material which can be used to build an explosive device. The county board passed the ordinance after a boy blew off his hands trying to use black gunpowder to remove a tree stump in his dad's field as a Father's Day surprise. What additional crimes, if any, have Ray, Jed, and Bill committed?

Answer:

1. *Crime Committed by Ray.* Ray is potentially guilty of conspiracy to sell bombmaking materials to a minor. He implicitly agreed with Jed to buy the materials (actus reus); he intended to have Jed commit a crime by selling the materials (mens rea); and he actually purchased the materials (overt act). Ray, however, is not eligible for prosecution because he is a member of the class of persons the law is intended to protect.

2. *Crimes Committed by Jed.* Jed is potentially guilty of selling bombmaking materials to a minor and conspiracy to sell bombmaking materials to a minor.
Selling Bombmaking Materials to a Minor. Jed sold the materials and the statute does not require a purposeful or even knowing mens rea; therefore, he is guilty of the sale.

Conspiracy to Sell Bombmaking Materials to a Minor. Jed implicitly agreed to sell the materials to Ray (actus reus); intended to commit a criminal act (mens rea); and actually sold the materials (overt act). Therefore, Jed meets the requirements for conspiracy.

Bill may be guilty of the sale of bomb parts as a co-conspirator, but at common law he is not a party to Ray and Jed's conspiracy, because he never agreed to the sale, i.e. there is no actus reus. This leaves Ray and Jed as the only two members of the conspiracy to sell, and Ray is ineligible for prosecution. In a unilateral jurisdiction, Ray's ineligibility is not a factor. Jed believed he was conspiring with another to commit a crime and this is enough to be guilty of conspiracy.

Ray's ineligibility is a factor if this is a bilateral jurisdiction. The general rule in a bilateral jurisdiction is that there must be at least two chargeable conspirators or "guilty minds." Under this rule, Jed is not guilty of conspiracy to sell. Ray's ineligibility, however, is a form of immunity much like diplomatic immunity, and it is likely that a judge would not apply the bilateral rule, meaning that Jed is guilty of conspiracy to sell bombmaking materials to a minor.

The Model Penal Code provides a different approach regarding who is included in the conspiracy to sell bomb materials. According to the MPC, Bill is guilty of conspiring with Jed because he knows that Ray has conspired with Jed, even though he does not know Jed's identity. In this way, there are three conspirators in the sale of bomb materials. Therefore, if Ray is eliminated as an eligible suspect, Bill and Jed remain as conspirators and the bilateral rule is not an issue.

3. *Crimes Committed by Bill.* Bill is potentially guilty under *Pinkerton* liability for the sale of bombmaking materials to a minor and conspiracy to sell bombmaking materials to a minor. Bill and Jed are both members of a chain conspiracy with Ray as the middleman. Bill did not know directly of Jed's actions, but he knew that someone would have to sell bomb materials to Ray in order for the plot to succeed. Bill and Jed are therefore co-conspirators, and as such, Bill is liable for any criminal act by Jed in furtherance of the conspiracy, i.e. reasonably foreseeable. It was reasonably foreseeable that someone would sell materials to Ray and that Ray and that person would conspire in that sale. Bill is, therefore, guilty of selling bombmaking materials to a minor and conspiracy to sell bombmaking materials to a minor. As discussed above, Bill is also guilty of conspiracy to sell under the MPC, because he knew Ray was conspiring with someone to buy the materials.

DEFENSES

CHAPTER OVERVIEW

In practice, the first defense in a criminal case is to challenge whether the government has proven the elements of the crime. Several defenses, discussed in earlier chapters, relate directly to challenges to specific elements of a crime:

- Involuntary Acts — Chapter 3
- Mistake of Fact — Chapter 3
- Mistake of Law — Chapter 3
- Impossibility — Chapter 8
- Abandonment/Withdrawal — Chapter 11

Once the prosecution has proven the elements of a crime, however, a defendant may assert additional defenses, traditionally known as affirmative defenses. There are two types of affirmative defenses: justifications and excuses.

Justification defenses are permitted as a recognition that the defendant did the right thing in a difficult situation. From society's perspective, the defendant's acts were "justified." Justification defenses include:

- Self-defense
- Defense of Others
- Protection of Property
- Law Enforcement
- Necessity—(Choice of Evils)
- Euthanasia

Each of these defenses will be discussed in Chapter 12.

The common law has also traditionally recognized a number of excuses to criminal behavior. An excuse defense differs from a justification defense in that the excused conduct is socially *undesirable*, but the defendant is not held liable. An excuse defense is allowed because the defendant has acted under some disability, which renders the defendant free of blame or subject to less blame. In other words, excuses recognize that people are only human and, under certain circumstances, they will do bad acts for which they are not blameworthy. The excuse defenses discussed in Chapter 12 include:

- Duress (Coercion)
- Intoxication
  - Involuntary
  - Voluntary
- Mental Disorders
  - Insanity
  - Diminished capacity
- Infancy
- Entrapment
- Consent

Just as crimes are composed of "elements," so are defenses. Chapter 12 will review the rationale behind each defense and its elements.

PART I. JUSTIFICATION DEFENSES

INTRODUCTION

The law recognizes a number of defenses that are premised on the rationale that, given the situation the defendant was in, the defendant made the right decision to commit what otherwise might be considered a crime. Justification defenses include:

- Self-defense
- Defense of Others
- Protection of Property
- Law Enforcement
- Necessity (Choice of Evils)
- Euthanasia

A. RATIONALE BEHIND JUSTIFICATION DEFENSES

Justification and excuse defenses are premised on different rationales, but both ordinarily provide a complete defense.

1. Justifications

Justification defenses recognize that even though the defendant caused some harm, given the particular situation facing the defendant, he or she made the socially correct decision. The primary example of a justification defense is "self-defense." A defendant who acts in self-defense may hurt someone, but given the high value society places on protecting human life, the law recognizes the defendant made the correct decision. A justification defense recognizes that the defendant made the right decision given the circumstances.

2. Structure of Justification Defenses

All justification defenses have the same internal structure:

a. Triggering condition that requires the defendant to act;

Example. An attack triggers self-defense;

b. Necessity element that gives the defendant no choice but to act; and

c. Proportionality requirement that places limits on how the defendant may respond.

> **STUDY TIP**
>
> There is no longer any legal significance to the labels "justification" or "excuse" for defenses. But the labels make it easier to remember the rationale for a defense and what elements are required. For example, because self-defense is a justification, it becomes clear that the defense can only be used when there is a serious and imminent threat to human life. Otherwise, the decision to protect one's life by harming another would not be warranted.

B. SELF-DEFENSE

Under both the common law and the Model Penal Code, a defendant is justified in using force to protect himself from the threat of immediate and unlawful force.

1. Rationale for the Defense

Under the law, human life holds the highest value. When someone's life is threatened, he may take necessary steps to protect his life. Both excuse and justification theories support the doctrine of self-defense. At early English common law, self-defense was treated as an excuse. The defendant's act of killing was excused because the law would not blame a person for acting on instinct to protect his life.

By contrast, self-defense today is considered a justified act. From a utilitarian viewpoint, if someone must die, it is better that it be the aggressor who has demonstrated antisocial conduct. Moreover, self-defense can, over time, lead to a greater savings of life as aggressors are deterred from attacking others who are allowed to defend themselves. From a moral perspective, one might argue that an aggressor forfeits his life by attacking another or that the right of an innocent person to life is morally superior to an aggressor's right to life.

2. Common Law

Self-defense has long been recognized as a defense under common law. When all of the elements of the defense are met, the defendant enjoys a full defense to the crime. Even when the defendant has not satisfied all of the requirements for the defense, a partial defense may be available. See sec. B7 infra.

a. **Elements of self-defense.** Under the common law, the requirements for self-defense are:

- Defendant had an honest and reasonable fear of death or great bodily harm.
- The perceived threat to defendant was unlawful and immediate.
- Defendant reacted with a proportional response.
- The defendant was not the initial aggressor.

In some jurisdictions, a fifth requirement has been added that did not exist under traditional common law:

- Duty to retreat.

b. **Honest and reasonable fear.** Self-defense may only be used when a defendant both honestly and reasonably fears the use of unlawful force. Before deadly force may be used in self-defense, a defendant must fear death or grave bodily harm. People v. Goetz, 68 N.Y.2d 96 (1986).

i. **Honest fear.** Self-defense is proper when the defendant honestly fears the use of unlawful force. Self-defense cannot be used as an excuse to kill for illicit purposes.

Example. A enters B's office with a gun behind his back. B does not believe A has a gun, but he takes the opportunity to shoot A who has been attempting to fire him from his job. Because B did not honestly fear that A would attack him, B cannot claim self-defense.

ii. **Reasonable fear.** Self-defense requires that a defendant had a reasonable fear of unlawful force. An objective reasonableness requirement means that the defendant's conduct is justified only when society agrees with the defendant. Without a reasonableness requirement, each individual would have license to hurt another whenever his aberrational or bizarre beliefs dictate that he should do so.

(a) **Example.** Defendant sees his long-time enemy and boss waiving a plastic knife at the company picnic. Because of the run-ins he has had with his boss, defendant believes that his boss may actually try to attack him, so defendant shoots him first. Assuming defendant had an honest fear of injury, his fear was unreasonable (the only threat was a plastic knife) and would not warrant self-defense.

(b) **Reasonableness standard.** A major issue in applying the elements of self-defense is determining what standard should be used to define the "reasonable person." How objective is the reasonableness standard? Recently, courts have made that standard more subjective.

(c) **Reasonable person in defendant's situation.** The reasonableness standard for self-defense is *not* strictly objective. The jury must determine the reasonableness of the defendant's acts by evaluating the "circumstances" facing the defendant. Factors frequently considered include:

- physical attributes of persons involved
- defendant's prior experiences
- physical movements and comments of the potential assailant

Example. In State v. Wanrow, 88 Wash. 2d 221 (1977), the court held that the self-defense standard should allow for subjective characteristics of defendant's gender, physical size, and past experiences.

Example and Analysis

In *People v. Goetz*, supra, Goetz was charged with shooting four youths he claimed were trying to assault him on a New York subway. Goetz claimed he acted in self-defense, but none of the youths had displayed a weapon and when Goetz shot one of the victims, Darryl Cabey, the youth was simply sitting on a bench. Defendant admitted he intentionally shot the youth after commenting to him, "You seem to be all right, here's another." Defendant claimed his fear of the youths was based upon their race, mannerism, and his past history of having been mugged.

Issue. The question before the court was whether the grand jury had received the correct jury instruction on self-defense. N.Y. Law stated that "a person may . . . use physical force upon another person when and to the extent he *reasonably believes* such to be necessary to defend himself . . . from what he *reasonably believes* to be the . . . imminent use of unlawful physical force by such other person." Goetz claimed that the standard was a purely subjective one because the law used the term "*he* reasonably believes."

Holding. Self-defense requires an objectively reasonable belief that force is necessary in the defendant's situation. The standard for reasonableness is a semiobjective one. The focus must be on a reasonable person in the defendant's situation.

Note. The *Goetz* court expressly rejected the Model Penal Code subjective standard for fear. Under MPC §3.09, a defendant's honest but mistaken belief that force was necessary would be sufficient. See Sec. 2(e)(iv) infra.

(d) **Actor's belief need not be correct.** Even though defendant's fear of force must be "reasonable," the law does not require that the defendant correctly evaluate the threat facing him.

Example. Defendant sees a person point a gun at him so he shoots first to avoid injury. The gun turns out to be a starter pistol. If a reasonable person had made the same mistake, it would be irrelevant that there was no actual threat of harm.

(e) **Race as a factor.** The reasonableness standard may allow race to be used as a factor in evaluating a threat, if the ordinary person in society would also consider it as a factor. Therefore, beliefs that persons of a particular race are more inclined to commit crime can become one of the factors jurors use in deciding whether the defendant's fears were reasonable. In *Goetz*, for example, defendant claimed that he reasonably feared the youths on the subway because they were black. Some commentators have argued that even if racial fear is *typical*, it should not be considered *reasonable*, and courts should therefore exclude race evidence from trial.

iii. **Compare MPC Subjective Approach.** Under Model Penal Code §§3.04, 3.09(2), a defendant's subjective belief that force was necessary is sufficient for self-defense unless defendant is charged with a crime requiring only recklessness or negligence.

(a) **Rationale for subjective standard.** Proponents of the subjective standard argue that it is fairer and more realistic than the reasonableness standard because no person is reasonable when he or she believes death or severe bodily harm is imminent. Under these circumstances, a person's actions are governed by emotion, not reason. "Detached reflection cannot be demanded in the presence of an uplifted knife." Holmes, J., Brown v. United States, 256 U.S. 335, 343 (1921).

iv. **Imperfect self-defense.** In some jurisdictions, if the defendant has an honest but unreasonable belief in the need to kill, or uses more force than is reasonably necessary, defendant's crime is mitigated to voluntary or involuntary manslaughter under the doctrine of "imperfect self-defense."

Example. In *People v. Menendez*, two brothers were charged with killing their parents, while the parents watched television, ate ice cream, and completed college applications for their son. The sons claimed that they feared for their lives because of prior abuse by their parents. If the jurors had believed that the defendants had an honest but unreasonable fear for their lives, the proper verdict would have been voluntary manslaughter.

v. **Alternative approach: involuntary manslaughter.** In some jurisdictions, imperfect self-defense leads to involuntary rather than voluntary manslaughter on the theory that the defendant's killing was akin to a criminally negligent or reckless killing. These jurisdictions apply this theory even though the actual killing was intentional, albeit precipitated by reckless or negligent beliefs in the need to kill. Shannon v. Commonwealth, 767 S.W.2d 548 (1988). The MPC applies a similar approach by holding that a mistake as to the need for force is a defense *except* for offenses which only require recklessness or negligence. MPC §3.09(3).

vi. **Battered spouse syndrome impact on "reasonableness" requirement.** Special issues arise when a battered spouse kills her husband in an act of alleged self-defense. In such cases, the perceived need to kill is often based upon a history of abuse and a belief that there is no reasonable alternative. Recently, courts have been willing to accept evidence on the battered spouse's syndrome so that a jury can decide whether a reasonable person in the battered spouse's situation would have believed she was in imminent danger of death or serious injury. See, e.g., State v. Leidholm, 334 N.W.2d 811 (1983).

(a) **Nature of battered spouse syndrome.** Battered spouse syndrome describes a relationship in which one spouse repeatedly batters another. The abuse runs in cycles. In phase one, the batterer engages in minor battering incidents. In phase two, the batterer engages in a serious, violent attack on the spouse. In phase three, the batterer begs forgiveness and seeks to compensate for his conduct by acts of affection and contrition. The cycle then begins anew. The psychological power wielded by the batterer combined with social and economic factors make it difficult for the victim to escape her situation. Trapped by their own fear, some battered spouses respond by killing the attacker when he is vulnerable, rather than waiting for the onset of another attack. See, e.g., State v. Stewart, 243 Kan. 639 (1988).

EXAMPLE AND ANALYSIS

In State v. Kelly, 91 N.J. 178 (1984), a wife killed her husband with a pair of scissors and unsuccessfully sought to offer evidence of the battered spouse syndrome to support her self-defense claim. The appellate court held that such evidence should have been admitted. The husband had repeatedly abused the wife and, at the time of the killing, was approaching her with his hands raised. Evidence of the battered spouse syndrome could have helped the jury decide whether the wife honestly and reasonably feared for her life.

Note. Upon retrial, the court allowed evidence of battered spouse syndrome, but the jury still convicted the wife of murder.

(b) **Expert testimony.** Evidence of battered spouse syndrome is ordinarily presented by an expert. Otherwise, jurors may not understand why, given the victim's situation, it was reasonable for her to stay in the abusive relationship. Today, courts overwhelmingly accept battered spouse syndrome as scientifically reliable evidence. See, e.g., Cal. Evid. Code, §1107(b) (1991); Tex. Penal Code, §19.06 (Vernon Supp. 1992).

(c) **Scope of expert testimony.** Some courts will allow battered spouse syndrome evidence only on the issue of whether the defendant had an honest fear for her life, not on whether that fear was reasonable. These courts insist on a purely objective evaluation of what the hypothetical reasonable person would have done in the situation. See People v. Aris, 215 Cal. App. 3d 1178 (1989). The more recent trend is to allow experts to testify as to whether a "reasonable person" in the defendant's position would have believed she was in imminent danger. People v. Humphrey, 13 Cal. 4th 1073 (1996).

(d) **Objections to battered spouse syndrome defense.** The validity and desirability of battered spouse syndrome is not universally accepted. Criticisms of the syndrome's use include:

- challenges to the research underlying the theory of the syndrome; and
- concerns that the defense institutionalizes negative stereotypes of women as helpless victims.

(e) **Note.** Even if a jurisdiction does not recognize the battered spouse *syndrome*, evidence of the relationship between the defendant and the spousal victim may still be relevant to determine what a reasonable person would have done *in the defendant's situation.* Such an approach coincides with the more traditional approach to the self-defense doctrine.

vii. **Other syndrome evidence.** The use of "syndrome" evidence to support claims of self-defense has expanded to other areas, including the "battered child syndrome," the "Holocaust survivor syndrome," the "battered parent syndrome," and the "policeman's syndrome." These syndromes are offered to get the jury to evaluate the defendant's use of self-defense from a more subjective point of view; i.e., What would a reasonable person in the defendant's situation and with the defendant's history and/or syndrome have done under the circumstances?

> **EXAM TIP**
>
> Prosecutors try to apply the most objective standard of reasonableness. The defendant, on the other hand, wants to specify and individualize the reasonable person to fit the defendant's attributes and experiences.

c. **Immediate, imminent, unlawful threat.** Self-defense is limited to situations in which the defendant faces an immediate, imminent threat.

   i. **Rationale for imminency requirement.** Killing is only justified when the defendant has no other alternative than to use force against another. If the threat is *not* imminent, there are usually alternative measures available.

   ii. **Example.** Gerry tells the defendant that some day Gerry will kill him. Defendant kills Gerry on the spot. The imminency requirement has not been met. Defendant had plenty of alternative means to stop Gerry from killing him.

   iii. **Objective standard.** Traditional common law uses an objective standard to determine whether the defendant faced the threat of imminent harm.

   iv. **No preemptive strikes.** Under the traditional approach, a defendant is *not* allowed to launch a preemptive strike. Other lawful alternatives must be found.

   v. **Criticisms of imminency requirement.** The traditional imminency requirement has been criticized for requiring a defendant to wait too long to use force against someone he or she knows will be an assailant.

Example. In State v. Schroeder, 199 Neb. 822 (1978), a 19 year-old inmate stabbed his older cellmate, who had threatened to make a "punk" out of him by morning. The court found that there was no evidence of an imminent threat and, therefore, defendant was not entitled to use self-defense.

vi. **Battered spouse cases.** The imminency requirement poses special problems in battered spouse cases. Because of the pattern of violence, the battered spouse may believe a threat is imminent, even though the abuser is making no overt threat at the moment of the killing. Courts are split on whether the imminency requirement may be relaxed in such cases. Some courts hold to the strict rule that the batterer must pose an objectively immediate threat before force can be used. See State v. Norman, 324 N.C. 253 (1989) (self-defense instruction denied because battered wife killed husband in his sleep). Other courts allow the jury to view imminency through the *subjective* eyes of the defendant and to decide, given defendant's overall situation, whether it was reasonable to believe there was an immediate threat of harm.

(a) **Note.** The use of battered spouse syndrome evidence to relax the imminency requirement has been extended by some courts to battered and abused children. See, e.g., State v. James, 121 Wash. 2d 220 (1993).

(b) **Note.** Even in those cases where the imminency requirement is viewed from the defendant's subjective viewpoint, courts have not permitted the defendant to hire another person to launch a preemptive attack on the batterer. See, e.g., People v. Yaklich, 833 P.2d 758 (Colo. App. 1991) (*impending* harm cannot be used as substitute for *immediate* harm).

vii. **Model Penal Code approach.** MPC §3.04(1) relaxes the imminency requirement by providing that it is sufficient if the actor reasonably believed that the use of defensive force was "immediately necessary . . . on the present occasion." This more subjective standard does not require that self-defense be triggered by an actual assault. Rather, a threat can support self-defense if a reasonable person in the defendant's situation would believe that the threat will be carried out.

(a) **Concerns about subjective standard.** By relaxing the imminency requirement, defendants may be more prone to use self-help to combat a potentially threatening situation than they would be under traditional standards. Moreover, abusers could be summarily executed because the abused believed that self-help was necessary. Jahnke v. State, 682 P.2d 991 (Wyo. 1984) (battered child's syndrome evidence not allowed when son waited for hours to shoot his father, who had been abusing him).

viii. **Unlawful force.** A person may not defend himself against lawful force, no matter how imminent. For example, if police officers use force while lawfully arresting the defendant, defendant may not use force to resist.

d. **Proportional response.** A person may only use force that is necessary. Accordingly, no excessive force is permitted and the force used in self-defense must be proportional to the threat facing the defendant. As a corollary to this rule, deadly force may only be used when the defendant faces the threat of deadly force or serious bodily injury.

i. **Example.** Mary threatens to pinch Joan. It would be excessive force for Joan to respond by shooting Mary.

ii. **MPC approach.** MPC §3.04(2)(b) limits the use of deadly force to cases where the threatened danger is "death, serious bodily harm, kidnapping, or sexual intercourse compelled by force or threat." Many jurisdictions have followed the MPC's lead and have expanded the situations in which deadly force can be used to include those crimes that easily escalate into a threat of deadly force or great bodily harm. See, e.g., N.Y. Penal Sec. 35.15(2) (cited in *People v. Goetz*, supra, authorizes the use of deadly force to combat a kidnapping, forcible rape, forcible sodomy, or robbery).

iii. **Force may only be used against attacker.** Self-defense only authorizes the use of force against one's attacker; it is not a justification for using force against a third person.

Example. Defendant's cellmate pulls a knife and threatens to kill him. Defendant then strikes a guard to distract the cellmate. Defendant may not claim self-defense.

iv. **Risk of injury to others.** Generally, if a defendant acts in self-defense against an attacker and an innocent party is accidentally injured, the defendant is not responsible for the third party's accidental injury. People v. Adams, 9 Ill. App. 3d 61 (1972). If the defendant, however, was negligent or reckless as to risks to innocent parties, he may be held responsible for the injury. MPC §3.09(3).

(a) **Example.** A rival gang member shoots at defendant. Defendant shoots back at the gang member but the bullet passes through the attacker's body and hits an innocent third party. Defendant is not responsible for the shooting of the third party.

(b) **Compare.** A rival gang member who is shooting at the defendant runs behind a bus bench. Although there are several innocent children sitting on the bench, defendant returns fire, striking and killing one of the children. Defendant may be responsible for negligent homicide.

e. **Defendant was not the initial aggressor.** A defendant cannot assert self-defense if the defendant was the initial aggressor.

i. **Rationale for the rule.** The use of force is justified only in those situations where the defendant was forced to defend himself. It would be contrary to this principle to recognize self-defense where the defendant generated the necessity to kill.

Example and Analysis

In United States v. Peterson, 483 F.2d 1222 (D.C. Cir. 1973), Peterson spotted the victim, Keitt, trying to remove the windshield wipers from one of Peterson's junked cars. Peterson protested and went back into his house to get a gun. Keitt was about to leave when Peterson threatened to shoot. Keitt then grabbed a lug wrench and headed toward Peterson. When Keitt would not stop, Peterson shot him. The court held that Peterson was not entitled to assert self-defense because he had provoked the threat of deadly force.

ii. **Initial aggressor vs. instigator.** In some situations, it can be difficult to determine who was the initial aggressor. A person may be an instigator without being an initial aggressor. The initial aggressor is the first person to escalate a confrontation by the use or threatened use of force. A person is not an aggressor if his conduct, albeit provocative, is lawful conduct.

Example. Defendant hears that rival gang members will be meeting at a particular park. Knowing that his presence may provoke violence, defendant nonetheless goes to the park. True to their colors, the rival gang members threaten defendant with deadly force, to which he responds with force. Although defendant may have instigated the confrontation, he was not the initial aggressor.

iii. **Returning from safe haven to place of violence.** A defendant who has reached a point of safe haven and then intentionally returns to a scene of violence and confrontation is generally considered an aggressor who is *not* entitled to use self-defense.

(a) **Example.** In Laney v. United States, 294 Fed. 412 (1923), defendant escaped from a mob into a safe backyard. Rather than remain in a place of safety, defendant loaded his gun and went out to confront the mob. Defendant's actions deprived him of the opportunity to invoke self-defense.

(b) **Example.** In Rowe v. United States, 370 F.2d 240 (D.C. Cir. 1966), defendant left the scene of an argument, went home to load his gun, and returned. Defendant was *not* entitled to assert self-defense because he had returned to the confrontation from a safe haven.

iv. **Initial aggressor may use nondeadly force.** Although an initial aggressor loses the right to use deadly force, the aggressor retains the right to use nondeadly force.

v. **Exception to initial aggressor rule.** An initial aggressor may reclaim the right to use self-defense by communicating to his adversary his intent to withdraw and then by attempting to do so in good faith.

vi. **Model Penal Code approach.** The MPC takes a more flexible approach to an initial aggressor's use of force. Under MPC §3.04, an initial aggressor only loses the privilege of self-defense if he or she provokes the use of force *with the purpose of causing death or serious bodily harm.* Therefore, if an initial aggressor only provokes a moderate, nondeadly use of force and the victim escalates the encounter into one involving the threat of deadly force, defendant may defend himself against the deadly attack. Defendant may be guilty of the initial, nondeadly attack, but he does not lose the right to assert self-defense when the situation escalates.

f. **Duty to retreat.** At traditional common law, a person did not have a duty to retreat before resorting to deadly force. However, many jurisdictions have added this duty as a prerequisite to asserting self-defense. In jurisdictions with this requirement, a person has the duty to retreat, if possible, before resorting to deadly force. State v. Abbott, 36 N.J. 63 (1961).

i. **Rationale for retreat rule.** Jurisdictions have adopted the retreat rule because of the high value afforded to human life, and the belief that self-defense should only be used when absolutely necessary. At common law, the retreat rule was not adopted because society believed that men should hold their ground rather than retreat in what was perceived as cowardice.

ii. **When duty to retreat applies.** The duty to retreat only arises if the defendant uses deadly force. If the defendant does not use deadly force, there is no duty to retreat. *State v. Abbott*, supra.

Example. Defendant is attacked by a man with a knife. Defendant is able to distract his attacker and kick the knife out of his hand. Defendant had no duty to retreat because he did not resort to deadly force.

iii. **Duty is only applicable when defendant can reach complete safety.** Even when there is a duty to retreat, the defendant need only do so when he knows he can reach complete safety by retreating. If the defendant cannot safely retreat, there is no duty to do so. MPC §3.04(2)(b)(ii).

iv. **Exception to duty to retreat.** A majority of jurisdictions that impose a duty to retreat make an exception when the defendant is attacked in his own home. ("Castle Rule") Most jurisdictions make an exception to the retreat rule when the defendant is attacked in his own home because his home is his castle and there is usually no other place to which he can escape.

Note. Some jurisdictions require the defendant to retreat if the attacker is another lawful occupant, but do not require the defendant to retreat if the attacker is an intruder.

v. **Timing of duty to retreat.** The duty to retreat arises only at the moment force is used. Therefore, even if a defendant hears that he is going to be attacked, he does not have a duty to retreat and avoid the confrontation.

Example. A is picketing in front of a grocery store when he is told that B is walking over to attack him with a knife. A is not required to leave the grocery store in anticipation of B's attack.

g. **Summary of common law self-defense.** In order to claim self-defense at common law, the evidence must meet the following requirements. However, if the evidence fails to demonstrate one of the required elements, the defendant may still be able to argue for an imperfect defense which will mitigate a murder charge to either voluntary or involuntary manslaughter.

i. **Defendant had an honest and reasonable fear of force.** Reasonableness should be measured by a reasonable person in the defendant's situation. Subjective factors that may be considered include: the actors' relative sizes; the defendant's past experiences; and the attacker's actions and words.

ii. **Defendant faced an immediate/imminent threat.** Preemptive strikes are not allowed under common law, although evidence of battered person's syndrome may be used to relax the imminency requirement.

iii. **Defendant responded with proportional force.** Defendant may not use excessive force in response to an attack. Deadly force may only be used in response to a threat of great bodily harm or death.

iv. **Defendant was not the initial aggressor.** If the defendant was the initial aggressor, he loses the right to claim self-defense.

v. **Defendant had no duty to retreat.** At traditional common law, a defendant had *no* duty to retreat. The modern approach is to impose such a duty but only if the defendant *knows* he can retreat in complete safety.

h. **Burden of proof.** Most jurisdictions place the burden on the prosecution to disprove self-defense beyond a reasonable doubt. A minority of courts impose the burden on the defense to prove self-defense by a preponderance of the evidence.

3. Model Penal Code

The Model Penal Code takes a more flexible approach than traditional common law to the requirements of self-defense. In particular, MPC §3.04 allows for self-defense when the following requirements are met:

a. **Honest belief by actor that force is necessary.** MPC §3.04(1) provides a subjective standard for determining when the use of force is necessary. As long as the defendant has a good faith belief that the use of force is immediately necessary, the actor is entitled to use self-defense.

i. **Limitation.** Although the MPC uses a subjective standard for deciding when force is necessary, if the defendant is reckless or negligent in his belief that force is necessary, he cannot claim self-defense for reckless or negligent offenses, such as manslaughter or negligent homicide. MPC §3.09(2).

EXAMPLES AND ANALYSIS

Defendant is told that he will be visited that evening by children selling candy for their school. However, when defendant hears noise outside his home during the evening hours, he automatically assumes it is an unlawful attacker. Defendant shoots at the noise through his draped window. A child is hit and killed. The self-defense doctrine will not protect the defendant from a charge of manslaughter or negligent homicide.

Defendant is riding in a subway when he is approached by four youths of a different race. Defendant can see that the boys are unarmed, but he shoots them out of fear. If defendant is charged with murder, he may argue self-defense. However, he could still be charged with manslaughter or negligent homicide because of his unreasonable fear of the victims.

> **STUDY TIP**
>
> Common law and the MPC rules use different terminology, but the end result under either approach is no self-defense for a negligent or reckless crime. The common law reaches this result by requiring that the defendant *reasonably* believe he is being threatened, but allowing a conviction of a lesser offense under the imperfect self-defense doctrine. The MPC uses a subjective standard regarding the threat, but explicitly denies self-defense for any crime requiring a reckless or negligent mens rea, thus making the defendant guilty of such lesser offenses.

b. **Flexible concept of immediacy.** Under the MPC, the immediacy of the threat facing the actor is viewed from the actor's standpoint; it is a subjective standard. MPC §3.04(1).

   i. **Limitation.** If the actor is recklessly or negligently mistaken as to the immediacy of the threat faced, he does not have a defense to crimes requiring recklessness or negligence. MPC §3.09(2).

c. **No excessive force.** Under MPC §3.04, the defendant may use that force he believes is necessary to protect himself against an unlawful threat of force. Deadly force may be used when the actor believes such force is necessary to protect himself against one of four categories: death, serious bodily injury, kidnapping, or sexual intercourse compelled by force or threat.

   i. **Limitation.** A mistake as to the amount of force necessary is treated under the same provision as a mistake as to the nature and immediacy of the threat. MPC §3.09(2).

   ii. **Force to resist arrest.** In a departure from common law, under the MPC a person may not use force to resist an arrest, even an unlawful one, as long as the officer is not using excessive force. MPC §3.04(2)(a)(i).

d. **No initial aggressor.** The MPC also recognizes the initial aggressor limitation on the use of self-defense. Use of deadly force in self-defense is not justified if, with the purpose of causing death or serious bodily injury, the actor provoked the use of force against himself in the same encounter. MPC §3.04(2)(b)(i). The MPC's initial aggressor rule differs from the common law in that 1. the actor is only considered an initial aggressor if he had the *purpose* of causing death or serious bodily harm; and 2. the right to use self-defense can be regained if the initial aggressor does not use it in the same encounter in which he or she was the provoker.

e. **Duty to retreat.** MPC §3.04(b)(ii) recognizes a duty to retreat before using deadly force if the defendant knows he can do so with complete safety.

i. **Note.** It is very difficult to prove that a defendant facing immediate attack knows he can retreat with complete safety.

ii. **Exceptions to duty to retreat.** There are three situations where an actor is *not* obliged to retreat:

1. He is in his dwelling and is not the initial aggressor. MPC §3.04(2)(b)(ii)(1).
2. He is in his workplace and is not the initial aggressor. MPC §3.04(2)(b)(ii)(1).
3. He is a public officer who is using force in the performance of his duty MPC §3.04(2)(b)(ii)(2).

4. Risk of Injury to Others

In most jurisdictions, if a defendant is lawfully using self-defense, but accidentally strikes a third person, he will still be entitled to use the defense. However, if the defendant is reckless as to the safety of the third person, he may not be entitled to invoke the defense because of the charge of reckless homicide.

a. **Example.** Defendant, acting in self-defense, shot and killed his assailant, who was threatening defendant's life. The bullet passed through the assailant and struck and killed a woman sitting next to him. The court held that defendant was entitled to assert self-defense for both killings. People v. Adams, 9 Ill. App. 3d 61, 291 N.E.2d 54, 55-56 (1972).

b. **Model Penal Code approach.** Under the Model Penal Code, a defendant can assert self-defense when he hits a bystander, unless he has acted recklessly or negligently with regard to the bystander's safety. MPC §3.09(3).

Example. Defendant is being shot at by a sniper in a school. Defendant blows up the classroom, and all the children in it, to protect himself.

Defendant has acted recklessly as to the lives of innocent victims and may be liable for manslaughter or negligent homicide.

FIGURE 12-1

Self-Defense	
Common Law	*Model Penal Code*
1. Honest and reasonable fear 2. Immediate threat 3. Proportional response (No excessive force) 4. Defendant not initial aggressor 5. Duty to retreat (Modern law)	1. Fairly subjective standard 2. More flexible 3. Limits on use of deadly force 4. Limit on initial aggressor 5. Duty to retreat

Review Question and Answer

SELF-DEFENSE

Question: Hollis Brown spent 11 months rebuilding his V-twin power, dual exhaust, Harley Davidson motorcycle so he could wow the other bikers at the big annual biker rally in Sturgis, South Dakota. Clad in classic biker attire — torn black Harley insignia T-shirt, scuffed leather boots, and ripped studded Levis — Hollis parked his large, overweight-from-beer-consumption body on the motorcycle's seat, and let the engine roar.

Much to Hollis's chagrin, however, the usual beer-drinking, rough-riding, tattoo-sporting crowd was absent from Sturgis. Instead, Hollis found clusters of middle-age lawyers and urban professionals — some of whom had towed their motorcycles to the area because of their back problems — discussing tax brackets and real estate investments.

Hollis scoffed at the crowd, calling the men "sissies" and "posers." The loud insults angered one of the aging preppies, who approached Hollis on his Honda motorcycle. Hollis shouted, "Get your cowardly tricycle out of my way, shorty! I'm blowin' this wimp convention!" But before Hollis could leave, the perturbed man pulled out his six-inch, Swiss army knife and retorted, "Don't call *me* a coward, you hog-riding dirtbag. You're going to die." Hollis threw a beer bottle at the knife-toting man, knocking him prone. The man later died from a serious head injury.

Hollis is charged with homicide. He alleges the act was committed in self-defense. Discuss.

Answer: *Self-defense.* Hollis's act of throwing the beer bottle is justified if the following requirements are met: 1. he had an honest and reasonable fear of death or great bodily harm; 2. he perceived an imminent or immediate threat; 3. he reacted with proportional response; and 4. he was not the initial aggressor. In addition, some jurisdictions require that 5. he had no duty to retreat.

1. *Reasonable Fear.* In order to be entitled to the right of self-defense, Hollis must have had an honest and reasonable fear of death or grave bodily injury. Hollis will argue that he honestly feared for his life when the perturbed man confronted him, took out a knife, and told him he was "going to die." But whether this fear is justified depends upon which "reasonable" test the jurisdiction follows. Under traditional common law, a physical assault was considered legally adequate provocation. Today, the reasonableness of a defendant's fear is evaluated by considering the circumstances facing the defendant in his situation. In this case, given that Hollis was a large, tough-looking man who was used to rough crowds, and the alleged aggressor was merely a short, aging businessman among a group of so-called "wimps" and "sissies," Hollis's fear was probably unreasonable.

Other jurisdictions (and the MPC) define reasonableness solely in terms of the defendant's subjective belief. Because Hollis honestly believed his life was threatened, the reasonable requirement would necessarily be met. But under the MPC, the application of the defense is also subject to the limitation of section 3.09(2), which provides that if defendant was reckless or negligent in believing his use of force was justified, he is culpable for reckless or negligent offenses. In other words, if Hollis is charged with reckless or negligent homicide, and the prosecution can establish that he was reckless or negligent in believing it was necessary to throw a beer bottle, Hollis has no right to self-defense.

2. *Imminent Threat.* Further, the right to self-defense is limited to situations where the defendant faces an imminent or immediate threat. Hollis will argue that he had to throw the beer bottle to prevent the alleged aggressor from immediately stabbing and killing him. But the prosecutor may argue that the Swiss army knife was incapable of causing grave bodily harm, and the statement "You're going to die" was too broad to constitute an immediate threat.

3. *Proportional Force.* The force used in self-defense must be proportional to the threat facing the defendant. Hollis was threatened with a knife and responded by throwing a beer bottle. Thus, even though the alleged aggressor died unexpectedly, Hollis may claim self-defense because the force he used was proportional. If Hollis threw the bottle at the businessman's head intending to kill him, however, Hollis' right of self-defense depends on whether his use of lethal force was justifiable, that is, whether the six-inch knife also constituted a deadly threat.

4. *Not Initial Aggressor.* A defendant cannot assert self-defense if he was the initial aggressor. Hollis was not the aggressor but merely an instigator. Even though Hollis insulted the businessman, indirectly calling him a "sissy," "poser," and "wimp," words alone are rarely sufficient to provoke a reasonable man to become violently outraged and reveal a knife. Further, there is no evidence that Hollis used or threatened to use force against the perturbed man, and it was the latter's actions of displaying a knife that generated the necessity to use violence. Moreover, even if the defendant was in fact the initial aggressor, there is evidence that he communicated to his adversary his intent to withdraw. Hollis told the businessman to get out of his way and said he was leaving.

5. *Duty to Retreat.* Under traditional common law, there was no duty to retreat. However, some jurisdictions and the MPC require that the defendant retreat, if possible, before resorting to deadly violence. Once again, this element only arises if throwing the bottle constituted deadly force. If it did, Hollis had a duty to retreat. In any event, there is evidence that Hollis wanted to retreat but could not because the alleged aggressor's Honda motorcycle stood in the way.

C. DEFENSE OF ANOTHER

Under certain circumstances, a person may use force to protect another person. There are two common law approaches to defense of another, and the Model Penal Code adopts a third approach.

1. Common Law Approaches

Most courts allow the defense of another if the defendant reasonably believes the use of force is justified. A minority of courts requires that the defendant be correct in his assessment that self-defense was justified.

a. Majority approach (Reasonableness standard). Most courts allow the use of force when the defendant reasonably believes such force is necessary to defend a third person from imminent unlawful attack. See, e.g., N.Y. Penal Law 35.15 Commonwealth v. Martin, 369 Mass. 640 (1976) (inmate entitled to assert defense of another when he came to another inmate's aid during prison melee).

Example and Analysis

In People v. Young, 210 N.Y.S.2d 358 (1st Dept. 1961), *rev'd*, 11 N.Y.2d 274 (1962), the defendant saw two middle-aged men beating and struggling with a youth. Believing the men were unlawfully assaulting the youth, the defendant entered the affray and injured one of the men. The men were plainclothes police officers making a lawful arrest. In a majority of jurisdictions, the defendant could assert defense of another because he reasonably believed that the youth was entitled to defense. The *Young* court, however, followed the minority approach. Subsequently, the state's legislature adopted the reasonableness standard.

---

i. **Rationale for majority approach.** By allowing defendants to have a defense, even when they make a reasonable mistake, the law encourages Good Samaritans to help others.

b. **Minority approach (Alter ego or act at peril rule).** Some courts require that the defendant "stand in the shoes" of the person being defended. Defense of another is authorized only if the person being defended had the right to use defensive force.

i. **Example.** In *People v. Young*, supra, the court denied defendant's claim of defense of another because the youth did not have the right to resist arrest. The court held that "one who goes to the aid of a third person does so at his own peril. . . . [T]he right of a person to defend another ordinarily should not be greater than such person's right to defend himself." Id. at 319-320.

ii. **Rationale for minority approach.** Encouraging people to take the law into their own hands and interfere in altercations is dangerous, especially when the police may already be involved. The defendant must be sure in his assessment of a situation or take the risk of not being able to claim defense of another.

2. **Model Penal Code Approach**

MPC §3.05 allows defense of another when the defendant believes the use of force is necessary. The standard is a subjective one. If the defendant is mistaken in his belief that the defense of another is necessary, however, the defendant is responsible for any reckless or negligent offense. MPC §3.09(2).

Exam Tip

In determining whether the defense of another is authorized, first analyze whether the person being defended would have been entitled to use self-defense, then decide whether the defense of another is justified under the two common law and Model Penal Code approaches.

FIGURE 12-2

Defense of Another	
Majority Approach	Reasonable belief force necessary
Minority Approach	Defendant stands in shoes of other person; if person being defended is not entitled to self-defense, neither is the defendant.

Review Question and Answer

DEFENSE OF ANOTHER

Question: Dan is devastated by a fire that just destroyed his home. All that is left of his house are his law school notes and a metal post from his brass bed. While Dan is rummaging through the ashes, he sees John, the person he believes set the fire. In a rage, Dan approaches John. John is still carrying a gas can and matches. John laughs at Dan and says, "Pretty soon, I'll make sure you and your notes look as good as the rest of your house." Hearing this, Dan runs back and grabs the bed post. John then pulls out a gun. Seeing what is occurring, Millie, a passerby, shoots and kills John before he can shoot Dan. What possible defense may Millie raise?

Answer: *Millie's Liability*

A. *Defense of Another.* In a minority of courts, a defendant's right to defend another is no greater than the defended party's right to protect himself. Thus, Millie's use of force to protect Dan is only justified if Dan meets the requirements for self-defense.

1. *Dan's right to self-defense.* Dan was entitled to a right of self-defense if he honestly and reasonably feared an imminent threat of death or great bodily harm; if he used reasonable force to combat the aggressor; and if he was not the initial aggressor.

In this case, Dan probably had an honest fear of an *imminent threat* of great bodily harm. John told Dan he was going to "make sure" Dan looked "as good as the rest of the house." Given that the house was destroyed, Dan probably interpreted the statement as a threat to his life. Further, since John was carrying a gas can and matches, Dan inferred that John was a dangerous arsonist.

But there is the question as to whether Dan's fear is reasonable. First, the statement, "Pretty soon, I'll make sure you and your notes look as good as the rest of your house," was ambiguous and perhaps not a threat at all. John was laughing at the time and possibly joking. And even if John was threatening Dan, the words "pretty soon" made the statement too general to pose an immediate threat. Second, if John was just threatening to destroy Dan's notes, Dan could not use deadly force to protect property alone.

The issue as to whether John was the *initial aggressor* is also unclear. The facts occurred as follows: first, Dan confronted John in a rage; then John, who was holding a gas can and matches, said some words to Dan; next, Dan grabbed a bed post to use as a weapon; and finally, John pulled out a gun. On the one hand, Dan may be viewed as the initial aggressor because he brandished a weapon before John pulled out a gun. When the facts are viewed in this way, Dan is not entitled to a right of self-defense. On the other hand, if John's words constituted a threat, and the gas and matches constituted a weapon, John was the initial aggressor and Dan's use of force was justified. Depending on whether or not John threatened Dan with imminent harm and was the initial aggressor, Dan may or may not have been entitled to act in self-defense.

2. *Millie's right to defense of another.* In a majority of jurisdictions, Millie would not be able to claim defense of another because it is questionable whether Dan had a legitimate claim to self-defense. However, the majority of courts hold that force used in defense of another is justified when the defender *reasonably believed* that force was necessary to defend another person from imminent danger. Given that John was holding a gun and Dan was holding a bed post, it was reasonable for Millie to believe that Dan was in great danger and in need of forceful assistance.

Finally, the MPC approach is only slightly different from the majority test. It allows the defense of another when the defendant subjectively believed her force was necessary to defend another, but does not allow the defendant to escape prosecution for reckless and negligent crimes when she formed her belief recklessly or negligently. In this case, Millie clearly meets the subjective requirement because she honestly believed Dan needed protection. But if Millie was negligent or reckless in her belief that force was necessary, she will be liable for reckless or negligent homicide.

D. DEFENSE OF PROPERTY

Limited force may be used to defend property. However, because property is not as valuable as human life, deadly force may *not* be used solely to defend property.

1. Common Law

At early common law, deadly force could be used to prevent any felony, including burglary. The law is now well-established that deadly force may only be used to protect human life, not property.

a. **Rationale for rule.** The rationale for the rule that deadly force cannot be used solely to protect property is a simple one: Human life is more valuable than property.

EXAMPLE AND ANALYSIS

In People v. Ceballos, 12 Cal. 3d 470 (1974), defendant set up a spring gun in his garage to protect his property. Defendant's living quarters were above the garage. When two unarmed youths broke into the garage, the spring gun shot one in the face. Defendant was charged with assault with a deadly weapon. The court denied defendant's claim of defense of property and person. Because defendant was not present at the time of the break-in, he could not claim self-defense. As for the threat to his property, the court held that deadly force may not be used solely to protect property. See also Bishop v. State, 356 S.E.2d 503 (Ga. 1987).

b. **Residential burglary.** As established in *Ceballos*, supra, deadly force cannot be used to defend against a burglary if the resident of the home is *not* present. If a burglary occurs when a resident is present, however, the resident may use deadly force, if she reasonably fears the use of force against himself or another.

Example. In the middle of the night, a homeowner hears someone breaking into her home. She cannot tell if the person is armed. Fearing for her life, she shoots the intruder. Because she reasonably feared for her life, the homeowner meets the ordinary requirements for self-defense and is, therefore, entitled to use deadly force.

EXAM TIP

In general, mechanical devices may only be used to protect one's home if they do not use deadly force. Use of deadly force mechanical devices is only justified when the defendant is home and meets the ordinary requirements for self-defense.

2. Model Penal Code Approach

The Model Penal Code offers very detailed rules for use of force to protect property. MPC §3.06. These rules allow, under certain conditions, the use of nondeadly force to prevent trespass or the theft of property. MPC §3.06(1). Deadly force is only allowed when:

- a person is being dispossessed of his dwelling;

  or

- an intruder is committing a felony against the defendant's property (like burglary or arson) and has used deadly force against the defendant;

  or

- an attempt to use force, other than deadly force, to prevent a felony would expose the defendant to substantial risk of serious bodily harm.

3. Application of Common Law and MPC Rules

In a well-publicized case, a homeowner, Rodney Peairs, killed a young Japanese exchange student, who rang the doorbell and inadvertently frightened his wife. Because the students were not able to speak English, they could not explain their harmless purpose to Peairs or his wife. Peairs was unable to ascertain whether the students were there to cause harm. When one of the students advanced, Peairs shot him. Under the common law, Peairs would only be able to use deadly force if he honestly and reasonably believed his or his wife's life was in imminent peril. He could not use deadly force to protect his house or the property therein. Under the Model Penal Code, if Peairs honestly believed the students were committing a felony and threatening deadly force, then he could use force in response. There were no facts indicating that either student had a weapon.

Note. Even when defendants do not meet the technical requirements of a defense, a jury might acquit because they identify with the defendant's dilemma and choice of action.

FIGURE 12-3

DEFENSE OF PROPERTY	
Early common law	Deadly force to prevent felony
Modern rule	No deadly force to protect property

REVIEW QUESTION AND ANSWER

DEFENSE OF PROPERTY

Question: Sally lives in a terrible neighborhood. Nightly, she hears the roar of police helicopters above her house. To protect herself, Sally buys a pit bull dog. The dog is perfectly capable of killing a person. Sally leaves the dog in her house when she goes to work. At night, the dog sleeps at the foot of her bed.

One day, while Sally is at work, two neighborhood children hit their ball into Sally's kitchen window. The window shatters and the children decide to go into the house to get the ball. The dog attacks and kills one of them. Sally is charged with involuntary manslaughter.

What defense, if any, can Sally raise to the charge against her?

Answer: Sally may try to raise defense of property but this defense is likely to fail. The general rule is that deadly force may not be used to defend property. In this case, the pit bull dog was much like a mechanical device that would indiscriminately kill an intruder. There was no evidence that Sally reasonably feared for her life since she was at work at the time of the attack. There was also no warning about the dog. Accordingly, Sally's actions, although somewhat understandable, do not satisfy the requirements for defense of property.

E. LAW ENFORCEMENT DEFENSE

Law enforcement officers, and those acting on their behalf, are justified in using force to apprehend criminal suspects. There are limitations, however, on this use of force.

1. Force in Apprehending Misdemeanants

Both common law and the Model Penal Code allow law enforcement to use only nondeadly force in apprehending a misdemeanant. Durham v. State, 199 Ind. 567 (1927); MPC §3.07. However, if the misdemeanant threatens the life of the arresting officer, the officer may act in self-defense.

EXAMPLE AND ANALYSIS

In *Durham v. State*, supra, a deputy game warden tried to arrest a fisherman for poaching. As the deputy was making the arrest, the fisherman started to beat him on the head. At that point, the warden shot the fisherman in the head. Normally, only nondeadly force may be used to apprehend a misdemeanant, but the fisherman's assault on the warden justified the use of deadly force.

2. Force in Apprehending Felons

Until 1985, the common law permitted law enforcement to use deadly force to prevent the escape of an unarmed suspected felon. However, in Tennessee v. Garner, 471 U.S. 1 (1985), the Supreme Court held that deadly force may not be used to prevent escape unless the officer reasonably believes, under all the circumstances, that the suspect poses a significant threat of death or serious physical injury to the officer or others.

EXAMPLE AND ANALYSIS

In *Tennessee v. Garner*, supra, police responded to a residential burglary. They saw a young man fleeing unarmed from the house. When the young man failed to respond to a command to halt, an officer shot and killed him. The Court held that the use of force was not justified because the suspect was unarmed. The dissent in *Garner* unsuccessfully argued that household burglaries inherently pose a risk of serious harm to others.

Study Tip

Two types of evidence tend to justify the use of deadly force against a fleeing felon:

- evidence that the felon is armed
- evidence that the felon just committed a crime involving violence

3. Arrests by Private Citizens

A private citizen has the right to arrest a person who has committed a felony in his presence or a person he reasonably believes committed a felony, as long as the felony was in fact committed. Unlike law enforcement officers, private citizens act at their own peril. If no felony was committed, and a private citizen uses force to effectuate an arrest, the citizen cannot assert the law enforcement defense. United States v. Hillsman, 522 F.2d 454 (7th Cir. 1975).

Example. In *Hillsman*, supra, an undercover police officer shot a person in an act of self-defense. Not realizing that the shooting did not constitute a crime, Hillsman shot at the undercover officer. Hillsman was not entitled to assert the law enforcement defense because, in fact, the person he shot at was justified in using force and, therefore, had not committed a felony.

4. Model Penal Code Approach

The common law restricts the use of extreme force to felony arrests. MPC §3.07(2)(b)(i). The defense is even more restricted under the Model Penal Code. Unlike the common law, the Model Penal Code allows a law enforcement defense only when:

- the defendant, under the law of the jurisdiction, is authorized to act as a peace officer or is assisting persons whom he believes are authorized to act as peace officers, MPC §3.07(2)(b)(ii);
- there is not a substantial risk of injury to innocent bystanders, MPC §3.07(2)(b)(iii); and
- the offender used or threatened deadly force or posed a substantial risk of death or serious bodily injury if apprehension was delayed, MPC §3.07(2)(b)(iv).

FIGURE 12-4

LAW ENFORCEMENT	
Common Law	
Apprehending Misdemeanant	No deadly force
Apprehending Felon	Deadly force only if felon poses threat of death or serious bodily injury
• Arrest by police officer	Reasonable belief
• Private citizen arrest	Must be correct in assessment of situation
Model Penal Code	
Use of force to arrest	1. Law enforcement or agents only 2. No substantial risk to bystanders 3. Offender poses substantial risk of death or serious bodily injury

REVIEW QUESTION AND ANSWER

LAW ENFORCEMENT DEFENSE

Question: Officer Keen was driving on his nightly rounds when he saw David Prince drive through a stop sign. Keen stopped Prince's car and ordered him out. Prince complied. When Keen looked into Prince's car, he saw that Prince had a large amount of cash on his front seat. Some marijuana was also seen on the seat, but no weapon was in sight. At that point, Prince started to run away. Keen ordered Prince to stop but Prince kept on running. Keen pulled out his weapon and shot and killed Prince. If Keen is charged with Prince's death, what defense, if any, does he have?

Answer: Keen would try to assert a law enforcement defense, but there are some significant problems in raising the defense in this case. In *Tennessee v. Garner*, the Supreme Court held that deadly force could only be used to prevent the escape of a felony suspect who poses a significant threat of death or serious physical injury. Although there was probable cause that Prince was involved in some type of offense involving narcotics, there is no clear evidence that it was a felony or that Prince posed a threat of death or serious physical injury to another. There was no evidence Prince had a weapon or would harm another. Under these circumstances, the Constitution does not allow the use of deadly force.

F. NECESSITY

A person who commits a crime because it is the lesser of two evils can invoke the "necessity" defense. The necessity defense is also called the "Choice of Lesser Evils." Self-defense is actually a form of necessity because the defendant is allowed to commit a wrongful act in order to avoid an even greater wrong, i.e., death or injury. Necessity, however, is a broader justification which applies to any situation where the defendant faces two evils and chooses the better alternative.

1. Examples

a. **Mountain climber trespassing to avoid storm.** Defendant is caught in an unexpected snowstorm while hiking. She breaks into a cabin to seek shelter during the storm. Because trespassing is a lesser evil than loss of life, the defendant is justified in her actions and may be afforded a defense.

b. **Distributing needles to avoid HIV.** Defendant distributes clean hypodermic needles to drug addicts, even though there is a law prohibiting such distribution programs. Defendant may argue that the harm of breaking such a law is less than the harm of allowing thousands of people to become infected with the deadly HIV virus.

c. **Stealing food to avoid starvation.** Defendant steals food to avoid dying of starvation. If there truly were no alternative, and if the court does not view the case as one of economic necessity, the defendant may claim she chose the lesser evil.

d. **Violating traffic laws to speed patient to hospital.** Defendant exceeds the speed limit while rushing a friend to a hospital emergency room. Defendant may argue that the emergency circumstances justified violating the minor traffic laws.

e. **Breaking dam to avoid flooding village.** A dike at the top of a village is ready to burst. It will either flood a farmhouse or wipe out an entire village. In an effort to save lives, defendant causes the dam to break over the farmhouse. It floods and kills its innocent occupants. Depending on whether the jurisdiction allows the necessity defense in homicide situations, defendant may have a necessity defense.

f. **Escaping from intolerable prison conditions.** Defendant escapes from prison to avoid the immediate threat of an assault. Under certain circumstances, defendant may have a necessity defense.

2. Rationale for Defense

The law recognizes that even well-drafted statutes cannot account for every real-life situation. Sometimes people are forced by unexpected circumstances to engage in illegal behavior. If a defendant is faced with a choice of evils and chooses the one least harmful to society, the defendant is not deserving of punishment. Defendant has chosen the best course of action given the circumstances. His actions are not blameworthy and need not be deterred. In necessity cases, jurors act as supplemental lawmakers. By applying the necessity defense, they can find that the legislature, had it been given the precise facts of the defendant's case, would not have found the defendant's conduct illegal.

3. Common Law Elements

Necessity is a defense recognized at common law. There are four requirements for the defense at common law:

1. Defendant faces a choice of evils.
2. There are no apparent legal alternatives.
3. There is an immediate threat.
4. Defendant chooses the lesser harm.

Additionally, the courts recognize the following limitations on the use of necessity:

- Defendant did not create the necessity.
- No specific legislative decision to the contrary.

The courts have interpreted these requirements and limitations as follows:

a. **Choice of evils.** Necessity only applies when the defendant faces a choice of evils. The choice is ordinarily between immediate physical harm and committing a crime.

i. Examples

(a) An inmate faces an imminent brutal attack unless he escapes. The inmate chooses to escape. People v. Unger, 66 Ill. 2d 333 (1977) (see discussion in Sec. 5(b)(i) infra).

(b) As the captain of a ship, defendant faces losing the ship and its crew if he does not immediately dock. Accordingly, defendant docks without a permit.

(c) Defendant is in an overcrowded lifeboat. In order to keep everyone from drowning, defendant throws several men out. In this situation, defendant sacrificed a lesser number of people to save a greater number, but courts are extremely reluctant to apply the necessity defense to intentional homicides. See Regina v. Dudley & Stephens, 14 Q.B.D. 273 (Eng. 1884); United States v. Holmes, 26 F.Cas. 360 (Pa. 1842) (discussed in Ch. 12 (F)(8) infra).

ii. **Economic necessity insufficient.** Economic necessity alone will not justify commission of a criminal act.

(a) **Example.** Defendant is about to lose his job and his home. Accordingly, he embezzles money from his employer. Economic necessity is not a defense.

(b) **Example.** Defendant is homeless so he breaks into an empty house. Courts have been reluctant to extend necessity to situations of economic necessity. See Borough of Southwark v. Williams (1971), 2 All E.R. 175.

b. **No apparent lawful alternatives.** For the necessity defense to apply, the defendant must not have any lawful alternative. Necessity is a defense of "last resort." If there is a lawful alternative, defendant must select it.

Example. Defendant's wife is very ill. Rather than taking her to an emergency room, he breaks into a local pharmacy for drugs. Because defendant had a lawful alternative, the defense of necessity does *not* apply.

c. **Immediate threat.** The defendant must have faced an immediate threat. If the threat is in the future, then the defendant has time to find another alternative.

Example. While hiking, defendant hears on the radio that a storm will hit within the next two days. Defendant has time to hike down from the mountain, but decides to break into a cabin and wait out the storm so he can complete his hike. Defendant did not face an immediate threat and is not entitled to claim necessity.

d. **Defendant chose the lesser harm.** The most important element of necessity is that the defendant, when faced with the choice of evil, chose the lesser harm. Defendant's decision is evaluated by an objective standard—Did the defendant, from society's point of view, pick the lesser evil?

iii. **What are greater and lesser evils?** In general, loss of life is a greater evil than loss of property. In some jurisdictions, the loss of more lives is a greater evil than the loss of fewer lives. But note: Many courts refuse to allow the defense of necessity in homicide cases. See section 8 infra.

(a) **Example.** While A and B are driving to a movie, B suffers a heart attack. In order to rush her to a hospital, A drives through a red light. A has chosen the lesser evil because this minor traffic violation may allow him to save B's life.

(b) **Example.** A swelling river threatens to flood a town. To divert the flood, A intentionally floods a nearby farm. A has chosen the lesser evil.

(c) **Example.** Three mountain climbers are roped together while hiking. One falls. Unless he is cut loose, all of them will die. In those jurisdictions where necessity is recognized as a defense to intentional homicide, the hikers are justified in cutting the third hiker loose because they have chosen the "lesser evil" by choosing the lesser number of deaths.

e. **Not self-created.** A defendant cannot create a necessity and then use that necessity as an excuse to violate the law.

i. **Example.** Defendant negligently starts a fire. The only way to stop the fire from burning down the neighborhood is to divert the fire into his neighbor's vacant guest house. The defendant is charged with arson for burning down the guest house. At common law, defendant could not assert the necessity defense.

(a) **Compare MPC.** Under MPC §3.02, a defendant who creates her own necessity does not lose the right to assert the defense for intentional crimes. She may, however, be prosecuted for negligent offenses because she was negligent in creating the situation. Thus, the defendant above has a necessity defense to arson (the purposeful destruction of those homes), but can still be charged with criminal mischief for her negligent acts.

f. **No contrary legislative intent.** If there has already been a legislative judgment that a particular necessity does not outweigh society's support for a particular law, then the defendant may not claim necessity for violating that law.

i. **Civil disobedience cases.** Defendants in civil disobedience cases often claim that violating the law is justified by an interest in preventing a greater harm. The necessity defense does not usually work in these cases because: a. the harm faced is not imminent; b. defendants have other lawful alternatives, such as trying to change the law through the democratic process; and c. society, by passing a particular law, has already determined that the defendant's assessment of the two evils is incorrect. There are two types of civil disobedience cases: direct civil disobedience and indirect civil disobedience.

(a) **Direct civil disobedience.** Direct civil disobedience involves protesting a law by breaking that law or preventing its execution.

- **Example.** To protest the draft, defendant burns his draft card. Although the defendant may claim he is trying to stop the greater evil of an unjust war, Congress has already made the legislative judgment that there should be a draft.
- **Example.** In needle exchange programs no necessity defense is allowed because the legislature has specifically addressed the AIDS/drug use issue and decided to make needle exchange illegal.

(b) **Indirect civil disobedience.** Indirect civil disobedience involves violating a law or interfering with government policy that is not, itself, the object of protest.

- **Example.** To protest United States involvement in El Salvador, defendant obstructs the activities of the Internal Revenue Service. Necessity is not a defense to indirect civil disobedience because there are lawful alternatives for changing the law and, until changed, the legislative policy dictates against defendant's choice of evils. See United States v. Schoon, 971 F.2d 193 (9th Cir. 1992).

4. Model Penal Code Elements

MPC §3.02 provides for a "Choice of Evils" defense. Under MPC §3.02(1), a defendant may engage in criminal conduct to avoid harm if:

- The harm avoided is greater than the harm done. MPC §3.02(1)(a).
- There is no specific prohibition to the use of a choice of evils defense for this offense.
- There is no clear legislative purpose to exclude the choice of evils defense in defendant's situation.

a. **Model Penal Code vs. common law necessity.** The Model Penal Code necessity defense is broader than the common law defense in three ways:

i. **No imminency requirement.** There is no imminency requirement under the MPC. Rather, the imminency of injury is one factor to be considered in deciding whether the defendant had a lawful alternative.

ii. **No absolute prohibition on self-created necessity.** A defendant does not lose her necessity defense even if she was at fault in creating the situation. Instead, the defendant is only responsible for any crimes of recklessness or negligence caused by her actions.

iii. **Necessity may be applied in homicide prosecutions.** While most common law jurisdictions do not allow the necessity defense in homicide situations, the Model Penal Code does not put such limitations on the doctrine. See Ch. 12 (F)(8) infra.

> **EXAM TIP**
>
> If a defendant is "forced by forces of nature to commit a criminal act," necessity, *not* duress, is the proper defense to assert. Only another human being can cause duress; people or natural forces can generate necessity.

5. Special Necessity Cases

Traditionally, there are certain types of cases in which necessity is invoked.

a. **Prison escape cases.** Necessity is recognized as a defense to prison escape, but the Supreme Court has added an additional requirement in these cases. To claim necessity, the defendant must:

- face a choice of evils;
- have no apparent lawful alternatives;
- face an immediate threat;
- choose the lesser harm;
- surrender immediately upon reaching a place of safety. United States v. Bailey, 444 U.S. 394 (1980), adopting surrender rule of People v. Lovercamp, 43 Cal. App. 3d 823 (1974).

i. **Note.** Though surrender is treated as a separate requirement, it is actually an expansion of the "no legal alternative" concept. The fact that a defendant surrendered shows that he would have chosen a legal alternative, if one had been available.

EXAMPLE AND ANALYSIS

In People v. Unger, 66 Ill. 2d 333 (1977), defendant was threatened by other inmates with rape and death. Defendant did not seek the help of prison authorities because he feared retaliation. Instead, defendant escaped. Authorities apprehended him two days later in a motel room. The appellate court held that defendant was entitled to a necessity instruction. Because the case was prior to *Bailey*, defendant was *not* required to prove that he tried to surrender himself immediately upon reaching a point of safety. Instead, defendant's conduct after his escape was only partial evidence regarding the credibility of his claim that he was forced to escape.

ii. **Rationale for surrender rule.** Although courts are willing to recognize that there are some rare situations where an inmate must escape, these circumstances must be narrowly circumscribed. Otherwise, there could be wholesale use of the defense and a breakdown in prison discipline and control.

iii. **Note.** Some escape cases may also be analyzed under the defense of "duress." See Ch.12 (II)(A) infra.

b. **Needle exchange programs.** Defendants have claimed a necessity defense when prosecuted for operating needle exchange programs, in violation of the law, in an effort to avoid the spread of acquired immunodeficiency syndrome (AIDS). Courts have held that the threat the defendant tried to avoid was speculative, *not* immediate. See, e.g., Commonwealth v. Leno, 415 Mass. 835 (1993).

c. **Use of marijuana.** Defendants have claimed necessity when prosecuted for illegal use of marijuana. There is evidence that marijuana can serve a medicinal purpose for some diseases. Society, however, has already determined through legislation that authorizing the use of drugs is a greater harm than the negative impact defendants would suffer by not having the drug. See, e.g., Commonwealth v. Hutchins, 410 Mass. 726 (1991).

6. Who Decides Whether the Necessity Requirements Have Been Met?

a. **Common law and MPC.** Traditionally, the court decides whether to give a necessity jury instruction and allow evidence on the issue. Then the jury decides whether the defendant has satisfied the requirements for the defense.

i. **Note.** Defendants typically have more success arguing necessity to juries than to courts. Appellate courts overwhelmingly refuse necessity instructions or bar defendants from introducing evidence on the issue. Juries, however, are sympathetic to the defense, especially if they identify with the defendant's cause or perceive an unfairness in the law.

b. **Statutory revisions.** Some jurisdictions make the question of necessity a matter of law for the court to decide. In this way, the judicial system has more control over how the necessity defense is applied. N.Y. Penal Law 35.05.

c. **Prosecutorial discretion.** Some commentators have suggested that necessity *not* be a considered as a defense, but rather a factor influencing the case-by-case discretion of prosecutors in charging cases. This position, however, has been rejected.

7. Criticisms of the Necessity Defense

Several objections to the necessity defense have been raised.

a. **Historical abuse of defense.** Juries have often improperly applied the necessity defense. For example, in the Bisbee Deportation Case, a posse improperly rounded up and deported 1200 striking miners. When charged with kidnapping, the defendants argued necessity. The jury acquitted, although the evidence clearly showed that the roundups were politically motivated and were not based upon genuine necessity.

b. **No clear definition of necessity.** The necessity defense allows 12-person juries to decide society's priorities. The result is inconsistent verdicts.

c. **Theoretical contradictions.** The necessity defense, if applied too broadly, undermines societal notions of individual responsibility. In theory, a homeless person who breaks into a warehouse for shelter or a poor person who steals money for food for her family is acting out of necessity, because her petty crimes prevent the greater harms of exposure and hunger. Society is generally not prepared to extend the defense of necessity to situations created by poverty, but such defendants are not much different from the defendant who floods a farm to save his town.

8. Necessity in Homicide Cases

The majority of courts do *not* recognize the necessity defense in intentional homicide cases. In those jurisdictions where the defense is allowed for homicide, a lesser number of lives may be sacrificed to save a greater number.

a. **Majority approach: No necessity defense in intentional homicide cases.** A belief that the value of each individual life is paramount leads to a bar on the necessity defense for intentional homicides. Even if a fewer number of lives are being sacrificed to save a greater number, the utilitarian approach will not prevail. Rather, the moral principle that it is wrong to sacrifice the life of an innocent person for another bars application of the necessity defense in homicide situations.

Examples and Analysis

Three mountaineers slip while hiking and are left hanging from a ledge. For any to have a chance of surviving, two of them must cut one of the hikers loose. The majority of courts would not view this decision as two lives vs. one life. Rather, each of the persons being saved would be choosing his or her life over that of the innocent person being sacrificed and that is morally and legally impermissible.

In *Regina v. Dudley & Stephens*, supra, four shipmates were adrift on a lifeboat. In order to save themselves, three of the sailors killed and ate one of their sicklier shipmates. Although one life was sacrificed to save three others, the court did not allow the necessity defense because, in fact, each of the saved shipmates chose his life over the sacrificed victim.

In United States v. Holmes, 26 F.Cas. 360 (C.C.E.D. Pa. 1842), 8 seamen and 32 passengers were adrift on a lifeboat. Because the lifeboat was grossly overcrowded, the first mate and crew ejected some of the passengers. Because each life is as valuable as the next, the court held that the defendants were not entitled to a necessity defense.

---

b. **Minority approach: Taking fewer lives to save more lives.** In some jurisdictions, the necessity defense is permitted if the defendant sacrifices fewer lives to save more lives. In these jurisdictions, the value of each life is treated equally, even though, in reality, some people may make more of a contribution to society than others.

   i. **Example.** Defendant realizes that the dike above a village is about to break. In order to save the whole town, he breaks the dike in a different place, knowing that it will flood one farmer's home and kill several people. Because he sacrificed a lesser number of lives to save more, defendant may assert a necessity defense.

   ii. **Example.** In a minority jurisdiction, mountaineers at risk on a mountain, see supra, could argue a necessity defense because two lives were saved by the sacrifice of one.

c. **Model Penal Code approach.** The Model Penal Code allows the use of a necessity defense in homicide cases as long as a lesser number of lives are lost to save a greater number. MPC §3.02. This rule applies even if the lives lost are innocent ones.

   i. **Note.** The rule that a greater number of lives are valued over a lesser number does *not* apply when a person is being threatened by an attacker. In that situation, the person exercising self-defense may kill more people to save fewer people. For example, if a defendant is being attacked by a terrorist, he may kill the terrorist and his accomplices if the force is necessary for self-defense.

d. **Danger of allowing necessity in homicide cases.** Many courts consider it immoral to allow necessity in homicide cases because, when taken to its logical extreme, necessity may allow the sacrifice of innocent people any time there is a chance of saving a greater number.

For example, one could kill innocent people in order to harvest their organs to save many. Allowing necessity in homicide cases can become a slippery slope.

9. Summary of Necessity Defense

The necessity defense, also known as "Choice of Evils," provides a full defense at common law when the evidence demonstrates:

- Defendant was faced with a choice of evils.
- There was no lawful alternative.
- The threat of harm was immediate.
- Defendant chose the lesser harm.

a. **Defendant must choose lesser harm.** In assessing whether defendant chose the lesser harm, an objective standard is used. Unless the defendant made the decision that society decides was the "right" one, the defendant does not have a defense.

b. **Necessity generally not allowed in homicide cases.** Courts are reluctant to recognize the necessity defense in homicide cases. Where it is recognized, a fewer number of lives may be sacrificed to save a greater number.

c. **Civil disobedience cases.** Necessity is often raised in civil disobedience cases. Ordinarily, the defense is not successful because the defendant has other lawful alternatives in the political process and there has already been a legislative judgment that the action is impermissible.

FIGURE 12-5

NECESSITY	
Requirements	1. Choice of evils 2. No apparent alternatives 3. Immediate threat 4. Defendant chooses lesser harm

FIGURE 12-5

(CONTINUED)	
Limitations on Defense	1. Not self-created (No MPC limitation) 2. No contrary legislative intent (Common law and MPC limitation) 3. Economic necessity insufficient (No MPC limitation) 4. Surrender requirement in escape cases (Incorporated in MPC definition) 5. Not in homicide cases (No MPC limitation)

REVIEW QUESTIONS AND ANSWERS

NECESSITY

Question: Alfred, an off-duty firefighter, takes his girlfriend Yvonne for a ride in a new, fully equipped, Super Scooper fire fighting airplane. From the air, Alfred spots a brush fire flaring two hundred yards south of the quaint mountain community of Acornville. The fire appears to be moving toward the town, but firefighters have the fire mostly contained and it no longer poses a grave threat. Concerned for the safety of the town's three thousand inhabitants, and eager to show off in front of Yvonne, Alfred immediately releases 1400 pounds of fire retardant, intentionally dousing the blazing brush and the surrounding fields.

Tyson operated a hermaphroditic worm farm on a field north of the blaze. As a result of Alfred's fire fighting efforts, thousands of Tyson's earthworms drowned in vast pools of fire retardant. Alfred is charged with the unlawful destruction of Tyson's property.

Does Alfred have a necessity defense?

Answer: *Necessity*. At common law, Alfred is not liable for the destruction of Tyson's property if: 1. he faced a choice of evils; 2. he had no lawful alternative; 3. there was an immediate threat; and 4. he chose the lesser harm. In addition, the MPC recognizes the following limitations: 5. defendant did not create the necessity and 6. there was no legislative decision to the contrary.

1. *Choice of Evils.* Alfred faced a choice of evils: flood the areas surrounding the blaze with fire retardant (Tyson's farm included) or let the fire continue on its path toward a populated town.

2. *No Lawful Alternative.* It is not clear whether the only way to combat the fire was to destroy Tyson's property. Alfred, who wanted to show off in front of his girlfriend, may have acted too quickly without considering other available options. Perhaps Alfred could have contacted the local fire department from his "fully equipped" plane. If so, Alfred's solo attempt at fire fighting is most likely unlawful.

3. *Immediate Threat.* Although the fire appeared to be moving in the direction of Acornville, which was only 200 yards away, it did not immediately threaten the town's inhabitants. The local fire department had the fire nearly contained and it no longer posed a serious threat.

4. *Chose the Lesser Harm.* If the fire had constituted an immediate threat to the town's inhabitants, then Alfred would have chosen the lesser harm by sacrificing Tyson's property in order to prevent the loss of lives. But the fire was not immediately threatening the townsfolk, therefore, the lesser evil was to allow the fire to continue on its course.

5. *Not at Fault in Creating the Necessity.* Even though Alfred did not start the fire and did not create the necessity, he may have been culpable in his belief that it was necessary to battle the blaze. Thus, under the MPC, if defendant formed this belief negligently or recklessly, then he may be liable for negligent or reckless crimes.

6. *No Legislative Intent to the Contrary.* The facts are not clear as to whether there was express legislative judgment forbidding acts such as Alfred's. It is questionable, however, whether the legislature would sanction the use of firefighting equipment by off-duty firefighters to fight fires on their own accord.

Question: It is 1982, and Katya is a young pacifist protester, who believes that war and weaponry are objectively evil. Katya decides that she can destroy the great evil of America's nuclear capability and bring about world peace by sabotaging the Pentagon's strategic defense computer. With the help of some friends, Katya is able to sneak into the computer room at the Pentagon. Once inside, she chooses the biggest computer she can find and blows it up with a small stick of dynamite. Security personnel immediately capture Katya and turn her over to the U.S. Marshals. Unfortunately for Katya's plan, the computer she destroyed had nothing to do with nuclear weapons or strategic defense; the computer managed the Defense Department payroll and its destruction only caused paycheck delays for thousands of federal employees. Dora Manila, the federal prosecutor on the case, decides to charge Katya with destruction of government property.

Katya tries to claim necessity or "choice of evils." Should she be allowed the defense?

Answer: Katya can claim necessity if she was faced with a choice of evils; there was no lawful alternative; the threat of harm was immediate; and the defendant chose the lesser harm. Katya will claim that she was forced to choose between the evil of not acting to eliminate the nuclear threat and the evil of breaking the law. She will also argue that the threat of harm was immediate because any foreign policy crisis could lead to worldwide nuclear destruction and lawful alternatives work too slowly.

Courts, however, are very unsympathetic to this type of necessity defense. As in cases regarding needle exchange programs, the court would likely find that the threat is only speculative. Courts are also reluctant to allow individuals to usurp the power of the legislature and the democratic process. In this case, the legislature, representing the people, has chosen nuclear weapons as an effective defense or deterrent to foreign threats. Katya may believe differently, but the majority has already spoken on this issue. There are legal means available to Katya, such as lobbying Congress or in some other way working through the democratic process.

Finally, there is no causal link between Katya's stated goal of bringing about world peace and her action of blowing up a payroll computer. Even if the computer had controlled strategic defense, its destruction would not have lead to world peace. In fact, Katya's actions could have easily caused a war by destabilizing a delicate and strategic balance of power. Therefore, Katya's choice was not the lesser of two evils.

JUSTIFICATION DEFENSES

Question: The Yatz family (Papa, Mamma, and Baby) is driving to San Francisco when California is hit by a devastating earthquake. The highways crumble before their eyes. In order to avoid the crumbling roads, Papa Yatz drives the van across a field next to the highway. The field has a sign, "No Trespassing."

Mr. Farmer becomes enraged when he sees the Yatz family van destroying his fields. The fields are his only means of feeding his poor family of ten. Accordingly, Mr. Farmer shoots at the Yatz van. He hits the van's tire, causing the van to flip over and kill Papa and Mamma Yatz.

1. What defense could Yatz raise to a trespass charge?
2. What possible defenses may Farmer raise to a homicide charge?

Answer:

1. *Yatz's Defense to Trespass.* Papa Yatz is guilty of trespass unless his acts are justified by the necessity defense.

Necessity

At common law the defense of necessity is available when the defendant meets four requirements: a. he faced a choice of evils; b. he had no lawful alternative; c. he was threatened by immediate harm; and d. he chose the lesser harm.

Yatz will argue that he was faced with the choice of evils—death to his family or trespassing. He will argue that there was no lawful alternative because the roads were crumbling before his eyes and the threat was immediate. Finally, Yatz will argue that he chose the lesser harm because loss of human life is more serious than damage to crops.

2. *Farmer's Defenses to Homicide*

Defense of Property

Common Law. Generally speaking, the common law places a high value on human life, and deadly force may not be used solely to defend real or personal property. Moderate force may be used, however, as long as the force is necessary.

Farmer will argue that he used moderate force when he shot the van's tire with a gun. Further, Farmer will contend that he used the amount of force necessary to stop the van from destroying his fields. But the prosecutor will counter that Farmer used deadly force when he shot a gun in the direction of the Yatz family; thus, even if the amount of force were necessary to protect the fields, its use was unlawful.

MPC. Deadly force to defend property is also prohibited under the MPC, except in three limited circumstances: 1. the intruder was attempting to dispossess the defendant of his dwelling; 2. the intruder was committing a felony and threatened defendant with deadly force; or 3. the defendant would have been exposed to a substantial danger of serious bodily harm had he used nondeadly force to prevent a felony.

The facts of this case do not fall within any of the above-stated exceptions: the Yatz family did not dispossess Mr. Farmer of his dwelling; the Yatz family never threatened Mr. Farmer with deadly force; and no evidence suggests that Mr. Farmer would have been at risk of serious bodily injury if he had attempted to use nondeadly force to stop the van.

Necessity
The majority of courts do not recognize the necessity defense in homicide cases. Under the MPC, however, it is permissible to use the necessity defense for homicide cases if the number of lives saved is greater than the number of lives sacrificed. Thus, in an MPC jurisdiction, Farmer will argue that he defended his crops, which were his family's only means of sustenance, in order to prevent his entire family from starving to death. Therefore, because he sacrificed two lives in order to save ten he should be entitled to the necessity defense.

Self-defense
In all jurisdictions, in order for a defendant to raise self-defense, the following elements must be established: 1. the defendant must have had an honest and reasonable fear or death or great bodily harm; 2. the threat to defendant must have been imminent or immediate; 3. the defendant must have acted with proportional response; and 4. the defendant was not the initial aggressor

Farmer is not entitled to the right of self-defense. Even if Farmer honestly believed that he would starve if his crops were destroyed, there is no evidence that the trespasser would have physically harmed him; thus, any fear of bodily harm was unreasonable. Nor was the perceived threat to the defendant imminent. Rather, the threat of starvation was speculative because Farmer may have been able to find food elsewhere. Also, Farmer did not act with proportional response; he used a deadly weapon to ward off an unarmed intruder. Finally, even though Yatz was a trespasser, he was not the initial aggressor, and it was the defendant who committed the violent acts.

Defense of Another
Most courts will allow the defendant to use force to defend another person when the defendant reasonably believes that such force is necessary to defend a third person from the imminent use of unlawful physical force by another.

Farmer might argue that he is entitled to claim defense of another because he was protecting his family from the imminent threat of starvation due to the unlawful destruction of his crops. But for the same reasons that Farmer was not entitled to the right of self-defense, he is not entitled to the defense-of-another defense.

G. EUTHANASIA

The last justification defense is euthanasia. Where euthanasia is lawful, a person can help another person die. Consent is usually *not* a defense to a crime, but if the victim consents and wishes to exercise the right to die, some jurisdictions hold euthanasia to be justified killing. Many jurisdictions, however, do not accept that euthanasia, which involves the killing of an innocent person, prevents a greater evil of undue suffering.

1. Right to Die

The Supreme Court has yet to decide whether there is a constitutional right to die and to assist another who wishes to end his or her life. Even courts that have assumed that such a right exists are cautious about letting defendants exercise that right without strict procedural protections.

EXAMPLES AND ANALYSIS

Cruzan v. Director, Mo. Dept. of Health, 497 U.S. 261 (1989). In *Cruzan*, after Nancy Cruzan had lived for years in a persistent vegetative state, her family sought the right to terminate all procedures, including nutrition and hydration, that would prolong her life. The Court held that a State could require clear and convincing evidence that the patient would want withdrawal of treatment before a request for euthanasia would be granted. Even if one assumed that there is a constitutional right to die (the Court did not decide that issue), that right does not prohibit a State from imposing procedural protections on the use of euthanasia.

People v. Kevorkian, 447 Mich. 426; 527 N.W.2d 714 (1994). In *Kevorkian*, the Michigan Supreme Court upheld that State's law prohibiting persons from assisting suicide. The court held that there is no constitutional right to die or to assist a suicide. Accordingly, any such killing is *not* justified.

Compassion in Dying v. State of Washington, 79 F.3d 790 (1995) (en banc). The Ninth Circuit (Reinhardt, J.) held that the provision of the Washington statute prohibiting assisted suicide violated the due process clause of the U.S. Constitution for terminally ill patients who wished to use drugs prescribed by a doctor to hasten their own deaths. To reach its finding, the court weighed state interest in preserving life, preventing suicide, precluding arbitrary, unfair, or undue influence by third parties, protecting children and loved ones, and protecting the integrity of the medical profession against the individual's liberty interest in choosing when and how to die. The court found that the individual liberty interest outweighed any state interest in preventing the deaths.

Quill v. Vacco, 80 F.3d 716 (2d Cir. 1996). The Second Circuit struck down a New York statute penalizing assisted suicide as violating the Equal Protection clause. The court held that the law did not meet the rational basis test, stating that the law should afford the greatest autonomy to the individual to decide on medical treatment.

---

a. **Dangers of legalizing euthanasia.** Courts are extremely reluctant to recognize euthanasia as justifiable killing. Euthanasia is suspect because:

1. It can be abused by those who do not want to provide proper treatment for the elderly and ill.
2. Doctors are not necessarily in a good position to determine a patient's wishes because few are trained to diagnose depression, especially in complex cases of the terminally ill.
3. It may take the decision to die away from the patient, who might change his or her mind at the last minute.
4. The inevitable honest mistakes that will be made and the not-so-honest abuses create evils that outweigh the evils euthanasia is designed to prevent; namely, the pain suffered by the terminally ill.

REVIEW QUESTION AND ANSWER

EUTHANASIA

Question: Peter Payne is a first-year law student, and life has been treating him rather poorly. He cannot keep up with his classes and he feels like a fool every time he gets called on in class. Outside of school things are not much better. Peter's car was recently destroyed in an accident; he caught a terrible flu virus just before exams; and worst of all, his wife recently left him for a man "who doesn't talk about mens rea and res ipsa all the time." Peter has reached the conclusion that life is a pain and he wants it to end. He asks his ex-wife, who is also an ex-Girl Scout, to help him commit suicide by making a noose in a long piece of rope and tying the other end to a high tree branch. If Peter's ex-wife agrees to assist him, will she be able to claim a euthanasia defense?

Answer: Peter's ex-wife will not be able to claim a euthanasia defense if she helps Peter kill himself. Most courts do not recognize a constitutional right to die, and laws prohibiting assisted suicide have been upheld in Michigan and elsewhere.

Even courts that recognize a right to die do so only in very narrowly defined circumstances. The Ninth Circuit has found a right to die only when the person is terminally ill and wishes to use doctor-prescribed drugs to hasten an inevitable death. Peter is perfectly healthy aside from the flu, and his wife is not a doctor. No court has recognized a right to die or euthanasia defense under these circumstances because the law places a high value on human life. Society at large does not believe that mental or emotional depression in an otherwise healthy person is sufficient reason for suicide.

PART II. EXCUSE DEFENSES

INTRODUCTION

The law recognizes a limited number of defenses when the defendant makes the socially wrong choice by engaging in certain conduct, but does so because he was not fully capable of controlling his behavior. This lack of control renders the defendant free of blame or subject to less blame. Excuse defenses include:

- Duress
- Intoxication
- Insanity
- Diminished Capacity
- Infancy
- Entrapment
- Consent

Some commentators divide excuse defenses into three categories:

1. Involuntary Actions

The first category of excuses includes "involuntary actions," discussed in Chapter 3 supra. The defendant's conduct is excused because it was not the product of a voluntary bodily movement.

Example. Defendant is pushed downstairs and causes others to fall. Defendant's motion of pushing others is excused because it is not a "voluntary act."

2. Inability to Choose

The second category of excuses includes those actions that a defendant commits because of an inability to know better (e.g., mistake, accident, or diminished capacity) or because she was forced by another to commit the act (duress).

a. **Example.** Defendant believes he is shooting a deer but, in fact, shoots a person dressed like the animal. Defendant's actions are excused as a mistake of fact.

b. **Example.** Defendant is threatened with great bodily harm unless he robs a bank. Defendant's actions are excused because he was under duress.

3. Inadequate Capacity for Rational Judgments

The third category of excuses focuses on the individual's inability to make a rational judgment. The foremost example of this category is insanity, although infancy may also be included.

A. DURESS

If a defendant is compelled by another person's use of force or threat of force to commit a crime, the defendant may claim the defense of "duress."

1. Example

A threatens to shoot B if B does not burn C's car. If B burns C's car, B has a defense to arson because he acted under duress.

STUDY TIP

A key difference between duress and necessity lies in the rationale for each. Necessity *justifies* a defendant's actions because the defendant made the right choice given the choice of evils facing him. Duress *excuses* a defendant's behavior because the threats by another person deprived the defendant of a fair opportunity to exercise free will. The duress defense applies even if the defendant did not choose the lesser evil. If a defendant is excused from a crime because of duress, the person who forced the defendant to commit the crime is guilty of the offense that the defendant committed.

2. Compare Involuntary Acts

If a person's brain is not controlling his actions, he is engaged in an "involuntary act." This is not an affirmative defense. Rather, it is treated as a failure by the prosecution to prove the actus reus of the crime. If the defendant knows what he is doing, but is being forced to do so by another person, then the defense of duress applies.

3. Rationale for Duress Defense

As an excuse, the duress defense relieves a defendant of liability if he was forced to commit a crime. In these coercive situations, the defendant has acted without a fair opportunity to exercise free will and therefore is not deserving of punishment. Likewise, punishment is not likely to deter a person who acted reasonably under the coercive circumstances.

4. Elements of Duress

The elements for duress are different under the common law and Model Penal Code.

a. **Common law elements.** The elements of duress under common law are:

- a threat of death or grievous bodily harm
- imminently posed
- against the defendant or a close friend or relative
- creating such fear that an ordinary person would yield
- defendant did not put himself in the situation
- defendant did not kill another person

b. **Model Penal Code elements.** The elements of duress under MPC §2.09 are:

- a threat of unlawful force
- against defendant or any person
- of the type that would cause a person of "reasonable firmness" in the defendant's situation to yield
- the defendant did not recklessly put himself in the situation
- the defense is available for any crime, including homicide

c. **Common law and Model Penal Code elements**

i. **Type of threat.** The common law only allows a duress defense when there is a threat of death or great bodily harm. Under the

Model Penal Code, there is a sliding standard. The greater the crime, the more serious a threat must be to excuse the defendant's conduct. For lesser crimes, the Model Penal Code provides an excuse, even if the defendant did not face death or great bodily harm.

EXAMPLE AND ANALYSIS

In State v. Toscano, 74 N.J. 421 (1977), a chiropractor received calls threatening retaliation against him or his wife if he did not help in a scheme to submit fraudulent insurance forms. One call stated, "Remember, you just moved into a place that has a very dark entrance and you leave there with your wife . . . You and your wife are going to jump at shadows when you leave that dark entrance." Under common law, the threat may not be specific enough because it did not state that defendant faced death or serious bodily harm. However, under the Model Penal Code, even general threats suffice, especially if the defendant's crime is a less serious one.

(a) **No economic duress or threat to reputation.** Neither the common law nor the Model Penal Code recognizes a duress defense when the threat is of economic harm or damage to the defendant's reputation. There must be a threat of bodily injury to a person.

- **Example.** An employer threatens to fire the defendant unless she participates in a fraud scheme. Defendant is *not* entitled to assert a duress defense.
- **Example.** B threatens to burn A's house while A is at work if A does not help B commit a bank robbery. Threat of damage to A's property is insufficient to raise a duress defense under either common law or the Model Penal Code.

ii. **Imminency requirement.** At common law, the pending harm must be imminent. There is no similar requirement under the Model Penal Code. Under the Model Penal Code, the imminency of the harm is one factor in determining how serious the harm was and whether a person of "reasonable firmness" would resist.

Examples and Analysis

In *Toscano*, supra, the threatening calls to defendant did not specify when the attack against him or his wife would take place. Under common law, the threat would not meet the imminency requirement. Under the Model Penal Code, however, threats of future harm may suffice for a duress defense.

In United States v. Fleming, 23 C.M.R. 7 (1957), an Army officer was court-martialed for collaborating with the enemy. The defendant claimed that the enemy threatened to send him on a death march if he did not collaborate. Because it was not clear when he would have to start the march or that the march would lead to death, defendant was not entitled to assert the duress defense.

In United States v. Contento-Pachon, 723 F.2d 691 (9th Cir. 1984), drug dealers threatened a Colombian taxi driver and his family if he did not smuggle cocaine. The court relaxed the "imminency" requirement and held that defendant could claim a duress defense because he had no reasonable avenue of escape. This approach is similar to the Model Penal Code view of imminency.

---

iii. **Threat to defendant or third person.** Under early common law, the defendant himself had to be threatened. Later, common law recognized threats to close relatives of the defendant. By contrast, the Model Penal Code recognizes threats to any person.

Example. Defendant receives word that his neighbor will be injured unless the defendant participates in a scheme to defraud the telephone company. Under common law, defendant would not have a duress defense because the threat was not against him or a close family member. Under the Model Penal Code, defendant would have a duress defense.

iv. **Reasonableness requirement: ordinary person would yield.** Both the common law and Model Penal Code impose a reasonableness requirement on the duress defense. The common law standard is usually more objective than the Model Penal Code standard. Under common law, the threat to the defendant must induce "such a fear as a man of ordinary fortitude and courage might justly yield to." The Model Penal Code, however, directs the jury to determine whether a "person of reasonable firmness in defendant's situation" would have been unable to resist the threat. The Model Penal Code standard allows the jury to consider subjective factors, such as the defendant's size, strength, age, and health in making its decision. Only matters of temperament are excluded.

Examples and Analysis

In People v. Romero, 10 Cal. App. 4th 1150 (1992), defendant was a battered woman who was ordered by the man she lived with to participate in a robbery. He threatened to kill her if she did not assist him. Under the common law, the woman may have a difficult time introducing evidence of the battered woman's syndrome to explain why it was reasonable for her to succumb to his threat. Under the Model Penal Code, battered woman's syndrome is admissible as evidence of "defendant's situation."

Although it ordinarily works to the defendant's advantage to have the trier of fact consider how a person "in defendant's situation" would have reacted, this element can work to a defendant's disadvantage. For example, in United States v. Fleming, 23 C.M.R. 7 (1957), defendant was a captured prisoner of war, who was convicted of collaborating with the enemy. The defendant's duress argument failed because other prisoners "in defendant's situation" had been able to resist their captors' threats.

---

v. **Contributory fault: did not bring upon self.** Both the common law and the Model Penal Code deny the duress defense to anyone who puts himself into a situation leading to duress, even if the defendant does so negligently. The Model Penal Code standard is a bit more forgiving than the common law standard. The defendant retains a duress defense, unless he recklessly places himself in a situation where it is probable he will be pressured into committing a crime.

(a) **Gang membership.** Defendant joins a gang to engage in petty thefts. When the leader decides to rob a bank, defendant refuses to go along, but is threatened with great bodily harm if he does not participate. Under the common law, defendant cannot assert a duress defense to the robbery because he voluntarily put himself into a situation where he could be pressured to participate in the robbery. Under MPC §2.09(2), if defendant had no reason to believe that the gang ever participated in more serious offenses, he may be able to claim that he did not recklessly put himself in a situation that could lead to coercion to commit bank robbery.

(b) **Mistaken threat.** If the defendant perceives a threat, when none occurred, most common law jurisdictions deny a duress defense. For example, if a particularly timid person believed that a glance of another person was actually a threat of death, the duress defense could not be asserted. The language of the Model Penal Code does not cover this situation, but the commentary suggests that the defendant would have a defense as long as the crime committed was not one of recklessness or negligence. MPC §2.09(1).

(c) **Brainwashing.** In some jurisdictions, brainwashing may substitute for a specific threat against the defendant. Under brainwashing, a defendant is deprived of free will through psychological indoctrination. The defendant is coerced through this indoctrination rather than by specific threats. Other jurisdictions, however, may view brainwashing cases simply as situations where the defendant changes loyalties and has, therefore, brought the coercive situation upon herself.

Example. In the Patty Hearst robbery case, Hearst alleged she had been kidnapped and brainwashed into participating in a bank robbery with members of the Symbionese Liberation Army. The court allowed the jury to consider this as a form of duress, but the jury decided Hearst had not been coerced, but had freely chosen to join her captors' group.

vi. Unavailability for murder cases. The common law strictly precluded the use of a duress defense in murder cases. Regina v. Howe, 1 App. Cas. 417 (1987). The majority of jurisdictions still do not allow a duress defense to murder, but the Model Penal Code does not have a similar restriction.

EXAMPLE AND ANALYSIS

A man with two guns in his hands approaches a woman who is pushing a baby carriage. The man takes one gun and puts it at the head of the woman's baby. He takes the other gun and gives it to the woman, stating: "Shoot the next person you see or I'll kill your baby." Under common law, and the law of most jurisdictions, the woman has no duress defense if she shoots and kills a passerby. Under the Model Penal Code, the woman could argue for a duress defense.

(a) **Imperfect duress.** In some jurisdictions duress can be used to mitigate a homicide from murder to voluntary manslaughter on the theory that a defendant who kills under duress is acting under extreme emotional distress. See Chapter 5 supra.

(b) **Defense to felony-murder.** Courts are divided on whether duress is a defense to a murder that occurs while the defendant is participating in a felony. Compare State v. Hunter, 241 Kan. 629 (1987) (duress available) with State v. Rumble, 680 S.W.2d 939 (Mo. 1984) (duress not available).

EXAMPLE AND ANALYSIS

Defendant is compelled to participate in a robbery. During the robbery, one of the other robbers accidentally shoots a bystander. Under the common law approach, defendant is more likely to be responsible for the felony-murder because duress is not a defense to a homicide. However, the Model Penal Code and some common law jurisdictions would allow a duress defense for felony-murder because the defendant was coerced to commit the underlying robbery.

---

5. Common Law vs. Model Penal Code Duress

Duress under the Model Penal Code is broader than the common law in several ways:

a. **Model Penal Code abandons deadly force and imminency requirements.** The MPC does not have specific deadly force or imminency requirements. Rather, these are factors for the trier of fact to consider in deciding whether a person or reasonable firmness in defendant's situation would have committed the offense. The threat of "unlawful force" is sufficient under the Model Penal Code. Even brainwashing may qualify as sufficient force for Model Penal Code duress. The more serious the crime the defendant committed, the more serious and imminent the threat must have been for the defendant to be entitled to a duress defense.

b. **Model Penal Code recognizes threat to any person.** Under the common law, defendant must react to a threat to himself or to a close relative. Under the Model Penal Code, the threat may be to any person.

c. **Model Penal Code's reasonableness requirement includes aspects of defendant's situation.** The Model Penal Code's standard allows the trier of fact to consider subjective factors regarding the defendant in deciding whether a person of reasonable firmness would have succumbed to the defendant's situation. Evidence such as the "battered woman's syndrome" has a better chance of being introduced under the Model Penal Code standard.

d. **Model Penal Code duress can be applied in homicide situations.** Under the Model Penal Code, there is no prohibition against using duress as a defense in homicide cases.

6. Duress vs. Necessity

It is often difficult to distinguish between duress and necessity because, in both situations, the defendant is faced with a choice of harms. For example, escape cases are analyzed under both duress and necessity theories. However, there are important distinctions between the two:

a. **Justification vs. Excuse.** Necessity is a justification because, given the circumstances, the defendant chose the solution that was most advantageous to society. Duress is an excuse because, though the defendant was not acting with free will, he still committed an act harmful to society.

Example and Analysis

A threatens to break B's elbow if B does not rob a store. B robs the store, leaving the proprietor and his family without the means to eat or pay their rent for months. Although it is questionable which harm would have been worse — a broken elbow or a starving family — defendant is entitled to a duress defense.

Prison escape cases may be defended under the duress defense, instead of the necessity doctrine. The benefit to a defendant in asserting the duress defense is that the jury need not decide which is the worse evil—a dangerous criminal being brutally assaulted in prison or escape of that criminal into society. Instead, the focus is on whether a threat of immediate and serious force compelled the defendant to flee.

Note. The limitation that an escapee immediately surrender to authorities following his or her flight applies whether the defendant asserts a necessity or duress defense.

---

b. **Natural threat or threat by person.** Many jurisdictions, including the Model Penal Code, allow the necessity ("choice-of-evils" defense) regardless of the source of the peril. By contrast, the duress defense is only allowed when the threat comes from another person.

Example. Faced with a potentially deadly snowstorm, the defendant breaks into another person's home. The defense is necessity. Faced with a threat of bodily harm or death, defendant breaks into another person's home. The defense is duress.

c. **Coercer is culpable.** If a defendant acts under necessity, no one is guilty of a crime. If the defendant acts under duress, the coercing party is responsible for defendant's crime. The coercing party has used the defendant as an instrument to commit the crime.

FIGURE 12-6

DURESS	
Requirements	1. Threat of death or SBH (MPC: Threat of unlawful force) 2. Imminently posed (MPC: No separate requirement) 3. Against defendant or close relative (MPC: Against any person) 4. Such fear ordinary person would yield (MPC: Person of reasonable firmness in defendant's situation)
Limitations on defense	1. Defendant did not put himself in situation (MPC: Recklessness standard) 2. Not available for homicide (MPC: Allows for homicide)

Review Question and Answer

DURESS DEFENSE

Question: Johnnie Jones is a taxi driver in New York, and his job has given him no end of trouble. He has been robbed no less than 13 times since he began driving a year ago. One day he picks up a man who asks to be taken to the First National Bank. When the cab pulls up in front of the bank, the man hands Johnnie a toy gun and tells him to rob the bank. The man has another gun in his hand, and he says that if Johnnie does not come out of the bank with at least $50,000, the next three passersby will "get it, just like the people in the last place I held up." The man's gun looks suspiciously like a water pistol, but Johnnie has not survived 13 robberies by quibbling with armed thugs. He dutifully robs the bank and returns to the cab. Unfortunately, the man's gun is real, and it accidentally goes off as Johnnie and the man are fleeing the scene. The bullet ricochets off a lamppost and kills a mime, who happened to be performing on the sidewalk outside the bank.

Johnnie is charged with bank robbery and felony-murder; what defenses, if any, are available to him?

Answer: Duress as a defense to robbery—common law. The duress defense is available if the defendant faced an imminent threat of great bodily harm or death to himself or a close friend or relative; the threat created such fear that an ordinary person would yield; the defendant did not put himself in the situation; and the defendant did not kill anyone. Johnnie's situation meets several of these requirements. The man threatened death or great bodily harm to bystanders if Johnnie did not rob the bank. The threat was serious and imminent because the man had a gun and could use it at any time to carry out his threat. Johnnie did not put himself in the situation because he simply picked the man up and took him to a requested location without knowing the man's intentions. Johnnie also did not kill anyone. Two of the common law duress requirements are problematic for Johnnie's case. First, it is questionable whether the man's threat would have caused an ordinary person to yield, because it was not even clear to Johnnie that the man's gun was real. Second, the man did not threaten a close friend or relative of Johnnie; at common law, a threat to unrelated bystanders is not enough. Therefore, Johnnie cannot receive a duress jury instruction.

Duress as a defense to felony murder—common law. Duress would not be a defense to felony-murder in Johnnie's case, because there is no duress defense for the underlying robbery.

Under the Model Penal Code, a defendant has a duress defense if there is an unlawful threat of force against a person that is of the type that would cause a person of reasonable firmness in the defendant's situation to yield. In addition, the defendant must not have put himself in the situation recklessly.

In this case, Johnnie faced an imminent unlawful threat to bystanders and did not recklessly put himself in the situation as discussed above. The important issue is whether a person of reasonable firmness in Johnnie's situation would have yielded. Johnnie is more likely to meet the MPC reasonableness standard than the common law ordinary person standard because the jury would be allowed to take into account the 13 times Johnnie has been robbed. This individualization of the standard works to Johnnie's advantage because the jury would understand why he was especially cautious even when he was not sure that the man's gun was real. Under the Model Penal Code, Johnnie would probably have a duress defense to robbery.

Johnnie would also have a duress defense to felony-murder under the MPC because he was forced to participate in the underlying robbery and was not personally responsible for the killing.

B. INTOXICATION

In criminal law, there are two types of intoxication defenses. Involuntary intoxication can provide a complete defense to a crime. Voluntary intoxication generally does not completely excuse a defendant's actions; rather, it reduces a defendant's culpability.

1. Involuntary Intoxication

Involuntary intoxication is a complete defense if it causes the defendant to commit a crime he would not have otherwise committed. Involuntary intoxication may also cause legal insanity; that is, affect the defendant's substantial capacity either to appreciate the criminality of one's conduct or to conform one's conduct to the law. Regina v. Kingston, (1994) 3 All E.R. 353; City of Minneapolis v. Altimus, 306 Minn. 462 (1976); MPC §2.08(4).

a. **Example.** While defendant is not looking, a person slips a drug into his drink. After drinking, defendant hallucinates and commits a crime. Defendant has a full defense to the crime if, in the hallucinated state, he was unaware of the criminal nature of his acts. The involuntary intoxication negated defendant's mens rea for the crime and caused him to lose control. Regina v. Kingston, (1994) 3 All E.R. 353.

b. **Definition of involuntary intoxication.** Involuntary intoxication can take the following forms:

- Unwitting intoxication,
- Coerced intoxication,
- Pathological intoxication.

City of Minneapolis v. Altimus, 306 Minn. 462 (1976).

i. **Unwitting intoxication.** If a person is unaware that he is ingesting alcohol or a drug, the intoxication is "involuntary."

Example. A person spikes the defendant's food or drink or substitutes a person's medication with a drug that has intoxicating effects. Defendant's intoxication is involuntary.

ii. **Coerced intoxication.** If a person is forced to ingest a drug or alcohol, the intoxication is "involuntary."

Example. Defendant is forced at gunpoint to swallow LSD. Defendant's intoxication is involuntary.

iii. **Pathological effect.** If medication or alcohol produces an unexpected grossly excessive effect, then that intoxication may be considered "involuntary."

(a) **Example.** Defendant takes an aspirin. The pill has the same effect on him as LSD would have on others. If defendant had no reason to know that aspirin would have that effect on him, the resulting intoxication is considered involuntary.

(b) **Warning.** Pathological intoxication only applies if the defendant has no warning as to the possible effect of the drug or alcohol and its effects were unpredictably extreme in that case. However, if the defendant voluntarily ingests an illegal drug but does not realize how drastic its impact will be on him, his intoxication is still voluntary. People v. Velez, 221

Cal. Rep. 631 (1985) (defendant "voluntarily" intoxicated after smoking marijuana cigarette laced with PCP).

2. Voluntary Intoxication

The common law takes a more restrictive approach to voluntary intoxication. Generally, voluntary intoxication can only be used as a defense to specific intent crimes (i.e., crimes requiring a particular purpose, motive, or sophisticated mental state). Commonwealth v. Graves, 461 Pa. 118 (1975). Intoxication can show that the defendant was unable to form the mens rea necessary for the offense.

a. **Example.** In Roberts v. People, 19 Mich. 401 (1870), the defendant was charged with assault *with intent to murder.* Defendant claimed that he was too drunk at the time of the assault to form the intent to murder. The court agreed that voluntary intoxication could be used as a defense to a crime that requires a specific intent to cause a particular result.

b. **Specific vs. general intent.** The distinction between specific and general intent crimes is an elusive one that developed as a judicial response to the problem of the intoxicated offender. At early common law, intoxication was never a defense. Then, as courts became troubled by this rigid rule, they permitted an intoxication defense for those crimes for which the defendant needed to form a sophisticated intent. For those offenses which simply require a reckless physical act, however, an intoxication defense is not permitted. See generally People v. Hood, 1 Cal. 3d 444 (1969).

i. **Specific intent.** Crimes that require a purposeful mens rea, i.e., an intent to cause a future result, or premeditation, are viewed as specific intent crimes. If the defendant was intoxicated, he can argue that he could not form the intent for that crime and is guilty, if at all, for a lesser offense.

Example. Defendant is charged with first-degree murder. He claims he was too intoxicated to premeditate the crime. If the jury finds that the defendant could not have premeditated the killing, he is only guilty of second-degree murder.

Study Tip

If a crime requires that a defendant have the "intent to" cause a specific result or cause a further crime, the defense of voluntary intoxication is available.

Example. If defendant is charged with burglary with intent to steal or intent to assault, voluntary intoxication may negate the mens rea for the intent to commit a further crime. However, the defendant would still be guilty of breaking and entering, a general intent crime. *Commonwealth v. Graves*, supra.

ii. **General Intent.** Crimes that require very little thinking or planning are typically categorized as general intent crimes for which voluntary intoxication is *not* a defense.

Examples and Analysis

Battery and assault are the classic examples of general intent crimes. It takes very little mental activity to decide to hit another person, and intoxication does not impair this activity. If a defendant hits another person while drunk, there is no intoxication defense to the crime of battery.

In *People v. Hood*, supra and People v. Rocha, 3 Cal. 3d 893 (1971), the defendants were charged with "assault with a deadly weapon." Because assault does not require a sophisticated intent, the courts denied voluntary intoxication as a defense. The *Rocha* court specifically designated the assault as a "general intent" crime.

(a) **Rationale.** Because so many crimes are committed when defendants are drunk or under the influence of drugs, courts are very reluctant to afford a defense to every person who acts illegally while intoxicated. In addition, if individuals voluntarily choose to drink, they should be responsible for their actions when they are drunk. The defense is limited to crimes that require a specific, sophisticated mental activity of which an intoxicated person may not be capable. It is not applied to those crimes that typically occur when people are drunk such as battery.

(b) **Reckless conduct.** Crimes that involve reckless conduct are considered general intent crimes and the defense of voluntary intoxication does not apply.

- **Example.** Arson is a crime involving recklessness. Voluntary intoxication is not a defense to arson.
- **Exception.** In California, most crimes of recklessness are considered general intent crimes. However, a charge of second-degree murder based on gross recklessness is considered a specific intent crime and evidence of intoxication is admissible.

c. **Alternative common law approaches.** Some courts have rejected the traditional approach because they find there is no principled way to distinguish between specific and general intent crimes. These courts adopt their own intoxication rules.

i. **Alternative #1/Restrictive view of intoxication defense.** In some jurisdictions, the intoxication defense is only allowed for first-degree murder or when the defendant has such a prolonged history of using drugs or alcohol that he or she has become insane. State v. Stasio, 78 N.J. 467 (1979).

ii. **Alternative #2/Liberal view of intoxication defense.** In a significant minority of jurisdictions, intoxication is allowed as a defense to any crime, including reckless crimes.

3. Model Penal Code Approach

Under the Model Penal Code, involuntary and voluntary intoxication are defenses. MPC §2.08.

a. **Involuntary intoxication.** Under MPC §2.08(4), intoxication which is not self-induced or is pathological can serve as a full defense, if it has the same impact as insanity, i.e., it causes the actor to not know what he is doing or to lose the ability to conform his conduct to the law.

b. **Voluntary intoxication.** Under MPC §2.08(1), voluntary intoxication can be used to negate the mens rea of any crime, except for reckless or negligent crimes. MPC §2.08(2).

Example. Defendant is charged with fourth-degree arson; i.e., recklessly damaging a building by lighting a fire. Although voluntary intoxication would be a defense to a charge of first-degree arson, which requires an intentional burning of the building, it is *not* a defense to the charge only requiring recklessness. People v. Tocco, 138 Misc. 2d 510 (1988).

4. Voluntary Intoxication Leading to Insanity

Even in jurisdictions that take a restrictive approach to the voluntary intoxication defense, if the defendant has used drugs and alcohol over such a prolonged period that he has become insane, voluntary intoxication is usually recognized as a defense. Voluntary intoxication cannot be used to argue "temporary" insanity. Rather, the defendant's repeated intoxication must have led to permanent mental damage.

5. Degree of Intoxication

The mere intake of alcohol or drugs is insufficient to demonstrate intoxication. There must be a "prostration of the defendant's faculties" such that the defendant is incapable of forming the mens rea necessary for the crime. State v. Cameron, 104 N.J. 42 (1986).

a. **Factors for determining intoxication.** To determine whether the defendant has ingested enough alcohol or drugs to be intoxicated, courts consider the following factors:

- quantity consumed;
- time period of consumption;
- defendant's conduct, as perceived by others;
- odor of alcohol;
- blood-alcohol content;
- actor's ability to recall significant events.

b. **Using liquid courage is not allowed.** A defendant who forms the intent to commit a crime and then drinks to give himself courage to complete the task is not entitled to claim intoxication. Defendant formed the intent for the crime before becoming intoxicated.

6. No Constitutional Requirement that Intoxication Defense Be Recognized

The Supreme Court recently held that a defendant is not constitutionally entitled to raise a voluntary intoxication defense. State statutes may bar juries from considering evidence of voluntary intoxication as an element of the defendant's mental state. Montana v. Egelhoff, 96 D.A.R. 6469 (1996).

7. Compare Status Prosecutions

A person cannot be prosecuted merely for being an addict or alcoholic. Robinson v. California, 370 U.S. 660 (1962). (See full discussion in §12H infra.) However, acts done by addicts, such as being intoxicated in a public place, are prosecutable. Powell v. Texas, 392 U.S. 514 (1968).

8. Summary of Intoxication Defense

The defense of intoxication is summarized in Figure 12-7.

FIGURE 12-7

INTOXICATION	
Involuntary Intoxication • Definition of Involuntary	Full defense "Involuntary" includes: • Unwitting ingestion • Forced intake • Pathological effect
Voluntary Intoxication • Definition of Intoxicated	Affects specific intent crimes • Lowers level of mens rea "Prostration of faculties"

Review Question and Answer

INTOXICATION

Question: Two brothers, Larry and Barry, are out enjoying one of their favorite Saturday night pursuits—driving around in their VW bug looking for trouble. They stop at the local "Gas & Sip" for snacks and beverages, and that's where the trouble begins. Larry buys a pint of vodka to go with his cola, even though he knows about his severe allergic reaction to alcohol, which causes him to "go crazy-like" whenever he drinks. As Larry is drinking his vodka cola, he also slips about half the pint into Barry's Mountain Spew. Barry, by his own admission, is a "heck raiser" and has often been in trouble with the law, but he is also a complete tea totaler and has never touched a drop of alcohol in his life.

A short while later, Barry stops at a traffic light in front of a piano store. Without a word, Larry jumps out of the car, runs to the store, and smashes his head through the plate glass window. He shouts back to Barry that he always wanted a piano when he was growing up. Barry and Larry then enter the store through the broken window. Once inside, they are confronted by a security guard. Barry punches the guard in the face and Larry smashes the vodka bottle over the guard's head, knocking him cold. A short time later, the police arrive to find the brothers playing a duet of "Chopsticks" on one of the store's pianos.

Larry and Barry are both charged with breaking and entering with intent to steal and battery. What intoxication defenses, if any, are available to them?

Answer: *Barry—Involuntary Intoxication.* Barry has an involuntary intoxication defense because he was unaware that he was drinking alcohol in his Mountain Spew. Prosecutors may argue that Barry must have tasted the alcohol in his drink because it contained half a pint, but Barry has never tasted alcohol before, and it is conceivable that he was completely unwitting as to the alcohol in his drink. Barry will have a complete defense to both breaking and entering with intent to steal and battery, if he can show that he was so drunk that he could not appreciate the criminality of entering the store and hitting the guard nor understand that the conduct was illegal but could not control his actions. Such a claim would be at least somewhat believable because this is the first time he has ingested alcohol.

Larry— Voluntary Intoxication. Larry can only claim a defense of voluntary intoxication. In all likelihood, Larry had a strong allergic reaction to the alcohol in his drink, which is at least partly responsible for his behavior. But Larry also had past experiences with the allergy and, therefore, cannot claim a defense of involuntary or pathological intoxication.

In general, voluntary intoxication is a defense only to specific intent crimes. Battery is a general intent crime, because it does not require a sophisticated mental process to have the intent to hit someone. Battery is also precisely the type of crime drunk people are more likely to commit. Therefore, Larry would not have intoxication defense for battery.

Breaking and entering with intent to steal is a specific intent crime because to be guilty a defendant must have formed a relatively sophisticated intent to take and keep items from the building. Larry will have the defense of voluntary intoxication, if he can show that the alcohol and his allergic reaction to it rendered him incapable of intending to steal something from the store. Larry will probably be able to get medical testimony regarding his "crazy-like" reaction to alcohol, but the prosecution will argue that Larry's statement that he always wanted a piano is evidence of his intent to take one of the pianos. On the other hand, the defense will argue that Larry only had a hazy, alcohol-clouded desire to play the piano. It also seems unlikely that Larry intended to steal the piano because he and Barry made no effort to remove it and could not have transported it away from the store in their VW anyway. Therefore, Larry may be able to successfully argue a voluntary intoxication defense to the specific intent offense, breaking and entering with intent to steal. However, he is probably still guilty of simple breaking and entering.

C. INSANITY

Insanity is a mental disorder that provides a full defense to a criminal charge. In addition, insanity may preclude a defendant from being tried or executed for an offense. The legal standard for insanity differs according to the issue to which it is being applied. This discussion of insanity covers the following subjects:

- Competency to Stand Trial
- Competency for Execution
- Insanity Defenses for Trial
  - Definition of "disease or defect"
  - Tests for legal insanity
    - M'Naghten
    - Deific command exception
    - Irresistible impulse test
    - Durham/Produce rule
    - Model Penal Code standard
  - Administration of insanity defense

1. Competency to Stand Trial

Competency to stand trial examines the defendant's mental state at the time of trial. If the defendant is mentally incompetent at the time of trial, he may not be tried. An incompetency ruling usually results in the defendant's commitment to a mental facility, until it is determined whether defendant will become competent to stand trial. If defendant is unlikely to become competent, criminal prosecution is dropped and civil commitment is pursued.

a. **Competency standard.** The test for mental competency to stand trial is whether the defendant has sufficient ability: 1. to consult with his attorney, and 2. to rationally understand the proceedings against him. Dusky v. United States, 362 U.S. 402 (1960).

b. **Forced medications.** Some courts have permitted forcible medication of defendants in order to make them competent to stand trial. See, e.g., Khiem v. United States, 612 A.2d 160 (D.C. 1992). However, the Supreme Court has held that forcible medication may be a violation of due process, if other treatments are available to render the defendant competent to stand trial. Riggins v. Nevada, 112 S. Ct. 1810 (1992).

c. **Amnesia.** A defendant who is suffering from total amnesia but is otherwise in full command of her faculties is competent to stand trial. State v. Wynn, 490 A.2d 605 (Del. Super. 1985).

2. Competency to be Executed

All states bar execution of a condemned prisoner who becomes insane. The Supreme Court has held that execution of the insane violates the Eighth

Amendment's proscription of "cruel and unusual punishment." Ford v. Wainwright, 477 U.S. 399 (1986).

a. **Definition of insanity.** In order to be executed, a prisoner must have "the mental capacity to understand the nature of the death penalty and why it was imposed." *Ford*, supra.

b. **Rationale for rule.** The law prohibiting execution of the insane is based upon a three-part rationale:

   i. As a moral issue, defendants should be able to mentally and spiritually prepare for their death;

   ii. The retributive force of the death penalty depends on the defendant's awareness of the penalty's existence and purpose;

   iii. The spectacle of executing an insane person would be cruel and "uncivilized."

c. **Mentally retarded prisoners.** It is constitutional to execute mentally retarded prisoners, even those with a mental age of seven. Penry v. Lynaugh, 492 U.S. 302 (1989). Many states, however, have enacted legislation barring the execution of offenders who are "seriously mentally retarded."

d. **Restoring sanity to execute.** Often an inmate can be restored to sanity through the use of medication, but is unclear whether it is constitutional to force a condemned prisoner to take such medication in order to face execution. In Washington v. Harper, 494 U.S. 210 (1990), the Supreme Court found that forcibly medicating a mentally ill inmate was not a violation of due process rights, if the prisoner was dangerous to himself or others, or the treatment was in the defendant's medical interest. The Court declined, however, to decide whether prisoners may be forced to take medication to become sane for execution. To date, only Louisiana and Maryland have held that such treatment cannot be compelled.

e. **Procedures to determine insanity.** There are many different procedures to determine whether a condemned prisoner has become insane. Constitutionally, a state need not provide a full adversarial proceeding, but the prisoner must be afforded an opportunity to present evidence and argument on his sanity before an impartial officer or board independent of the executive branch. *Ford*, supra. California, for example, impanels a special jury of 12 persons to decide whether the condemned inmate is insane. Cal. Penal Code, §§3705, 3706.

3. Insanity Defense to Crime

A defendant is excused from committing a crime if he was legally insane during the commission of the offense.

> **STUDY TIP**
>
> Insanity examines the defendant's mental capacity at the time of the crime. Competency examines the defendant's mental capacity at the time of trial. Only insanity is a defense to a crime.
>
> | Time 1 | | Time 2 |
> |---|---|---|
> | Crime | ----- | Trial |
> | (Insanity) | | (Competency) |

a. **Rationale of the insanity defense.** The insanity defense is recognized as an excuse for criminal conduct because:

- A person who does not know what she is doing or cannot control her acts cannot be deterred;
- The insane person should be incapacitated in a mental institution without the added stigma of being classified a "criminal";
- For the safety of the insane defendant, as well as that of other inmates, it is better for the insane defendant to be institutionalized in the civil, not penal, setting;
- The spectacle of punishing a person who does not have control over his or her reason is tantamount to punishing an animal or infant who is incapable of reasoning;
- The underlying principle of criminal law is that the defendant operates with free will and, therefore, should be punished when he or she chooses to commit a crime. Insane defendants are deprived of free will by a mental disease or condition. Without this free will, they lack moral responsibility for their actions.

b. **Legal concept.** Insanity is a *legal* standard. Although medical findings are considered in the legal determination, ultimately, whether a person will be excused from responsibility because of insanity is a legal, social, and moral determination.

c. **Definition of disease.** The basic requirement for any insanity defense is that the defendant be suffering from a mental disease or defect. "Mental disease" is a legal, not medical, concept. Not all diseases recognized for medical purposes are recognized for an insanity defense. State v. Guido, 40 N.J. 191 (1963) (psychiatrists may change their opinion as to disease and insanity depending on the legal standards adopted by the court). Legal diseases are defined by their impact on the defendant's behavior rather than by their scientific characteristics.

i. **General legal definition of disease.** A disease is "any abnormal condition of the mind which substantially affects mental or emotional processes and substantially impairs behavior controls." McDonald v. United States, 312 F.2d 847, 850-851 (D.C. Cir. 1962).

ii. **Factors for determining when a mental condition constitutes a disease.** Because the definition of a "disease" is so vague, it is helpful to consider the factors that courts use to determine whether a mental condition is a "legal disease:"

- Does the condition have clear symptoms?
- Do the medical and scientific communities support the recognition of this condition as a criminal defense?
- Is this a condition defendants are likely to bring upon themselves?
- Is this condition easily feigned?
- How many cases are likely to be covered by this disease?
- Are there other policy reasons to exclude or include this condition as a disease?

iii. **List of diseases.** The following disorders are often raised under the insanity defense, but are not necessarily accepted as legal diseases.

(a) **Battered spouse syndrome.** Trial courts often admit battered spouse syndrome evidence, but appellate courts have been reluctant to find it a mental disease for purposes of the insanity defense.

(b) **Compulsive gambling disorder.** Most courts have rejected compulsive gambling disorder because there is insufficient scientific consensus on its status as a disease. United States v. Gould, 741 F.2d 45 (4th Cir. 1984).

(c) **Premenstrual syndrome (PMS).** Courts are beginning to consider PMS a disease. There is resistance to its recognition because it is easily feigned and recognition might undermine the status of women in society and the workplace by strengthening gender stereotypes.

(d) **Postpartum disorders.** Postpartum psychosis has repeatedly qualified as a mental disease for purposes of the insanity defense.

(e) **Multiple-personality disorder.** Multiple-personality disorders and schizophrenia have been recognized as diseases for purposes of the insanity defense.

(f) **Post-traumatic stress disorder (PTSD).** Because of the large numbers of veterans who suffer from PTSD, courts have been reluctant to recognize it as a disease qualifying for the insanity defense. In extreme cases, however, where the defendant's mental history is well-documented, PTSD has been recognized.

(g) **Alcohol and drug addiction.** Because large numbers of criminal defendants abuse drugs and alcohol, courts are extremely reluctant to recognize addiction as a mental disease, unless there has been prolonged use that has permanently affected the defendant's brain.

(h) **Personality disorders.** In general, personality disorders are *not* recognized as mental conditions or diseases for the purposes of the insanity defense.

(i) **Psychopathy.** A psychopath is an offender with a long history of antisocial conduct. Courts generally do *not* afford an insanity defense to psychopaths merely because they have a predilection to commit crimes. However, in extreme cases, courts have recognized such a condition. See State v. Werlein, 401 N.W.2d 848 (Wis. Ct. App. 1987).

- **Model Penal Code approach.** MPC §4.01(2), the "caveat paragraph," provides that "the terms 'mental disease or defect' do not include an abnormality manifested only by repeated criminal or otherwise antisocial conduct." Accordingly, it excludes from the concept of disease the so-called "psychopathic personality."

- **Note.** Psychopaths are treated as criminals and not insane because: 1. the description may apply to a broad range of defendants; and 2. psychopaths need to be confined and would endanger other patients and staff in a mental hospital environment.

d. Tests for insanity. Courts have used a variety of tests to determine whether a defendant is insane.

i. Overview of tests. The following tests have been adopted for legal insanity. Each of these tests is discussed in detail in this chapter.

(a) Traditional M'Naghten standard. Did the defendant know the nature and quality of his acts and did he know his acts were wrong?

(b) Deific command exception. Was the defendant operating under a delusional belief that he had been commanded by God to commit the crime?

(c) Irresistible impulse test. Would the defendant have been able to control his behavior even if a police officer had been at his elbow?

(d) Durham product rule test. Were the defendant's actions the product of a mental disease or defect?

(e) Model Penal Code standard. Did the defendant lack substantial capacity either to appreciate the wrongfulness of his conduct or to conform his conduct to the requirements of the law?

ii. Traditional test/M'Naghten standard. The traditional test of legal insanity is referred to as the M'Naghten test. Under this test, a defendant is presumed sane. To prove insanity, it must be demonstrated that:

- at the time of the commission of the offense,
- defendant was laboring under a defect or disease of the mind, and
- defendant did not know:
  - the nature and quality of his acts, or
  - that his acts were wrong.

M'Naghten's Case, House of Lords, 10 Cl. & F. 200, 8 Eng. Rep. 718 (1843).

iii. **Background of M'Naghten case.** The M'Naghten standard emerged after a jury returned a verdict of "not guilty on the ground of insanity" in a famous case. The defendant, M'Naghten, admitted he had come to London to murder the Prime Minister, Sir Robert Peel, but had mistakenly killed the prime minister's secretary, Edward Drummond. Defendant claimed he murdered Drummond because the tories were persecuting him. M'Naghten hired the best psychiatrists of his day and convinced the judge to give a general jury instruction authorizing an acquittal if defendant did not know he was doing a wicked act. In order to prevent more such acquittals, Queen Victoria ordered the House of Lords to set forth a more definitive standard for insanity. The result was the M'Naghten test.

iv. **Rationale for M'Naghten test.** In King v. Porter, 55 Commw. L.R. 182 (1933), the court explained the rationale for adopting the M'Naghten rule:

(a) People who are insane should not be punished; they should be medically treated;

(b) The focus of any insanity rule must be on the condition of the mind (a disease, disorder, or disturbance);

(c) A defendant should be excused if he did not know what he was doing or that his acts were wrong.

v. **Analysis of M'Naghten standard.** Under the M'Naghten test, a defendant is insane if he does not know the nature and quality of his acts or that his acts are wrong.

(a) **Nature and quality of acts.** If the defendant, as a result of a mental disease or defect, does not understand his own physical action, he is legally insane.

Example. Defendant is operating in a hallucinogenic state and believes he is using a hatchet to open a melon. In fact, he is chopping open a person's head.

(b) **Know his acts are wrong.** Even if a defendant understands the physical nature of his acts, he must know that his acts are "wrong." The meaning of the term "wrong," under the M'Naghten standard, has been hotly debated. Most jurisdictions interpret the term to include "morally wrong" (based upon society's morals, not the individual defendant's) and "legally wrong." Because laws are based upon society's morals, the two are ordinarily synonymous.

EXAMPLE AND ANALYSIS

In State v. Crenshaw, 98 Wash. 2d 789 (1983), defendant killed his wife on their honeymoon. He claimed he did so because she had been unfaithful and his Moscovite religious faith prescribed death as the penalty for adultery. The defendant, however, seemed to know that society as a whole would find the killing wrong because he took actions to hide the killing and escape detection. Even though the defendant's personal morality sanctioned the killing, defendant was not legally insane because he knew his actions were legally and morally wrong, according to society.

(c) **Morally wrong vs. legally wrong.** Generally, if a defendant knows something is legally wrong, she will know it is morally wrong, and vice versa. Some courts, however, have held that knowledge of an act's illegality does not defeat a M'Naghten defense. An insane person may know an act is illegal but may not understand the moral basis for the law. Psychosis may prevent a person from comprehending why a punishable act is inherently wrong. People v. Serrano, 823 P.2d 128 (1992).

Example. Defendant knows that he is cutting open a child's head and could go to jail for it, but because of a mental disease, has no idea why such an act is wrong and illegal.

vi. **Criticisms of M'Naghten test.** Dissatisfaction with the M'Naghten test led many jurisdictions to formulate different or additional standards for insanity. See section vii infra. These criticisms include:

(a) M'Naghten allows a finding of sanity whenever the defendant "knows" the nature of his acts and that they are wrong. Some mentally ill people may have a cognitive understanding of their actions but do not appreciate why such actions are wrong.

(b) M'Naghten focuses only on the cognitive aspects of the personality; i.e., the ability to know right from wrong. It does not address the person who is unable to control his acts because of a mental disease. This concern led to the "irresistible impulse" test, infra.

(c) Because the M'Naghten standard is so narrow, mentally ill people serve prison terms and are eventually released, having received little or no treatment for their underlying mental problems.

(d) M'Naghten unrealistically shackles psychiatric testimony because a psychiatrist may only testify as to a defendant's logical and cognitive functions.

vii. Expansions of insanity test. Since *M'Naghten*, courts have recognized several alternative tests to prove insanity. These include:

(a) **Deific command exception.** Most jurisdictions recognize an insanity defense when the defendant, due to a mental illness or disease, believes that God or a Supreme Being ordered him to commit the crime. In such cases, the defendant may know his actions are contrary to society's morals and legally wrong, but he believes that a "deific command" has overridden society's morals.

EXAMPLES AND ANALYSIS

While shopping, a mentally ill woman hears what she believes to be the voice of God. The voice tells her to kill the next person she sees. Although the woman knows that it is unlawful to kill, she follows the command. If her delusional state is due to a mental disease or defect, she will be entitled to assert the insanity defense.

In State v. Cameron, 100 Wash. 2d 520 (1983), defendant stabbed his stepmother 70 times, left her in a bathtub, and hit the road in only a pair of women's stretch pants and a housecoat. When apprehended, he said that God had commanded him to kill his stepmother, who he claimed was practicing sorcery. Defendant claimed he was the messiah. Defendant knew his actions were legally wrong, but he did them because he had been directed by God. Defendant was entitled to assert the deific command insanity defense.

(b) Deific command vs. religious faith. Deific command does not apply to defendants who kill because of their religious beliefs. Rather, it is limited to those who claim they actually heard the "voice of God."

- **Example.** In *Crenshaw*, supra, defendant killed his wife because of his devotion to his Moscovite faith. He was *not* entitled to assert the deific command exception.
- **Example.** David Koresh orders his followers to kill their children. Unless the follower has a mental disease and believes Koresh is God, the command is not a basis for asserting the deific command exception.

(c) Irresistible impulse test. Another extension of the insanity test is the "irresistible impulse" or "policeman at the elbow" test. Under this test, an accused is legally insane if, due to a mental disease or defect, he would have been unable to stop himself even if there had been a policeman at his elbow at the time he committed the crime. Insanity has destroyed defendant's power to choose between right and wrong. Parsons v. State, 81 Ala. 577 (1884).

- **Example.** Defendant has a long history of mental disease. In front of hundreds of people, he attacks a speaker at a conference. Defendant knew his action was wrong, but because of a mental disease, he could not control himself.

- **Criticisms of irresistible impulse test.** Some courts reject the irresistible impulse test because it is difficult for experts to distinguish between offenders who could not control themselves and those who chose not to control themselves. There is a strong suspicion that violent criminals will fraudulently use the irresistible impulse defense to evade punishment. The irresistible impulse test may also not be necessary because persons who cannot control their actions probably cannot appreciate the wrongfulness of their conduct. They would, therefore, pass the regular M'Naghten test anyway. United States v. Lyons, 731 F.2d 243 (5th Cir. 1984) (en banc).

(d) Durham test/Product rule. In Durham v. United States, 214 F.2d 862 (1954), Judge Bazelon proposed an insanity rule that eliminates the "right-wrong" dichotomy of the traditional M'Naghten standard. According to this test, a defendant is excused for insanity "if his unlawful act was the product of mental disease or defect." This test has not been widely accepted because it fails to give the fact-finder any standards by which to determine insanity. As long as a psychiatric expert makes some connection between the defendant's acts and a mental disease, that defendant can be adjudged insane.

viii. Model Penal Code approach. The Model Penal Code provides a standard for insanity that is more lenient than the traditional M'Naghten approach. Under MPC §4.01, a person is not responsible for criminal conduct if he *lacks substantial capacity* to either *appreciate the criminality* (wrongfulness) of his conduct or to *conform his conduct* to the requirements of the law.

ix. Analysis of Model Penal Code approach. The Model Penal Code approach relaxes the requirement that a defendant "know" the difference between right and wrong. It focuses instead on whether a defendant "lacks substantial capacity to appreciate" the nature or consequences of his acts.

(a) Lacks substantial capacity. Under the traditional M'Naghten test, the issue is black and white: either the defendant is so seriously mentally ill that he does not know the nature or wrongfulness of his acts, or the defendant is sane. This traditional test requires an impairment so extreme that few defendants qualify. The Model Penal Code is more lenient. By focusing on whether the defendant "lacks substantial capacity" to understand or control his actions, the Model Penal Code allows a partially impaired person, like a schizophrenic, whose disorientation is extreme but not total, to qualify.

(b) **Appreciate the criminality.** The traditional M'Naghten test takes a hard line: if a defendant cognitively "knows" his actions are wrong, he is deemed sane. By contrast, MPC §4.01(1) broadens the "knowledge" test by focusing on whether the defendant has a genuine understanding of the consequences of his acts.

Example. Defendant hits a child in the head with a hammer. The defendant knows he is breaking the child's skull and that society considers his actions "wrong," but the defendant does not understand why it is wrong to break a child's skull.

STUDY TIP

Appreciation = knowledge + emotional understanding (i.e., affect).

(c) **Conform his conduct. . . .** With this clause in MPC §4.01(1), the Model Penal Code expressly adopts the common law irresistible impulse test.

(d) **Inclusion of all common law tests into Model Penal Code standard.** The Model Penal Code standard broadly encompasses all common law insanity standards. Therefore, any defendant who is deemed insane at common law would also be insane under the MPC. See figure 12-8. For example, if a defendant does not know his acts are wrong, he also will not appreciate that they are wrong. Likewise, if a defendant is operating under a deific command, he will not appreciate that his acts are wrong.

FIGURE 12-8

C/L Insanity Tests	MPC Insanity Tests
Defendant presumed sane	Defendant presumed sane
At the time of the offense defendant suffered from mental disease or defect	At the time of the offense defendant suffered from mental disease or defect
Defendant did not know (M'Naghten) a. nature and quality of his acts, or b. his acts were wrong	Defendant did not have substantial capacity to a. appreciate criminality of his conduct, or
Deific command rule	
Irresistible impulse test	b. conform his conduct to the requirements of the law

e. **Policy arguments regarding the insanity defense.** From its inception, the insanity defense has generated controversy.

i. **Arguments against insanity defense.** The insanity defense is subject to abuse. Where there is a lenient standard for insanity, criminals can feign mental illness and evade responsibility. Additionally, the insanity defense relies on experts who make crucial subjective determinations based on unscientific and vague standards.

EXAMPLE AND ANALYSIS

In 1982, John Hinckley was found not guilty by reason of insanity for the attempted assassination of President Ronald Reagan. The verdict led to a widespread backlash against the insanity defense and the substantive and procedural standards for its use. Many states using the MPC standard have returned to the more restrictive M'Naghten test. There is little empirical evidence, however, that different formulations of the insanity defense produce different practical results.

ii. **Arguments in support of insanity defense.** Supporters of the insanity defense argue that its detractors grossly overestimate the number of people who are acquitted under an insanity defense. In fact, jurors and judges are generally skeptical about the defense and expert testimony. Even those who are found insane are isolated from society by long-term commitment to mental hospitals. Finally, there may be no precise way to ensure a person is insane, but the insanity defense is necessary to guarantee that only those who are morally blameworthy are punished. See United States v. Lyons, 731 F.2d 243 (5th Cir. 1984).

f. **Administering the insanity defense.** Many procedural questions arise in administering the insanity defense.

i. **Who may raise the defense?** In most jurisdictions, the decision to raise an insanity defense is within the defendant's control because it is the defendant who must bear the consequences of that decision. United States v. Marble, 940 F.2d 1543 (D.C. Cir. 1991).

ii. **Instructing jury on consequences of insanity acquittal.** Most courts have held that jurors should not be told the consequences of an insanity verdict. See, e.g., People v. Goad, 421 Mich. 20 (1984). Prosecutors fear that jurors will be more likely to acquit if they know that the defendant will still be committed if acquitted. However, a substantial minority of state courts now hold that a jury should be informed that a defendant will be detained until she is found no longer mentally ill. Commonwealth v. Mutina, 355 Mass. 810 (1975). The Supreme Court has held that in federal court juries should not be informed of mandatory commitment provisions. Shannon v. United States, 114 S. Ct. 2419 (1994).

iii. **Burden of proof.** All jurisdictions presume the defendant was sane at the time of the offense. In federal court, the burden is now on the defendant to prove insanity by clear and convincing evidence. 18 U.S.C. §17(b) (adopted in response to *Hinckley* verdict). States are divided between requiring the defendant to prove insanity by a preponderance of the evidence or requiring the prosecution to disprove insanity beyond a reasonable doubt. A law requiring a defendant to establish insanity beyond a reasonable doubt is constitutional. Leland v. Oregon, 343 U.S. 790 (1952).

Note. It is very difficult for the prosecution to succeed when it carries the burden of proving the defendant was sane. Bizarre conduct by a defendant, coupled by defense expert testimony, will almost always be sufficient to establish a reasonable doubt as to the defendant's sanity. State v. Green, 643 S.W.2d 902 (1982) (defendant's use of meaningless phrases, loner personality, and prior psychiatric treatment were sufficient to create a reasonable doubt).

iv. **Constitutionality of abolishing insanity defense.** Courts are split on whether it is constitutionally permissible to abolish the insanity defense. Some courts have found a due process right by the defendant to show he is not blameworthy for his crime. State v. Strasburg, 60 Wash. 106 (1910). Other states, however, have held that the insanity defense can be abolished as long as evidence of mental illness is admissible to show that the defendant did not have the mens rea for the crime or should receive a lesser punishment. State v. Korrell, 213 Mont. 316 (1984). At least two states have abolished the insanity defense. Idaho Code §18-207 (1982); Utah Code Ann. §76-2-305 (1990).

v. **Commitment after acquittal.** A defendant acquitted by reason of insanity may be hospitalized for a period longer than he might have served in prison had he been convicted. Jones v. United States, 463 U.S. 354 (1983). A finding of not guilty by reason of insanity is a sufficient foundation for indefinite commitment for purposes of treatment and protection of society. Id. In some states, a defendant is automatically committed after an acquittal; in other states, the authorities hold separate civil commitment proceedings.

(a) **Opportunity to seek release.** An insanity acquittee is presumed to suffer continuing insanity. He or she must petition for release from confinement. Courts typically set release hearing dates at regular intervals after confinement, but a defendant may waive such a hearing. 18 U.S.C. §4243. Once a person is no longer mentally ill, he must be released from a mental hospital even if he could be a danger to himself or others. Foucha v. Louisiana, 112 S. Ct. 1780 (1992).

vi. **Guilty but mentally ill.** In order to prevent the release of defendants who receive treatment for their illness but continue to pose a danger to society, some jurisdictions have enacted the verdict of "guilty but mentally ill" (GBMI). This verdict is available when a defendant was not insane, but only mentally ill at the time of the offense. Using this verdict, a court can send a defendant to prison with the direction that he receive psychiatric treatment, as needed, in that setting.

vii. **Automatism and insanity.** When automatism results from mental disorder, most American jurisdictions allow the defendant to plead insanity, involuntariness, or both. The English rule only allows the defense of insanity when the automatism is the result of a mental disease. Defendants may favor the automatism defense because it does not automatically result in commitment of the defendant after acquittal. To determine whether an automatic act should be treated as an involuntary act or as insanity, courts often look to whether an internal condition of the mind caused the act or whether it was triggered by external factors, like a failure to take medication.

4. Insanity Summary

Insanity is a complete defense to a crime. The defendant is excused from responsibility because he did not have the capacity to understand or control his actions. Different jurisdictions use different standards for deciding insanity. All jurisdictions, however, require that a defendant have a "mental disease or defect" to trigger the defense. Approaching an insanity issue:

a. **Was there a mental disease or defect?** Discuss factors that determine mental diseases.

b. **Which insanity standard does the jurisdiction use?**

i. **M'Naghten.** Defendant is presumed sane. At the time of the offense, did the defendant know the nature and quality of his acts, or that his acts were "wrong"? Discuss moral vs. legal wrong.

ii. **Deific command exception.** Even if defendant knew his actions were legally and socially wrong, did he commit them because of a deific command? Distinguish religious beliefs from deific commands.

iii. **Irresistible impulse.** Even if defendant knew his actions were wrong, did he commit them because he could not control himself due to a mental disease or defect?

iv. **Durham/product rule.** Were the defendant's actions the product of a mental disease or defect?

v. **Model Penal Code approach.** Did the defendant have substantial capacity to appreciate the wrongfulness of his acts or control his behavior?

c. **What are the consequences of the defendant being adjudged insane?** Imprisonment vs. civil commitment.

D. DIMINISHED CAPACITY

Diminished capacity is a controversial defense that has been abandoned by many jurisdictions. When applied, diminished capacity is similar to a voluntary intoxication defense—evidence of a defendant's mental condition is used to prove that the defendant did not form the mens rea necessary for a specific intent crime. Like voluntary intoxication, diminished capacity is usually only a partial or mitigating defense.

1. Example

Defendant has an undiagnosed mental condition. She has been charged with first-degree murder. Defendant may claim that her mental condition made her incapable of premeditating and that she is, therefore, not guilty of first-degree murder.

EXAM TIP

If a question asks what "mental defenses" the defendant could raise, it is best to analyze the problem for both insanity and diminished capacity. If there is a problem in arguing insanity, because defendant's condition does not qualify as a disease or defendant knew her acts were wrong, the alternative defense of diminished capacity may apply.

Example. Defendant argues that a personality disorder caused him to commit a crime. Because a personality disorder does not qualify as a mental disease or defect, defendant's case must be analyzed under diminished capacity.

2. Rationale for Defense

Although some mental conditions will be insufficient to trigger a full insanity defense, they may demonstrate that the defendant was unable to form the mens rea for the crime. Accordingly, diminished capacity should be allowed to negate the mens rea for the crime, especially if it is a specific intent offense (i.e., an offense that requires a sophisticated intent). United States v. Brawner, 471 F.2d 969 (D.C. Dir. 1972).

3. **Objections to Defense**

The most prevalent objection to diminished capacity is that it allows a defendant to evade responsibility based upon vague psychiatric testimony and nebulous standards for mental disabilities.

EXAMPLE AND ANALYSIS

In State v. Sikora, 44 N.J. 453 (1965), defendant was charged with first-degree murder. He claimed diminished capacity because he was stressed over nasty remarks he heard about his separation with a woman. The court excluded psychiatric testimony on how defendant's personality disorder had led him to shoot his victim. The court criticized the diminished capacity defense because it directs the jury to focus on a defendant's unconscious, not conscious, thoughts. Using this approach, too many defendants would have a defense to a crime.

4. **Partial Defense**

Most often, when diminished capacity is recognized as a defense, it is only a partial defense to specific intent crimes. The defendant can claim that because of a mental condition, he could not form the intent for the more serious specific intent crime and is only guilty of a lesser offense. *Brawner*, supra.

Example. Defendant is charged with assault with intent to kill. Defendant claims diminished capacity and is only found guilty of assault.

5. **Application of Defense**

Different jurisdictions take different approaches to the diminished capacity defense.

a. **Using diminished capacity for specific intent crimes.** Most courts only apply diminished capacity as a partial defense, allowing a defendant charged with a specific intent crime to argue he is guilty of a lesser-included general intent offense. *Brawner*, supra.

i. **Example.** First-degree murder may be reduced to second-degree murder based upon psychiatric testimony that the defendant could not form the intent for premeditation.

ii. **Note.** Most jurisdictions will only allow diminished capacity for specific intent crimes when there is a lesser-included offense. McCarthy v. State, 372 A.2d 180 (Del. 1977). In the past, some jurisdictions have allowed it as a defense to specific intent crimes, whether or not there was a lesser-included offense for which the defendant could be convicted. People v. Wetmore, 22 Cal. 3d 318 (1978) (diminished capacity recognized as a defense to burglary because defendant could not form intent to steal).

b. **Rejection of defense.** Recently, there has been a trend toward rejecting the diminished capacity defense entirely. Under this approach, psychiatric testimony is inadmissible unless it can support a complete insanity defense. The reasons for rejecting the diminished capacity defense include:

i. It is unnecessary in jurisdictions that use a flexible standard for insanity;

ii. It is unnecessary if the jurisdiction considers mental illness a mitigating factor for sentencing;

iii. Juries improperly use diminished capacity to reach compromise verdicts in cases where there is contradictory evidence as to a defendant's mental condition;

iv. Even if a person has a mental disorder, her capacity to form mens rea will virtually never be obliterated. If it is, the defendant will most likely be able to assert an insanity defense;

v. It is illogical to use diminished capacity only for specific intent crimes, yet jurisdictions are not prepared to exonerate defendants completely by applying the defense to general intent offenses.

State v. Wilcox, 70 Ohio 182 (1982); Chestnut v. State, 538 So. 2d 820 (1989); See also Stephen J. Morse, Undiminished Confusion in Diminished Capacity, 75 J. Crim. L. & Criminology J. 1, 42-43 (1984).

c. **Model Penal Code approach.** Under MPC §4.02(1), diminished capacity may be raised as a defense to any crime. In the few jurisdictions that adopt the Model Penal Code approach, expert psychiatric evidence may be used to negate the mens rea for any crime, even if this leads to a full defense.

Example. Defendant is charged with reckless driving. He claims that because of a mental condition, he did not realize the risks posed by his driving. If diminished capacity is allowed as a defense, defendant may be acquitted of the charges against him.

6. Expert Psychiatric Testimony

In some of those jurisdictions that have sought to eliminate the diminished capacity defense, the defendant may still introduce expert evidence of his mental disease and use that testimony to argue that the defendant did not actually form the mens rea for the offense. See Cal. Penal Code §28(a). However, the expert may not discuss the defendant's "capacity" to commit the crime, nor may she opine as to whether the defendant actually formed the intent in that particular case. In those jurisdictions where diminished capacity is allowed, the defendant may introduce expert testimony as to whether he had the "capacity" and did, in fact, form the intent for the crime. In most jurisdictions where diminished capacity is abolished, no psychiatric evidence is allowed as to defendant's guilt.

7. Distinguish Diminished Responsibility

Diminished capacity involves the use of evidence of mental disorder to negate a required mens rea; "diminished responsibility" involves using evidence of mental disorder to mitigate a defendant's sentence. Thus, the key difference is that "diminished capacity" transfers partial sentencing authority from the judge to the jury.

FIGURE 12-9

DIMINISHED CAPACITY	
Partial Defense Specific Intent	Diminished capacity may be used to negate proof of specific intent crime; Reduces specific intent crime to general intent offense General Intent
No Defense	No psychiatric evidence allowed on issue of defendant's mens rea for the crime
MPC Approach General Intent	Diminished capacity may be used to negate mens rea for any crime, including general offense crimes. No crime

REVIEW QUESTION AND ANSWER

INSANITY AND DIMINISHED CAPACITY

Question: Bob had suffered long enough. For three years he had been subjected to the indignities and pressures of law school. He could no longer eat or sleep; he suffered from constant headaches. The doctors were unclear as to the precise nature of his condition, but were willing to analogize it to "battle fatigue."

On the day before his contracts final, Bob saw another student's outline sitting on a library table. Bob grabbed it and ate it page by page to "digest" the knowledge it contained. Bob was charged with stealing the outline. The elements for stealing are:

a. knowingly taking an object;
b. without permission;
c. with the specific intent of depriving the owner permanently of it.

When confronted with his acts, Bob said, "I knew that I would get in trouble, but I couldn't help myself. After studying law so much, it is hard to tell the difference between right and wrong."

What mental defenses may Bob have to the theft charges?

Answer: Bob has the potential defenses of insanity and diminished capacity. His success in arguing these defenses depends on the approach followed in his jurisdiction.

I. Insanity

Mental Disease or Defect. Under both the common law and the Model Penal Code, Bob would be presumed sane. The court would first have to decide whether Bob's condition qualifies as a legal mental disease or defect. Law school battle fatigue is not currently recognized by the courts as a disease for the purposes of the insanity defense. It may be similar to the Post-Traumatic Stress Disorder. Since courts are reluctant to recognize PTSD as a disease, they are likely to be reluctant in Bob's case for the same reasons, namely, there is a potential floodgates problem with large numbers of students claiming "battle fatigue" as a defense to a myriad of crimes. Ultimately, the court will recognize several factors to determine whether to recognize Bob's condition as a disease: 1. whether the condition has clear symptoms; 2. whether the medical community supports the use of the condition as a criminal defense; 3. whether this is a condition defendants bring on themselves; 4. whether the condition is easily faked; 5. how many cases will be covered; and 6. whether there are specific policy reasons to disallow the defense. In Bob's case, this is a condition defendants bring on themselves by choosing to go to law school, and it seems that any law student would either have the condition or be able to fake it. The court would need more facts to determine the medical/scientific stance on the condition and whether there are any other policy considerations. Overall, it seems unlikely that a court would recognize Bob's condition as a disease. Assuming, however, that the court holds that the condition is a disease, common law and MPC jurisdictions diverge in their approaches to the defense.

Common Law Standards. Under the common law, there are various forms of the insanity test: the M'Naghten test; the deific command rule; the irresistible impulse test; and the Durham product rule test

1. M'Naghten Test. Under the M'Naghten test, a defendant has a defense if, at the time of the offense as the result of his disease, he did not know either the nature and quality of his acts or that his acts were wrong. Whether or not Bob is held to have known the nature and the quality of his acts depends upon how the courts interpret the word "know." Traditionally, courts have interpreted the word narrowly: if the defendant understood his physical action, he was sane. Thus, according to this standard, Bob would not be entitled to the defense if he knew he was eating the outline. On the other hand, if Bob was acting in a hallucinatory state, thinking he was studying the material as he ate the outline page by page, he probably did not know the nature and quality of his acts.

The definition of the word "wrong" in the M'Naghten test is also debated. Most jurisdictions interpret the term to mean "morally wrong," i.e. whether the defendant knew he was acting contrary to society's morals. Other jurisdictions interpret the word to mean "legally wrong." In this case, Bob would probably fare better if the court defined the word in the moral sense, because there is evidence that he had trouble distinguishing between right and wrong. On the other hand, if the court defined the word in the legal sense, Bob would not be entitled to the insanity defense; the facts clearly indicate that Bob knew he could get in trouble for stealing the outline.

2. Deific Command. Most courts recognize the insanity defense when the mentally ill defendant believed a Supreme Being ordered him to commit the crime. In this case, there is no evidence that Bob thought he was given a deific command.

3. Irresistible Impulse. Under the irresistible impulse test, an accused is legally insane if he was so out of control that he couldn't have stopped committing the crime, even if a police officer was standing at his elbow. In this case, Bob said, "I couldn't control myself." Thus, if Bob's will was so overcome that he acted from an impulse, he is entitled to the insanity defense.

4. Durham Test. According to this test, a defendant is excused for insanity if "his unlawful act was the product of mental disease of defect." Thus, under this standard, as long as a psychiatric expert can make a connection between Bob's acts and his mental defect, he can be adjudged insane.

Model Penal Code. The MPC standard is more lenient than the common law. A person is not responsible for his crime if he lacks substantial capacity either to appreciate the criminality (wrongfulness) of his conduct or to conform his conduct to the requirements of the law.

The lacks-substantial-capacity standard broadens the M'Naghten test and enables partially impaired defendants or defendants who do not have a general understanding of the consequences of their acts to qualify for the insanity defense. Here, there is a question as to whether Bob could truly discern what he was doing—i.e. whether Bob knew he was simply eating paper and not mentally "digesting" the material. If so, Bob may not have been able to appreciate the consequences of his acts. Furthermore, the MPC test encompasses all the common law insanity standards. There fore, if Bob could be deemed insane according to any of the common law standards, he may also be adjudged insane under the MPC.

II. Diminished Capacity

If Bob does not qualify for the insanity defense, he still may be entitled to the diminished capacity defense. In jurisdictions applying diminished capacity, evidence of a defendant's mental condition may be introduced to prove that the defendant was unable to form the necessary mens rea for the crime.

No Diminished Capacity. Some jurisdictions reject the diminished capacity defense. Thus, in these jurisdictions, evidence of Bob's mental condition may only be introduced to prove insanity.

Specific Intent. Diminished capacity is generally applied as a partial defense; a defendant charged with a specific intent crime may argue that he is only entitled to a lesser (including general intent) offense. For instance, if diminished capacity is applied in this case, Bob, who committed a specific intent crime of theft, will argue that he should only be convicted for a crime of general mens rea. In this case, however, there may not be a lesser included offense for theft. If not, most jurisdictions will not allow Bob to raise the diminished capacity defense.

Model Penal Code Standard. Under the MPC, diminished capacity may be raised as a defense to any crime. Thus, Bob could introduce expert testimony to prove that, because of his mental condition, he lacked the intent of permanently depriving the owner of his notes, and be acquitted of the theft charges.

E. INFANCY

The law excuses the acts of children who are too young to be criminally responsible for their actions. Children under a certain age are presumed incapable of forming the intent required for a criminal offense. Different jurisdictions choose different ages for the defense of "infancy." Some jurisdictions afford an automatic full defense; others afford a rebuttable presumption that the child was too young to commit the crime.

1. Common Law

Under the common law three arbitrary limits are placed on the prosecution of minors, as shown in Figure 12-10.

a. **Under seven.** Common law conclusively presumes that a child under age seven does not have the cognitive capacity to form the mens rea for a crime.

b. **Age 7-14.** A minor between the ages of 7 and 14 is presumed incapable of committing a crime, but the prosecution can rebut this presumption by demonstrating that the youth was capable of understanding the nature and consequences of his acts and of distinguishing right from wrong. In Re Devon T., 85 Md. App. 674 (1991).

c. **Over 14.** A youth over age 14 has no infancy defense.

FIGURE 12-10

SUMMARY	
Under 7	Conclusive presumption
Age 7-14	Rebuttable presumption
Over 14	No presumption

2. Statutory Revisions

Many jurisdictions now have separate courts for the prosecution of minors. In addition, some courts, like California's, have eliminated the conclusive presumption and provide a rebuttable presumption for all minors under a certain age, usually 14.

3. Model Penal Code Approach

Under MPC §4.10, a person under the age of 16 years at the time of an offense must be tried in Juvenile Court. The Model Penal Code does not set forth an age at which a defendant is not responsible for his acts.

REVIEW QUESTION AND ANSWER

INFANCY

Question: Two young boys are arrested for kicking an infant to death. One boy is eight years old; the other is six years old. Both boys were arrested previously for an incident involving shoplifting and assault, but they were released under the supervision of their parents. The prosecution wants to charge both boys with first-degree murder. What defenses are available to each of the two boys?

Answer: Common Law. Under the common law approach, children under age seven are conclusively presumed unable to commit a crime. Therefore, under the common law, the six-year-old boy would have a complete defense.

For minors between the ages of 7 and 14, there is a rebuttable presumption that the child is incapable of committing a crime. Under this approach, the eight-year-old would be presumed unable to commit the murder. The prosecution would try to rebut this presumption by arguing that the eight-year-old must understand the wrongful nature and consequences of his actions, because he has been picked up previously by the police. On the other hand, the defense would argue that the prior arrest and release actually shows that the boy does not understand his actions because the boy has behaved badly his entire life and has never been disciplined or made to understand that his actions have consequences. More facts would be needed to decide whether the eight-year-old understands the nature of his actions.

Statutory Revisions. In California and other jurisdictions with similar statutory revisions, both boys would be subject to a rebuttable presumption that they were incapable of committing the offense. The prosecution and defense arguments would be the same as for the eight-year-old under common law above.

Model Penal Code. Under the MPC, the boys would be tried in juvenile court because they are under 16, but there is no specific age at which the boys would not be held responsible for their actions.

F. ENTRAPMENT

A defendant may be excused of criminal behavior because the government unfairly induced the defendant to commit the crime. There are two primary standards used to determine whether a defendant has been entrapped: the subjective ("predisposition") standard and the objective ("government inducement") standard. Entrapment is a full defense to a crime.

1. Rationales for Entrapment Defense

a. **Discourage police misconduct.** The entrapment defense discourages police from using overreaching tactics.

b. **Ensure defendants have criminal intent.** The entrapment defense ensures that police focus on those who are most inclined to commit crimes and not on law-abiding persons who may bend to a police scheme or undue pressure.

2. Requirements for Entrapment

Two elements are required for the entrapment defense:

a. Inducement by government official or informant; and

b. Defendant was not predisposed to commit a crime (subjective standard);

or

The government's conduct would have induced a law-abiding person to commit a crime (objective standard).

3. Analysis of Elements

a. **Undercover agents and informants.** The entrapment defense only applies when a government official induces the defendant to commit a crime. Government officials include those who officially work for law enforcement, as well as private individuals, such as informants, who are cooperating with the government. A defendant cannot be entrapped by a third party who is not working for or with the government.

EXAM TIP

The first step in assessing whether there is entrapment is to determine whether an individual associated with the government was involved in inducing the defendant to commit the crime. If no such individual was involved, there is no entrapment.

b. **Subjective vs. objective test.** Under the common law, there are two different standards used to determine whether there has been entrapment.

i. **(Subjective) predisposition test.** In federal court and several state courts, the test for whether a defendant was entrapped is the subjective "predisposition" test. If the defendant was predisposed to commit the crime and law enforcement agents only offered him the opportunity to do so, then there was no entrapment. United States v. Russell, 411 U.S. 423 (1973) (adopting Sorrells/Sherman subjective approach).

(a) **Example.** Defendant, M. Barry, asks his friends for cocaine. An undercover officer hears defendant's request and offers to sell defendant cocaine. Defendant was *not* entrapped because he had a predisposition to purchase cocaine.

(b) **Proving predisposition.** Factors to be considered in determining predisposition include:

- defendant's prior criminal behavior;

- defendant's statements regarding his attitude toward committing the offense;
- defendant's motive for participating in the illegal conduct;
- who instigated the criminal behavior;
- defendant's level of involvement in the crime.

(c) **Note.** Prosecutors favor the "predisposition" standard because it allows them to bring in evidence of the defendant's prior bad acts to prove criminal predisposition.

(d) **Exception.** Even in those jurisdictions that focus on the defendant's predisposition, if the government's conduct is particularly outrageous, the court may find a due process violation and dismiss the charges for "outrageous government misconduct." Dismissals under this theory are rare and only occur when the government constructs the crime from beginning to end. See, e.g., Greene v. United States, 454 F.2d 783 (9th Cir. 1971).

(e) **Jacobson v. United States.** The Supreme Court reaffirmed in Jacobson v. United States, 503 U.S. 540 (1992), that the predisposition standard applies in federal court but added that the defendant must be predisposed to commit a crime, not just predisposed to engage in marginally acceptable social behavior. In *Jacobson*, defendant purchased mail-order pornography. In a sting operation, the government sent child pornography to the defendant. Although defendant was predisposed to purchase pornography, there was no evidence that he was predisposed to purchase illegal child pornography and, therefore, as a matter of law, he was entrapped to commit that offense.

ii. **(Objective) Government misconduct test.** Some courts use an objective standard to determine whether there has been entrapment. These courts hold that there is entrapment when it is likely that the government's conduct would have induced a law-abiding person to commit the crime. Under this standard, the focus is on the government's conduct, not the defendant's predisposition. People v. Barraza, 23 Cal. 3d 675 (1979).

(a) **Example.** In *Barraza*, supra, defendant was charged with selling heroin to undercover narcotics agents. While the defendant was in a detoxification center, undercover agents used a female decoy to pressure defendant to make the sale. The decoy made constant requests to get him to succumb. Given the conduct of the officer, the court held that an entrapment instruction should have been given.

(b) **Note.** The objective standard is not completely objective because the trier of fact can look at defendant's circumstances to determine whether law enforcement used proper investigative techniques.

EXAM TIP

Defense lawyers prefer the objective standard because it keeps the jurors focused on the government's misconduct and not on the defendant. Also, the objective standard does not allow for the introduction of a wide range of evidence describing the defendant's prior criminal conduct. By contrast, prosecutors argue for the "predisposition" test.

iii. **Model Penal Code standard.** MPC §2.13 adopts the objective approach to determining entrapment but leaves the decision to the court, not the jury. MPC §2.13(2). The decision is left to the judge because judges are less inclined to conclude that because undercover methods were used, there was entrapment. Unlike the ordinary juror, judges are accustomed to the government's use of undercover investigation techniques. Under the Model Penal Code, the entrapment defense is unavailable in cases involving serious bodily injury. MPC §2.13(3).

4. Alternative Defenses

In most jurisdictions, a defendant need not admit he committed the crime before asserting the entrapment defense. The defendant may offer the alternative defenses of: 1. he did not commit a crime; and 2. if the prosecution proves the elements of the crime, defendant was entrapped.

FIGURE 12-11

Entrapment	
Predisposition	Subjective standard • Focus on defendant's predisposition
Government Inducement	Objective standard • Focus on government's conduct
MPC	Court decides based on objective standard

Review Question and Answer

PRACTICE ENTRAPMENT QUESTION

Question: For three years the police have suspected that Mary, a state legislator, has been extorting money from tenant groups by threatening to vote in favor of pro-landlord legislation if she is not paid a regular "honorarium." No specific complaint has been forwarded to the police, but the rumors about her activities are well-known.

Reacting to these rumors, the police send a decoy into Mary's office. The decoy, who formerly worked as a police officer, claims to be the head of a tenant's group. The first thing the decoy does is place an open brown envelope filled with cash on Mary's desk. With tears in her eyes, the decoy then asks Mary if Mary would agree to "honor" the decoy's tenant group. The decoy says she won't take no for an answer. Mary grabs the envelope without any questions. She states that she would be glad to help the decoy's group, as she has helped others.

Mary's only prior criminal record is for falsifying her income tax returns. She forgot to list some gifts she received from major lobbying groups. Discuss whether Mary may raise the entrapment defense.

Answer: Mary may have a defense of entrapment.

1. *Government Officials Only.* The entrapment defense is only available when a government official induces the defendant to commit the crime. In this case, even though the decoy no longer formally worked as a police officer, she was working in cooperation with the police and, therefore, qualifies as a "government" official."

2. *Common Law Tests.* Under the common law, there are two different standards used to determine whether there has been entrapment: (subjective) predisposition test and (objective) government misconduct test.

(Subjective) Predisposition Test. Under the predisposition test, if Mary was predisposed to commit extortion and the decoy only offered her an opportunity to do so, there was no entrapment. Hence, the prosecutors will introduce evidence of Mary's prior conduct and character to prove that she was predisposed to commit extortion. For instance, the prosecutor will argue that since Mary had a criminal record of falsifying her income tax returns, suspiciously leaving off "gifts" from lobbying groups; had a well-known reputation for making her political decisions contingent upon the receipt of "honorariums;" and readily "grabbed" the envelope without any questions, Mary had the criminal intent to accept a bribe long before the decoy gave her the envelope full of money.

Mary's attorney will argue that the prosecution's evidence does not establish Mary was predisposed to commit extortion. People frequently make mistakes on their tax returns, and it is common for public officials to receive gifts and honorariums. The attorney will also point out that Mary had no prior criminal record for extortion. Mary did not ask for the money and, because it was in an envelope, it is unclear whether Mary knew there was money in the envelope. Thus, Mary was not predisposed to commit the crime and should be entitled to the entrapment defense.

(Objective) Government Misconduct Test. Under the government misconduct test, if the decoy's conduct would have induced a law-abiding person to commit the crime, there was entrapment. Prosecutors will not introduce a wide range of evidence concerning defendant's prior conduct, but rather the defense will turn the focus of the trial to the government's conduct. Mary's attorney will argue that any reasonable person would have succumbed to the pressure exerted by the decoy: she went to Mary's business claiming to be a powerful head of an organization; she set an open envelope full of money within Mary's reach; she broke into tears and pleaded with Mary to help her; and she refused to accept "no" for an answer. Thus, the defense will say that given the extreme tactics used by the decoy, any reasonable person would have engaged in misconduct.

(Objective) Model Penal Code Standard. The MPC adopts the objective standard discussed above but leaves the decision to the judge and not the jury. A judge who is more accustomed to undercover investigative techniques may be less sympathetic toward Mary and deny her the right to the entrapment defense.

G. CONSENT

In general, consent is not a defense to a crime, especially when the crime can lead to great bodily injury. Consent is only an effective defense when "lack of consent" is an element of the offense.

1. Example

The crime of "rape" has lack of consent as one of its elements. If the victim consents, the defendant is not guilty of the offense.

2. Model Penal Code Exceptions

Under MPC §2.11(2), even if lack of consent is not an element of the offense, consent can be a defense if: a. the harm involved is not serious; b. it occurs during an athletic contest; or c. the harm occurs during authorized discipline. MPC §3.08.

Example. Defendant and the victim freely and jointly decide to play football against each other. If the victim is harmed, defendant is not guilty of battery.

3. Consent Ineffective

If consent would negate an element of the crime, such consent is ineffective under the following circumstances:

a. **Victim legally incompetent.** The victim is legally incompetent to provide consent; e.g., a girl consents to statutory rape.

b. **Victim incapacitated.** Youth, mental disease or defect, or intoxication prevents the victim from making a reasonable judgment.

c. **Forced consent.** The victim's consent is induced by force, duress, or deception. MPC §2.11(3).

FIGURE 12-12

CONSENT	
General Rule	Consent is not a defense.
Exceptions	Element of crime is lack of consent.
Ineffective consent	1. Victim legally unable to consent (e.g., statutory rape) 2. Victim incapacitated 3. Forced consent

REVIEW QUESTION AND ANSWER

CONSENT

Question: Every morning Monica called 1-900-GOD-TALK to receive her personalized message from the Heavenly Father. One day, the recorded voice of God told Monica to "break a leg." Monica, who was eager to please God, took this message very seriously: she slammed her car door on her leg, trying to crack the bone. Unfortunately, this painful effort was unsuccessful and she needed to make another attempt. This time she drank a bottle of whiskey so she wouldn't feel the pain. Then, she summons her friend Aron to help her with the ugly task. Aron willingly agreed to help; he had just purchased a new sledgehammer. Aron is charged with battery. Discuss whether Monica's consent is a defense.

Answer: Consent is only a defense to criminal charges in limited circumstances: when lack of consent is an element of the crime; when the crime is a minor assault or battery; and under the MPC, when the harm involved is not serious or occurs during an authorized discipline. In each of these circumstances the victim's consent must be effective.

Aron is not entitled to the consent defense. Even though Monica asked Aron to break her leg, victim's consent is never a defense in cases involving the infliction of great bodily harm. Further, Monica's consent was ineffective. She was unable to make a reasonable judgment because she was intoxicated and may have been mentally ill.

H. DEVELOPMENTS IN EXCUSE DEFENSES

Depending on society's view of different types of behavior, additional excuses may be recognized by the courts. The law assumes "free will" and recognizes deviations "where there is a broad consensus that free will does not exist." United States v. Moore, 486 F.2d 1139 (D.C. Cir. 1973) (Wright, J. dissenting).

1. Status Defense

In the past, the Court has held that the law cannot criminalize a defendant's status.

a. **Example.** In Robinson v. California, 370 U.S. 660 (1962), the Supreme Court held that a defendant could not be convicted of being a narcotics addict. People may only be punished for their acts, not their status.

b. **Status vs. act.** Courts have been reluctant to expand the rule set forth in *Robinson*, supra. Accordingly, if a defendant is an alcoholic, she may not be prosecuted because of her status, but she may be prosecuted for the "act" of being intoxicated in a public place. Powell v. Texas, 392 U.S. 514 (1968).

c. **Public policy.** The more concerned courts are with a particular societal problem, the less likely the court is to excuse a defendant's conduct related to that problem. Thus, if alcoholism is viewed as a disease treatable by society, then it is more likely that the alcoholic will be afforded a "status" defense. State Ex rel. Harper v. Zegeer, 296 S.E.2d 873 (W.Va. 1982). However, as concerns grow regarding the drug trade, the court's are more likely to find addicts are acting with free will and less likely to excuse their actions. See, e.g., United States v. Moore, 486 F.2d 1139 (D.C. Cir. 1973).

2. Reluctance to Expand Excuse Defenses

Courts are generally reluctant to expand the list of excuse defenses. Their reasons include:

a. People should be encouraged to exercise their free will;

b. Everyone faces some type of disability that he or she might want to use to excuse criminal behavior;

   Example. A defendant who is raised in extreme poverty might want to assert RSB (Rotten Social Background) as a defense. United States v. Alexander, 471 F.2d 923, 957-965 (Bazelon, C.J., dissenting).

c. Most disabilities are not permanent;

d. Disabilities are easily feigned;

e. Society operates on the presumption that people will be responsible for their behavior.

3. Extreme Proposals

Rather than constructing individual excuse defenses, some commentators propose eliminating mens rea for all crimes and replacing the current system with one that deals with excuses only in deciding how a defendant should be punished. See Barbara Wooton ["Lady Wooton"], Crime and the Criminal Law (1963).

Theft Offenses and Other Crimes Against Property

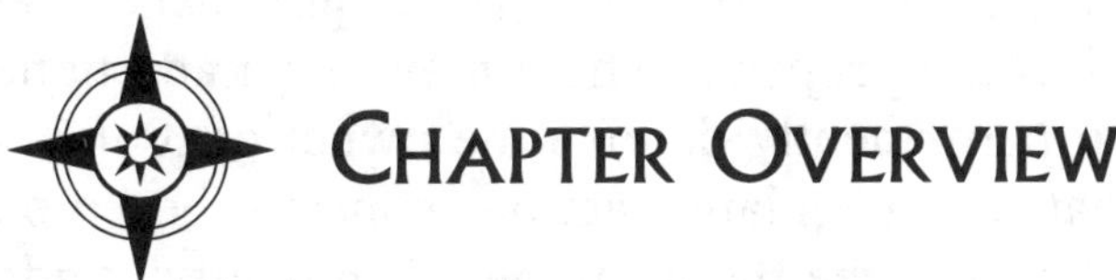

Chapter Overview

The law of theft offenses concerns itself, to a significant degree, with the historical evolution of crimes against property. Legislatures have tried to simplify the law of theft by adopting general theft and fraud statutes, but common law principles still influence the courts in their interpretations of these laws.

Chapter 13 reviews the history and elements of crimes against property. In particular, it discusses:

- History of Theft Crimes
- Elements of Theft Crimes
  - Actus reus — Means of acquisition
    - Larceny (trespassory takings)
    - Robbery
    - Misappropriation and embezzlement
    - False pretenses
    - Fraud
    - Blackmail
    - Statutory theft crimes
  - Mens rea
    - Intent to permanently deprive
  - Definition of "property"
    - Traditional theft
    - Theft of services
    - Intangible property
    - Mail and wire fraud
  - Defenses to theft crimes
- Other Crimes Against Property
  - Burglary
  - Arson

A. INTRODUCTION

Distinctions among larceny, embezzlement, obtaining property by false pretenses, extortion, and other theft crimes are the result of the historical evolution of the criminal laws protecting property. Today, many statutes lump together the various theft crimes under the broad category of "theft" or "fraud." Nonetheless, the courts still rely on common law principles regarding the elements of theft crimes to interpret modern day laws.

Theft crimes are crimes against property. Like crimes against persons, they have three components: actus reus, mens rea, and circumstances. The actus reus varies according to the type of theft crime. The mens rea requirement is an intent to do that act which acquires the property. There may be an additional requirement, such as an intent to permanently deprive the owner of property. Finally, the key circumstance, that the defendant's actions concern the "property" of another, makes it crucial to analyze the meaning of "property" under various theft laws.

B. HISTORICAL DEVELOPMENT OF CRIMES AGAINST PROPERTY

The law of theft did not develop in a smooth manner. Originally, only theft crimes that posed a physical danger to others, i.e., robbery, were punishable. Gradually, both the courts and lawmakers expanded the law of theft to cover other types of offenses such as larceny, embezzlement, and obtaining property by false pretenses (fraud).

1. Evolution of the Law of Theft

Originally, the law of theft focused on violent property crimes (robbery). Then, theft law expanded to all takings from another's person without consent (larceny). Later, courts recognized misappropriation of property by a person who already has possession of the property (embezzlement). Throughout the 18th century, lawmakers expanded embezzlement to include conversions by all types of persons entrusted with property. Eventually, the law created breach of trust crimes that cover the theft of both tangible and intangible property.

2. Evolution of the Law of Fraud

Fraud was never regarded as serious a crime as the physical taking of property without consent. Common law originally recognized only the misdemeanor of "cheat," which prohibited the use of false weights in transactions with the public. It was not until 1757 that the broader crime of obtaining property by false pretenses—the ancestor of fraud crimes—was created.

Originally, obtaining property by false pretenses only covered elaborate swindling schemes. Simply lying during a business transaction was not considered a crime. As competition became more regulated, legislatures recognized a broader range of fraud crimes involving intentional and material misrepresentations.

Time Line
Evolution of Law of Theft and Fraud

Early Common Law ———————————— Modern Day

Thefts

Violent thefts (robbery) → Takings (larceny) → Misappropriation (embezzlement) → Breach of Trust

Fraud

False weights (misdemeanor of cheat) → Swindles to obtain property (felony false pretenses) → Misrepresentations (fraud)

C. THEFT CRIMES

Each common law theft crime has its own distinct elements. But many theft crimes share common elements such as a "trespassory taking" of "property" from another.

1. Larceny

Larceny was the most basic theft crime at common law. Although many jurisdictions still retain the term "larceny," the modern equivalent is "stealing."

a. **Definition.** Larceny is the trespassory taking (taking and carrying away) of the personal property of another with intent to permanently deprive that person of the property.

b. **Elements.** The elements of larceny are:

i. **Actus reus**

- Trespassory taking
  - taking and
  - carrying away (asportation)
  - no consent

ii. **Circumstances**

- Property in possession of another

iii. **Mens rea**

- With intent to permanently deprive another of the property

c. **Analysis of elements.** The elements of larceny are interpreted as follows:

i. **Trespassory taking.** To constitute larceny, the defendant must take and carry away (asportation) the physical property. The taking is "trespassory" because the person who lawfully possesses the property does not consent to the taking.

trespassory taking = taking and asportation

(a) **Example**. Defendant takes a purse off a woman's lap and carries it away. Defendant has engaged in a "trespassory taking" because he took and moved the property of another.

(b) **Slight movement sufficient.** The crime of larceny is satisfied with a slight movement of the taken property; the defendant need not transport the property far nor succeed in permanently obtaining the property.

- **Example**. Defendant picks up an item in a store and slips it into her jacket. As she takes a step toward the door, a security guard apprehends her. Defendant has engaged in a "trespassory taking." People v. Olivo, 52 N.Y.2d 309 (1981).
- **Example**. Defendant moved an air conditioner from its base in the window to the floor near the door. Defendant had engaged in a "trespassory taking." State v. Carswell, 249 S.E.2d 427 (N.C. 1978).
- **Note**. On rare occasion, courts may dispense with the requirement of actual movement if the defendant otherwise evidences complete possession and control over the object. People v. Alamo, 34 N.Y.2d 453 (1974) (defendant's presence in stranger's car with ignition on was sufficient for "trespassory taking.").

(c) **Using another as an instrument.** A taking can be completed by using an innocent third party to take and carry away the property.

Example. In State v. Patton, 364 Mo. 1044 (1954), the defendant purported to sell concrete blocks, not his own, to an innocent purchaser, who himself carried the blocks away.

(d) **Model Penal Code approach.** MPC §223.2(1) eliminates the asportation requirement and substitutes the requirement that the defendant "exercise unlawful control" over the movable property.

Example. Defendant surreptitiously attaches a "Sold" tag to an item of merchandise, listing himself as having paid for the item. Under common law, there has been no larceny because defendant has not yet removed the item. Under the Model Penal Code, defendant has exercised unlawful control and is therefore guilty of theft.

(e) **No consent.** The term "trespassory" assumes that the victim has not consented to the taking. If the victim agrees to give the property to the defendant, there is no larceny. Topolewski v. State, 130 Wis. 244 (1906).

Note. If the victim sets a trap for someone he suspects is stealing, there is a possibility a court will find "consent" to the taking. *Topolewski*, supra. Most courts, however, determine whether there was consent by examining the state of mind of the defendant who does not know that a trap is being laid for him. United States v. Bryan, 483 F.2d 88 (3d Cir. 1973).

ii. Property. Traditional theft laws cover only the taking of tangible personal property. Tangible personal property includes: money, objects, fixtures, or crops severed from the land, and animals. It does not include real estate, services, or intangible property rights, like guarantees. State v. Miller, 192 Or. 188 (1951); Lund v. Commonwealth, 217 Va. 688 (1977) (unauthorized use of computer services not larceny). See also discussion of property in sec. 13E infra.

(a) **Example.** Defendant convinces a painter, who shows up to paint his neighbor's residence, to paint defendant's house instead.

(b) **Model Penal Code approach.** MPC §223.0(6) takes a broad view of "property" and includes anything "of value," ranging from real estate to tangible and intangible personal property to contract rights and food.

iii. **In possession of another.** Larceny applies to the taking of property in the possession of another, even if the defendant is the owner of the property.

Example. Defendant takes his car in to be repaired. When the repairs are completed, he refuses to pay his bill and drives his car away. Even though defendant is the owner of the car, he has taken it out of the lawful possession of another person.

EXAMPLE AND ANALYSIS

In Commonwealth v. Tluchak, 166 Pa. Super. 16 (195), defendants sold their farm and most of the personal property thereon. Before the new owners moved in, defendants removed some fixtures from the farm. Because defendants were in possession of the property and did not take the items "from the lawful possession of another," they were not guilty of larceny. Instead, defendants should have been charged with a different crime—fraudulent conversion.

- **Custody vs. Possession**. Because the common law crime of larceny only applies when a defendant takes property out of the lawful possession of another, the issue arises as to what crime applies if the defendant, who had been granted temporary physical control of property, then decides to keep it. In this situation, the defendant could argue the property was already in his possession, thereby negating one of the elements of larceny. In such situations, courts have found that the defendant had mere "custody" of the item, not possession, and therefore could still be guilty of larceny when he decided to keep it.
- **Example**. A store owner asks his delivery girl to deliver a box of merchandise to another store. Instead, she keeps the box of items. Larceny has occurred because the delivery girl had mere custody of the items and took them out of the possession of the owner when she decided to keep them.
- **Breaking Bulk**. Beginning with the *Carrier's Case*, the courts created a legal fiction that a bailee who opens a

container and removes its contents has engaged in larceny because the bailee had possession of the container but mere custody of its contents.

iv. **Mens rea: intent to permanently deprive.** A defendant is not guilty of larceny unless she intends to permanently deprive another of possession. Merely borrowing an object is insufficient for the common law crime of theft.

(a) **Example.** Defendant took a boy's bicycle, but he never intended to keep it. Defendant may be guilty of trespass, but he is not guilty of larceny. People v. Brown, 105 Cal. 66 (1894).

EXAM TIP

If a defendant "borrows" an item, he does not have the requisite intent for larceny because he intends to return the object. For example, "joy riding" is not larceny because the defendant intends to return the car. It may, however, be a separate crime under joy-riding statutes.

(b) **Exceptions.** Some jurisdictions hold that a defendant who takes an object and abandons it or recklessly exposes it to loss meets the intent requirement, even if defendant claims he did not intend to permanently deprive the owner of the property. N.Y. Penal Law §155.00(3).

(c) **Purpose of intent requirement.** The intent requirement ensures that a person who is convicted of stealing acted dishonestly in taking the property. Without a requirement that the defendant have the intent to permanently deprive, bad business deals or misunderstandings could lead to criminal convictions. People v. Jennings, 69 N.Y.2d 103 (1986) (no larceny when defendant made interest from the short-term use of the victim's money).

(d) **Repayment insufficient.** If a defendant takes an object with the intent to keep it, it is no defense that he later repays the victim or returns the object. MPC §2.06(1)(c).

(e) **Theft of property, lost, mislaid, or delivered by mistake.** If a person finds property and knows it belongs to another, he must take reasonable measures to return the item. If not, defendant acts with an intent to permanently deprive another of property and is guilty of larceny. MPC §223.5.

- **Abandoned Property**. If the defendant reasonably believes that the property has been abandoned, not lost, taking the property is not larceny. United States v. Smiley, 27 F. Cas. (1864).

2. Aggravated Thefts

To protect victims from the physical danger of certain thefts, the common law developed the crime of robbery and modern legislation created the crime of extortion.

a. **Robbery.** Robbery is the taking of property from another person with force or intimidation. Its elements include:

- taking of property
- from the victim's person or presence
- by force or intimidation
- with intent to permanently deprive

Robbery is a combination of the crimes of larceny and assault.

larceny + assault = robbery

i. **From victim's person or presence.** The property must be forcefully taken from the victim's person or the victim's presence.

Example. Defendant threatens to shoot the victim unless he steps away from his motorcycle and lets defendant drive it away. If the defendant takes the motorcycle, he has committed robbery.

Study Tip

In everyday speech, laypersons misuse the term "robbery." For example, a person who finds that his car or home has been broken into will often exclaim, "I've been robbed." According to the legal definition, no robbery has occurred because nothing has been taken from the person or presence of the victim.

ii. **Force or threat of force.** Either the use of force or the threat of force is sufficient for robbery. The defendant need not cause actual injury to the victim; slight force is sufficient. If a threat is used, it must be of immediate and unlawful injury. Threats of future injury constitute a different crime of "extortion."

(a) **Example.** Defendant grabs a purse from the victim's arm. Because the defendant used force against the victim, the taking constitutes a "robbery." Commonwealth v. Brown, 506 Pa. 169 (1984).

(b) **Example.** Defendant approaches victim and threatens to shoot her unless she gives him her jewelry. Victim complies. Defendant's threat of immediate and unlawful injury satisfies the requirement for robbery.

(c) **Contrast.** Defendant slips a wallet out of the pocket of an unconscious drunk. Because defendant has used *no* force, the crime is larceny, not robbery.

EXAM TIP

If the facts state that the defendant "snatched" or "grabbed" the property, or used force to render a victim helpless and then took the property, there has been sufficient force for robbery.

iii. **No claim of right defense.** A defendant may not use violence to collect debts that he claims were owing to him. "Claim of right" is not a defense to robbery. Commonwealth v. English, 446 Pa. 161 (1971). Some jurisdictions, however, have recognized the claim of right defense as negating defendant's intent to steal. See People v. Butler, 55 Cal. Rep. 511 (1987).

b. **Extortion.** Extortion is the taking of property by threat of future violence. It sometimes goes by the name "blackmail." Its elements include:

- taking of property
- from another
- by threat of future violence, release of harmful information, threat of criminal charges, or similar harm

i. **Threat of future violence.** The key difference between robbery and extortion is that extortion involves the threat of future violence.

Example. A sees B on the street and threatens to burn B's house down the next day if B does not give A his wallet.

STUDY TIP

robbery — threat of present violence
extortion — threat of future violence

ii. **Other extortionate threats.** Many different types of threats may suffice for extortion or blackmail. Depending on the jurisdiction, threat of one the following may suffice:

- bodily harm
- exposure of secret and/or embarrassing information
- official action against the victim
- future criminal charges
- causing a strike
- testifying or withholding information, or
- other harm to the victim, MPC §223.4; People v. Dioguardi, 8 N.Y.2d 260 (1960) (using threat of strike constituted extortion).

EXAMPLE AND ANALYSIS

In State v. Harrington, 128 Vt. 242 (1949), defendant, an attorney representing a woman divorcing her husband, hired another woman to seduce the husband into having sex. Defendant had their lovemaking recorded and busted in on the naked pair to take photographs. Defendant then threatened to embarrass and ruin the husband with the information unless he agreed to the wife's divorce proposal. The court upheld defendant's extortion conviction.

- **Note**. Courts are cautious about expanding the list of threats recognized as extortion or blackmail because threats are common both in personal and business interactions. For example, it is not uncommon for an employee to state, "Give me a raise, or I will quit." Extortion law is not meant to cover such remarks.

- **No Threats to Collect Debts**. A defendant may be charged with extortion when he threatens harm to collect a legal debt. People v. Fichtner, 281 A.D. 159 (1952).

iii. **Taking.** In some jurisdictions, the mere threat for the purpose of obtaining property is sufficient, even if the defendant never actually takes the property. In other jurisdictions, actual misappropriation is required.

iv. **Hobbs Act violations.** The Hobbs Act, 18 U.S.C. §1951 is a federal statute that prohibits extortion by government officials. The Hobbs Act prohibits elected officials from providing quid pro quos in exchange for so-called campaign contributions. McCormick v. United States, 500 U.S. 257 (1991). A promise to provide a quid pro quo is sufficient; the official need not actually fulfill his part of the agreement. Evans v. United States, 112 S. Ct. 1881 (1992).

3. Misappropriation and Embezzlement

Courts and lawmakers have expanded theft crimes to include the conversion of property that is already in the defendant's possession. Such conversion is called "misappropriation" and it is the criminal act that characterizes the crime "embezzlement."

a. **History of embezzlement as a crime.** In Rex. v. Bazeley, 2 Leach 836 (1799), a bank teller pocketed a depositor's bank note after he credited the depositor's account. Because the defendant did not take the money from the possession of another, he could not be prosecuted for larceny. In response to this case, Parliament enacted the first laws against embezzlement.

b. **Definition of embezzlement.** Embezzlement is the unlawful conversion of another's property that is in the possession of the defendant. Its elements are:

- a fraudulent
- conversion of ("misappropriation")
- the property of another
- that the defendant already possesses

EXAMPLES AND ANALYSIS

Defendant is the manager of a store. He decides to take home and keep one of the televisions sets that his store is selling without paying for the item. As the manager, defendant is in lawful possession of the items in the store, but he does not have authority to convert the items to his own use. Defendant is guilty of embezzlement.

In United States v. Titus, 64 Fed. Supp. 55 (N.J. 1946), the defendant worked as a manager at a local military base post exchange. Defendant would take cigarettes from the base, sell them off base at a profit, pocket the profit, and return the rest of the money to the base. Defendant's conversion of the cigarette stock constituted embezzlement.

c. **Larceny vs. embezzlement.** If property is taken from the possession of another, the crime is larceny. If the defendant already has possession of another's property and converts it to his own use, the crime is embezzlement.

STUDY TIP

Property in another's possession — larceny
Property in defendant's possession — embezzlement

EXAMPLES AND ANALYSIS

In Nolan v. State, 213 Md. 298 (1957), defendant was the office manager of a finance company. Defendant stole money from his employer by taking deposits out of the cash drawer. Because defendant was not to have access to the money in the drawer until later, his crime involved the taking of property from another (his employer) and therefore was larceny, not embezzlement.

In Government of the Virgin Islands v. Leonard, 548 F.2d 478 (3d Cir. 1976), defendant was charged with embezzling 49 rolls of chicken wire. Because defendant did not have control of the storeroom or its contents, defendant committed larceny, not embezzlement, when he took the chicken wire.

---

i. **Note.** In the past, having separate offenses for larceny and embezzlement was a problem because defendants were often charged with the wrong technical crimes and therefore released. As a result, many jurisdictions eliminated the distinctions between larceny and embezzlement and consolidated all theft crime under one statutory provision. See, e.g., N.Y. Penal Law §155.05 (defining larceny to include common law larceny, embezzlement, obtaining property by false pretenses, and common law larceny by trick); Cal. Penal Code, §484 (broadly defining general crime of "theft."

d. **Persons capable of embezzling.** Originally, embezzlement was used only for a narrow category of individuals who by their status had possession of another's property. This primarily included servants who were entrusted with their masters' property. The laws gradually expanded to include agents, servants, and clerks, such as brokers, merchants, bankers, attorneys, and trustees.

Example. In State v. Riggins, 8 Ill. 2d 78 (1956), defendant operated a collection agency. He intentionally kept some of the collected money instead of turning it over to the client who hired him to do collections. Even though the defendant operated independently, the court held he was an agent of the client and, therefore, guilty of embezzlement.

e. **Misappropriation.** The actus reus of embezzlement is misappropriation, i.e., the conversion of another's property to one's own use. Sometimes, the courts call the crime "misappropriation" instead of embezzlement, when the converted property is found by the defendant or given to him by a third party.

Example and Analysis

In *Burns v. State*, a police officer arrested an insane suspect who had thrown away a roll of money during the police pursuit. Another officer gave the defendant officer the money to hold as a "bailee"; i.e., until the money would be introduced as evidence in the case. Instead of properly accounting for the money, the defendant spent it. Although the court called the crime "larceny as bailee," it is also properly characterized as misappropriation.

Converting Found Property. If a person comes into control of property of another that he knows to have been lost, mislaid, or delivered by mistake, and uses it with the purpose to deprive the owner of its possession, the defendant is guilty of theft by misappropriation.

---

4. Danger of Expanding List of Theft Crimes

The list of theft crimes has expanded considerably since early common law. The danger, however, of expanding the list is that every nonperformance or breach of contract that results in the transfer of property may be treated as a basis for criminal punishment. Sometimes these breaches occur because of the defendant's lack of funds. In those situations, criminalizing the defendant's failure to pay money may come dangerously close to reinstituting debtor's prison, which is contrary to American tradition and may be unconstitutional.

D. FRAUD CRIMES

In addition to unlawfully taking property from another, a defendant may cheat another out of property. Fraud occurs when a person knowingly gives property to another, but does so because of false representations. Common law divided fraud crimes into different technical offenses.

1. Historical Evolution of Common Law Fraud

At early common law, using deception to obtain property was not criminal. As one judge stated, "[W]e are not to indict one for making a fool of another." Regina v. Jones, 91 Eng. Rep. 330 (1703). Slowly, however, fraud as a legal concept developed. Initially, common law criminalized only the use of false weights, measures, or tokens. Later, fraud was made a misdemeanor and eventually a felony.

2. Types of Fraud Crimes

There are many types of fraud crimes, including false pretenses, larceny by trick, and mail and wire fraud. In each of these crimes, the defendant obtains property by the use of false representations or other deceit.

a. **False pretenses.** The crime of false pretenses occurs when a defendant:

- takes title and possession of the property of another
- by knowingly false representations
- with regard to a material present or past fact
- with an intent to defraud

EXAMPLES AND ANALYSIS

The bank erroneously credits defendant's account with $43,000. Realizing the bank's mistake, defendant withdraws the money. Defendant obtained the money by "false pretenses."

In Locks v. United States, 388 A.2d 873 (D.C. 1978), defendant used a friend's worthless check to buy merchandise at stores. Because defendants obtained the property by false representation as to the value of the check, defendants were guilty of false pretenses.

Note. In some jurisdictions, title does not pass until a check clears. In these jurisdictions, defendants would be guilty of larceny by trick. See Ch. 13 (C)(2)(b) infra.

In Brown v. Commonwealth, 656 S.W.2d 727 (1983), defendant auto mechanic falsely told a customer that his transmission was defective and needed to be replaced. The customer paid the replacement price, but defendant only repaired the transmission. Defendant obtained property, i.e., the payment, by false pretenses.

---

b. **Larceny by trick.** Larceny by trick is an offshoot of traditional larceny. It applies when a defendant obtains possession, although not title, to property by the use of deceit. Larceny by trick occurs when a defendant:

- takes possession of the property of another
- by false representations or deceit
- with intent to defraud

EXAMPLES AND ANALYSIS

Defendant hires a horse and promises to return it at the end of the day. Instead, he keeps it. Defendant is guilty of larceny by trick. Rex v. Pear, 1 Leach 212 (1780).

Defendant offers to hold the victim's ring while the victim swims. Defendant then leaves with the ring. The victim voluntarily gave the defendant possession, not title, of the ring based upon defendant's false representations. Defendant has engaged in larceny by trick.

Defendant drives into a gas station and asks for a fill up. He leaves the gas station without paying. Defendant did not have lawful title to the gas, but he did have possession. He is therefore guilty of larceny by trick. Hufstetler v. State, 37 Ala. App. 71 (1953).

Defendant, an attorney, obtains money from a client by telling the client that extra funds are needed to bribe a police officer. In fact, the attorney keeps the money that was supposed to be a bribe. Because defendant obtained his client's funds by false representations, defendant is guilty of larceny by trick. Graham v. United States, 187 F.2d 87 (1950).

---

i. **Compare false pretenses and larceny by trick.** False pretenses applies when the defendant obtains both title and possession through deceit. If the defendant only obtains possession, the crime is larceny by trick.

False Pretenses	—	Obtain title & possession by deceit
Larceny by Trick	—	Obtain possession by deceit

Example. Defendant offers to swap what he says is a gold watch for the victim's gold ring. The victim agrees. In fact, defendant's watch is worthless. Because the victim gave both possession and title to the defendant under false pretenses, defendant is guilty of false pretenses.

ii. **False promises vs. false representations.** Another distinction between false pretenses and larceny by trick is that a false promise is inadequate for a conviction for false pretenses, but is sufficient for a conviction for larceny by trick. For false pretenses, the defendant must make a material misrepresentation of fact.

EXAMPLES AND ANALYSIS

Defendant promises to give the victim money for the victim's watch. The defendant takes the watch but never pays the victim. Under common law, defendant's promise is not a material misrepresentation of fact and is therefore insufficient for a false pretenses conviction.

But see. In People v. Ashley, 42 Cal. 2d 245 (1954), defendant obtained loans by promising the lenders that her money would be secured by a first mortgage and loan money would be used to build a theater. In fact, defendant never obtained property to post as security and never used the loan funds to build a theater. In a jurisdiction where larceny by trick and false pretenses are consolidated under a single theft statute, defendant was properly convicted.

---

iii. **Inferring intent to defraud.** Both false pretenses and larceny by trick require intent to defraud. A defendant's intent to defraud can be inferred from his statements, actions, and the results of his actions.

Example. In Nelson v. United States, 227 F.2d 21 (1955), defendant offered to give a car that he said he only owed $55 on as security for a debt. In fact, he owed more than $3000 on the car. It was proper for the jury to infer from defendant's false statements and acts an intent to defraud.

E. CONSOLIDATED THEFT AND FRAUD CRIMES

Modern statutes tend to group theft and fraud offenses together in order to avoid arcane distinctions that lead to technical loopholes. For example, under the Model Penal Code, theft crimes have been consolidated. MPC §223.1. In other jurisdictions, theft crimes are all treated as a type of "larceny" or simply as "theft." This includes taking by fraud. See, e.g., N.Y. Penal Law, §155.05; Illinois Ann. Stats., §16; Cal. Penal Code, §484.

F. EXPANDING CONCEPT OF "PROPERTY"

The concept of what "property" is protected by the criminal law has expanded over the years. The traditional requirement was that the property must be tangible personal property to be covered by the theft laws. However, over the years, statutes have expanded the concept of "property" to include:

1. Services

- Chappell v. United States, 270 F.2d 274 (9th Cir. 1959) (e.g., painting services)

2. Use of Property

- State v. McGraw, 480 N.E.2d 552 (Ind. 1985) (unauthorized use of computer services)

3. Intangible Property, Such as Confidential Information

- United States v. Girard, 601 F.2d 69 (2d Cir. 1969) (release of confidential information in DEA files)
- United States v. Jones, 677 F. Supp. 238 (S.D.N.Y. 1988) (release of overheard prosecution discussions)
- Dreiman v. State, 825 P.2d 758 (Wyo. 1992) (copying of unlisted telephone number)
- United States v. Bottone, 365 F.2d 389 (2d Cir. 1966) (copies of secret processes for manufacturing antibiotics)

a. **Concerns regarding intangible property.** Including confidential information as a form of intangible property subject to the theft laws has been controversial. Traditionally, there has been free access to information in the United States. It is also often difficult to know when information has ceased to be confidential. Finally, courts prefer that any expansion of the concept of "property" be done by legislative action so that there is public concurrence as to how far the law should extend. See Regina v. Stewart, 50 D.L.R. 4th 1 (1988) (court reluctant to recognize employee list of names and addresses as property subject to theft laws); Oxford v. Moss, 68 Crim. App. 183 (Eng. Div. Ct. 1978) (borrowing page proof of exam did not constitute stealing "property").

b. **Temporarily withheld property.** Under MPC §223.0(1), temporarily withholding property from its owner can be treated as a permanent deprivation if the taker uses up the property's economic value.

i. **Example.** A "borrows" B's season pass to hockey and does not return it until after the season is over.

ii. **Example.** A "borrows" B's battery and returns it when the battery's power is exhausted.

c. **Jointly owned property.** Under common law, a partner could not be convicted of larceny or embezzlement for appropriating partnership funds to her own use. Today, courts are divided on the issue. Under MPC §223.2, taking jointly owned property is stealing even if the defendant has an interest in the property.

i. **Example.** A and B jointly own a racehorse. B takes the horse to another state, racing it and keeping all of the profits.

ii. **Interspousal theft.** One can steal from one's spouse, but if the item taken is a household item normally accessible to both spouses, it is only theft if the parties have ceased living together. MPC §223.1(4).

d. **Secured property.** The prevailing view is that taking property from the possession of another, who has a legal interest in it, like a lien, is considered theft of property. People v. Travis, 275 A.D. 444 (1949). The Model Penal Code treats such thefts as a separate crime, the misdemeanor of defrauding secured creditors. MPC §§223.0(7), 224.10.

e. **Unsecured property.** Courts are split on whether disposing of property constitutes a fraud on unsecured creditors. In California, such an act is criminal. Cal. Penal Code, §154. However, the Model Penal Code has rejected this approach. MPC §224.10.

G. MAIL AND WIRE FRAUD

Some of the most dramatic changes in theft law during the last decade occurred in the area of mail and wire fraud. Mail and wire fraud is a federal offense, defined as the use of the mail or wires in a scheme to defraud another person out of property. Until 1987, courts were split as to whether defrauding a person out of intangible rights constituted fraud. See United States v. Siegel, 717 F.2d 9 (1983). Federal prosecutors had been charging corrupt corporate and public officials with fraud for cheating shareholders or the public out of honest service while in office. In 1987, the Supreme Court held that federal mail and wire fraud statutes did not cover this type of fraud. McNally v. United States, 483 U.S. 350 (1987). The Court was concerned that there had been overcriminalization of corporate and political affairs, giving too much discretion and power to prosecutors. The Court held that such matters should be handled by the civil law unless expressly criminalized by Congress. In response to *McNally*, Congress amended the federal laws to prohibit frauds involving the intangible property right to honest corporate or public service. 18 U.S.C. §1346.

EXAMPLE AND ANALYSIS

In McNally v. United States, 483 U.S. 350 (1987), defendant was a public official who engaged in a kickback scheme. In exchange for financial benefits, he selected particular private agencies for government contracts. The government charged a scheme to defraud the citizens of Kentucky out of their intangible right to honest government. The Court reversed the conviction, holding that intangible rights are not property covered by the fraud statutes, unless expressly recognized by Congress. Today, McNally's actions would be covered by the more recently enacted 18 U.S.C. §1346.

Note. *McNally* requires that a fraud deprive the victims out of some type of tangible property. In response to *McNally*, many prosecutors began to charge that dishonest politicians had deprived the citizenry of the money paid for their services as loyal public servants. The need to use such creative theories was obviated by the passage of 18 U.S.C. §1346.

---

1. Mailings in Furtherance of Fraud

If a mailing is part of the execution of a scheme to defraud, as originally conceived by the perpetrator, it does not matter that the mailing does not actually further the scheme to defraud. In fact, in hindsight, it may prove to be counterproductive. The mailing element of the mail fraud offense is extremely broad. Schmuck v. United States, 489 U.S. 705 (1989).

H. DEFENSES TO THEFT AND FRAUD CRIMES

As with other offenses, a defendant charged with a theft crime can both contest the evidence of the *prima facie* case, and raise affirmative defenses.

1. Contesting Prima Facie Cases

a. **No property taken.** Defendants can contest whether the item taken constitutes "property" under the law. See Ch. 13(E) supra.

b. **Consent.** A taking must be against the owner's will to be theft. Accordingly, consent may be a defense to traditional theft crimes like larceny.

c. **No intent to permanently deprive.** If a defendant, at the time the goods were taken, intended to return the goods or money, then the defendant did not act with the intent to permanently deprive the owner and, therefore, is not guilty of larceny. Regina v. Feely, 2 W.L.R. 201 (1973).

   i. **Intent to restore property.** Intent to repay or return the property is not a defense if it is formed after the defendant takes the property. Likewise, it is not a defense to embezzlement or false pretenses charges. People v. Weiger, 100 Cal. 352 (1893).

2. Affirmative Defenses

There are very few affirmative defenses to theft crimes.

a. **Claim of right.** On rare occasion, a defendant charged with a theft crime can claim that she is the true owner of the goods or money, and that she was just trying to reclaim her right to it. Claim of right generally is not a defense for a theft crime that involves violence or the threat of violence, such as robbery or extortion. People v. Reid, 69 N.Y.2d 469 (1987). The Model Penal Code recognizes an affirmative defense if the defendant reasonably believed that she was recovering property that was owed to her. MPC §223.1(3).

I. OTHER CRIMES AGAINST PROPERTY

There are other crimes against property that do not require theft:

- burglary
- arson

1. Burglary

Burglary is a special type of crime against property. It does not have to involve theft. The common law definition of burglary is "breaking and entering of the dwelling house of another at nighttime with the intent to commit a felony inside." Thus, a burglary is committed if the defendant enters a dwelling with the intent to commit any felony, not just when he intends to steal something from the house.

a. **Elements.** The elements of common law burglary include:

- breaking and
- entering
- the dwelling house of another
- at nighttime
- with intent to commit felony inside

b. **Application of elements.** Each of the common law elements has a specific meaning and application.

i. **Breaking.** Opening a door or window of a dwelling constitutes a "breaking." It does not matter if the door or window was unlocked or already partially opened. If the defendant opened it wider, or defrauded another into opening his residence, the requirement is met. State v. Neely, 582 S.W.2d 352 (1979). However, if the entry is completely consensual and without fraud, then there is no burglary. Regina v. Collins, 2 All E.R. 1105 (1972).

(a) **Constructive breaking.** The courts have recognized types of constructive breaking:

- by threat
- by fraud and misrepresentation
- by exceeding the scope of entry to which there was consent

ii. **Entering.** Burglary is a crime inside a home. The law's greatest concern is for the safety of individuals and their homes. An entering can be complete or partial, such as reaching into a window that the defendant has opened. Franco v. State, 42 Tex. 276 (1875).

(a) **Using instruments to enter.** The entry requirement is met if the defendant uses a physical instrument, or another person, to make entry into the dwelling. People v. Tragni, 113 Misc. 2d 852 (1982) (entry made by inserting grabbing instrument through hole in the wall).

iii. **Dwelling house of another.** At common law, burglary only covered residential buildings. Statutes have now expanded burglary to include commercial buildings.

(a) **Note.** A person may not be guilty of burglary for breaking and entering into his own residence.

iv. **At nighttime.** At common law, an illegal entry was only burglary if it occurred at night. Otherwise, it was only trespass. Today, many jurisdictions have eliminated the nighttime requirement.

v. **Intent to commit a felony.** The mere entry of a home is not a burglary. Burglary occurs only when the defendant enters with intent to commit another crime inside, such as larceny, rape, kidnapping, murder, or arson. If the defendant commits the other crime, he is then guilty of two crimes: burglary and the other felony committed in the home.

(a) **Specific intent crime.** Because burglary requires that the defendant have a specific intent when he enters the dwelling, intoxication can serve as a defense to burglary.

(b) **Intent to commit any felony.** An intent to commit any felony inside the dwelling is sufficient for burglary. It need not be an act that poses physical danger. People v. Salemme, 2 Cal. App. 775 (1992).

2. Arson

The common law definition of arson is "the malicious burning of the dwelling house of another."

a. **Elements.** The elements of common law arson include:

- burning
- dwelling house
- of another
- with malice

b. **Application of elements.** Each of the common law elements has a specific meaning and application.

i. **Burning.** The actus reus of the crime of arson is burning. Common law requires that there be an actual burning of some part of the structure. Damage to property inside the structure was insufficient. Likewise, smoke damage to the building itself was insufficient. There must be actual charring of the structure. State v. Hall, 93 N.C. 571 (1885).

ii. **Dwelling house.** At common law, arson only applied to a residential building. Most jurisdictions have statutorily expanded arson to include commercial buildings.

iii. **Of another.** Like burglary, common law arson required that the dwelling burned be in the possession of another. An owner of a dwelling could be guilty of arson, however, if at the time of the fire, the building was lawfully occupied by a tenant.

iv. **With malice.** The mens rea requirement for arson is "malice." Like the malice required for murder, there is no requirement that the defendant act with ill will. Rather, it is sufficient if the defendant acted purposely, knowingly, or with gross recklessness. If a person sets a fire, realizing there is a high risk that the structure will burn, the defendant has acted with malice.

Example. Defendant sets off fireworks inside his neighbor's living room. Defendant does not intend to burn down his neighbor's home, but he realizes there is a substantial and unjustifiable risk that the structure will burn. Defendant has acted with malice.

- **Note**. At common law, damage to a structure from an explosive alone was insufficient for arson. The explosion must have caused a fire that damaged the dwelling. State v. Landers, 47 S.W. 100 (Tex. 1898).

J. SUMMARY OF THEFT CRIMES

Figure 13-1 presents a summary of theft crimes.

FIGURE 13-1

SUMMARY OF THEFT CRIMES
Larceny
• intentional taking and carrying away • personal property • in the possession or presence of another • without consent [trespassory taking] • with intent to permanently deprive other of the property
Larceny by Trick
• obtaining possession of • personal property • of another • by fraud and deceit
False Pretenses
• acquiring title and possession of • personal property • of another • by fraud and deceit
Embezzlement
• converting to personal use ("misappropriation") • property belonging to another • defendant already has custody of • with intent to permanently deprive

FIGURE 13-1

(CONTINUED)
Robbery
• taking property of another • from person or presence of another • by force or intimidation • with intent to permanently deprive
Extortion/Blackmail
• acquiring property of another • by threat of future harm
Mail and Wire Fraud
• acquiring property of another • by false representations • using the mail or interstate wires

K. SUMMARY OF OTHER CRIMES AGAINST PROPERTY

Figure 13-2 presents a summary of other crimes against property.

FIGURE 13-2

SUMMARY OF OTHER CRIMES AGAINST PROPERTY
Burglary
• breaking and • entering • dwelling house of another • at nighttime • with intent to commit felony inside
Arson
• burning • dwelling house • of another • with malice

Review Question and Answer

THEFT CRIMES AND OTHER CRIMES AGAINST PROPERTY

Question: For weeks, Gerry has coveted his neighbor's new big screen television. The picture on the television was unbelievable. When Gerry heard that his neighbor, Manuel, was going on an extended three-month business trip, Gerry asked Manuel to loan him the television. Manuel said he would think about it, but he left on his trip before he could get back to Gerry.

Gerry, seeing that Manuel was gone, decided he would borrow the set anyway. He used an emergency key that he had for his neighbor's door and went inside. The television was kept in a locked den, so Gerry had to use a screwdriver to help him open the door to the den. For the next few weeks, Gerry watched the television in Manuel's house. He then decided that it would be easier if he moved the television to his house.

With the help of some friends, Gerry moved the television to his own home. He even called Manuel's television repairman and, posing as Manuel, told him to help Gerry set up the television at his friend, Gerry's, house. Gerry told the repairman to add the cost to Manuel's regular bill.

One week before Manuel was to return home, Gerry decided that he would be embarrassed if Manuel found out what he had done, so Gerry decided to sell the television and tell Manuel that there had been a break-in at his home. Gerry sold the television and kept the proceeds. He added the money to $1800 he had collected at Manuel's request from Manuel's tenant at a nearby rental house. Gerry used the money to send himself on a vacation.

What theft crimes can be charged against Gerry?

Answer:
1. *Burglary*. It may be difficult to charge Gerry with burglary for his entry into Manuel's house. Burglary is defined as the breaking and entering of the dwelling house of another at nighttime with intent to commit a felony inside.
Breaking. Gerry used a key to enter Manuel's house. If he had Manuel's general permission to enter the house, then there is no breaking. However, when Gerry used a screwdriver to go beyond where he was authorized to enter, then the breaking requirement was fulfilled.
Entering. Gerry physically entered the premises, so the entering requirement is met.
Dwelling house of another. Gerry clearly met this requirement for burglary. The house he entered belonged to his neighbor, Manuel.
At nighttime. The facts are ambiguous as to whether Gerry entered the residence at night. If he did not, at traditional common law, there would be no burglary.

With intent to commit a felony inside. The biggest problem with a burglary charge is that, at the time Gerry entered Manuel's home, he did not have the intent to steal the television or commit any other felony inside. Accordingly, although Gerry may be guilty of trespass, he has not met the crucial mens rea requirement for burglary.

2. *Larceny.* Defendant may be charged with larceny for taking Manuel's television. Larceny is defined as the trespassory taking of the personal property of another, with intent to permanently deprive that person of the property. The key issue in this problem is: When did the larceny take place?

Unauthorized watching of the television. No larceny occurred when Gerry watched Manuel's television without permission. Larceny involves the taking of "personal property." Unauthorized use of an electronic device is not the taking of personal property. Under the Model Penal Code, Gerry's actions may have constituted larceny because the Code defines property as "anything of value."

Initial taking of the television. There is also a problem with charging Gerry with larceny for when he first moved the television to his house. When Gerry first removed the television, his intent was only to borrow the set. Larceny requires that the defendant have an intent to permanently deprive another of the property. Because Gerry did not have that intent, he was not guilty of larceny when he first removed the set.

Selling the set. Larceny took place when Gerry sold the television. At that point, he did intend to permanently deprive Manuel of his property. His taking of the property had been trespassory, since there had been a physical removal and carrying away without consent. Gerry's offense was not embezzlement, because he did not have Manuel's consent to have possession of the television when he sold it.

Use of the repairman. Under common law, Gerry also could not be charged with larceny for getting the repairman to provide him services and bill Manuel. The taking of "property" at common law did not involve services. Under the Model Penal Code, the taking of such services would constitute larceny.

3. *Embezzlement.* Gerry is also guilty of embezzlement for using the rents he collected for Manuel to go on a vacation. Embezzlement is the fraudulent conversion or misappropriation of the property of another that the defendant already possesses. Gerry served as Manuel's agent for the collection of the rent and, therefore, already had possession of the money. He did not, however, have authority to spend the money. Accordingly, he misappropriated the property of another and is guilty of embezzlement.

Sample Exam Questions

Question: Tisha, a recent immigrant from the Soviet Union, opens a grocery store in an area of town where many Puerto Ricans live. Tisha and her family live in the back of her grocery store. In the short time that Tisha has lived in the neighborhood, she has been robbed twice by two different Puerto Rican youths. Other Russian immigrant store owners have been killed during robberies. Tensions between the two communities are high.

On Monday, during school hours, two large, Puerto Rican girls, Ana and Maria, enter Tisha's store. They wander through the aisles. As Maria places different items in and out of her backpack, Ana looks around to see if anyone is watching them. As they approach the counter, Tisha insists that Maria open her backpack. She refuses to do so. When the smaller Tisha tries to grab the backpack, Maria strikes her in the face. Tisha grabs a gun that she had placed under the counter when she saw the girls enter. Tisha had vowed to herself that she would never be robbed again. As the girls turn to walk out of the store, the gun goes off in Tisha's trembling hand and hits Maria in the back of the head. Instead of staying to help Maria, Ana runs from the store without the backpack. Maria bleeds to death.

In investigating the shooting, the police are told by classmates of Ana and Maria that the Friday before the incident, they had heard the two girls planning to steal from Tisha's store. At first, Ana did not want anything to do with the plan. She told Maria, "I don't want a felony on my record." Maria, however, told Ana that if she did not participate, she might not like how Ana and her family would be treated by some of Maria's gang friends: "You do for me, or we'll do to you."

In her statement to the police, Tisha tells them that she has no specific recollection of how the shooting occurred. All she can say is "It was like a bad dream."

What crimes could Tisha and Ana be charged with and why? What defenses would you expect them to raise? Where the Model Penal Code and Common Law standards are different, apply each.

Answer: Crimes of Tisha

Homicide. Tisha is potentially responsible for Maria's death.

Actus Reus. The first requirement for any homicide offense is a voluntary act. A voluntary act must be the result of conscious or volitional movement. Tisha may have only picked up the gun in order to scare the girls out of the store. Once Tisha was holding the gun, her hand began trembling from fear, and it was this trembling that caused the gun to go off, not a conscious desire to pull the trigger on Tisha's part. She also told the police that the shooting was like a bad dream, which suggests that she was not voluntarily causing her finger to pull the trigger. However, involuntariness is usually defined very narrowly, and guns usually do not just go off in someone's hands. The MPC lists several kinds of involuntary actions: actions while under hypnosis; actions while sleepwalking; bodily movement not the product of the effort or determination of the actor; reflexes or convulsion. Tisha could argue under the MPC that the movement of her finger was a convulsion or reflex caused by extreme fear, but this is somewhat suspect. This was a robbery and Tisha was trying to protect her store; it is more logical to believe that firing the gun was the result of conscious thought. Whether it was purposeful is discussed below.

Mens Rea. Assuming that Tisha committed a voluntary act in firing the gun and killing Maria, the next issue is what level of mens rea accompanied the action.

First-Degree Murder. In many jurisdictions first-degree murder requires premeditation—the purpose to kill. In light of the discussion above, it does not seem that Tisha's goal or aim was to kill Maria. She did not even know Maria and she may have just been trying to scare the two girls to get them out of her store. On the other hand, the tension between the Russian and Puerto Rican communities was high; other Russian immigrants had been killed; Tisha had been robbed before; and she kept a gun in the store and had sworn never to be robbed again. From those facts we might infer that Tisha wanted revenge or she wanted to carry out her own version of vigilante justice. These motives support a theory that Tisha's goal was to kill one of the robbers to carry out her revenge.

Although premeditation can be formed in a matter of seconds, it does require some time of cool reflection. [*Carrol*] Moreover, in some jurisdictions, there must be a preconceived design to kill as demonstrated by the manner, motive, and planning of the killing. [*Anderson*] In this case, even if Tisha had a motive to kill, there was little opportunity for her to engage in cool reflection. It is unlikely the killing would be viewed as premeditated.

Second-Degree Murder. If Tisha did not have the purpose to kill Maria, she may be guilty of *second-degree extreme recklessness murder* if she acted with an extreme indifference to the value of human life. Pointing a gun at Maria and firing it was an extremely reckless act because Tisha knew that there was a great risk of harm, and she took that risk anyway. Shooting someone in the back over a few groceries also shows indifference to the value of human life. Therefore, Tisha is probably guilty of second-degree murder.

Voluntary Manslaughter. If Tisha did have the purpose to kill, her crime can be mitigated to *Heat-of-Passion Voluntary Manslaughter* if she can show: 1. she killed while actually in a state of passion; 2. there was legally adequate provocation; and 3. there was insufficient cooling time following the provocative act.

Tisha was definitely very excited when the killing took place. She was trembling, and she said later that it was all like a bad dream. The killing took place in the midst of a robbery. Tisha had just been slapped by one of the robbers, and the robbers were getting away. It appears that Tisha was actually in the heat of passion. Second, even under the most stringent of common law standards, a physical assault was considered legally adequate provocation. It is the type of provocative act that might very well make a normally reasonable person upset enough to lose control or be incapable of cool reflection. Third, events were unfolding quickly. There is no indication that Tisha had an opportunity to cool off after Maria's provocative acts. Tisha has a strong argument for partial mitigation to voluntary manslaughter.

Involuntary Manslaughter. Tisha is guilty of involuntary manslaughter if her actions constituted gross negligence, i.e., if an ordinary person in her situation would not have taken the risk of firing a gun at someone's back from relatively close range. At the very least, Tisha is guilty of gross negligence. Any reasonable person would know that firing a gun at the back of someone's head could kill them.

Tisha's Defenses

Self-Defense. Tisha's most obvious defense to a homicide charge is self-defense. Tisha can successfully claim this defense if 1. she had an honest and reasonable fear; 2. there was an imminent threat; 3. she had no duty to retreat; 4. she was not the initial aggressor; and 5. she did not use excessive force.

Tisha, a small woman, was faced with two much larger robbers. She had also been robbed before and knew that her neighbors had been killed in robberies. These factors support Tisha's claim that she was honestly afraid of Maria. Moreover, in judging whether a reasonable person would have feared for her life, the jury must consider a reasonable person in Tisha's situation. A reasonable person, with Maria's past experiences and relative size, might well be afraid in that situation. It is very questionable, however, whether Tisha faced an imminent threat. The girls had turned to walk out of the store when Tisha fired at Maria. Even though Maria had struck her previously, the threat of harm had subsided by the time Tisha pulled out the gun.

Assuming Tisha was faced with an imminent threat, Tisha probably had no duty to retreat because she was in her own store, which was also her home. Even in those jurisdictions where there is a duty to retreat, there is ordinarily not a duty to retreat from one's own home. Tisha was not the initial aggressor even though she tried to grab the backpack from Maria, because Tisha was within her rights in demanding to check the bag.

Finally, even if Tisha had been threatened with further slaps from Maria, using a gun to defend herself against this threat was excessive force because a person must use force proportional to threat. It is generally illegal to use deadly force unless one is faced with a life-threatening situation.

Defense of Property. Deadly force cannot be used to defend property. Life is more valuable than property. Accordingly, unless

Tisha was entitled to use self-defense, she was not entitled to use deadly force to defend her property.

Law Enforcement. Under modern common law, deadly force may only be used to apprehend a fleeing felon if the felon poses an imminent danger to the safety of others. Deadly force may not be used to apprehend a fleeing misdemeanant. Under the MPC, deadly force is justified to protect property if 1. the victim was attempting to commit a felony; 2. the victim threatened to use violent force against the defendant; and 3. the force was necessary to prevent the felony.

There are two problems for Tisha invoking the law enforcement defense. First, shoplifting is not a felony in most jurisdictions. Second, even if it were, Maria did not appear to be a threat to others. Tisha is unlikely to prevail with a law enforcement defense.

Crimes of Ana

Ana is potentially guilty of Conspiracy to Rob, Aiding and Abetting, Larceny/Robbery, Felony Murder, and Murder.

Conspiracy. Conspiracy requires: 1. agreement; 2. purpose to commit the underlying offense; and 3. and overt act toward the commission of the underlying offense. Ana explicitly agreed to help Maria rob the store. Ana joined the plot to protect her family and this motivation shows that despite her reluctance, she probably intended for the robbery to succeed. Finally, she was a lookout while Maria actually put things in her backpack, which constitutes an overt act toward the commission of the crime. Maria is guilty of conspiracy to rob even though the robbery never succeeded.

Aiding and Abetting Larceny/Robbery. Aiding and abetting requires: 1. purpose to assist the primary action and 2. an act of actual assistance or encouragement. Ana's goal or aim was to help Maria steal from the store because she thought Maria would hurt her family if she did not. She also played the critical role of lookout, which assisted Maria in robbing the store. It does not matter that Maria was apprehended before she could leave with the items. It is sufficient for larceny that there was an unconsensual taking and movement of the items with intent to permanently deprive the owner. Moreover, by using force (striking Tisha), the larceny was converted to a robbery. Therefore, Ana aided and abetted the robbery.

Felony Murder. Ana is guilty of felony murder if: 1. there was a killing 2. during her commission of 3. an inherently dangerous act 4. that was an independent felony; and 5. the killing was in furtherance of the felony. Maria was killed while Ana and Maria were committing the felony of robbery, as discussed above. If considered in the *abstract*, shoplifting is not *inherently dangerous* because in general there is no threat to life and the robbers try to avoid detection. In this particular case, however, the prosecution could argue that robbing a store when there was great interethnic strife in the community—and it was generally known that many shopkeepers were armed to the teeth—was an inherently dangerous act because the likelihood that any confrontation could lead to violence was very great. Moreover, robbery is considered inherently dangerous because it involves force. If this were found to be inherently dangerous, it is clearly *independent* of the homicide. Robbery does not merge into homicide. It has a purpose apart from causing serious bodily injury or killing another.

Even if the first four prongs of the test for felony murder are met, in either an agency or proximate cause jurisdiction, it is unlikely Ana would be guilty of the death of her cofelon. In an agency jurisdiction, Ana would not be responsible because she did not fire the shot that killed Maria. In a proximate cause jurisdiction, Ana could argue that Maria and Ana were running away when Tisha fired. There was no gun battle and Tisha acted for her own purposes. The killing was not in furtherance of the felony. Finally, in most jurisdictions, a cofelon is not responsible for the death of a cofelon because such killings are viewed as justified.

Homicide by Omission. Ana may also be guilty of homicide by omission because she left Maria to bleed to death. Ana would be guilty under this theory only if she had an affirmative duty to act. Maria was not a member of Ana's immediate family, and there is no evidence of any statutory or contractual duty for Ana to help her. It may be argued under theories of felony murder that Ana in some way put Maria in danger, but it seems clear that Tisha and Maria herself were primarily responsible for the dangerous situation. There is also a causation problem. Even if Ana had stopped to help, it is very likely that Maria, having been shot in the back of the head, would have died anyway. Therefore Ana could not be considered the proximate cause of Maria's death.

Ana's Defense

Duress. Ana's best defense is to claim duress. This defense requires that the defendant: 1. was faced with imminent threat of harm; 2. to herself or a third party; 3. such that an ordinary person would yield; and 4. the defendant did not bring the situation on herself. The threat by Maria against Ana's family was probably too vague and remote for a duress defense. There was no specific time stated and it was unclear exactly what Maria was threatening to do. At common law there must be a threat of great bodily harm or death. Under the MPC the threatened harm must only be enough to make the reasonable person yield. Clearly, Ana would have a better argument under the MPC. Even under the common law, Ana might argue that she knew Maria and her family were very dangerous people and that in her neighborhood such threats usually mean death and are usually carried out quickly. If Ana's argument on the first two requirements is successful, prong three is probably met as well. Faced with such a serious threat, the ordinary person would probably yield to helping in a relatively harmless shoplifting scheme.

Finally, Ana did nothing to bring the situation on herself. She was not a member of a criminal gang and had no desire to be involved in the plot. If Ana can show that despite the vague language used, Maria's threat was very real, serious, and imminent, then she can use the defense duress.

Question: Tommy is hooked on video games. He developed this habit while he was a law student. Although he is now an associate in a prominent law firm, he still sneaks out during his lunch break to go to a video arcade. During his off hours, Tommy sometimes pretends to be a character from his video games. His friends have told him to seek counseling for his bizarre behavior.

One day, after staying up all night working, Tommy's senior partner came to him and told him that he could no longer play video games because it gave the firm a bad image. Tommy exploded in anger. He screamed at the partner, "I have been working my guts out for you. Last night I took at least six amphetamines just so I could finish your stupid pleading. You have no right to abuse associates. I practically live at this place, and I can play video games whenever I want. You'd better be careful. A voice from within tells me society would be better off without you."

When the partner started to yell back and march toward Tommy, Tommy shoved the partner against the coat rack. The partner hit his head and fell bleeding on the floor in Tommy's office. Although the partner begged for help, Tommy stepped over him and headed for lunch. To calm his nerves, Tommy had a few beers and played a few video games. Then he returned to finish the pleading. The other hard working associates at the firm ignored the partner's cries for help, and he eventually bled to death after crawling into the firm's reception area.

Despite his condition, Tommy managed to finish the pleading. It consisted of a Securities and Exchange Commission (SEC) filing, in which Tommy was required to attest to the accuracy of his client's financial disclosures. Anxious to get home, Tommy did not read the papers carefully and signed them even though they mistakenly reported that the company had assets of $100,000,000. In fact, the company only had $10,000 in assets. Tommy did not worry about the accuracy of the papers because he mistakenly believed, from misreading a statute, that the legal penalties for signing a false form applied only to the company, not the attorney who signed the form.

Based on the foregoing events, Tommy is charged with the homicide of the partner. The Department of Justice is also considering one of the following SEC charges against him:

§222 — Filing a false financial disclosure form with intent to deceive the SEC.
Penalty — 10 years in jail

§444 — Filing an SEC disclosure form that contains a false statement.
Penalty — 6 months in jail

1. Who is responsible for the partner's death? What is the degree of culpability (level of homicide) and what, if any, defense could be raised?

2. Which SEC charge should the Department of Justice file and why?

Answer (Question 1):

Homicide. Tommy is primarily responsible for the death of the partner. He voluntarily chose to shove the partner, and this is a sufficient actus reus for homicide. The critical issue is Tommy's level of mens rea. Tommy is probably not guilty of first-degree murder, which may require premeditated purpose to kill. Tommy did have purpose to kill. He said that society would be better off without the partner, which shows that he had the partner's death as his goal when he shoved him. There is no evidence, however, that Tommy planned to kill the partner, and he had no real motive for killing the partner, that would indicate that he thought the killing out beforehand. On the other hand, some courts hold that premeditation can occur in a very short amount of time. A prosecutor could argue that Tommy's words about wanting to get rid of the partner showed enough thinking and reflection for premeditation.

Tommy's crime can be mitigated to Voluntary Manslaughter if: 1. he was actually provoked/actually in the heat of passion; 2. there was legally adequate provocation; and 3. there was an inadequate cooling off period. The fact that the two men were in the midst of an argument and yelling at each other shows that Tommy was actually in the heat of passion when he shoved the partner. There is also a strong argument that a reasonable person in Tommy's position would not have been capable of cool reflection. Although words alone are traditionally insufficient provocation, working in a law firm can be very stressful and the partner was chewing Tommy out and marching toward him. A reasonable person in Tommy's situation may also have become very angry. Note that Tommy does not have to show that a reasonable person would have killed in this situation — only that a reasonable person would have become very upset.

Under the Model Penal Code, Tommy could certainly claim extreme emotional distress. It appears that he had been constantly abused at the law firm and was operating under extreme emotional strain. If the Model Penal Code test is used, there is no need to prove a specific act of provocation. Tommy must be evaluated by someone from the perspective of a reasonable person in Tommy's ongoing situation. The jurors could also consider pressures put on Tommy by other persons. Overall, Tommy would have a convincing argument under the Model Penal Code.

There was no cooling time between Tommy's confrontation with the partner and his acts in response. However, an argument can be made that Tommy had plenty of time to cool off from his passion while the partner slowly bled to death. Tommy tried to calm his nerves with beers and video games, but his time alone may have only made him think about the injustice of the partner's remarks more, which continued to enrage him. On the other hand, if Tommy cooled down and calmly decided not to go back and help the partner, he would be guilty of first-degree murder. This would be an omission on his part, but he put the partner in danger in the first place and therefore has a duty to act.

Finally, there is a causation problem in convicting Tommy. It might be argued that the failure of the other associates to help the partner was the real cause of his death, but the associates' omission is only criminal if they were under some affirmative duty to act. Absent a contractual or statutory duty, there is no general affirmative duty to help someone in need. The associate's relationship to the partner is probably insufficient.

Defenses. In addition to mitigating the homicide to Voluntary Manslaughter, Tommy may also have the affirmative defenses of self-defense, insanity, diminished capacity, and voluntary intoxication.

Insanity. For an insanity defense, Tommy must first show that he had a mental disease or defect. Although there is no evidence that Tommy has been treated in the past for mental illness, many of his friends have suggested that he seek psychiatric help. Tommy hears voices, acts bizarrly, pretends to be a video character, and takes medication. Depending on expert testimony, Tommy may have a recognized disease or defect of the mind.

If the defense can show that Tommy has a mental disease or defect, there are several tests for insanity. Under the common law M'Naghten test, Tommy was insane if he did not know: 1. the nature and quality of his actions; or 2. that his acts were wrong. Given his hallucinations, Tommy may claim that he did not know the nature of his acts. On the other hand, Tommy said that society would be better off without the partner, so it is likely that Tommy knew that he was killing the partner. If he knew the nature and quality of his acts, there are no facts to support an argument that Tommy did not know his actions were wrong. Under the M'Naghten test, it will be difficult for Tommy to claim he was insane.

Under the Model Penal Code, a defendant is insane if as the result of mental disease or defect the defendant lacked substantial capacity: 1. to appreciate the criminality of his actions; or 2. to conform his conduct to the law. Under this broader test, Tommy would argue that his mental state made him unable to control his actions. Although Tommy was able to go out, buy beer, play video games, and finish his work, he lacked substantial capacity to appreciate his acts or control them because he went in and out of reality. Also, the Model Penal Code would allow Tommy to argue that he could not control his acts, even if he realized they were wrong. Finally, Tommy may claim that he was following a deific decree to kill the partner because he heard a "voice from within."

Diminished Capacity. If Tommy cannot show a mental disease or defect, he may try to claim diminished capacity. He can argue that his mental state made it impossible for him to form the purpose mens rea necessary for murder. Most courts allow this type of mens rea diminished capacity defense only for specific intent crimes such as intentional murder. However, the MPC would allow Tommy to argue to the jury that he was unable to form a purpose mens rea and therefore should only be convicted of involuntary manslaughter.

Self-Defense. Tommy would also claim the defense of self-defense. This defense requires that the defendant: 1. faced imminent danger; 2. honestly and reasonable feared death or great bodily harm; 3. did not use excessive force; 4. did not have a duty to retreat; and 5. was not the initial aggressor. Tommy was not the initial aggressor because the partner was advancing toward him, and most jurisdictions do not require the defendant to retreat. It is questionable whether Tommy faced imminent danger. The partner was advancing toward him, but he did not have a weapon and there is no other evidence that the partner would have harmed Tommy physically. Tommy's fear was probably not reasonable because in an office with other people around, it is highly unlikely that the partner really would have attacked him. Even if he did have reason to fear an imminent physical attack from the partner, Tommy used excessive force when he tried to kill the partner because the partner did not have a weapon, and there is no evidence that Tommy's life was in danger. Finally, if he was able to do so in many jurisdictions, Tommy had a duty to retreat before using deadly force.

Intoxication. Tommy's final possible defense for homicide would be voluntary intoxication. Tommy had taken six amphetamines before his encounter with the partner and may have still been intoxicated from them. As a public policy matter, courts are very unwilling to allow voluntary intoxication as a defense because drug use is such a large societal problem. Voluntary intoxication is only a defense when the effects of the drug effectively negate some element of the defense. Second-degree murder only requires gross recklessness, so it is unlikely that Tommy could successfully argue that his intoxicated state is a defense. Furthermore, he was able to do his work, which shows that he probably had a sufficiently lucid mental state to form malice.

Answer (Question 2):

Section 222 has two basic elements: 1. filing false documents; and 2. intent to deceive. This is probably a felony because it penalizes a defendant with more than one year in jail. The purpose of this stiff penalty seems to be to punish only those defendants who have the specific purpose to deceive the government. The DOJ should not charge Tommy with this offense. Tommy did not know for sure that the papers were false and had no purpose to deceive the government. His mens rea was, at most, reckless.

The DOJ should charge Tommy with Section 444. It is not clear from the wording of the statute what the mens rea for this crime is. Because this is a regulatory crime and the penalty is relatively light, this may be a strict liability offense. If that is true, Tommy is guilty because he has fulfilled the material elements of: 1. filing a form 2. that has a false statement. His mental state regarding the truth or falsity of the statement makes no difference.

There are strong arguments, however, against construing Section 444 as a strict liability offense. Many courts require specific language in the statute in order for the crime to be strict liability. Although six months in jail means this crime is a misdemeanor, it is also a much greater penalty than most regulatory crimes, which have only monetary penalties. If 444 is not a strict liability offense, recklessness is usually the default mens rea at common law. As discussed above, Tommy probably did take an unjustifiable risk that the papers he was signing would be false, and he filed the papers. Therefore, he is guilty of 444.

Question: Al, Bob, and C.J. had always been the best of friends. From the time they were in college together, they vowed to help each other no matter what troubles they faced.

One day, Al and Bob heard that their best friend, C.J., was going to be arrested for allegedly killing his wife. Al rushed over to C.J.'s house and found C.J. running around his house with a gun in his hand. Before Al had a chance to talk to him, C.J. dashed out the door and ran toward his Bronco car. Afraid that his friend might try to kill himself, Al ran after C.J. and jumped into the driver's seat of the car. C.J. threatened to kill both himself and Al unless Al drove him to the border. At that point, Al began to drive. Out of the corner of his eye, he saw a gun, a passport, and large wad of cash in C.J.'s hand. C.J. promised to share the money with Al if they made it to the border.

As they drove toward the border, Al saw large crowds gathering on the side of the highway. They were cheering Al and C.J. as they drove along the empty freeway at 35 miles per hour. At one point, the crowd accidentally pushed one of the rooters into the path of the Bronco. Al tried to avoid the pedestrian, but it was too late. The car hit and killed the pedestrian.

During the drive, C.J. used the cellular phone to call Bob, asking him to wire money to Mexico under an assumed name. Bob agreed to do so even though he believed his actions would violate international currency transaction laws. (Unbeknownst to Bob, the law does not require that a person use his or her own name when wiring money internationally. The other relevent laws for the jurisdiction are set forth in the Appendix at the end of the question.) Bob then wired the money. He felt guilty, however, about his actions and decided to call 911 to report the direction in which he believed the Bronco was headed. Unbeknownst to Bob, he gave the police incorrect information.

For two hours, while they drove toward the border, Al repeatedly asked C.J. if he wanted to surrender. C.J. reminded Al that they had promised to stick by each other and that he felt he had no choice but to leave the jurisdiction given the charges he faced. Because Al continued to drive slowly, the police finally caught up with the Bronco and surrounded it. Al, Bob, and C.J. were arrested.

What crimes have Al and Bob committed and what defenses would you expect them to assert? Where applicable, apply both common law and Model Penal Code standards.

APPENDIX

In addition to the common laws you studied, the following laws are also applicable in the jurisdiction:

Penal Code §32:

"It is a felony for a person to flee the jurisdiction with the intent to avoid arrest or trial for a violent felony."

Penal Code §48:

"It is a misdemeanor for a person to drive slower than 45 mph on a freeway unless required to do so because of traffic."

Penal Code §522:

"It is a misdemeanor to report false information to the police. If a person knowingly reports false information, that person shall be guilty of a felony."

Answer:

Crimes of Al

Aiding and Abetting Escape. Al is guilty of aiding and abetting C.J.'s attempted escape if: 1. he had the purpose to help or encourage C.J., and 2. he committed an actual act of assistance. The fact that C.J. promised to share his money with Al if Al helped, and that Al thought C.J. might kill himself if Al did not help him show that Al had it as his conscious object to assist C.J.'s flight to the border. Al also acted to provide actual assistance by driving the car for C.J. Al is therefore guilty of aiding and abetting C.J.'s flight.

Conspiracy. Al is also guilty of the separate crime of conspiracy to escape if there was: 1. agreement; 2. purpose to commit the underlying offense; and 3. an overt act toward the commission of the offense. Al did not specifically state his agreement to join C.J.'s planned escape, but he ran to the car, jumped into the driver's seat, and began to drive — all of which showed his agreement to join the plan. Al also knew that C.J. was going to be arrested for a violent felony. On the other hand, Al could argue that he never really agreed to the plan and was only going along to slow C.J. down so he would turn himself into the authorities. Nonetheless, it seems safe to infer agreement from Al's actions. As discussed above, Al had the purpose to help C.J. escape and committed overt acts toward the completion of that offense. He is, therefore, guilty of conspiracy to commit Section 32 escape.

Homicide. Al may also be charged in the death of the rooter. The rooter simply fell into the road and there is no evidence of plan or deliberation, so Al is not guilty of first-degree premeditated murder. Al also did not seem to be aware that he might cause the death of a random bystander. Therefore, he is not guilty of Second-Degree Murder or Voluntary Manslaughter, which requires subjective awareness.

Al may be guilty of unlawful act involuntary manslaughter. Under this doctrine a defendant is guilty of involuntary manslaughter if he kills another during the commission of an unlawful, nonfelony act. Al was driving in violation of Section 48 because he was only driving 35 mph and the highway was empty. However, this violation was not malum in se and driving too slowly was not the proximate cause of the death.

Al may also be guilty of felony murder because the rooter was killed during the commission of Section 32 which is a felony. For its crime, a court would first have to decide if Section 32 is an inherently dangerous felony. In the abstract, escaping from arrest for a violent felony may not be considered inherently dangerous. There are many ways to escape that do not pose a danger. If viewed in the abstract, the felony may not be considered inherently dangerous. However, if the facts of this case are considered, especially that C.J. was wanted for murder and was carrying a gun, the felony may be viewed as inherently dangerous. Al's driving the car was an act in furtherance of the felony of escape and could thereby trigger the felony murder doctrine.

Finally, there is some argument in Al's favor that he was not the proximate cause of the rooter's death because someone in the crowd pushed the rooter into Al's path. Someone else pushed the rooter into the path of the car when he had no chance to avoid the person. However, C.J. and Al's flight from authorities caused the crowd to gather and set up the entire situation. In this way, it is unlikely that Al would not be the cause of the person's death.

Accessory After the Fact. Al may also be an accessory after the fact if: 1. the felony was actually committed; 2. he knew the felony had been committed; and 3. he aided the felon in evading authorities. We would need more facts as to whether C.J. actually committed the crime. Al definitely knew that C.J. was about to be arrested for homicide, and he drove C.J. in order to evade authorities. Therefore, if C.J. committed the underlying offense, Al is an accessory after the fact.

Al's Defenses

Necessity. If charged with aiding and abetting and conspiracy, Al will probably claim the defense of necessity. For this defense to be successful, Al must show that: 1. he faced choice of evils; 2. he had no legal alternatives; 3. the harm was imminent; 4. he chose the lesser harm; 5. he did not bring the choice upon himself; 6. there was no contrary legislative intent. Al will argue that the choice was between letting C.J. kill himself or going along with C.J. to try to talk him out of it. C.J. could also argue that he had no legal alternatives and the harm was imminent because C.J. was dashing out of the house and there was no one else around to help him. Al will argue further that he did his best to drive slowly to allow the police to catch up and take C.J. in a nonviolent manner. However, it will be difficult for Al to argue that it was the lesser of two evils for him to go along with C.J. and help him elude police, especially when a pedestrian was killed in the process. There was also a clear contrary legislative intent to Al's actions, which is manifested in Penal Code Section 32. It is also not at all clear from the facts that preventing C.J.'s suicide was Al's only motivation. C.J. did offer Al money.

Duress. Al can use a duress defense if he can show: 1. there was an imminent threat of death or great bodily harm 2. against himself or another; 3. a reasonable person under the circumstances would yield; and 4. Al did not bring the circumstances upon himself. C.J. had a gun and directly threatened to kill both himself and Al unless Al helped him, which shows an imminent threat of harm against C.J. Faced with a gun and a crazed friend who may have just killed his wife, it seems that the normal, reasonable person would yield to his demands much in the way a bank teller faced with an armed robber will give him the money. The problem for Al, however, is that he may have voluntarily placed himself in a situation where he would be placed under duress. Also, at common law, duress would not be a defense to the homicide.

Crimes of Bob

Accomplice. Bob is guilty as an accomplice to C.J.'s escape if: 1. he had the purpose to assist C.J.; and 2. he committed an actual act of assistance. Bob agreed to help C.J. even though he thought he was breaking the law by wiring the money and he knew that C.J. was about to be arrested and was trying to escape to Mexico. This shows that it was his purpose to help C.J. escape. He also wired the money, which assisted C.J. Therefore Bob is guilty as an accomplice.

Conspiracy. Bob is also guilty of the second crime of conspiracy to commit Section 32. Conspiracy requires: 1. agreement; 2. purpose to commit the underlying crime; and 3. an overt act toward the commission of the offense. Bob agreed to take part in the escape plan. When C.J. called him on the phone, he said he would wire the money. Bob's purpose is shown in the act of intentionally wiring the money when he knew C.J. would be using it in his escape plan, and actually wiring the money as part of the plan was sufficient overt action.

Section 522—Reporting False Information. Bob is also potentially guilty of violating Section 522. Bob did not know the information he submitted was false, so he is not guilty of the felony count. The wording of the statute does not set out a particular mens rea for the misdemeanor offense. However, because this is a misdemeanor and the penalties are probably relatively light, this may be a strict liability offense. This analysis is supported by the fact that the legislature included the work "knowingly" when describing the felony offense, but did not include any mens rea language for the misdemeanor offense, which means that such language was intentionally left out. If this is a strict liability crime, Bob is guilty because he committed the actus reus in reporting false information.

By contrast, Bob would not be guilty of the felony to "knowingly" report false information because his mistake of fact—mistakenly reporting the wrong destination of the Bronco—negatived the mens rea requirement for the offense.

Attempt to Violate Currency Transaction Laws. Finally, Bob may also be guilty of attempt to wire money illegally. Bob believed that it was illegal to wire money under an assumed name, but Bob's actions in this regard were actually not illegal. This is true legal impossibility. Bob was not mistaken as to any of the facts of the situation; he was only mistaken about the law. Under both common law, this is a complete defense to attempt charges. There is simply no crime that the defendant could have committed here. Likewise, under the Model Penal Code, Bob may have grounds for dismissal of the charges. Although if the laws were as he believed them to be, he would have been guilty of an offense, his conduct in wiring the funds posed no danger to society and did not reflect, in itself, culpable behavior.

Bob's Defenses

Abandonment. As a defense to the conspiracy charges above, Bob may try to claim that he abandoned the plan. Most jurisdictions hold that abandonment is no defense. The MPC allows abandonment as a defense if the defendant thwarted the success of the conspiracy, showing a voluntary renunciation of his criminal purpose. The fact that Bob called the police on the phone telling them which way he thought C.J. was headed does not seem to be enough to meet this standard. The information he gave to police was not what thwarted C.J.'s escape, and Bob did not turn himself in or attempt to cancel the wire transfer. Bob's abandonment defense would probably not be successful.

Necessity and Duress. Bob may also try to claim necessity or duress as Al did above, but there is no evidence that he knew that C.J. was threatening to kill himself or Al. In addition, unlike Al, Bob was faced with no imminent danger. It is also hard to understand how wiring C.J. money would avoid the evil of C.J. committing suicide or killing Al because C.J. would not even know whether Bob had wired the money until he was in Mexico. Therefore, necessity and duress are unlikely to be successful defenses.

Question: Angered by the voters' failure to pass Proposition 128 ("Big Green"), Tom Hatem, an ardent environmentalist, decides he will teach people a lesson before it is too late. Hatem plans to dump toxic waste into a small reservoir that serves approximately 12 percent of the local population. Although he knows some people may be killed before he can hold a press conference to alert them, he sincerely believes his radical tactic is necessary to save the greater society from doom.

In preparation for the dumping, Hatem contacts his old friend, Willie Blue. Because Hatem has previously threatened to poison

Blue's pets, Blue agrees to steal some toxic chemicals from an oil refinery at which Blue works.

At night, Blue enters the refinery after closing hours. Hatem stands guard at the gate. Hatem is accompanied by his friend, Frank Unreal. Unreal is unaware of the plot and thinks that Blue has returned to work to retrieve his lunch box.

Blue manages to steal some of the toxic chemicals and conceal them in a large ice chest. While he is leaving the refinery, he triggers an alarm. The police respond and start shooting. They hit and kill Unreal, but Blue and Hatem get away.

Blue gives Hatem the chemicals and says that he wants nothing further to do with the plan. He then goes home and tells no one of their escapades. Hatem proceeds directly to the reservoir where he pours the chemicals into the water. Unknown to Hatem, the city has stopped using the reservoir for anything other than fishing. After Hatem has poured in his chemicals, a local boy comes by to fish. The boy catches a fish, eats it, and dies.

What crimes, if any, have Hatem and Blue committed and what defenses might they assert?

Answer:

Crimes of Hatem

Aiding and Abetting Larceny. Hatem is potentially guilty of aiding and abetting larceny. Larceny is the trespassory taking of the personal property of another with intent to permanently deprive that person of the property. In order to be guilty of this crime, the defendant must: 1. have the purpose to encourage or assist the primary actor; 2. commit an act of assistance or encouragement; and 3. the primary actor must actually commit the offense. In this case we know that Hatem intended to help Blue steal the chemicals because it was Hatem who suggested they do it. Hatem also committed clear acts of encouragement and assistance when he asks Blue to join his plot and when he stands as a lookout while Blue is in the refinery. Blue did actually take the chemicals with the intent to keep them. The property was not in the possession of Blue even though he worked in the refinery. Accordingly, there was a larceny and Hatem was an accomplice to it.

Aiding and Abetting Burglary. Even though Blue and Hatem entered the refinery at night with an intent to commit a felony therein, they would not be guilty of burglary because common law burglary only applies to the breaking and entering of a residential building. Here, Blue and Hatem entered a commercial structure.

Attempted Murder. Hatem can also be convicted for attempted murder of the reservoir drinkers. Attempted murder requires: 1. purpose to kill and 2. a substantial act strongly corroborative of intent (the MPC language). The prosecutors will argue Hatem had as his purpose the killing of another person, but that he was willing to kill them to get across his message. The defense will argue that although Hatem knew of a risk to others but did not have it as his purpose, as required by common law. Hatem certainly took enough steps for his conduct to satisfy the actus reus requirement for attempt. He took the last step of pouring the toxic chemicals into the water. The fact that the population no longer used the reservoir for drinking would not be a defense. Factual impossibility is not a defense at common law or under the Model Penal Code. If the facts had been as Hatem believed them to be, almost 12 percent of the population may have been killed.

Homicide. Hatem may also be culpable for the death of the boy who ate the contaminated fish. Hatem acted with gross recklessness and arguably knowingly when he poured the chemicals in the reservoir. There is no evidence that Hatem actually knew that there was a risk of someone eating fish from the water, but his actions may have nonetheless constituted malice for a murder charge. He showed extreme callousness toward human life and, even though he had an arguably good motive for his actions, he still acted with the intent (gross recklessness) that satisfies for malice. Moreover, in this case, we can transfer Hatem's level of mens rea regarding the drinkers to the end result, which was the death of the boy. Under the doctrine of transferred intent, Hatem may be guilty of the murder of the boy.

Felony Murder. Hatem is also potentially guilty of felony murder for the death of Unreal. Under traditional common law a defendant is guilty of felony murder if someone is killed during the commission of certain enumerated felonies. However, larceny, unlike burglary, may not constitute an inherently dangerous felony in the abstract. Even with the facts of this case, defendants were not armed, and they were only breaking into an unoccupied refinery. Finally, it is unclear that the felons provoked the gun battle that killed Unreal.

As for the death of the boy, if poisoning is considered the underlying felony, prosecutors will have a problem with the merger (independent felony) rule. Poisoning is an integral step toward killing someone and, therefore, cannot be used as an underlying felony for the felony murder doctrine.

Conspiracy. Finally, Hatem is probably guilty of the separate crime of conspiracy to steal and kill. A defendant is guilty of conspiracy if there was: 1. agreement to commit the crime, 2. purpose to commit the crime, and 3. an overt act toward the commission of the crime. In this case Hatem solicited Blue to help him in his plot, which shows that there was an agreement. Purpose to steal is shown by Hatem contacting Blue to help him and in the plan to dump the chemicals and make a political statement. However, as discussed above, Hatem probably did not have the purpose to kill and would therefore not be guilty of conspiracy to kill. Finally, for conspiracy to steal, there was definitely an overt act toward the commission of that crime because Hatem and Blue actually took the chemicals. Therefore, Hatem is guilty of conspiracy to steal.

Hatem's Defenses

Necessity. Hatem would probably try to use a necessity defense for his actions. To be successful Hatem will have to show that: 1. he faced a choice of evils; 2. there were no lawful alternatives; 3. he chose the lesser harm; 4. the threat of harm was immediate; 5. he did not bring the choice of evils on himself; and 6. there was not a contrary legislative intent. Hatem would argue that his choice of evils was either endangering the lives of reservoir water drinkers or allowing the continued destruction of the environment, which could lead to the end of all life on earth. In this way there may have been a choice of evils, but a court would probably find that Hatem had legal alternatives, such as petitioning the legislature or staging a protest demonstration. The threat of environmental harm is also not the type of immediate danger usually required especially when Hatem's protest involved endangering the lives of human beings. The environment and all human life may ultimately be destroyed by toxic dumping, but the threat is not immediate. Hatem's necessity defense, therefore, will probably not be successful.

Crimes of Blue

Conspiracy. As discussed above, Blue is guilty of conspiracy to steal. He is not guilty of conspiracy to kill because he did not have it as his purpose that someone would die as a result of his stealing the chemicals. There is also no evidence that Blue knew what Hatem planned to do with the chemicals. In this way, Hatem's actions after the theft may be outside the scope of the conspiracy. On the other hand, if Blue knew what Hatem planned to do, he is guilty as a coconspirator for all Hatem's actions after the larceny. It is not a defense that Blue went home and did not take part in those activities.

Pinkerton Liability. Blue may be responsible under the *Pinkerton* doctrine for the acts of his coconspirator in furtherance of the conspiracy. In this case, Hatem poured chemicals in the water that ended up killing the boy. Unless Blue has successfully withdrawn from the conspiracy, he is automatically liable for his coconspirator's acts if a jury finds that they were in furtherance of the original conspiracy.

Blue's Defenses

Withdrawal. Under the common law, once a person joined a conspiracy, he is guilty of all crimes in furtherance of that conspiracy until the objectives of the conspiracy are achieved or abandoned. Although Blue advises his coconspirator that he no longer wants to participate in the plan, under the common law, abandonment was not a defense. Even under the Model Penal Code, Blue would only be relieved of responsibility for ongoing acts of the conspiracy once he notified his coconspirators of his withdrawal. To be relieved of liability for the underlying conspiracy, Blue would have had to thwart the efforts of the conspiracy.

Duress. Blue's most obvious defense to his criminal activities is duress. At common law, Blue has a duress defense if: 1. he was threatened with imminent death or great bodily harm to himself or a family member; 2. he reasonably believed there was no way to avoid the threat except to carry out the crime; and 3. he was not at fault in being in the coercive situation. Blue may have believed there was no way out except to commit the crime, and it was not his fault that he was in the situation, but Hatem had threatened at some time in the past to poison Blue's pets. This threat was not imminent at the time Blue agreed to steal the chemicals because it has occurred in the past and was not specific enough. It is also doubtful that a threat against a person's pets is serious enough for a common law defense. Therefore, Blue would have no necessity defense.

Under the MPC, however, duress requires only that: 1. the defendant was coerced to commit the crime by a threatened use of unlawful force; and 2. a person of reasonable firmness in the defendant's situation would not have been able to resist. The MPC rule is broader in not requiring imminence, and there may be some argument that in the face of threats to a pet, the person of reasonable firmness would steal toxic chemicals, but the threats are still only against animals and not other humans, which makes it extremely questionable even under the MPC.

MULTIPLE-CHOICE QUESTIONS

Question 1: Defendant Cori Anderson has been charged with a violation of the Modern Marine Act (MMA). Section 4 of the MMA provides: "It is a felony to harass a blue dolphin." Anderson was arrested when Coast Guard officials found him shooting his gun off his boat in an area where blue dolphins live. Anderson was not shooting his gun at the dolphins; rather, he was shooting in the air so that the dolphins would scatter and he could fish without fear of catching the dolphins in his nets.

Anderson confesses that he was trying to harass the dolphins, but that he never knew that the dolphins in the area were blue dolphins. They looked like bottle-nosed dolphins to him. Section 4 of the MMA was drafted after scientists complained that blue dolphins were becoming extinct.

What is Anderson's best defense at trial?

a. He did not commit the actus reus for the crime.
b. Factual impossibility.
c. Mistake of fact.
d. Legal impossibility.

Question 2: During a fire in the Malibu area, Stan Brakeswitch decides to stay and protect his home. In order to do so, he breaks into his neighbor's garage. Stan steals his neighbor's hoses, shovels, and other tools that could be useful in fighting the fire. His neighbor, Bill Barney, has already evacuated the area. When Bill returns after the fire, he is furious to learn that Stan stole his tools. Miraculously, both homes were saved from the fire.

If Stan is charged with the theft of Bill's tools, what is his best defense?
a. Self-defense.
b. Duress.
c. Temporary insanity.
d. Necessity.

Question 3: Bob Brains, a student at Byola Law School, studies in the law library. Brains is a very competitive student. He is currently number two in the class. Late one night before finals, Brain sees the number one student, Alvin Einstein, have an asthma attack in the library. Brain just stands there and watches. He makes no effort to call for help or administer artificial respiration. Rather, Brains is delighted that his competition may be eliminated. Einstein collapses and dies. Brains is charged with homicide.

Is Brains quilty?
a. He is guilty of first-degree murder because there was sufficient time for him to deliberate over Einstein's death.
b. He is guilty of first degree because he watched with malice.
c. He is guilty of negligent homicide because the benefit of being number one in law school is outweighed by the costs.
d. He is not guilty.

Question 4: Judge Flevinson is outraged by the number of unpunished acquaintance rapes on college campuses. Accordingly, when the next defendant convicted of this crime appears before her, Flevinson throws the book at him and imposes the maximum sentence. Flevinson tells the defendant that even though he has a spotless record and has shown full remorse for the crime, she must send a message to others that acquaintance rape is a serious crime.

What is Flevinson's stated purpose of punishment?
a. Rehabilitation.
b. General deterrence.
c. Specific deterrence.
d. Incapacitation.

Question 5: George M. Shugah is furious at President Clinton for his failure to intervene in the Bosnian atrocities. Shugah writes complaint letters to Senators Newt Greenwich and Jesse Holmes, who respond with almost identical notes:

"Dear Faithful Citizen:

> You're right. We have tried in every way we know to get rid of Bumbling Bill. Now, it is up to you, true citizens. The government belongs to you. As long as you believe in your heart that democracy still lives with the people, you can take back your White House. The law is what the people say it is!"

Sincerely,

Senator Greenwich
and
Senator Holmes

After reading this note, George decides to kill Clinton. He buys a high-powered rifle, travels to Washington D.C., and stands in line to get into the White House. A Secret Service Agent spots George's rifle and arrests him for attempting to kill the President. As it turns out, even if George had shot at the White House, the President was in another state giving a campaign speech.

At trial, what is George's best defense to the charge of attempted murder?

a. Mistake of law.
b. Insufficient mens rea.
c. Factual impossibility under the Model Penal Code test.
d. Insufficient actus reus under the original common law test.
e. Entrapment.

Question 6: Defendant Herman Ferrari is charged with reckless driving. Ferrari claims that he did not intend to drive in a reckless manner, but only did so because he had a few too many drinks during a celebration after his ACJ class. Ferrari felt peer pressure to have a few drinks at the celebration.

In the majority of common law jurisdictions, does Ferrari have an intoxication defense?

a. No, because voluntary intoxication is not a defense to the crime with which Ferrari has been charged.
b. No, because voluntary intoxication is never a defense.

c. Yes, if Ferrari can prove he did not form the intent for the crime.
d. Yes, because Ferrari was suffering from involuntary intoxication.
e. Yes, because duress is a common law defense.

Question 7: Mary decides to rob a bank because she needs money to buy holiday gifts. She buys a mask, gets a toy gun, and plans the robbery. Unbeknownst to Mary, Joan also needs money for gifts and decides to rob the same bank on the same day. On that day, Mary enters through the front door of the bank while Joan enters through the rear. Mary robs the tellers; Joan loots the vault. Neither sees the other and each runs out to her respective car to escape.

What may Mary and Joan each be charged with?
a. Bank robbery, conspiracy, and aiding and abetting each other's bank robberies.
b. Bank robbery.
c. Aiding and abetting the other's bank robbery.
d. Conspiracy and bank robbery.
e. No crime because each defendant would have a duress defense.

Question 8: Linette asks Angela to help her smuggle illegal aliens across the border. Out of friendship, Angela agrees and they set a date for the smuggling. Linette rents a van to transport the aliens, she recruits two other people to help, and calls Angela. Angela tells Linette that she has changed her mind. Linette goes ahead anyway and transports the illegal aliens across the border.

If Angela is charged in a Model Penal Code jurisdiction with both conspiracy to transport the illegal aliens and the substantive charges of transporting illegal aliens, what will she likely be found guilty of?
a. Guilty of conspiracy only.
b. Guilty of conspiracy and the substantive charges of transporting illegal aliens.
c. Not guilty of any crime because she abandoned the conspiracy.
d. Not guilty of any crime because she did not commit an overt act.
e. Not guilty of any crime because she did not reach an explicit agreement with all members of the conspiracy.

Question 9: Max Melvin is a collector of war memorabilia. His friend, Shawn Thomas, visits Melvin one day and offers to buy some of the memorabilia. They stand in the open doorway of Melvin's home and try to negotiate a sale. Melvin, however, is not interested in selling. Melvin grabs an old civil war sword and yells, "Get out, you scoundrel. I'm going to kill you. How dare you try to part me from my precious collection." Melvin then starts flailing at Thomas. Thomas, believing that Melvin is going to kill him, pulls out a gun and shoots Melvin. Melvin dies and Thomas is charged with murder.

Under traditional common law, if Thomas raises self-defense, will his defense fail or succeed?

a. Likely fail because he was the initial aggressor.
b. Likely fail because he had a duty to retreat before using deadly force.
c. Likely fail because he did not have an honest and reasonable fear for his life.
d. Likely fail because there was no immediate threat of violence.
e. Likely succeed.

Question 10: Defendant Carl Gata-Kilher is angry at his neighbor so he shoots at his neighbor through his window. The bullet ricochets off his neighbor's window frame and kills a passerby.

What is Carl guilty of?

a. Not guilty of murder because he did not intend to kill the passerby.
b. Guilty of murder.
c. Guilty of involuntary manslaughter.
d. Not guilty of murder because he did not have a motive to kill the passerby.

Answers:

1. c. Anderson's best defense is mistake of fact. Anderson will argue that knowing whether the dolphins are bottle-nosed or blue is a material element of the crime. The statute does not specify the mens rea requirement for that circumstance, but the statute is a felony which makes it more likely that it is not a strict liability offense. a. is incorrect because the act of shooting constitutes harassment. b. is incorrect because it actually was possible and Anderson did harass blue dolphins. d. is incorrect because there was a law barring his activities.

2. d. Stan would argue that he was faced with a choice of evils (necessity) and that he chose the lesser evil by stealing Bill's tools and saving homes from fire. a. is incorrect because Stan was not threatened with harm from another person. b. is incorrect because he was not forced by another person to commit a crime. c. is incorrect because there is no evidence of mental disease or defect.

3. d. Brains had no duty to help Einstein. Therefore, the general rule applies that an omission does not fulfill the actus reus requirement for a crime. a., b., and c. are incorrect because there was no actus reus for the crime.

4. b. By sending a message to others, Flevinson is adopting a general deterrence theory for punishment. The goal of general deterrence is to use the defendant as an example so others, in the future, will not commit the same offense. a. is incorrect because Flevinson said nothing about helping the defendant change. c. is incorrect because Flevinson wanted to send a message to the public at large, not just this defendant. d. is incorrect because Flevinson did not express any concern about the defendant's continued threat to others.

5. d. Under the original common law standard for attempt, the defendant had to take the last step toward commission of the crime. Although George is in line at the White House, he has not taken the last step of aiming at the President and pulling the trigger. a. is incorrect because the Senators did not have authority and did not tell George that killing the President was legally permissible. b. is incorrect because George had the purpose to kill the President. c. is incorrect because there is no indication that it would not have been physically possible to kill the President if George had not been stopped. d. is incorrect because a normal law-abiding person would not have responded to the letter by trying to kill the President. Also, it appears that George was predisposed to kill the President.

6. a. Voluntary intoxication is not a defense to a crime requiring only recklessness. Ferrari has been charged with reckless driving. b. is incorrect because voluntary intoxication can be a defense to specific intent crimes. c. is is incorrect because recklessness can be formed even when a defendant is intoxicated. d. is incorrect because peer pressure does not constitute duress or involuntary intoxication. e. is incorrect because even though intoxication can be a defense, it would not apply in this situation.

7. b. Each defendant is responsible for her own robbery, but because the defendants did not agree to assist each other in the crime, there is no conspiracy or accomplice liability. a., c. and d. are incorrect because there was no agreement between the defendants nor purpose to help each other commit a crime. e. is incorrect defense because economic duress is not a recognized defense.

8. a. Under the Model Penal Code, a defendant can withdraw from a conspiracy if she notifies her coconspirators. However, if the defendant withdraws, she is still responsible for the original conspiracy, unless she can thwart the plan. Here, all Angela did is notify Linette that she was withdrawing. She did not thwart the plan. b. is incorrect because Angela would have a defense to the substantive charge once she withdrew. c. is incorrect because Angela is still responsible for the original conspiracy. d. is incorrect because only one conspirator need commit an overt act. e. is incorrect because an agreement may be inferred from circumstantial evidence. There need not be an express agreement.

9. e. Thomas met all the requirements of common law self-defense. a. is incorrect because he was not the initial aggressor. Although he went to Melvin's house, he did not threaten any harm. b. is incorrect because there was no duty to retreat under common law. c. is incorrect because a flailing sword would create an honest and reasonable fear for life; and d. is incorrect because there was immediate threat of force.

10. b. The doctrine of transferred intent applies in this case. Accordingly, Carl is guilty of murder. He had the intent to kill but hit the wrong victim. a. is incorrect because of the transferred intent doctrine. c. is incorrect because an intent to kill creates malice for murder, not manslaughter. d. is incorrect because motive is not an element of an offense.

Exam Tips for Essay Exam

In preparing for the exam

- Thoroughly review your course outline.
- Study both the well-established and vague areas of the law.
- Ask your professor about unresolved questions.
- Memorize the law correctly.
- Memorize key terms of art.
- Don't confuse terms of art with colloquialisms. For example, terms like "necessity" and "duress" or "malice" and "recklessness" have very specific legal meanings.

In taking the exam

- Read the instructions and "call of the question" carefully: Are you required to discuss both the crimes and defenses suggested by the fact pattern? Should you apply both common law and the Model Penal Code? Which defendants' culpability should you discuss?
- Unless otherwise instructed, use the "IRAC" approach: Identify the legal Issue, apply the correct Rule. Analyze the rule as applied to the facts and suggest a Conclusion.
- Unless otherwise instructed, argue both sides of an issue: prosecution and defense.
- For each crime and defense, set forth the elements that must be proved. Define key terms, like "premeditation" or "malice."
- Discuss issues relating to the prosecution's prima facie case, before discussing affirmative defenses.
- Do not skip over the basics. For example, carefully examine the facts to determine whether there is a voluntary actus reus and causation for the crime.
- Apply alternative tests for the issue if they exist. For example, if the question suggests an insanity defense, consider all possible insanity standards which might apply in that jurisdiction.
- Unless otherwise instructed, review all possible theories for liability. For example, if the facts suggest more than two or more defendants' involvement, analyze the problem for direct liability, accomplice liability, co-conspirator liability and, if there is a death involved, possible felony murder.

- Unless otherwise instructed, start your discussion with the most culpable defendant. Then, address the culpability of accomplices.
- If an ambiguity in the facts would change your conclusion, state why.
- If the facts involve a homicide, consider all levels of culpability—from first-degree murder to involuntary manslaughter.
- In discussing causation, discuss both actual cause and proximate cause.
- In applying a "reasonableness' standard, define who is the "reasonable person." What subjective factors, if any, regarding the defendant or his situation should the trier of fact consider?
- Use the purposes of punishment in analyzing policy questions. If the policy question asks whether a proposed change in the law should be adopted, first discuss the current state of the law and then identify how the proposed change would make a difference.

Exam Tips for Multiple-Choice Exam

- Read the entire question, including all possible responses, before designating your answer.
- If asked whether the defendant is quilty of a crime or has a defense, make sure to analyze the facts for all elements of the crime or defense.
- Look for why possible answers are wrong. Select the correct answer by process of elimination.

GLOSSARY

abandonment withdrawing from a criminal endeavor before its completion; not a defense at common law

absolute liability strict liability crimes that do not require the defendant have a culpable mens rea

accessory an accomplice to a crime

accessory after the fact a person who helps after a crime and has been committed by concealing the defendants or evidence of their crime, or helping their flight from justice

accomplice a person who helps another person commit a crime

actual cause defendant's acts that were a link in the chain of causation; also called "legal cause" or "cause in fact"

actus reus a voluntary criminal act; may be a positive act or a failure to act when there is a duty to do so

alter ego rule when defending a third person, the defendant stands in the shoes of that person to determine whether there was a right to use self-defense

arson the malicious burning of the dwelling house of another

assault the willful attempt or threat to inflict injury upon another person

attempt a substantial step toward completing a crime with the purpose that the crime succeed

attendant circumstance circumstances that define elements of a crime, other than the actus reus, mens rea, and result

bail release of a defendant pending the outcome of proceedings

battery injurious or offensive wrongful touching of a person without his or her consent

beyond a reasonable doubt the burden of proof in all criminal cases

bifurcated trial a trial divided into two phases, often the "guilt phase" and the "penalty phase"

bilateral rule requirement that there be two or more persons that can be prosecuted for conspiratorial activities

black letter law the specific definitions of crimes and defenses and how the courts interpret those requirements

burden of proof the legal obligation to present evidence to persuade the jury on a specific issue(s) in a case

burglary breaking and entering the dwelling house of another at nighttime with the intent to commit a felony inside

but-for cause determination that a harmful result would not have occurred without the defendant's acts

capital punishment the death penalty

cause-in-fact defendant's acts that lead to a harmful result

chain conspiracy conspirators participating along a distribution line

challenges for cause the excusal of a juror because of bias

claim of right a defense by which the defendant claims that the taking of property was lawful because the defendant was recovering his or her own property

common law principles of law established through a series of cases in England and the American colonies

concurrent causes acts by more than one person that simultaneously lead to the same harmful result

conspiracy agreement by two or more persons to commit a crime

cooling time period between act of provocation and defendant's killing of victim

culpability the extent to which a defendant's mental state shows the defendant should be punished for his or her acts

dangerous proximity defendant's physical nearness to completion of a crime

defendant person accused of a crime

dependent intervening causes causes that do not break the chain of causation

determinate sentencing a guideline approach to sentencing requiring the court to select a sentence based upon the nature of the defendant's offense and criminal history

deterrence punishment imposed to deter the commission of future offenses based on the theory that defendants weigh advantages and disadvantages of their acts before committing a crime

diminished capacity failure to form the mens rea necessary for a specific intent case

due process the fair processing of cases through the justice system

duress acting under the compulsion of another person

Durham test insanity test that focuses on whether the defendant's acts are the product of mental disease or illness

elements requirements of a crime or defense

embezzlement fraudulent conversion of the property of another that is already in the defendant's possession

entrapment improper inducement of a person to commit a crime

euthanasia early termination of a human life to end suffering or prolonged death

ex post facto "after the fact" crimes that impose criminal liability for acts that were not criminal at the time committed

extortion the taking of property by threat of future violence

factual impossibility common law doctrine that recognized that even though the defendant could not complete the crime because of unexpected facts, defendant was still guilty of attempt

felony offense which carries a maximum punishment of more than one year in jail

felony murder a felon's strict liability for murder for all deaths occurring during the course of a felony, even without a showing of malice

general intent a crime in which the defendant intends to commit the act but does not intend the specific consequences of the act

general verdict a verdict by a jury to acquit or convict without a detailed finding supporting the jury's verdict

gross negligence taking a substantial and unjustifiable risk that a reasonable person would not have taken under the circumstances and of which the defendant should have been aware

gross recklessness the conscious disregard of a substantial and unjustifiable risk which reflects a gross deviation from the standard of conduct a law-abiding person would observe in that situation

habeas corpus collateral attack on a conviction

homicide the unlawful killing of another human being

imperfect self-defense self-defense based upon an honest but unreasonable fear; usually mitigates crime to voluntary manslaughter

impossibility the inability to complete a crime

incapacitation punishment used to isolate a defendant from committing more harm to society

inchoate preparatory crimes of attempt, conspiracy, and solicitation

independent felony a felony that does not have as its underlying purpose the killing of another human being

indeterminate sentencing discretionary sentencing which allows the judge to impose a sentence ranging from probation to the maximum authorized by the statute

indictment formal charges brought by a grand jury

infancy a defense based upon the young age of the defendant

infanticide killing of a young child

information formal charges filed without grand jury

infractions less serious criminal offenses, often of a regulatory nature, typically punishable by fine as punishment

inherently dangerous felony a felony that, either in the abstract or as committed, is likely to pose a risk to human life

initial aggressor one who initiates a violent confrontation

insanity defect or disease of the mind, at the time of the crime, that prevents the defendant from knowing the nature or wrongfulness of his acts, or prevents the defendant from controlling those acts

intentionally acting with the purpose to cause a specific harmful result; acting with the awareness, but not the purpose, that one's acts may cause a specific result

intervening act an act that occurs between the time of defendant's act and a harmful result

involuntary intoxication intoxication that is under duress, unwitting, or from a pathological effect

jurisdictional facts elements of a crime provided only to set limits on the jurisdiction of the court

jury nullification a jury's decision to disregard the law and render a verdict contrary to it

justification a defense that recognizes the defendant made the right choice under the circumstances

knowingly virtual or practical certainty that conduct will lead to a particular result

larceny the taking and carrying away, without consent, of the property of another with intent to permanently deprive that person of the property

larceny by trick the taking of possession of another person's property by false representations

legal cause defendant's acts that lead to a harmful result

legal impossibility a common law defense afforded to attempted criminal action that could never constitute a crime no matter how hard the defendant tried

legality "lawfulness"—the principle that a person may not be punished unless that person's conduct was defined as unlawful before the defendant acted

magistrate a person who provides an initial review of the charges against a suspect

malice intentionally doing a wrongful act or acting with gross disregard as to the risk of injury to others

malicious engaging in conduct with a conscious disregard of the substantial and unjustifiable risk to others

malum in se crimes which are inherently dangerous or violate the most basic moral principles of society

malum prohibitum crimes which violate regulatory laws designed to maintain the orderly functioning of society

manslaughter the killing of another person without malice

material element elements of a crime for which the defendant must have a mens rea in order to be guilty

mens rea the level of awareness and intentionality with which the defendant acted

misappropriation unlawful conversion of property that is already in one's possession

misdemeanor an offense which carries a punishment of less than one year in jail

misdemeanor-manslaughter responsibility for a death that occurs during the course of a nonfelony criminal act

mistake of fact ignorance or mistake as to a material element of a crime that demonstrates a lack of the requisite mens rea

mistake of law ignorance or mistake as to the law charged or as to another law involved in the offense

Model Penal Code a model statute drafted by the American Law Institute in 1962, which has influenced but is not binding on legislatures or the courts

motive the cause or reason for the defendant's action

murder the killing of another human being with malice

necessity a defense based on a claim that the defendant was faced with a choice of evils

negligently taking a risk that a reasonable person would not have taken under the circumstances and of which the defendant should have been aware

omission failure to act when there is a duty to help

overt act any act taken to further a conspiracy

parole release from jail, prison, or other confinement after serving part of the sentence

pathological intoxication unexpected reaction to medication or alcohol

patricide killing of one's parents

peremptory challenge dismissal of a juror at the discretion of the litigant

***Pinkerton* liability** co-conspirator's liability for criminal acts of co-conspirators in furtherance of the conspiracy

precedent a case already decided that serves as an example or authority for a similar or identical question of law

premeditation purposeful and deliberate thought or killing with preconceived design

prima facie case prosecution's proof of the elements of a crime

probation the release of a convicted criminal under supervision of a probation officer in lieu of incarceration

prosecutor government official representing the public in a criminal case

proximate cause a determination that the defendant's conduct was sufficiently related to the harm that resulted to warrant criminal punishment

public welfare offense regulatory crimes that ordinarily do not require a culpable mens rea

purposely acting with the goal or aim to engage in particular conduct or achieve certain results

rape unlawful sexual intercourse with a woman without her consent by force, fear, or fraud

reasonableness the standard of care exercised by the ordinary, law-abiding person

recklessly consciously disregarding a substantial and unjustifiable risk of harm

rehabilitation punishment designed to correct criminal behavior by remedying deficiencies in the defendant

renunciation completely and voluntarily withdrawing from criminal conduct

res gestae the facts and circumstances surrounding the commission of an offense

res ipsa loquitor defendant's actions that speak for themselves to prove defendant's intent

respondeat superior corporate liability for acts of its agents

result the harm caused by defendant's acts

retribution punishment inflicted upon the defendant as a form of social revenge for the crime committed

RICO the Racketeer Influenced and Corrupt Organizations Act that prosecutes multifaceted, diversified conspiracies, including those by organized crime

robbery taking of property from another person with force or intimidation

self-defense using force to protect one's person

solicitation recruiting, encouraging, directing, counseling, or inducing another person to commit a crime

somnambulism a condition of sleep in which motor acts are performed

special verdict jury findings regarding specific issues in a case

specific intent a crime in which the defendant must act with either the intent to commit a crime or with an intent to cause a specific result

stalking intentionally harassing another and placing that person in immediate and reasonable fear for her safety

statutory rape unlawful sexual intercourse with a minor

strict liability minor crimes which do not carry a mens rea requirement

suicide the taking of one's own life

transferred intent injuring a victim other than the one intended

unilateral rule responsible for conspiracy as long as defendant believes she is agreeing with another person to commit a crime

unlawfully acting with no legal excuse for one's behavior

utilitarianism a doctrine which determines the right conduct by weighing its usefulness

venire the panel of potential jurors

vicarious liability a defendant's responsibility for the criminal acts of another person

voir dire questioning of jurors regarding their background and attitudes during jury selection

Wharton's Rule prohibition on charging conspiracy where the conspiracy has as its goal a crime that requires two persons

wheel conspiracy conspiracy in which a group of individuals are working with a common middleperson

willful blindness deliberate ignorance to criminal circumstances that is often treated as meeting the standard for "knowledge"

willfully acting with the purpose of violating the law; intentionally doing an act knowing of its likely consequences; intending the act where the act has harmful or illegal consequences

withdrawal abandoning a criminal endeavor

Table of Cases

Table of Statutes

Table of Model Penal Code Provisions

Index